Introducing Social Geographies

Rachel Pain

University of Durham

and

**Michael Barke, Duncan Fuller, Jamie Gough,
Robert MacFarlane, Graham Mowl**

University of Northumbria

A member of the Hodder Headline Group
LONDON
Co-published in the United States of America by
Oxford University Press Inc., New York

First published in Great Britain in 2001 by
Arnold, a member of the Hodder Headline Group,
338 Euston Road, London NW1 3BH

http://www.arnoldpublishers.com

Co-published in the United States of America by
Oxford University Press Inc.,
198 Madison Avenue, New York, NY 10016

British Library Cataloguing in Publication Data
A catalogue record for this book is available from the British Library

Library of Congress Cataloging-in-Publication Data
A catalog record for this book is available from the Library of Congress

ISBN 0 340 72005 0 (hb)
ISBN 0 340 72006 9 (pb)

1 2 3 4 5 6 7 8 9 10

Production Editor: Anke Ueberberg
Production Controller: Martin Kerans
Cover Design: Terry Griffiths

Typeset in 10/14pt Gill Light by Phoenix Photosetting, Chatham, Kent
Printed and bound in Great Britain by MPG Books Ltd, Bodmin, Cornwall

What do you think about this book? Or any other Arnold title?
Please send your comments to feedback.arnold@hodder.co.uk

To our students, past and present

Contents

Contents

List of contributors

This book was conceived and planned collectively. The contents page lists the individuals or teams responsible for first drafts of respective chapters. Rachel Pain edited the book, and Jamie Gough deserves special mention as copy editor.

Michael Barke is a Reader in Human Geography at the University of Northumbria. His teaching and research interests include the impact of housing policy change on local communities, the changing social geography of nineteenth- and twentieth-century Tyneside, and global change and development. His previous books include:

Barke, M. and O'Hare, G. P. (1984) *The Third World: Diversity, Change and Interdependence.* Edinburgh: Oliver & Boyd (2nd edn, Oliver & Boyd/Longman, 1991).

Barke, M. (1986) *Transport and Trade.* Edinburgh: Oliver & Boyd.

Barke, M. (1991) *Cast Studies of the Third World.* Harlow: Oliver & Boyd/Longman.

Barke, M. and Turnbull, G. (1992) *Meadowell: The Biography of an 'Estate with Problems'.* Aldershot: Avebury.

Barke, M. and Buswell, R. J. (eds) (1992) *Newcastle's Changing Map.* Newcastle upon Tyne: City Libraries and Arts.

Barke, M., Towner, J. and Newton, M. T. (1996) *Tourism in Spain: Critical Issues.* Wallingford: CAB International.

Duncan Fuller is a Lecturer in Social and Economic Geography at the University of Northumbria. His teaching and research interests include geographies of inclusion and exclusion, money, credit union development, poverty, disability, anthropological and psychoanalytical theories, and qualitative methods and academic activism.

Jamie Gough is a Senior Lecturer in Human Geography at the University of Northumbria. His teaching and research interests include industrial, economic and urban geography, particularly labour processes and their geography, urban and regional economies, flows of value within cities, and relationships between economic governance at different spatial scales. His previous books include:

Gough, J. and MacNair, M. (1985) *Gay Liberation in the Eighties.* Pluto: London.

Eisenschitz, A. and Gough, J. (1993) *The Politics of Local Economic Policy.* Basingstoke: Macmillan.

Gough, J. (2001) *Work, Locality and the Rhythms of Capital*. London: Continuum.

Robert MacFarlane is a Senior Lecturer in Geography and Environmental Management at the University of Northumbria. His teaching and research interests include the meaning and management of landscapes, urban nature conservation initiatives, landscape ecology and Geographical Information System applications in the developed and developing worlds.

Graham Mowl is a Senior Lecturer in Human Geography at the University of Northumbria. His teaching and research interests include geography of leisure, impacts of tourism development, disability, gender relations and ageing.

Rachel Pain is a Lecturer in Cultural and Social Geography at the University of Durham. Her teaching and research interests include geographies of crime, fear of crime and community safety, health, gender, ageing, and qualitative methods.

Acknowledgements

Every effort has been made to trace copyright holders of material reproduced in this book. Any rights not acknowledged here will be acknowledged in subsequent printings if notice is given to the publisher.

1
Introduction

1.1 What is social geography?

Social geography is concerned with the ways in which social relations, social identities and social inequalities are produced, their spatial variation, and the role of space in constructing them. It places particular emphasis on the welfare issues which affect people's lives, and aims to expose the forms of power which lead to social and spatial inequality and oppression.

Although it is traditional to study human geography within the spheres of social geography, economic geography, political geography and cultural geography, there can be no clear distinctions between the four. Increasingly, the subject matter of each crosses the artificial boundaries which academics have drawn in the past. After all, geography is literally 'earth-writing', a holistic discipline which takes account of all of the processes influencing particular human environments. But many would maintain that it is still useful to maintain the sub-disciplines 'to identify particular foci for intellectual study and analysis' (Hamnett, 1996: 3). Changing interests in geography and elsewhere in the social sciences mean that each sphere is constantly developing, and receives more or less attention from geographers at different times.

Box 1.1 Social geography before the 1980s

In the 1960s and 1970s, social geography was a thriving area of human geography. Its focus was on the spatial patterns of social welfare and inequality, which new techniques of mapping and statistical analysis were able to identify. Linked to the radical perspectives emerging at the time, many social geographers took structural approaches (which focus on social power) to explaining these inequalities. The predominantly urban literature focused on issues such as community, crime, health, housing, segregation and poverty.

In the 1980s, these traditional interests were challenged, firstly by new ways of theorizing the role of space (see Box 1.4) and, secondly, by the rapidly developing understanding of gender relations elsewhere in the social sciences. Since then, other forms of inequality have also become key interests – especially those around sexuality, disability and age – and the cultural turn (see Box 1.2) has shifted attention away from the traditional interests of urban socio-spatial inequality.

In particular, attention to social geography as a discrete area of study has been diffused in recent years as the subject of Cultural Studies has become more influential, a situation sometimes referred to as the 'cultural turn'. Boxes 1.1 and 1.2 outline what social geography was like before 1980, and what the cultural turn entailed. Today, 'social and cultural geography' are frequently grouped together. We welcome the invigorating effect that the cultural turn has had, but it has also had less the desirable effect of overshadowing some of social geography's central concerns.

> ## Box 1.2 The cultural turn and discourses
>
> The cultural turn describes a period of transformation in the concerns and theories of human geography during the 1980s and 1990s. The defining feature of the cultural turn is an emphasis on culture, and attention to the theories of cultural studies rather than to those of the traditional partner of social geography, sociology. Increasingly, human geographers have focused on the construction of society and space through 'discourses' – on sets of meanings, symbolism and signification.
>
> The cultural turn does not mean, as some imply, the death of theory based on material life or of political relevance in human geography. One welcome impact on social geography has been the greater recognition of the voices of diverse social groups and the incorporation of the concerns of those traditionally excluded from geography. However, with its emphasis on representation, ideology and meaning, and interest in literary and psychoanalytic theory, cultural geographers can sometimes be accused of underplaying or ignoring the issues of power, inequality and material welfare.

Informed by some aspects of the cultural turn and recent radical approaches in geography, our social geographies refocus attention on to inequality, social power and the material world. Drawing political and economic processes back into social geography is as important as acknowledging the power of culture.

1.2 A theoretical framework

We now need to tell you what sort of social geography it is that we are writing in this book. There is no one way of doing social geography. Every student, teacher, reader and writer develops her or his own perspective, influenced by their own positioning and beliefs (which we come to in the next section). The title of the book, *Introducing Social Geographies*, highlights this plurality. We present other geographers' geographies in the book as well as our own, and it would be wrong to pretend that there are no differences within our own writing team!

We do think it is important, though, for any account of social geography to have a theoretical stance and to be explicit about it. Our social geographies should not be read as a universal authority on the subject, nor as free-floating and apolitical. The five key themes for social geography, below, will help to let you know where we are coming from in writing this book.

1.2.1 Individuals are part of societies

First, social geography is about *society* (see Box 1.3). It cannot begin from describing or analysing individuals, but instead must focus upon the social relations between people. In terms of subject matter, social geography therefore has most to say about social reproduction: issues of families and households, as well as social identities of race, age, sexuality, disability and gender, and the sites of the home, the community and the nation.

Box 1.3 Society

'Society' denotes the ties that people have with others. These ties are 'social' relationships, 'social' being used in its widest sense. A slightly different meaning of 'society' is of people occupying a given area of geographical space and/or governed by a common political system. Societies are usually perceived as having a distinct identity and a system of meanings and values which members share. Societies are sometimes labelled to indicate their appearance in history ('pre-modern societies'), their geographical territory ('Danish society') or, more controversially, their 'progress' ('less developed societies'). Of course, given the size of most societies, they are very internally diverse.

Like 'community' (see Chapter 4), 'society' has different connotations and uses, depending on the political interests involved. When Margaret Thatcher, the former British prime minister, famously stated 'there is no such thing as society', it signified her view that people should look after themselves and ignore their ties to others. A socialist view of society, on the other hand, sees individuals as both enabled and constrained by the societies of which they are a part, so that the form of society is important.

1.2.2 Space and society

Social geography focuses on the relationships between societies and the spaces they occupy and use. Space has an important role in actively constituting society. Space and place are important means by which societies and social groups organize themselves, distribute resources, come into conflict, are given meaning or create meaning for themselves. Thus social geography has particular contributions to make to social theory and social problems. Box 1.4 outlines some of these different ways of conceptualizing the relationship between space and society.

1.2.3 The significance of the local and the everyday

The focus of social geography is on people's daily living spaces. Events and processes at different spatial scales can not be discussed in isolation from each other: for example, global processes shape local places and processes. However, the starting point for social geography is everyday experience, and therefore analysis is usually of events and phenomena at a *local* scale – the neighbourhood, the home, the local park, the workplace, and the body. Different meanings of place, and their relation to power, have been a central interest (see Box 1.5).

Box 1.4 Three relationships between space and society

First space: Space reflects social activity

For example, we can view highly segregated social areas as reflecting social inequalities of class, race, age and gender.

Second space: Space constructs social activity

We can also view space as having an active role in the creation or maintenance of social inequality. Continuing with the example of housing patterns, there are many ways in which where you live reinforces your social position. For example, some areas have fewer job opportunities than others and their reputations may make it difficult for residents to find work elsewhere. These areas also have poorer services, education and public transport.

Third space: Space is a means of resistance and celebration

Rather than accepting these social constructions of space, we might challenge them through our use of space. Spaces can be used to resist oppression and redefine social identity. Some of those that geographers have written about are metaphorical or imagined spaces (e.g. the spaces of music), but oppressed communities can use local spaces to contest and redefine their labelling, for example as living in a 'bad neighbourhood'.

(Source: Smith, 1999)

Box 1.5 Place

A place has locational properties – it may occupy a particular portion of space, or occupy an imaginary location conjured up by listening to music or reading a novel. A place also has subjective meaning to people – a 'sense of place'. Notions of place are not fixed nor universally shared, and social geographers have shown how dominant forms of power and social identities affect what places mean to different individuals and groups. These relationships to power, and access to place, define the boundaries which include and exclude certain people.

(Source: Rose, 1995)

1.2.4 Social relations and identities are power relations

The social relations on which social geographers have concentrated their attention – those of class, gender, sexuality, race, age and disability – are about power, oppression and the distribution of resources in society. Social geography is also concerned with identities, which are always linked to ways of life, and so are not just about ideologies but power and resources. The distinctions of identity which relate to power are the most important; gender relations, for example, create 'masculine' and 'feminine' identities.

People's perceptions of their own and others' identity are variable and subjective, and so social identities are not fixed but take variable forms in different places and times. To some degree individuals and social groups are able to resist and change these identities, and space and place have important roles in this process. However, as social identities are not infinitely mutable but strongly underpinned by power relations and given material circumstances, the relation between power and resistance is a central concern in social geography. Furthermore, we need to be aware not only that gender, race, age, class, disability and sexuality each influences the socio-spatial world, but that they intersect and work together. One cannot be fully understood without reference to the others.

1.2.5 Social geography is political and has a role in social policy

Because social geography is about power relations, it is inevitably political. Power is confronted by people through personal resistance strategies, through social movements, and may be influenced by the state through social policy. All of these forms of resistance are dealt with in the book, although the state is not assumed to be neutral nor even capable of solving particular social problems. There is a strong case for geographers to contribute to social policy issues and other forms of action.

1.3 Approaches to social geography and positionality

1.3.1 Approaches to social geography

At undergraduate level, human geography is about inquiry, rather than lists of facts. It is important to be clear from the start of your studies as a geographer that 'facts' are contested, and that 'truths' can be represented in many different ways. Above all, human geography is subjective, which means that different people may have widely divergent views about the same phenomenon, and it is impossible to make an objective judgement about who is right (though some views are better grounded than others). Human geography is situated, which means that beliefs and knowledge are rooted in the social and political positioning of those who construct it.

Box 1.6 briefly outlines some of the main approaches which social geographers have taken. The references at the end of the chapter will be helpful if you want to learn more about these. In reality, few geographers work only within one of these paradigms, but combine approaches. The most important thing is that as geographers we 'lay bare our own role as analysts' (Jackson and Smith, 1984). Not all textbooks do this – and not all lecturers and students do it either. As you read the book, bear in mind our philosophical and political stance in writing it. You are also encouraged to develop your own stance.

Box 1.6 Approaches to social geography

Positivist approaches

Positivists approach social geography as though it were a natural science, seeking to make general statements, model geographical phenomena and discover 'laws' to explain human/spatial interactions. Quantitative methods have usually been employed in support of these goals. In most positivist research social scientists are assumed to be capable of being objective, neutral, value-free observers. Although this position has been widely criticized, positivism has been a popular approach to social geography and dominant until relatively recently.

Humanistic approaches

Humanistic approaches offer a longstanding alternative which challenges deterministic explanations. Humanistic social geographies assert that there is no objective geographical world, but that geographies are both perceived and created by individuals' perceptions, attitudes and feelings. They give centrality to human agency, diversity and difference, and value the trivial, local and everyday human experience. They believe that science and scientists are subjective and involved, and indeed may alter what they are studying.

Radical approaches

Radical approaches emphasize power relations and social and political structures in explaining the social geographical world. Radical social geographers have an explicit political and moral commitment to the issues they study. The most influential have been Marxism, feminism and anti-racism, all of which apply important bodies of social theory to the analysis of society and space. Marxist geographies draw on the theories of Karl Marx, stressing the centrality of capitalist economic and political systems in underpinning social and spatial life, and adapting and refining theory to keep pace with current changes to society and economy. Feminist geographies draw on feminist theories, and have expanded their focus from examining women's lives and the importance of gender in constructing space to a concern with other forms of difference and oppression. Anti-racist geographies have highlighted and contested the racism endemic to western societies and in human geography itself. Radical approaches stress the need to constantly re-examine not only the content of social geography but the ways in which research and theory are done.

Postmodern approaches

Postmodern approaches to geography are disparate. Postmodernism denotes a supposedly new era for western societies, the idea that we are now beyond the 'modern' age. Postmodern approaches generally involve challenging the linear progress of history and social science; the fragmentation of traditionally discrete forms of explanation; and the rejection of realism, certainty and truth, including 'grand theories'. The term is often used to incorporate the cultural turn and postcolonial approaches. The perspectives it encompasses sometimes conflict. Some have viewed postmodernism as relativistic, while others claim it has opened up spaces for those previously excluded from geographical theory.

1.3.2 Positionality

Positionality concerns the diversity of views in social science, in three linked senses. Firstly, it refers to the variety of *philosophical* traditions in the discipline, the systems of theories which explain how things work (Box 1.6). It also describes the *political* value systems and beliefs which we all hold; thus there are conflicting theories in social geography, which are not clearly superior to each other but involve ideological positioning and value judgments. And finally, it describes our *social* position as students, teachers, readers or writers; our relation to power, depending on whether we live in more or less developed countries, whether we are rich or poor, black or white, female or male, disabled or able-bodied and so on. The notion of positionality has been used by humanist, radical and postmodern writers, though in slightly different ways.

Not everyone in geography favours the word positionality or the way it is sometimes used, as it can imply relativism. Extreme relativism would argue that there are an infinite number of biased positions from which individuals may write or read geography, and no way of telling which is better or worse. We disagree with wholly relativistic geographies. As we outline below, our approach in writing this book is to some extent pluralistic, though we have distinct preferences. However, this does not mean that 'anything goes' in social geography, the supposedly peculiarly postmodern crisis of not having a viewpoint, that any explanation is as equally useful (or useless) as the others. Rather, reference to different philosophical positions in exploring the socio-spatial world can be about acknowledging complexity; forging alliances between sets of theories that are not always incompatible; and recognizing the diverse ways in which different forces interact and different people respond. It can be viewed as a prerequisite for understanding a complex world, and does not mean abandonment of a strong political commitment. We write better geographies if we acknowledge our positionality and ground our writing in our experiences, and for most people these are too complex to fit into single boxes.

1.3.3 Our philosophical and political stance

In terms of our politics, Marxist and feminist approaches have been most influential in writing this book. Our stance is against socially created inequality, which needs to be challenged through social policy and forms of action by individuals and groups (see section 1.2.5). In terms of interpreting human behaviour, we view humanistic and qualitative approaches and methods as most enlightening. We recognize the contribution of postmodernist thought in geography in helping us rethink our ideas and values; again, not an 'anything goes' postmodernism but a critical and constructive one which stresses difference, challenges the authority of authors, and tries to make space for non-traditional voices to speak about their own geographies. While these are our own positions, and they organize the material of the book, we nevertheless consider many theories and ideas with which we disagree. You will need to make up your own mind.

1.4. A guide to the book

Any book on 'social geographies' has to be partial in its coverage. This book focuses on highly urbanized and highly industrialized societies, what are sometimes called the more developed countries (MDCs) – with particular focus on Britain and western Europe, but also drawing on case studies from North America, Australia, New Zealand and Japan. While these societies are diverse, they are different enough from other societies in the world to justify a separate focus. They are also home to ourselves and most of our readers: the best place for social geography to begin is on the doorstep.

In Part I, *Society, material life and geography*, we start to examine the basic sites of social life and their spatialities: the household, the neighbourhood, the community and the workplace. We introduce the major social practices of domestic work, paid work, consumption, leisure, and use of services. While paid work and production are usually the domain of economic geography, we begin in Chapter 2 by examining the ways in which they profoundly shape social life and vice versa. Chapter 2 also provides some context to several recent changes referred to later in the book. Much of this part of the book is concerned with the material aspects of life: employment and the incomes and resources which individuals derive from it, the work of providing basic necessities and caring, the goods and services which people buy; and the relations within households and communities which organize these. But as we shall see, these material practices also involve ideas, ideologies and individuals' consciousness – their desires, hopes and fears. These sites, practices and ideologies are seldom determined simply by nature, technologies or efficiency; they are profoundly marked by different types of power and social conflict. We get a first view of these in Part I of the book, and in particular we examine one form of power, class, in some detail. We also begin to see some of the intersections of various forms of power here; these are examined in greater detail in Part II.

In Part II, *Power, identity and social geography*, we go on to explore the spatial construction of identity and difference. We examine race and ethnicity, gender, sexuality, age and disability, and how these forms of power circumscribe people's lives and the environments they use. In these chapters we outline current understanding of the concepts and issues involved, and using case studies of geographers' work we demonstrate the importance of space and place in their operation in different times and contexts. We show that social identities are not fixed but take variable forms in different places and times, and that people who are oppressed resist and redefine their oppression. As Part II progresses, we demonstrate that although we have chosen to present these social identities in four separate chapters (and while 'class' is considered in detail earlier in the book), they must be seen as inter-related. We also highlight in these chapters the positioning of those who have predominantly studied and carried out research in social geography, and the implications this has had for knowledge construction.

In Part III, *Social geography and social problems*, we turn to look at four important social issues in order to demonstrate how a social geographical approach contributes to our understanding of them and informs our responses to them. They cover the problems of managing 'natural' landscapes and environments; the inequitable distribution of housing; the impact of crime on the spatial and social lives of individuals and communities; and the geographies of poverty. We review the range of work geographers have carried out in these fields. We draw out connections with the sites of social life discussed in Part I, and the social power relations and identities dealt with in Part II. We argue that each example is an important site of inequality, and that this has implications for present day social policy, underlining the relevance social geography has to the 'real' world outside of books, lectures and academic journals. The final chapter on geographies of poverty draws together many of the issues dealt with in previous chapters.

Summary

Social geography is not a discrete sub-discipline. It shares much subject-matter and many theories and methods with cultural, economic and political geographies. However, social geography has as a central concern the relations between people, people's identities, the spatial variation of these, and the role of space in their construction. It emphasizes the welfare issues which affect people's lives, and often involves moral and political positions which oppose social inequality and oppression.

Social geography has had a bumpy recent past, and can be expected to continue to change as the discipline of geography, other social sciences, and the world around us develop.

We have suggested that it is time for geographers to refocus their attention on social relations and power, on the local, on the material issues that affect people's lives, and on the social and spatial processes which cause inequality.

Our political, philosophical and social positioning affect the geographies we research, write, and read, and those we construct in the world. It is important to be explicit about positioning as it underpins different interpretations of the social world.

As a student of social geography, we encourage you to be aware of your positionality and to develop your own frameworks of understanding. Welcome to the book!

Further reading

These books will be a useful follow-up to this introduction, and also contain material which supplements the rest of the book.

- Johnston, R. J. (1997) *Geography and Geographers: Anglo-American Human Geography since 1945* (4th edn). London: Arnold.
  A thorough account of changing perspectives in the discipline.

- Hamnett, C. (ed.) (1996) *Social Geography: A Reader*. London: Arnold.

Contains a number of key articles by social geographers; a good companion to this book.

- Cloke, P., Crang, P. and Goodwin, M. (1999) *Introducing Human Geographies*. London: Arnold. A good introduction to human geography. Although it contains relatively little on social geography itself, it shows how the different spheres of geography intersect, and highlights common themes between them.

- Blunt, A. and Wills, J. (2000) *Dissident Geographies: An Introduction to Radical Ideas and Practice*. London: Prentice Hall.
  A useful introduction to radical perspectives and their effect on human geography and beyond.

PART I

Society, material life and geography

2
Work, class and social life

2.1 Introduction

We are accustomed to thinking of 'home' and 'work' as quite separate spheres of our lives, the first as concerned with the need to make money, the second with 'free time' and leisure. Yet the two spheres are, in the end, inextricable. The incomes and the skills which people acquire within waged work, and the relations with others which they form there, impact strongly on their social lives. The home itself is not simply for 'leisure' but is where we do a large part of the work to sustain ourselves. Moreover, social life and its geography react back onto the economy. The domestic and residential spheres are where workers, potential workers and future workers are produced; and the personal resources, character, values, attitudes and relationships developed within social life strongly affect the capacities which people bring to the economy. Social and economic geography, then, are thoroughly intertwined.

In this chapter we examine the combination or 'nexus' of economic and social spheres. We first examine how it is that 'work' and 'home' come to be regarded as so separate, that is, the *division* between the economic and social spheres within capitalist societies (section 2.2). We then examine the two spheres in turn. Sections 2.3 to 2.5 look at employment relations, their geography, and the connection of these to notions of class. Section 2.6 examines some economic dimensions of the social and residential sphere, the varied processes through which people produce themselves day to day. We then bring economic and social processes back together again, by discussing their mutual interaction within particular territories, whether nations or localities, and the actions by business, workers, residents and the state which shape these (sections 2.7 and 2.8). Finally, we discuss the particular forms which economic-social geography has taken over the last thirty years or so and the conflicts which are shaping it.

2.2 The split between 'economic' and 'social' life

Mature capitalist societies are marked by a split between what we now call the 'economy' and 'social life'. This split is so familiar that people in the MDCs tend to take it for granted. Yet it is a relatively recent historical development. In feudal Europe, the peasant household was responsible for all aspects of work and reproduction of its members: care of household members, agricultural and pastoral work, building, collection of fuel and water, preparation of food, and production of implements. Women, men, young and old had different roles; but the total work to be done was organized as a single project in a single space. Our modern distinction between 'work' and housework would have been meaningless.

These arrangements first started to erode with the growth of waged work in agriculture in the late Middle Ages, and were definitively broken with the rise of the factory system. Industrial capitalism instituted a clear divide between 'productive work' and the household. Manufacturing work was brought into a space, the factory, where it could be directly supervised by the firm. This enabled the firm to determine both the pace and the quality of work and to reap a surplus from it; this was the new capitalist system. This work took place on particular days and during particular hours of the day. The need to work routinely and dependably at predetermined times was completely new, an enormous cultural revolution. The spread of this form of work was resisted in myriad ways, but also reinforced by new practices and ideas of self-control and sobriety (Thrift, 1996). The household no longer supported itself through what it directly produced; instead, it depended on wages to buy commodities, which were then transformed through household labour.

A wholly new set of splits and distinctions was thus set up, which are with us to this day (Box 2.1; see also section 2, Chapter 6). Work in the capitalist factory, mine or farm was 'productive' since it produced a wage for the worker and a profit for the owner, whereas work in the home became merely 'housework', or simply 'consumption' or 'leisure'. The former was motivated by the 'rational' pursuit of maximum money income, whereas the latter was motivated by self-realization or by altruism. Waged work was

Box 2.1 Distinctions commonly made between 'work' and 'home'

work	home
work	not work
productive	unproductive
production	consumption
production spaces	residential areas
economic	social
public	private
creates value	creates good
controlled	free
self-interest	altruism
head	heart
hard	soft

Some of these distinctions are contentious. What is your view?

done under the direction of firms, whereas the work of the household was under its own control, albeit governed by internal power relations of gender and age (see section 6.2 of Chapter 6 and section 7.3.2 of Chapter 7). Household time was 'free time', distinct from the alienated time of the waged working day. Work now occurred in two distinct and separated spaces, the 'workplace' and the house; and with this change the house becomes a 'home' in the modern sense, with associations distinct from, and in many ways the opposite of, waged production. In parallel with the rise of new ideologies of the disciplined wage worker came new ideas about the home, increasingly idealized as a sphere of caring and self-determination, its 'softness' contrasted with the harshness of the money-making economy outside (Williams, 1987).

Capitalism thus splits many people's daily time and space into two. This is best seen as a difference in *social relations*: the economy and social life respectively consist of different relations between people, centred on the organization of work in its widest sense.

Yet the two spheres form a single system, in that people's needs and wants are met through the *combination* of the formal economy and the household. The economy depends on a labour force produced within residential spaces, while the activities of households would be impossible without wages and the commodities they can buy. There is thus both a fundamental split *and* a fundamental interdependence of the two types of space.

In the contemporary MDCs, the separation of income-earning and unwaged activity is not total since many people earn incomes while working at home or in family businesses. But the latter are a small minority: split times and spaces of work dominate our societies.

Figure 2.1 *Work and home in Wallsend, England. With the industrial revolution work and home became separated – but in some cases only just. Credit: Sirkka-Liisa Kontinnen.*

Figure 2.2 *A purely residential area. Over time the distances between home and work, and their location in separate zones, have generally increased. Credit: Longman GeoInformation, Cambridge, UK.*

Box 2.2 Theories of the split between 'work' and home

The nature of the relation between economic and social life has long been the subject of theoretical debate among social scientists. One set of theories focuses on the *differences and separation* between the two spheres, and only secondarily on their interconnections. In a general sense this has been true of mainstream social science since the nineteenth century, when 'economics', 'sociology' and 'psychology' emerged as distinct academic disciplines, corresponding to distinct professions and distinct branches of government. The separation was codified definitively by Max Weber, who worked in the late nineteenth and early twentieth century. Weber argued that society and social difference are organized in distinct spheres which are *constituted* separately from each other; in particular, class is constituted in the economy, and social status within the social realm. This kind of distinction has been institutionalized in the split between 'economic geography' and 'social geography'; and some geographers have explicitly adopted the Weberian approach (Mollenkopf, 1981; Wolch and Dear, 1989a; Savage and Warde, 1993). Within feminist theory, the 'dual systems' approach has argued that contemporary societies should be understood as constituted by two distinct systems, capitalism and patriarchy, associated with class and gender respectively (Young, 1981).

Others, however, see economic and social life as parts of a single system, as constructed *jointly*. Yet this system itself makes a division between the two spheres. This approach is adopted by some theorists who focus on 'discourses'. Discourses of the home as a realm separate from and opposed to 'work' are seen as important, even dominant. And yet, it is argued, this distinction can be reinterpreted and subverted by individuals, and may ultimately be arbitrary (Gibson and Watson, 1994, Part 1). In socialist–feminist theory and most Marxist work, economic and social life are seen as a single system for organizing the work which sustains people. The split between these spheres is then understood as produced by the different social relations and spaces organizing 'work' and housework respectively (Barrett, 1988; Little, Peake and Richardson, 1988; Harvey, 1989a). These approaches have led to a large amount of work in human geography which seeks to analyse the economic and social realms as a single, if split, system. Most of this chapter uses socialist–feminist and Marxist approaches.

We now examine in a little more detail the social relations of the two spheres and how geography enters into their construction. For clarity, we shall refer to the formal, waged economy as 'production' and work performed outside it as the 'reproduction of people' (see Box 2.3).

Box 2.3 'Reproduction'

In everyday language, 'reproduction' usually means biological reproduction. In social science, however, it is used to mean all the activities which sustain people's lives other than the capitalist production of consumer goods and services, especially housework, care of dependants, and welfare services. Marxists often refer to 'the reproduction of labour power', focusing attention on people's role as waged workers. However, we are interested here in 'the reproduction of people', which includes, but is not limited to, their capacity for waged labour. Reproduction is sometimes referred to as the 'social' or 'residential sphere', as distinct from the 'economy'.

2.3 Employment relations and space

Firms' profits, which are the life-blood of a capitalist economy, depend on employers being able to exert a certain power over workers. In the work process, firms must be able to exert sufficient discipline to ensure that the net product exceeds the wage bill. In the labour market, business needs some way of restraining the wage rises and reductions in hours that workers seek.

This power of capital over workers is normally secured through a combination of workers' dependence on the firm which employs, or may employ, them, and competition between workers for this employment. Most adults in the MDCs need to seek waged work in order to have a reasonable standard of living: state benefits may be adequate for a time, but in most MDCs are set at poverty levels; genuine self-employment is only a small minority of employment, and much is low income or insecure. People therefore have an interest in the stability and profitability of business which employs, or may employ, them. Moreover, workers are in competition with others to get (better) jobs.

This dependence and competition are intrinsically geographical (Gough, 1992). Most people have social ties to a particular territory – a neighbourhood, town, region or country – because of relationships with partners, family and friends or enjoyment of its social milieux, facilities or landscapes. These territorial ties vary enormously between groups in the population, particularly by age, gender, possession of a partner, and employment skills; nevertheless, they are important to some extent for most people (Cox, 1998). Because of these ties people are unwilling to move away from 'their' territory, and are therefore dependent on its firms. On the other hand, the capital which provides these jobs in general has different spatial horizons. If production is insufficiently profitable, it will seek to move elsewhere. The scale of capital's mobility is highly variable: retail workers may be threatened with redundancy as jobs shift to shops a few kilometres away; workers in clothing manufacturing may be threatened by shifts between continents. But all such shifts act as a disciplinary pressure on workers, enabling managements to keep work rates up and wages and conditions down.

It is often said that capital is globally mobile while labour is tied to locality. But this is too simple. It ignores the enormous differences in the mobility of both workers and types of capital. And it is the *relative* scales of mobility of capital and labour which matters: if the retail worker wants to keep her job because it is accessible to her home, or because her friends work in the shop, then a shift of jobs even a short distance is a threat; but for a young worker in finance with few social attachments or responsibilities, a shift of the banking sector between London and Frankfurt may not be too serious. The discipline of workers by capital is thus a function of the *relative* geographies of production and reproduction.

Cooperating with their employer to secure local jobs is not the only means by which workers can compete for employment. Workers from relatively privileged social groups – men, whites, ethnic nationals, the middle-aged – may also compete through formal or informal arrangements which reserve jobs for the social group to which they belong (Walby and Bagguley, 1989). Indeed, a major cause of such social divisions is this competition in the labour market. In the case of ethnicity, discrimination uses prejudice against people based on attributes of their (supposed) country of origin, particularly the socially-produced lower incomes of their economies. Thus a central cause of racism in the MDCs is the combination of under-development of the Third World with workers' competition for jobs (see Chapter 5).

Employers have to secure and reproduce their power over labour. But their task is more complex (even) than this. For speed and quality of production to be adequate, workers need to use their *initiative* in sorting out temporary problems in the production process. Employers can also benefit from workers' deep knowledge of the work they do in making long-term changes to production or products. Managements thus tend to pursue ever-shifting compromises between eliciting active cooperation and maintaining discipline (Friedman, 1977).

Box 2.4 Differences, dilemmas and conflicts in jobs

In all workplaces there are tensions between:

workers' autonomy	management's discipline over workers
high skill	low skill
good wages	low wages
secure employment	insecure employment
fixed hours	variable hours
promotion prospects	no promotion prospects

Each of these aspects is linked with the others in complex ways. Managements tend to accentuate the right-hand side attributes when they seek to reduce costs, and those on the left when they want to improve production and product quality. Particular jobs at particular times lean towards one side or the other of these tensions (Figs 2.3 and 2.4). For example, jobs in television in Britain from the 1950s to the 1980s were generally towards the left of the diagram, but since then many aspects have been shifted towards the right. Think where industries such as aerospace and hotels in your country today might lie.

Figure 2.3 *Work in a call centre usually involves strong management surveillance, close measurement of work, and penalties for workers who 'fail'. Credit: Network Photographers.*

Figure 2.4 *Workers in this architects' office have a substantial degree of autonomy in performing and scheduling their work, and interact with each other as well as with management. Credit: J. Gough.*

This tension is closely connected to other aspects of employment such as skill, wages, job security, hours and promotion prospects (Box 2.4). All these are the subject of conflict between workers and employers and pose dilemmas for management. Widely different temporary resolutions are found in different sectors, occupations and firms. These resolutions depend on many factors including the technical nature of the product and work process, the particular mix of quality and cost competition faced by firms, and the intensity of competition (Thompson, 1989). We shall see shortly that these differences and changes in jobs have major implications for social life.

2.4 Conceptions of class

The discussion so far enables us to examine different ideas of class and its relation to geography. There are two broad approaches to class: class as a *personal attribute* and class as a *relation* (Wood, 1995). The first approach is concerned to assign a class position or identity to individuals or households. This can be specified according to a number of variables: income, skill, social status, security of employment, type of knowledge or cultural competences possessed ('cultural capital'), accent, consumption pattern, and so on. Each of these variables has a continuum of values, and the variables can be combined and weighted in different ways; thus typologies of class can be constructed in an infinite number of ways, none of which is clearly superior. There are further dilemmas within this approach. Should one classify *individuals* (in which case the sharing of income and knowledge within households is neglected) or *households* (in which case one neglects differences in externally obtained incomes and work-related skills, which are often correlated with gender and age)? And to what extent are adults' class identities defined by the households in which they grew up, and to what extent their current situation?

The second approach to class, implicit in the discussion of employment above, is to see it as a set of relations between people and firms. People as isolated individuals do not have a class; they acquire class 'relationally', through entering into

Box 2.5 Politics and culture in theories of class

The two approaches also differ politically. Class-as-relation explicitly sees class as changeable and subject to struggle, and implicitly sees it as capable of radical revision or abolition; class-as-position takes class variation as given, and implicitly sees it as inevitable. Both approaches can be concerned with 'cultural' as well as 'economic' aspects of class. But whereas class-as-position takes for granted variation in cultural attributes (for example, that few manual workers read 'quality' newspapers), class-as-relation sees traits such as knowledge, status, individualism/collectivism and autonomy/conformity as constructed through the social organization of production and conflicts within it.

Figure 2.5 *Class relations in space: Petticoat Lane market in the East End of London, with the financial district of the City in the background. People using these two spaces have different class identities. But what are the relations between them? Credit: J. Gough.*

relations with others. The class nature of individuals is then constructed through disciplinary or cooperative relations with employers, and through relations with other workers with whom they compete or collaborate (section 2.3). These relations give rise to particular incomes, skills, work autonomy, status, and types of knowledge. These are not, then, fixed positions which people occupy but outcomes of dynamic and unstable processes. In this approach, the differences in income, skill, and so on are not taken as given but are to be explained (Harvey, 1982). The dilemmas in the positional approach concerning the class position of individuals, households and generations are approached by focusing on the *processes* involved, for example, how individuals' class position can be changed (or not) as they age, or how resources and work are shared (or not) within households.

The two approaches have different understandings of the *geography of class*. Since class-as-position is primarily concerned with classifying individuals or households, geographers using this approach analyse territories by the class characteristics of their resident populations. A body of work in this vein is the 'urban ecology' analysis of localities (Knox, 1995: 40–57). Within Britain, one could for example compare the internal class characteristics of Berkshire and County Durham. In contrast, geographers who regard class as a relation analyse the processes by which class attributes are *created* both within territories and across them (Allen, Massey and Cochrane, 1997). Study of the class character of County Durham, for example, is then concerned with the relations between capital and labour within the county, but also with the ways in which the mobility of capital in and out of County Durham creates class processes within it. Moreover, the headquarters and research and development work of companies employing people in County Durham may be located in Berkshire; there are thus class relations (management–workers, workers–workers) *between* Berkshire and County Durham – or more precisely, between people and institutions located within them. The relational approach to class thus lends itself to geography conceived as relations (Harvey, 1996a).

2.5 Geographical production processes and patterns

Only the slightest knowledge of the world is necessary to know that the formal economies of different nations, regions and localities differ sharply from one another. As we shall see, this uneven development in production has crucial implications for social life.

The uneven geography of production is produced by the interaction of *economic relationships within territories* and *economic flows between territories*; aspects of each of these are shown in Box 2.6.[1] The internal relationships within a territory may be successful in the sense of producing competitive firms, high profits and high investment rates; these are usually in specific industries, giving rise to a particular territorial specialization (Storper and Walker, 1989). The territory's economy then tends to be relatively stable. Flows between the territory and others may help its economy to

Box 2.6 Internal relationships and economic flows

The most important types of economic relationships (or 'linkages') within territories are:
- between firms and their labour force: employment practices and industrial relations
- between the labour force and resources for reproduction
- between firms and other firms which supply them or which they supply
- between firms and financial institutions
- between firms and transport and communications infrastructures
- between all the above and business organizations and parts of the state.

These webs of relationships, which collectively can be termed the territory's 'business culture' (Gertler, 1997), market rules (Christopherson, 1993) or its economic 'coherence' (Harvey, 1989b, Ch.5; Cox, 1993), can be very long-lasting.

Economic flows between territories include (Knox and Agnew, 1994; Dicken, 1998):
- trade in goods and services
- finance for investment or speculation
- labour
- production facilities
- economically useful knowledge

develop by providing markets, finance, inward investment, useful knowledge and labour. But these flows may also weaken or drain the territory's economy, causing it to decline. Moreover, some types of production are relatively 'footloose' in that their linkages are relatively few, unspecialized and easy to achieve. Box 2.7 provides an example. We shall

Box 2.7 Regional economies in Britain

Some regional economies in contemporary Britain have strong and successful internal relationships. An example is the financial industry of London, which benefits from a skilled labour force, dense and strong relations between firms, sympathetic regulation, and advanced communications. Other examples in south east England are the media industries, high-level business services, and software writing. All these industries benefit from international trade, financial flows and migration of skilled workers. Their location is stable.

On the other hand, there are localized industries of long standing with strong internal linkages which have nevertheless declined; this is true of many localities with mature manufacturing sectors. International flows are partly responsible for undermining these, by directing finance away from them, using their skills and knowledge in other places, and subjecting them to competition in widening markets.

The poorer regions of Britain have received footloose investment, such as low-skilled manufacturing, routine office work and call centres. These benefit – temporarily – from the mobility of production facilities and finance and from trade with other regions and nations. But these flows can just as easily undermine these types of production as they move to yet cheaper locations.

(See further Hudson and Williams, 1995).

Figure 2.6 *The many clothing firms concentrated in Whitechapel, London, are dependent on each other and on local skilled labour. The photo shows a former synagogue and a present-day mosque used by Bengalis, indicating the communities which have worked in the clothing trade at different times. Although the industry is rooted in the locality, the use of gender and racial difference by employers, and pressure of imports from lower-wage countries, have produced poor wages and insecure employment. Credit: J. Gough.*

Figure 2.7 *Part of a business park, Newcastle, England. Unlike the firms in Whitechapel, the workplaces located here are mostly branch offices of large firms, have little relation to each other, and the workers are mostly non-local, as suggested by the cars. These offices are located here mainly for the low costs characteristic of depressed regional economies, and in some cases to serve local customers. Credit: J. Gough.*

see later in the chapter that social life itself contributes to forming these uneven geographies of production.

What are the implications for the geography of jobs? Firstly, the quality of employment is highly variable between territories. Certain nations and regions, usually those with elaborate and politically successful internal relationships, generate jobs which are relatively skilled, high paid and secure; cooperation between capital and labour tends to both reinforce and be reproduced by these business cultures. At the other end of the spectrum are territories with weak internal relationships, where jobs tend to be low skilled, low paid and insecure, and where employers tend to exert authoritarian control over workers and the work process (cf. Box 2.4).

Secondly, the stock of jobs in a particular territory may change rapidly, sometimes positively, sometimes not. Footloose types of production may be moved to a territory which is cheaper or has freer or less demanding labour. But even workers in strongly integrated production complexes may see their jobs undermined by the growth of rival complexes elsewhere. As we saw in section 2.3, these mobilities of production can strengthen the hand of employers.

2.6 Reproduction work and its geographies

Just as production is organized through particular social relations, so too is the work of 'reproduction' (Box 2.3). Aspects of reproduction are discussed throughout the book. Here we focus on the more 'economic' aspects: the different kinds of *work* involved, the ways in which reproduction is moulded by private property, and how it is influenced by production. The argument of this section is pictured in Figure 2.8.

In a capitalist society many of the goods and services which people require are purchased from firms. Incomes and the 'commodities' (Box 2.8) they purchase may be used by individuals, but they may also be shared. This sharing, however, is limited by notions of private property, particularly in the developed countries. In North America and Australia some indigenous peoples share income within the clan; but the predominant form of sharing in the MDCs is within heterosexual or homosexual couples, families, or households of close friends. The boundaries of these units of sharing are strongly constructed by the fact that within mature capitalism incomes, whether from wages, profits or state benefits, are overwhelmingly *individual* incomes, and moreover

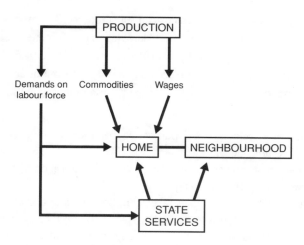

Figure 2.8 *The economics of reproduction work.*

vary enormously between individuals. This generates a 'property-based individualism' within which people are unwilling to share income beyond those closest to them. Moreover, because people are hired *individually* as wage workers, people are often forced to move to obtain suitable employment, severing ties with their communities. Thus the composition of households is profoundly influenced by the system of capitalist production.

Box 2.8 'Commodities'

In human geography 'commodities' usually refers to goods and services which are bought and sold. The simplest commodities are those which are produced by the production system just before they are sold. Other commodities, sometimes known as 'fictitious', are not produced, or have been produced long ago: examples are land, older buildings, and shares, bonds and financial derivatives. A person's ability to do waged work is a special kind of commodity, produced by reproduction work and sold to employers.

The household as the primary unit of purchase of commodities influences the nature of those commodities themselves. From housing to cars to ready-made meals, things are designed to be consumed by 'normal' households. And the form of these goods in turn influences the ways in which households can conveniently be formed.

Purchased goods require unpaid work to transform them. The majority of this work is organized within the same household units within which income is shared. In households with a mix of genders, however, this labour is not shared equally: women and girls organize and perform the majority of this work (see Chapter 6).

In certain ways, purchase of commodities can substitute for domestic work. Over the history of industrial capitalism, consumer durables have lightened domestic tasks (washing machines replace washing by hand), and purchased services have replaced work done in the home (take-aways replace cooking). These options are more available the higher the household's income. But purchased commodities can also, paradoxically, *increase* domestic work:

- Work is involved in selecting and purchasing commodities: shopping is now the largest single 'free time' activity.
- Many consumer commodities are associated with new activities, particularly hobbies and leisure, rather than labour saving.
- Repairs and replacement of durables takes considerable time and energy.
- The use of commodities tends to set higher standards which require more domestic work to achieve: shirts are worn for one day rather than a week before being washed.

A result is that the time spent on domestic work in the MDCs has not declined substantially during the twentieth century. Thus unpaid domestic work remains enormously important.

Social relations and scales other than the household are also involved in reproduction. A significant amount of unpaid work is organized through informal or semi-formal collaboration within neighbourhoods – child care, the care of the infirm, help with repairs, borrowing of things, watching out for people and property. These forms of collaboration are certainly *restricted* by the economic and ideological dominance of the private household, but they nevertheless survive, albeit in very different intensities and forms in different neighbourhoods (Pahl, 1984).

There are, however, vital aspects of reproduction which commodity purchase and unpaid labour together cannot adequately provide, and which have been taken up by services organized by the state and provided free or at a subsidized price – the 'welfare state'. These services are of two types. First is the *overall reproduction of particular social groups* such as children, people with severe disabilities, and the chronically sick. Over the last hundred years in the MDCs the state has increasingly provided services and incomes specifically for these groups. The need to do so has been increased by households becoming smaller, thus excluding or marginalizing those social groups. The organization of waged work has increased the need for care by public services of children and other dependants: time demands on working-age adults have increased, particularly with the increasing participation by women in waged work; and increasing migration for jobs disrupts household care.

Secondly, *particular aspects of reproduction* tend to be poorly achieved by household and neighbourhoods alone: these include education and training, health, and the regulation of the residential built environment (Chapter 10). Again, state provision in, or regulation of, these fields has grown since the late nineteenth century, though with large variations between MDCs. And again, changes in the production sphere have tended to increase the *need* for such state intervention. As production uses increasingly elaborate equipment and infrastructures, absences of workers through ill-health or domestic responsibilities become increasingly expensive. The deepening of technical skills in some occupations requires better education and training. The intensification of work is supported by education which inculcates work discipline (Bowles and Gintis, 1976), by promoting health, and by facilitating relaxation in 'leisure time'. The growth of state provision and regulation in these fields has in part been a response to pressure from people; but it has also often been supported by business with an eye on the quality of the labour force (I. Gough, 1979).

We have thus seen three types of reason why the functions of the welfare state have tended to expand:

- The production system makes increasingly stringent demands on workers, whose reproduction then needs more support.
- The technical requirements of some aspects of reproduction – for example work-related skills and health technologies – have tended to become more elaborate and thus beyond the means of households.

- It has become more difficult for households and neighbourhood cooperation to meet reproduction needs due to decreasing household size, enhanced household mobility, and women's waged employment – combined with men's avoidance of domestic work.

Thus we have the paradox that the development of production makes more demands on reproduction while at the same time reducing the ability of households to meet those demands.

To summarize the main points on reproduction:

- Reproduction is carried out through a variety of forms of work and property ownership – purchase of commodities, unpaid domestic work within households and neighbourhoods, semi-informal exchanges of work, and state services and regulation. The fit between these different forms is complex, varies between social groups, and changes over time. These divisions of responsibility are full of tensions.
- As section 2.2 above would suggest, these different types of reproduction are profoundly structured by the production system and its geography. The economy produces incomes of various kinds with which commodities are purchased; wage labour strongly influences the composition of households; incomes and household forms affect the ability of domestic provision to satisfy reproduction needs; and wage labour shapes people's needs and their aspirations in the social sphere.
- The reproduction sphere creates people with more-or-less adequate capacities for waged work, and hence influences production. The historical development of the forms of reproduction has been partly a response to demands placed on workers by the production system, demands articulated by both workers and employers.

Having examined the characteristic social–spatial forms of production and reproduction respectively, in the remainder of the chapter we look at how their combination develops in space.

2.7 The nexus of production and reproduction within nations and localities

We have seen that the reproduction sphere is strongly influenced by the production system, and that it in turn influences production. Since territories have very different economies (section 2.5), they are then likely to have varied social spheres too. Investigating this question will enable us to examine in more depth both the *separation* and the *interdependence* of the two spheres (section 2.2). We first consider the production–reproduction nexus in a fairly abstract way, and then look at examples in nations and localities. The shape of the argument of this section is shown in Figure 2.9.

Nations, regions and localities have specific mixes of types of jobs and workers, and these have many effects on the social life and culture of the territory:

- Wages, their temporal stability and long-term growth prospects have decisive impacts on the means for reproduction and social life.

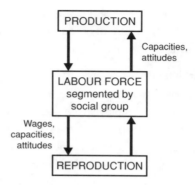

Figure 2.9 *The nexus of production and reproduction in a territory.*

- Gender, age and ethnic divisions of labour, and the wages, stability and hours of the respective jobs, strongly influence household formation and the divisions of labour within domestic work. They also have strong effects on popular prejudices about these social differences (*see further* Part II).
- Wages, security of employment, promotion prospects and skill strongly influence people's status in their own and others' eyes; and this status affects not only their 'position in society' but their friendships and intimate relationships.
- The possibilities for individuals to find work in other territories affects their relations within their household and their local social ties.
- Workers' career paths, skills, approach to work and attitude to employers shape their self-discipline, individualism and acquisition of knowledge – central elements of a person's personality.
- People's identities as workers and their relationships with others in production – similarity of jobs, degree of daily interaction, competition for promotion, cooperation against the employer – affect people's identification and sympathy with others in their territorial community, with impacts on their patterns of social contacts, neighbourliness and citizenship.

But it is not merely that production influences social life; social life has a profound influence on production. The work of reproduction in each territory produces a labour force specific to the territory with particular capacities and attitudes:

- The participation of men and women and people of different ages in waged work is conditioned by the composition of households, their income, and the way they share out domestic work.
- The participation of members of oppressed groups in waged work is affected by prejudices generated within social life.
- People's attitudes to employment and the capacities they bring to work are developed by roles and cultures in households and wider social life, including attitudes to knowledge. Welfare services such as education are also important here.

- People's membership of trade unions and their preparedness to oppose employers are conditioned not only by the nature of production but also by attitudes developed in the social life of the locality or nation (Martin, Sunley and Wills, 1996).

One effect of these mutual interactions of production and reproduction is to 'segment' the labour force. Different social groups have different types of jobs and employment relations due to the *combination* of employers' choices and workers' social lives (Peck, 1996). This segmentation of labour is specific to the particular territory.

However, a territory's labour force does not necessarily meet the wishes of employers. The possibility of such a 'mismatch' arises from the split between production and reproduction with which we began this chapter. The historical separation of workers from the means of employment and the creation of 'home' distinct from production mean that employers do not directly produce their labour force. The growth of production in ever larger urban areas has exacerbated this problem, since employers hire their workforce from labour pools over which they can have little direct influence. It is true that competition for jobs puts pressure on people to make themselves attractive to employers (section 2.3). But social and financial circumstances often prevent people from doing so, and people may anyway refuse to subordinate their lives to work in this way. The social sphere may thus fail, from the employers' point of view, to produce workers with the 'right' skills and the 'right' expectations of employment conditions and responsibilities within work. The household structure and local cultures may fail to

Figure 2.10 *An inner neighbourhood of Newcastle, England. The social and spatial coordination of employment, housing, privately supplied consumer services and public services – in this case a further education college – potentially presents many problems. These are felt by workers, residents and employers, albeit in different ways. Credit: J. Gough.*

deliver a (potential) labour force with the gender, age and ethnic composition desired by firms. Moreover, the spaces of social life may generate attitudes which lead to resistance to employers. A territory's social sphere, then, *may or may not* be functional to the profitability of its economy.

A territory's labour force also strongly affects the *long-term dynamics* of the economy. New investment in a territory is always dependent on the nature of the (potential) labour force. It may use the longstanding capacities of the workforce; this normally means investment in sectors in which the territory is already strong or in related sectors. On the other hand, new investment may be very different from existing production. In some British regions of declining industry, for example, the high rate of unemployment and an increase in women seeking waged jobs have attracted investment providing mainly semi-skilled jobs for women; the influence of the labour market on investment has thus led to radical shifts in sectors, employment conditions, and social groups employed. Such shifts lay down what Massey (1984a) has termed successive 'layers' of production within a territory, which coexist sometimes well, sometimes conflictually with each other.

To summarize this section so far:

- Employment within a nation, region or locality has major impacts on its household formation, social life, culture, reproduction practices and people's personalities.
- The specific forms of reproduction and social life in a territory mould the skills, attitudes and social composition of the labour force, with decisive impacts on the economy. These impacts are on both the short-term profitability and the long-term development of the economy.
- The socially produced labour force may or may not meet employers' requirements.

We now consider these processes at the particular scales of the nation and the locality, and give some examples.

2.7.1 Nations

The relation of social life and the economy within particular nations has been analysed by sociologists and historians more than by geographers; nevertheless, it is an important topic for us. Every change in economic relations within a nation has impacts on the social sphere and vice versa; the previous discussion should enable you to think of examples. Rather less obvious is that particular practices within production and reproduction and

Box 2.9 National social–economic settlements

Japan

In the late nineteenth century Japan experienced a very rapid industrialization, designed by the elite to catch up with the leading capitalist countries. This was effected through close cooperation between large companies and the state. Industry drew on large supplies of formerly peasant labour. After Japan's imperial expansion in the 1930s and its defeat in WWII, its model of industrialization was threatened by militant offensives by the trade unions, which were, however, defeated. From the mid-1950s, large firms were able to impose intense work discipline onto workers while also eliciting active cooperation, and an extensive small-firm sector remained in which worker organization was very difficult. This economic history has profoundly marked social life. Rapid industrialization has meant that social mores of rural society have continued to have a greater influence than in north-western Europe. Disciplinary industrial relations have given rise to a culture marked by strong commitment to work and, in large firms, to one's employer. The appropriation of existing technologies by Japanese firms has lent itself to a culture where disciplined application has been more highly regarded than creativity. In the post-war period, the availability of a pool of labour in the countryside meant that employers did not need to use married women as a labour force, affecting households and gender relations. The rapid rate of growth and corresponding power of business up to the 1980s inhibited radical social movements and reinforced 'traditional' social mores.

Australia

After the foundation of the unified Australian state and its independence from Britain in 1901, a settlement was reached between business and the unions which was to last until the 1980s. Business would pay wages to male workers sufficient to support a family, without need for married women to bring in an additional wage. Public service spending would be kept at a low level, thus saving business taxes; welfare was to be secured through the 'family wage'. Immigration would be limited to white people, which the unions believed would help to keep wages high. These wage levels were sustained initially by high productivity agriculture, and later mining, and privileged access to the British market. A manufacturing sector with good wages would be developed using high tariffs to protect it against imports, creating a further field of cooperation between Australian business and labour. This 'Federation settlement' was bound up with key social phenomena. It involved racism and an acceptance of strongly differentiated gender roles. It encouraged a nationalistic bond between workers and business. The weakness of welfare services and state benefits made people strongly dependent on family resources. The importance of the family unit was further enhanced by the high rate of immigration, due to the characteristic dependence of new migrants on family support (see Chapter 5). At the same time, the high profitability of the primary industries, and protection against dismissal afforded by the statutory industrial relations machinery, allowed a casual attitude of men to work and a suspicion of authority developed in the nineteenth century to continue through the twentieth.

the way they fit together can often be quite durable, lasting for decades; we may call these 'national settlements'.[2] These stamp the character of the society over long periods, and severely constrain social and economic change. Box 2.9 gives thumb-nail sketches of two such settlements, illustrating the sort of relationships that may be involved.

A number of general points can be taken from these sketches:

- The character of social relations within a national economy depends strongly on its external political and economic relations. Different scales are interdependent.

- National settlements are created by class, gender and ethnic conflicts, sometimes over substantial periods, and they in turn perpetuate particular assumptions about these identities (S. Duncan, 1994).
- Arrangements which at first sight might appear to concern production alone can also have profound implications for reproduction in the form of welfare services and household dependencies.

2.7.2 Localities

National settlements have different effects in each locality. Since most people work and live within the same locality, locally distinct production is associated with particular labour forces, which in turn may be associated with specific social structures (Warde, 1988). Changes in waged work can then have major impacts on the social sphere (Box 2.10). Moreover, for localities as for nations, one can find social practices spanning the two spheres which are durable over long periods – though not, of course, immutable. Thus localities may have distinctive, durable patterns of labour market regulation and industrial relations, created through class, gender and ethnic conflicts within both production and reproduction, and perpetuated through local institutions such as welfare services, training schemes and industrial bargaining arrangements (Eisenschitz and Gough, 1993; Peck,

---

Box 2.10 Employment, household work and gender in Mo i Rana

Mo i Rana is a town in northern Norway which became a major centre of publicly owned steel-making in the 1950s. The industrialization of Mo changed gender relations: in the small-scale farming and fishing which had previously dominated the region the work of both men and women was valued; in the new steel industry men took nearly all the jobs while their wives became full-time housewives. In the 1980s there was a sharp cutback in employment in steel, and a rapid rise in service jobs, both shaped by national government policies. Many women took jobs in services or undertook further education, encouraged by Norway's state benefits system whereby benefits paid to men did not decrease when their wives took paid employment.

These changes were accompanied by major changes within heterosexual households. In some cases, particularly among older people, the man became a full-time domestic worker while his wife went out to work. In most households men started to do far more domestic work. But women generally did not trust men to organize this, and they continued to do domestic tasks where cleanliness and care were particularly important, masculinity in Mo being strongly associated with dirt and roughness. There was therefore both continuity and change in gender roles. The older men often coped well with these changes, partly by reverting to the rural activities of their youth, which gave them a sense of worth; the younger men lacked such skills for self-realization (Sande, 1997).

Thus production, gender and age relations were closely intertwined and locally distinctive. Notice how each successive 'layer' of the local economy and household roles is conditioned by earlier ones. Notice also how national policies can condition the development of a locality in a unique way.

1996). At a smaller spatial scale, neighbourhoods are strongly differentiated by income and occupational identities (Harvey, 1989a, Ch. 4; Knox, 1995).

The dominant gender and sexual relations can differ markedly between localities, and these may be related to the local economy (McDowell and Massey, 1984). If one considers cities within England, for example, Newcastle and Liverpool have traditions of hedonism and strongly sexualized heterosexual nightlife, which may be related to the importance of casualized employment as well as to the influence of people removed from their families passing through the ports. Images of this character of the local populations, together with reputations for industrial militancy, have in turn affected the local economies through frightening off some types of investor. Nottingham, by contrast, has long had a large lesbian scene, predominantly working class, which has been based around the big food, tobacco and medical goods factories employing mainly women. Another contrast is provided by Sheffield, which up until the deindustrialization of the 1980s had a dominant model of sober and 'respectable' families based on a man's 'family wage', associated with a rather limited night life. This may have been linked to the main industry, specialist steel and castings, which employed men in mostly skilled and secure jobs, paying a wage which enabled wives to be denied wage jobs. Thus even sexual relations may be related to local traditions of employment.

2.8 Actively moulding the nexus of production and reproduction

The nexus of production and reproduction within nations and localities is to some extent formed unconsciously, but also through conscious action by business, labour, residents and the state. In this section we consider such strategies.

Employers often choose their location in order to mould their labour force and its reproduction to their benefit. They may maintain production in one location for a long time in order to build up cooperative relations with their workforce and to be able to exert long-term influence over local institutions of reproduction. This influence is perhaps most obvious in 'company towns', where one firm dominates local employment; in such cases, a firm may be able to exercise a paternalistic control over the population, using the carrot of welfare facilities and the stick of people's dependence on the firm (for example Beynon et al., 1989). But employers may find that relations with their workforce or local social conditions are escaping their control, and may then shift production to another locality. When relocation results in a substantially new workforce, the firm can set up new working and employment arrangements; this is especially the case where the industry has no history in the new location – a 'green workforce' (Gordon, 1984).

Active roles in shaping production–reproduction relations are also played by national and local governments. The state plays an important role in steering and supporting industry and in influencing its geography. But particularly relevant here are policies concerned with the interface between production and reproduction. Some industrial and regional policy – though by no means all – is directed at securing jobs in areas of high unemployment with the intention of maintaining the social fabric of the area, preventing

Figure 2.11 *Picket in coal miners' strike, Britain, 1984. Isolated communities, such as mining villages, can enable paternalistic control by employers. But they can also give rise to strong solidarity and organization among workers and residents. Credit: Network Photographers.*

out-migration and the deterioration of housing, infrastructures and welfare services; such intervention is sometimes a response to pressure from trade unions and residents. Another strategy at the intersection of the two spheres is community businesses run on a not-for-profit basis; these draw on community structures and loyalties, and, while providing jobs, also often provide useful services for residents of poor neighbourhoods (McArthur, 1993). Yet other state interventions are concerned directly with the reproduction sphere but are partly motivated by economic aims. For example, the support given by English town planners over the last hundred years to the development of leafy suburbs of 'family' houses reinforces an anti-industrial and anti-urban culture (Williams, 1993; *see further* Chapter 9); this has been expected by some of its advocates to construct an atomized, disciplined and sober workforce – though whether it actually has that effect is another matter (Short, 1991). A large part of national and local governments' social and economic interventions thus *span the divide* between the economic and the social, aiming to shape the two spheres simultaneously.

Territorial nexuses of production and reproduction are therefore *consciously* constructed through

- employers' wish to tap particular segments of labour,
- conflicts between employers and workers,
- employers' wish to influence reproduction,
- state actions in response to these conflicts and to 'mismatches' of economy and society.

2.9 The present period

There is wide agreement amongst human geographers and social scientists that, worldwide, the period since the 1970s has differed in important ways from the period lasting from 1945 until the late 1960s – though what underlies these changes is controversial (Harvey, 1989b). In this final section we examine some important, interlinked changes in the spatial economy, state welfare services and social life during the last thirty years or so.

2.9.1 Changes in employment

In the present period profitability and economic growth have been lower than in the world economic boom of the 1950s and 1960s. We saw in section 2.3 that relations between management and labour contain a tension between discipline and cooperation. In the present period this tension has resulted in sharp contrasts between occupations and rapid changes in many, and these have varied between different countries (section 2.7.1). The predominant change, arguably, has been towards management exerting sharper discipline over workers and downward pressure on employment conditions. This can be found in each of the dimensions of employment given in Box 2.4:

- Unemployment rates have increased in nearly all MDCs, hitting the less skilled, the young, older workers and ethnic minorities disproportionately.
- Wages, especially those of less skilled occupations, have been held down or, in some cases, reduced; in the US for example, real wages for the majority of jobs have not changed or have declined over the last thirty years. Wages have been increasingly linked to management's measurements of workers' output, to the profitability of the work unit, or to the firm's share price through employee share-ownership schemes.
- Insecurity of employment has increased, through greater use of short-term contracts and higher rates of enforced redundancies. In many workplaces weekly hours have been made unpredictable as workers are employed for periods which suit the employer. Overtime, both voluntary and enforced, has tended to increase, particularly for men. Domestic service, where workers are in the weakest position of all, has expanded massively (Gregson and Lowe, 1994).
- The number of workers legally defined as 'self-employed' has increased. In some cases this represents real independence. But many of the 'self-employed' are subcontractors and effectively work for firms but with no security.

- Participation rates in waged work have generally increased for women and declined for men. In many countries this has been connected to increases in part-time employment.
- In the organization of the work process, many workers have been required to perform a greater variety of tasks. The pace and intensity of work, and the physical and mental exertion required, have been increased (T. Smith, 1994).
- Trade unions have been weakened by the threat of unemployment, decline of strongly unionized sectors, and restrictive laws on industrial action. The weaker power of the unions has made it easier for employers to carry through the changes just described, and casualization, payment by 'results', and part-time work have produced further difficulties for union organization (Martin, Sunley and Wills, 1996).

These changes taken together are sometimes referred to as 'flexible labour markets'. Evidently, flexibility here is largely *of* the worker and *for* the employer rather than the reverse (Pollert, 1999).

In certain occupations, however, some contrary trends can be found. In fast-growing, higher-skilled occupations there have been chronic shortages of labour; particularly in high-profit sectors, these shortages have enabled workers to obtain substantial wage increases. These workers also tend to be given considerable autonomy in the organization of their work, partly to keep them from leaving the firm, partly because such treatment elicits better quality work; some are self-employed (cf. section 2.3). This section of the workforce, then, is 'flexible' in a very different way. Even these relatively privileged workers may, however, be subjected variously to deskilling, work intensification, casualization, effectively-compulsory overtime, and gender discrimination.

Increasing managerial discipline combined with superior conditions for some skilled workers have produced a large increase in *dispersion* in employment conditions and wages. Some authors have pictured this as a 'disappearing middle' in the range of conditions. Differences in the quality of jobs between localities and within them have increased (Hudson and Williams, 1995).

How can we understand these changes? Part of the explanation lies in the particular working out over the last thirty years of the *geographical* production processes discussed in section 2.5. New forms of economic relations within territories and economic flows between them have developed, producing new ways in which production can be immobile or footloose. For those jobs which are (more) geographically mobile, employers have used relocation or the threat of it to reduce wages, intensify work, make hours flexible and worsen conditions (Ross, 1983). On the other hand, in production which is (for a period) spatially stable, workers tend to have more bargaining power since they cannot so easily be replaced.

Just how mobile contemporary production is is controversial. Some authors have emphasized the increasing mobility of many types of manufacturing and office work both within and between countries (Peet, 1983). This is seen as enabled by improvements in transport and telecommunications and by the cumulative industrialization of previously peripheral territories, but also, crucially, powered by the wish of firms to cut costs and discipline labour. In contrast, other authors have emphasized the spatial stability of production arising from relations within regional economies (Storper, 1997). Slightly different accounts of such relations have been given: 'industrial districts', 'technopoles', and 'learning', 'innovative' or 'networked regions' (Simmie, 1997). Such areas tend to attract investment because of their specific suppliers, services, infrastructures, business cultures, and, especially, their labour forces and reproduction spheres appropriate for them (cf. section 2.5). It is argued that such production complexes have become stronger in recent decades as creation, circulation and use of knowledge have become more important.

The mobile and immobile views of contemporary production may be combined in models which examine the dispersal of different stages of production of a product between territories through 'production chains' and global networks. A particular version of this approach is the 'new spatial division of labour' model, in which high-skill activities and those which benefit from dense, local linkages are located in relatively stable, high income production complexes, while less-skilled activities and those which do not require dense local linkages are dispersed to ever-shifting low-cost locations (Massey, 1984a; Dicken, 1998). The current patterns of mobility and immobility of production are, evidently, very complex and differentiated; this is one reason for the contrasts in employment relations which we noted earlier.

These developments have occurred within a wider set of economic–political relations in which the dominant – but not the only – strategy has been *neoliberalism*. From the 1970s onwards, in response to low average profitability and intense political–economic conflicts, business increasingly adopted a strategy of 'free markets'. Labour markets were to be freed from influence by trade unions and 'excessive' regulation by the state, thus facilitating intensification of work and helping to hold down wages. State regulation of industry and finance was to be reduced, encouraging less profitable lines of business to be abandoned and enabling capital to flow into new activities, sectors and locations. Increased mobility of investment flows and the freeing of trade – often referred to as economic 'globalization' – are an integral part of the neoliberal strategy in that they enhance the freedom of business. Freer investment flows and trade then intensify the pressure on labour to accept employers' demands.

2.9.2 State welfare services

State welfare services have been radically reformed in the last thirty years; reforms have differed between countries, but there are some discernible similarities:

- State spending on benefits and services has tended to be restrained and, in some cases, reduced in real terms.
- Benefits have tended to become more selective and conditional; benefits for the unemployed, in particular, have been increasingly tied to the recipient undertaking training and accepting any job offered, a practice known as 'workfare'.

- Charges to users for many services have been increased, and units delivering services have often had to seek additional private or charitable sources of funding.
- Units of service, such as individual schools or hospitals, are encouraged to compete against each other for clients and for their share of public funds, and have sometimes come to specialize in a particular client group.
- In many cases the direct management of services has been transferred from national or local government to unelected boards or voluntary organizations. Some services have been contracted out to private firms.

Like the changes in employment already discussed, these reforms may be seen as part of neoliberalism. State spending on reproduction of people is to be cut in order to reduce taxes, especially those on business, and thus increase private profitability. Privatization and competition are to increase the intensity of labour of service workers. The transfer of control to boards, the voluntary sector or private firms fragments and diffuses pressures for better services. And increased selectivity of services and charges for them fit with the increasing divergences in wages and incomes (Cochrane, 1993).

These changes in state services have had some direct impacts on social life and its geography:

- Cuts in services have increased people's reliance on their private resources, whether money incomes or support from family or friends.
- Pressures on resources and the decentralization of control have made access to good services more dependent on the political clout of the particular social group; this power may be used not only to obtain greater public and private funding but also, as in the case of decentralized control of schools and land use planning, to exclude other clients from service units on the basis of their class or 'race'. Quality of services comes to vary more strongly with an area's income.
- Decline in public intervention into housing accentuates differences in housing prices and quality by area (see *further* Chapter 10).

Box 2.11 Neoliberalism and increasing inequality in London

Sharp inequalities in London are longstanding. As one of the major world centres of finance and corporate headquarters, as capital city and centre of a former empire, London is one of the main centres of the world elite. It has many high-paid professionals. There have been a substantial number of higher-paid male manual workers employed in utilities and manufacturing. There have also been a large number of low-paid, often casualized jobs in consumer services, infrastructures, clerical work and manufacturing.

Since the 1970s these inequalities have been deepened. High-paid jobs have grown with the expansion and strong profitability of high-level finance, business services and cultural industries. Skilled manual jobs have declined with the closure or relocation of manufacturing. Low-paid service work and domestic service have expanded to service the well-off. Increasing income differentials have thus been even more pronounced in London than in the rest of Britain.

The reproduction of the poor in London has long been problematic. This has been due to insecure incomes, high land prices and high costs of some services, excerbated by exclusion by the outer suburbs; the indifference of the elite has been accentuated by the fact that the poor are not employed in London's 'core' sectors. But since the 1970s the growth of profits, jobs and incomes in the core, coupled with cuts in welfare services and social housing, have not only exacerbated the high costs and low quality of reproduction of the poor but have widened these problems to the middle-income population (Sassen, 1991; Fainstein, Gordon and Harloe, 1992). This overall crisis of reproduction has in turn damaged business (Peck and Tickell, 1995).

- Finally, moves between localities are made more difficult both by barriers of housing affordability and by people's increased reliance on established family and neighbourhood networks.

2.9.3 Effects on social life

Changing patterns of employment, combined with reforms in state services, have had major impacts on social life, illustrated in Box 2.11:

- The distribution of money income has become increasingly unequal (Hills and Walker, 1996). This is partly due to the increasing disparities in individuals' wages already discussed. But household incomes have tended to diverge even more than this, due to the fact that households with two people in waged employment and households with none have become increasingly common. Income differences have been widened by the relative decline in the value of state benefits. Since the 1980s incomes of some of the richest individuals – those who live on dividends, senior company executives, and high-level workers in finance – have increased very rapidly. People on middle and high incomes have tended to gain from increased individual share ownership and speculation and, in countries where home ownership is common, from rapid inflation in house prices. Many of these sources of increasing income for the well-off are not derived from work, let alone work effort, but are rather results of the increasingly 'financialized', 'fictitious' and speculative nature of the economy (Harvey, 1989b).
- We saw in sections 2.2 and 2.4 that capitalist society is built on property-based individualism. The present period has emphasized this trait; in the words of Margaret Thatcher 'there is no such thing as society, only individuals and their families'. Personal competitiveness, toughness and indifference to others have seemed to become more necessary and have been celebrated in dominant cultures (Geras, 1998). This shift may be traced to some of the changes already discussed. Within waged work, increasing differences in wages, job insecurity, deregulation of labour markets and weakening of trade unions have all encouraged workers to compete against, rather than cooperate with, each other (Sennett, 1998). In addition, widening income differences and changes to the welfare state make individual and household resources more important. One expression of these forms of economic competition has been increasing racism and xenophobia.

- Present-day economic conditions tend to promote social and cultural conservatism. In many jobs, particularly non-manual ones, success has always required the adoption of particular modes of speech, dress, deportment and social attitude; intensified competition for jobs has made this conformity more important (Halford and Savage, 1997). To receive state benefits or good consideration from a state service may require one to present oneself as 'respectable' and hence worthy. Income- and occupational-differences in clothing, consumer durables, housing styles, residential location and cultural products consumed take on an added force in times of heightened inequality; desire to consume prestigious commodities intensifies as economic and social status become more insecure and polarized.
- Instabilities in waged employment tend to make people's social situation and identities more unstable. Migration for jobs breaks people's ties to their neighbourhoods and can weaken family ties. A sense of insecure identity, sometimes described as 'postmodern', may have material roots.
- Yet, paradoxically, people may be *more* dependent on their communities due to the pressures towards individualism and employment-associated instabilities in social life. Local community, in particular, can assume greater importance both as a source of material support and its promise of stable identity (see *further* Chapter 4). But at the same time, as we have seen, localities are becoming more unequal in terms of employment, income and reproduction facilities, so that people's lives and life chances have become more constrained by where they live (Christopherson, 1994). Thus, in different ways, *place* becomes increasingly important.
- People's relations to communities, however, are in conflict with the intensified material demands of jobs. Longer hours and intensified work can leave people with too little time and energy for relations with their households, neighbours and friends.

These social changes rebound back onto production, in particular through their effects on the reproduction of labour forces. Intensification of poverty in particular neighbourhoods together with inadequate state services undermine the production of a disciplined labour force for low-status jobs. Increasing barriers to migration between localities restrict the labour supply in high-growth areas. At the other pole, increasing spatial concentration of high incomes in particular localities causes inflation of living costs, upward pressure on wages, and a forcing out of low-wage workers. Thus the contemporary economy has created reproduction conditions and a labour force which in many ways fail to meet the demands of firms. Here again we see the *mutual* influence of the 'economic' and the 'social'.

Summary

- Capitalist society embodies a split between the public spaces of 'work' and the private spaces of the home, with many important practical and ideological implications. The reproduction of people depends on both spheres, yet their split gives the possibility of mismatches between them.
- Production and its geography are marked by conflicts between employers and

workers and dilemmas for both. These are one cause of differences within and between territorial economies and of instabilities in these economies.

- Class and its geography can be analysed either as the characteristics of individuals or as relationships between people and institutions.
- Reproduction of people is carried out through a great variety of forms of work and cooperation, property and uses of space, between which there are both synergies and tensions.
- Production and reproduction construct each other over varied time periods and at different spatial scales. These nexuses are partly constructed through the conscious interventions of different social actors. The two spheres do not, however, necessarily fit together well.
- The period since the 1970s has seen major changes to socio-economic life and its geographies, many connected with neoliberalism. These have tended to accentuate individualism, social competitiveness, insecurity and inequalities.
- Social geographies are therefore deeply marked by economic relations and their geographies.

Notes

1. The approach to production geography in this chapter is in the Marxist paradigm (Harvey, 1982; Blunt and Wills, 2000, Ch. 2), with a considerable overlap with institutionalist approaches and socio-economics (Granovetter and Swedberg, 1992).
2. 'National settlements' is a similar concept to the notions of national 'regimes', 'social structures of accumulation' and 'mode of regulation' used by some geographers.

Further reading

On the geography of production, see:
- Harvey, D. (1996b) The geography of capitalist accumulation. In Agnew, J., Livingstone, D.N. and Rogers, A. (eds), *Human Geography: An Essential Anthology*. Oxford: Blackwell.

For its contemporary patterns, see:
- Schoenberger, E. (1989) New models of regional development. In Peet, R. and Thrift, N. (eds), *New Models in Geography*. London: Unwin Hyman, Vol. 1, pp. 115–41.

For a specific focus on employee relations and their geography:
- Massey, D. (1984a) *Spatial Divisions of Labour*. London: Macmillan.

- Peck, J. (1997) *Work-place: The Social Regulation of Labour Markets*. New York: Guilford Press.

Useful on class are the following:
- Massey, D. (1984a) *Spatial Divisions of Labour*. London: Macmillan, pp. 30–9.

- Short, J. (1996) *The Urban Order*. Oxford: Blackwell, pp. 207–19.

- Abercrombie, N. and Ward, A. (2000) *Contemporary British Society*, 3rd edn. Cambridge: Polity, Ch. 3.

The role of welfare services in reproduction is discussed in:

- Pinch, S. (1989) Collective consumption. In Wolch, J. and Dear, M. (eds), *The Power of Geography*. Boston: Unwin Hyman.

On the relationship between production, labour markets and the reproduction sphere
  – within nations:

- Esping-Andersen, G. (1990) *Three Worlds of Welfare Capitalism*. Cambridge: Polity.
  – within localities:

- Pratt, G. (1989) Reproduction, class and the spatial structure of the city. In Peet, R. and Thrift, N. (eds), *New Models in Geography*. London: Unwin Hyman, Vol. 1, pp. 84–108.

- Eisenschitz, A. and Gough, J. (1993) *The Politics of Local Economic Policy*. Basingstoke: Macmillan, Ch. 6.

- Savage, H. and Warde, A. (1993) *Urban Sociology, Capitalism and Modernity*. Basingstoke: Macmillan, Ch. 4.

On employment, social life and their connection in the present period:

- Pacione, M. (ed.) (1997) *Britain's Cities*. London: Routledge, esp. Ch. 1.

3
The place of leisure

3.1 Introduction: why a geography of leisure?

Leisure and recreation have always been on the fringes of mainstream academic study in geography, and it is only in recent years that social geographers have begun to re-evaluate their importance. We might ask ourselves why this has been the case. A recent survey indicates that on average in Britain the population spends only about 15 per cent of their time in waged work (this figure rises to over 25 per cent for those who work full time), 27 per cent of their time asleep and 20 per cent of their time on other essential activities such as eating, chores and caring for children. This leaves nearly 40 per cent of time to spend as people choose, most of which is spent on leisure (Henley Centre, 1994). On average, therefore, people in Britain spend at least twice as much time at leisure than they do at work. Why then have geographers dedicated so much time and type-space to the study of the world of work, yet so little to the world of leisure? Is it because we spend so much time writing about other people's work that we have no time left for leisure and no concept of the term? Or is it because the geographer's work is never done, we never stop observing and interpreting people and places, and every holiday or outing becomes a fieldtrip?

For an increasing number of people in western society, their work involves the provision of goods and services for other people's leisure. Over the last twenty-five years leisure has become a major source of employment and a favourite site for investment and capital accumulation. In western capitalist economies, leisure goods and services represent a major growth area in the economy. At the time of writing (June, 2000), at least eighteen of the top 100 Financial Times Stock Exchange (FTSE) listed companies were directly and primarily involved in the production of leisure goods and services (e.g. luxury foods and alcoholic beverages; pub, restaurant and hotel chains; DIY retailers; home entertainments; television and media). Several of these companies, such as Allied Domecq, Bass, Diageo and Scottish and Newcastle, make clever use of branded leisure goods and services in order to cater for a broad range of customers each occupying seemingly separate and distinctive niche markets (see Box 3.1).

Economic geographers, it seems, can no longer ignore the leisure industry: leisure is part of the changing economic fortunes of people and places, it is part of the redevelopment of redundant post-industrial urban spaces, and it offers an alternative

---

Box 3.1 Profile of a leading Financial Times Stock Exchange (FTSE) listed leisure corporation

Bass

Turnover (1999) £4,686 million   Profit (1999) £824 million

Branded products – drinks

Carling, Carling Premier, Caffrey's, Worthington, Bass, Grolsch, Tennents, Staropramen, Hooch, Reef, Britvic, Tango, Robinsons, Pepsi, J₂O

Branded retail outlets – bars and restaurants (number of outlets)

All Bar One (50), Browns (11), Harvester (129), Vintage Inns (132), Toby Carvery (127), Edwards (32), O'Neills (107), It's a Scream (68), Bar Coast (15), Goose (15), Hollywood Bowl (20), Dave and Busters (2)

Hotel chains (2800 establishments)

Intercontinental, Crowne Plaza, Holiday Inn, Express by Holiday Inn, Staybridge suites

(Source: www.bass.co.uk)

---

land use and economic enterprise to agriculture in rural areas. But what do we mean by a social geography of leisure?

Other social scientists, including sociologists, anthropologists, psychologists and cultural theorists, have contributed to a well established 'leisure studies' literature. But until relatively recently, much of work by human geographers tended to focus on what could be described as the more geographically distant and socially exclusive end of the leisure spectrum, namely international tourism, active sport and outdoor recreation (see Box 3.2). Very few have focused on the less spectacular, everyday, localized leisure activities of most of the population. However, with the growing influence of cultural theory on human geography, described by some as the 'cultural turn' (see Chapter 1, section 1.1), together with an increased interest in post-industrial geographies of consumption, social and cultural geographers have begun to wake up to the fact that there is a whole area of social life out there with which they have so far had limited academic engagement (Crouch, 1999; Skelton and Valentine, 1998; Aitchison, 1999a).

In this chapter we outline and illustrate with examples three conceptual approaches to the social geography of leisure. The first has its primary research focus on individuals and social groups, examining the relationships between place, identity and their leisure behaviour patterns. The second approach focuses on places themselves and the role played by leisure in shaping and changing their identities. Our third approach explores the social construction of leisure spaces and the social conflicts that surround them. Before we can do this, it is necessary to first explore the contested concept of leisure *per se* and particularly how it is conceptualized relative to other important areas of social life such as work, reproduction, and consumption.

Box 3.2 Relationships between leisure, recreation and tourism

Figure 3.1 attempts to illustrate graphically the interrelationships between leisure, recreation and tourism. The distinction between them is subtle and, depending on their social and spatial context, all can potentially be considered as production, reproduction or consumption (see section 3.2.2). Not all leisure, for instance, occurs outside work time and space (e.g. professional sports, office parties, business tourism). Although the boundaries between these different activities should be regarded as permeable, we prefer to see both recreation and tourism as distinct sub-areas of the much broader, more inclusive term leisure. Tourism is essentially leisure in distant places, usually involving at least an overnight stay away from where we normally live and work. Recreation is the most difficult sub-area to distinguish from leisure and many authors therefore use the terms interchangeably. Recreation tends to be considered as active pursuits carried out during leisure time but the word itself suggests that these pursuits should perform some form of reproductive (re-creative) function (see section 3.2.2a). Leisure itself is a contested concept and can be defined in at least three different ways; as non-work time, as activity and as experience. We explore each of these in section 3.2.1.

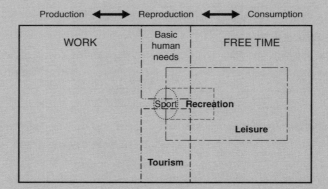

Figure 3.1 *Relationships between leisure, recreation and tourism. Note: The relative proportions of the different sub-areas in Fig. 3.1 are not fixed, but vary from one individual to another depending on variations in personal preferences and structural factors such as age, ethnicity, class, gender, sexuality and ability.*

3.2 Conceptualizing leisure and its relationship with work, reproduction and consumption

3.2.1 Different conceptualizations of leisure

Most contemporary leisure writers (e.g. Kelly 1983; Patmore, 1983; Haywood *et al.*, 1995; Horna, 1994) accept that leisure can be defined in at least three different ways; as time, activity, or experience. Each of these conceptualizations has its own limitations and there has been considerable debate amongst leisure theorists – as Patmore noted 'leisure is more readily experienced than defined' (1983:5). Let us now look at each of these definitions in turn and discuss their respective limitations.

a) Leisure as time

In the most popular and straightforward method of conceptualizing leisure, it is seen as a specific time free from other obligations such as work, domestic responsibilities and subsistence. This approach usually conceptualizes leisure in relation to work, most commonly paid work.

The idea that leisure is something that only takes place outside work time is by no means a universal one, as the temporal (and spatial) separation of work and leisure is a relatively modern and western concept arguably dating from the Industrial Revolution. Feminist writers (e.g. Deem, 1982; Green, Hebron and Woodward, 1990) in particular have been critical of this definition of leisure, because of its failure to adequately explain the position of leisure in the lives of those, increasingly numerous, individuals and groups who do not engage in formal paid work (e.g. full-time carers, the retired, unemployed, children, long-term sick and disabled, and parents caring for children). While we may be able to extend the concept of 'work' and 'other obligations' to include forms of unpaid reproductive work (e.g. child care, looking after sick relatives, education, and domestic tasks) the definition is still problematic for those other groups listed (e.g. the retired, unemployed) who are temporarily or permanently excluded from paid work. It would be false then to assume that all the time left available to the retired and the unemployed after they have completed the daily obligations necessary for subsistence (eating, sleeping, cleaning, etc.) could be considered as leisure. Some authors (Grossin, 1986; Glyptis, 1989) have used the term 'idle time' to describe this surplus of unobligated time. In order for this surplus time to be converted into leisure time, other important leisure resources such as money, space, legal rights and entitlements, knowledge and capabilities are required.

However, it would be a mistake to deny the importance of work (in its broadest sense) in defining the boundaries of leisure. Social historians (e.g. Malcolmson, 1973; Cunningham, 1980; Clarke and Critcher, 1985; Yeo and Yeo, 1981) have argued that the Industrial Revolution fundamentally changed the spatial and temporal settings of work. Work began to be undertaken in particular places (factories and offices) and at specific times. This spatial and temporal restructuring of work necessitated a concomitant restructuring of leisure. For the capitalist factory system to be efficient and successful, labour needed to be disciplined, regulated and controlled. From the early nineteenth century onwards relatively unregulated and anarchic forms of pre-industrial working-class leisure in Britain were consequently discouraged and suppressed, using specific government legislation (Clarke and Critcher, 1985; Yeo and Yeo, 1981). It would be simplistic to assume that the Industrial Revolution and its associated changes in work practice fundamentally reshaped the concept of leisure for all individuals, in all places at the same time, but it clearly was of considerable importance in redefining the nature of leisure for the mass of the population in western capitalist societies.

b) Leisure as activity

A second way of conceptualizing leisure is to see it as a group of specific activities which people choose to participate in during their free time; for example, going swimming, going to the pub, watching TV, doing the garden, and playing in the park. The use of this definition makes the measurement of people's leisure behaviour incredibly straightforward and planners and policy-makers consequently often use it in extensive surveys of people's leisure (e.g. the General Household Survey). Although this approach produces tidy and easily quantifiable results, the assumptions that lie behind it result in a number of limitations:

- The lists used by surveys can be culturally specific and are rarely all-inclusive. More formal, institutionalized, socially acceptable and publicly visible forms of leisure (e.g. golf, theatre, football) are over-emphasized at the potential expense of the informal, unstructured, socially deviant, and privatized forms (e.g. smoking marijuana, train-spotting or having sex).
- An individual may participate in a 'leisure activity' but not experience it at the time as leisure. Activities such as gardening, DIY, sports, gambling can sometimes be experienced as paid or unpaid work whilst other activities where the participant may also be responsible for the welfare of others (e.g. taking young children swimming) can be experienced as a chore.

It is not the activities themselves then that are important in defining leisure, but the context in which these activities take place and the feelings, emotions and obligations associated with them. This criticism leads to the next conceptualization.

c) Leisure as experience or a state of mind

'Leisure is defined by the use of the time, not the time itself. It is distinguished by the meaning of the activity not its form' (Kelly, 1983). For Kelly, leisure is about the quality of an activity, which he defines by relative freedom and intrinsic satisfaction. A fundamental defining quality of leisure is the nature of the leisure experience itself and how the individual perceives this. Kelly (1983:4) points out that a 'persistent element in defining leisure throughout the history of Western civilization has been a relative freedom of choice.' Leisure, in contrast to the constraints of work, is associated with the feelings of freedom, playfulness and pleasure.

In reality, though, very few leisure experiences are totally free from social role expectations, environmental constraints or resource limitations (Kelly, 1983). Some therefore prefer to describe leisure as only 'a relatively self-determined' activity where individuals at least feel they have scope for choice (Roberts, 1978:5). Thus Kelly (1983:5) suggests that leisure is 'not residual, but is a social space in which we not only retain, but insist on some freedom of choice'.

As we have seen, there is a considerable academic debate around how leisure should be defined. While we are not going to single out a definition of our own, the main points from this debate which we would like you to consider in reading the rest of this chapter are as follows:

- leisure is more than just non-work time
- in contemporary capitalist societies work has a fundamental influence on the spatial and temporal setting of leisure in many people's lives
- not all free time is leisure time
- leisure can involve both activity and inactivity
- the quality and context of the individual's leisure experience, not the leisure activity itself, is what is most important
- leisure experiences are relatively self-determined and contain an element of choice as well as constraint.

3.2.2 The role of leisure in contemporary capitalist society: consumption or reproduction?

There is an important distinction to be made between debates regarding the definition of leisure discussed above and those regarding its actual function or role in society.

a) Leisure as reproduction

To understand the role of leisure in capitalist society, Marxist social and cultural theorists argue that we need to first understand the role of work and particularly how capital–labour relations interact within the capitalist production process (e.g. Rojek, 1995; Clarke and Critcher, 1985). A Marxist analysis suggests that reproduction is needed to produce a suitable labour force for capital (see Chapter 2 for a detailed discussion of the relationship between production and reproduction). Leisure can be seen as contributing to this reproduction. Reflect for a moment on how 'unproductive' you as a student would become if, for example, you had no breaks for social activity during the day, week or academic year. The word 'recreation' (often used as a synonym for leisure) in its original form implied the 're-creation' of a readiness to work (Haywood et al., 1989). Without leisure, it is argued that the productive capacity of labour would decline as workers become increasingly tired, jaded and unhealthy. Leisure performs a reproductive function, as it rests, revitalizes and restores the labour force. Leisure also provides us with something to look forward to; a reward to work towards and to save for. In this sense, some Marxists would argue that leisure also pacifies and subdues the labour force by providing a palliative for the inadequacies of a repetitive and spiritually unrewarding capitalist production process. In addition, the increasing costs of commercial leisure create a perceived societal need for regular and stable paid work to accumulate the income necessary to purchase all these new leisure goods and services. In this way, too, it has a pacifying effect on the workforce. However, in order for the reproductive role of leisure to serve the interests of capital, leisure must be socially regulated, temporally and spatially limited, and legally controlled. Imagine trying to run a competitive business and producing goods to satisfy your market if, for instance, your workforce turned up when they felt like it and took time off whenever they liked and for as long as they wished. Some social theorists therefore see leisure as an important area of social control, although the level of this social control is fiercely debated. For example, members of the Frankfurt School whose ideas are typified by the work of Adorno (1991) use the term 'the culture industry' to describe 'the collection of entertainment industries dedicated to amusing the masses in their non-work time: film, jazz, and pop music, television, magazines and radio' (Rojek, 1995:17). Leisure appeals to workers because of the awfulness (alienation) of waged work and thus people's self-worth, self-development (and pleasure) is displaced from the work sphere to that of leisure. According to the views of the Frankfurt School, the 'culture industry' creates a climate of passive satisfaction and complacency amongst the masses, by feeding them with unchallenging entertainment loaded with overt and subliminal messages of patriotism and conservatism (e.g. royal visits to far-flung corners of the Commonwealth (empire), replays of the 1966 World Cup final, Coronation Street, game shows, and home and garden makeover programmes). The result, they argue, is an unquestioning, acquiescent working class which accepts the status quo and is thus unknowingly socially controlled by the dominant capitalist class.

This rather pessimistic and passive view of leisure and culture in working-class life has been heavily criticized by other cultural theorists such as Clarke and Critcher (1985). These commentators prefer to see leisure and culture as sites of everyday popular resistance, conflict and rebellion. Clarke and Critcher (1985) therefore attribute a much more active role to the working classes in challenging the forms of social control, which have historically been mediated through leisure by the dominant capitalist class. Thus, leisure is a site of cultural contestation and class conflict.

Certain leisure activities, such as narcotic drug use, could be seen to pose a threat to the productive capacity of labour and thus it is no surprise that in most capitalist societies these activities are subject to strict legal restrictions. According to Harvey (1989:126) the Ford motor company actually sent teams of social workers into the homes of their production line workers in order to 'ensure that their leisure activity was morally sound and consistent with "rational corporate expectations" ' (quoted in Rojek, 1995).

Although the degree to which people are able to resist social control through their leisure is debatable, the state (government, judiciary, police) through its powers of licensing, moral leadership and policing has historically tried to establish which forms of leisure are appropriate and legitimate and which are considered inappropriate and deviant in particular places. Later in this chapter, we will examine some contemporary examples of leisure activities that have become sites of cultural conflict because they have been considered by the capitalist state to be deviant and a threat to so-called 'civilized society'.

b) Leisure as consumption

In contrast to the discussion above, not all forms of leisure can be seen as fulfilling a reproductive function.

- For those who do not work (e.g. the retired, the unemployed and others permanently excluded from the world of paid work) leisure performs no reproductive function as their labour capacity is considered to be surplus to the requirements of the capitalist system of production. For these individuals, leisure is as much concerned with consuming resources (e.g. time, money, and physical capacity) as it is with reproducing resources (labour).
- Some leisure activities consume resources and arguably have little or no beneficial effects in terms of reproducing the productive capacity of labour (see Box 3.6). It tends to be these activities which in most capitalist societies are subject to closest regulation and social control. Recreational drug use such as drinking alcohol, smoking cigarettes, or using cannabis, cocaine or Ecstasy are either illegal or heavily regulated (both temporally and spatially) in most capitalist societies. In excess, all of these activities arguably impair our productive capacity.
- Other activities although performing no apparent reproductive function are socially acceptable and in some cases are actively encouraged. Whilst some shopping (see Chapter 2) plays an essential reproductive function in the labour process, other forms of shopping for 'non-essential items' are apparently purely consumption. However, it could be argued that shopping for luxury items such as 'leisure goods' (e.g. designer clothes, sports wear, music CDs, computer games) indirectly contributes to the reproductive role of leisure, by providing the raw materials that enable us to re-create our productive capacities through diversion, rest, and regeneration. Some individuals even talk of 'shopping therapy'.
- Leisure as consumption also provides markets for firms. As capital is increasingly heavily involved in the production of leisure goods and services, it makes economic sense for individual capitals (e.g. firms, sectors) to put pressure on the state to help further their interests by facilitating the increased consumption of leisure goods and services. In Britain, for example, the government during the 1980s liberalized trading laws in order to enable shops to open for longer hours (e.g. Sunday trading) and relaxed planning legislation which enabled the development of a proliferation of large out-of-town shopping centres like Tyneside's Metro Centre and Sheffield's Meadowhall.

It is, in reality, very difficult to separate production from reproduction, or leisure from work.

Having explored some of the important academic debates around the meaning and purpose of leisure, we go on to examine the contribution that can be made by social geographers to the understanding of leisure in contemporary society. First, we argue that space and place are central to the construction of leisure experiences and the understanding of individual patterns of leisure behaviour. Second, we argue that leisure contributes to the identity of places and is therefore a significant aspect of the politics of identity. Finally, we contend that leisure spaces themselves are socially constructed, socially contested spaces acting as sites of social conflict as well as arenas for the expression of social differentiation, power, and control.

3.3 The experience of leisure and the importance of place

Traditionally geographers have been interested in the spatial patterns of leisure behaviour. Much of the published work on recreation produced by geographers in the 1960s and 1970s was very much in a positivist, spatial science paradigm (Mowl and Towner, 1995; Aitchison, 1999a). Geography, in this work, was simply the spatial expression (or outcome) of leisure behaviour. As Massey (1984:4) argues, these geographers were 'simply mapping the outcomes of processes studied in other disciplines'. In post-war leisure geography, the primary concern was therefore 'space' as a neutral backdrop. But there is much more to the geography of leisure than simply mapping leisure spaces. We need to consider geography as an active participant (a process) in shaping leisure behaviour, not just an outcome (a pattern).

It has been argued that an appreciation of the distinction between the terms 'space' and 'place' is fundamental to our understanding of individual leisure behaviour (Mowl and Towner, 1995). The distinction between space and place used in this chapter is that while the former has absolute and relative dimensions and can be seen as distinct, objective and real, the latter has no such objective dimensions and is perceptually or socially produced. Objective spaces are therefore measurable, have clear, indisputable boundaries and are identifiable on conventional maps. Places, on the other hand, have different boundaries and different qualities for different individuals and groups. For the humanistic geographers who wrote extensively in the 1970s about the importance of place, places only existed within the minds of individuals and groups. Tuan (1975:152), for instance, defined places as 'centres of meaning constructed by experience'.

So while different people may have very different conceptions of New York as a place, depending on their perceptions, experiences, values and preferences, at the same time everyone can obtain maps which unambiguously demarcate New York as the same objective physical space. This distinction is important in developing an understanding of the geographical nature of leisure behaviour.

Mowl and Towner (1995) argue that we create places through our everyday leisure behaviour. Through the experience of leisure, spaces (e.g. beaches, mountains, urban streets, and derelict buildings) become 'centres of meaning'; they are transformed into leisure places. Leisure allows us to transcend the physical boundaries of space and to create places that have purely personal meaning and value. For example, when relaxing to a piece of music or reading a book we are able to 'travel' within the confines of our own minds, and to create imaginary places that provide a metaphysical spatial context for our leisure experience.

For each individual, their personal leisure geography consists of both leisure spaces and leisure places. Leisure places are those sites associated with more personal and meaningful leisure experiences; they represent centres of meaning, significance and emotion. Although they may be important to the individual, they may be irrelevant and even invisible to others. They may vary in scale and include almost anywhere and anything such as a certain chair in the living room, a favourite corner of the pub, or a particular walk through a favourite landscape. Our relationship with these places is infused with past and present experiences, with sensual memories of how they look, sound, feel, smell, and taste (Urry, 1999).

It is worth pointing out that not all our associations with leisure places are positive. An individual may have strong feelings towards a leisure place because of a frightening, threatening, oppressive or uncomfortable experience there in the past (see Chapter 11, section 4.2). Alternatively, we may just have negative associations with a place because of our attitudes towards or prejudices against other users of that place. The work of some humanistic geographers has been subsequently heavily criticized by feminist geographers such as Rose (1993) because of the overly positive and rather 'masculinist' way in which they conceptualized individuals' senses of place, and for their failure to recognize the importance of gender relations in structuring them (Mowl and Towner, 1995). We would further argue that we need to consider the influence of all social relations (age, ethnicity, class, sexuality and ability as well as gender) on individuals' senses of place. These influence the way we perceive and experience different places and consequently our attachment to these places. As Rose (1995) points out:

> Although senses of place may be very personal, they are not entirely the result of one individual's feelings and meanings; rather, such feelings and meanings are shaped in large part by the social, cultural and economic circumstances in which individuals find themselves.
>
> (Rose, 1995: 89)

We all favour different leisure places – we each have our favourite pubs, clubs, parks, landscapes and resorts to which we have some emotional attachment, but it is important not to take these attachments at face value, as they are conditioned by social, economic and political processes and structures. The case study in Box 3.3 about the changing nature of pubs in the Docklands illustrates this point. The Docklands is now a very socially mixed locality, with both professional middle classes and ethnic minority groups moving into what was traditionally a white working-class area. Broader processes and social structures are therefore important in shaping patterns of leisure behaviour and associated conceptions of place.

3.4 Leisure and the identity of place

There is a dynamic and complex three-way relationship between places, leisure, and identity. Notions of identity are important in defining our sense of self, of who we are and what we are, and in distinguishing ourselves from 'others' (Pile and Thrift, 1995). Leisure plays a crucial role in the process of identity formation, not only for individuals but also social groups and even places themselves. Leisure is therefore an integral part of the politics of identity.

Leisure also helps forge the identity of places. When asked to describe the characteristics of a group of people or a specific place (e.g. a nation or a region) we often refer to specific and sometimes distinctive forms of leisure behaviour. T. S. Eliot's famous characterization of England in the 1950s, for example, included nine leisure activities in a list of thirteen distinctive activities and interests, which were: Derby Day, Henley Regatta, Cowes, the twelfth of August, a cup final, the dog races, the pin table, the dart board, Wensleydale cheese, boiled cabbage cut into sections, beetroot in vinegar, nineteenth-century Gothic churches, and the music of Elgar. The extent to which these characteristics are real or just simple stereotypes is open to question, nevertheless they are an important part of our commonly held images, and consequently the identities, of people and places. Moreover, identities are contested, dynamic concepts, which should not be regarded as stable and fixed but subject to instability, conflict and change. Leisure, identity and place interrelate with one another at a variety of different spatial scales, producing geographically specific outcomes.

The idea that sub-national regions or localities develop their own unique, 'place-bound' leisure cultures, which in turn help establish distinctive regional identities, is increasingly difficult to illustrate. Global economic changes have destabilized some regional economies and their social structures, with places becoming socially and culturally more 'porous' and less bounded as geographical areas (Massey, 1995). It has been argued that 'spatial movement, interaction, influence and communication have become so extended, so fast, and so available, that the borderlands and boundaries which once used to define places as distinct and in some degree separate from each other are so often crossed that the notion of place which was previously viable has to be re-thought' (Massey, 1995:53).

As places have become more 'open', with people, products, money and ideas flowing in and out of their borders, so too have their identities become more fluid. Leisure in our daily lives is increasingly subject to global connections. Alternative leisure lifestyles are promoted internationally through television, cinema, global news media and the Internet. While there are many parts of the world that do not have access to the global communications media, very few individuals in the more developed countries (MDCs) are not exposed to it. Consequently, some now argue that distinctive, regionalized leisure identities are increasingly under threat and can be seen as somewhat romantic, nostalgic and outdated. At the same time, the cultural diversity and associated variety of leisure lifestyles which global change brings produces a unique, and some might say enriched, identity of its own (Massey, 1995; Rose, 1995). Alternatively, we may want to consider whether or not there are distinctive and dominant (Anglo-American) global leisure cultures that involve shared tastes in food, films, music, styles of dress, and even common languages (A.D. Smith, 1990). These changes in the identity of place are not welcomed by all and there may be resistance against some forms of social and cultural change by particular social groups who feel that their collective sense of identity is under threat from 'outsiders'. Globalization has therefore been accompanied by a rise in nationalist and regionalist movements and sentiments, often concerned with cultural and social, as well as economic and political, aims.

Leisure is inextricably bound up with notions of national identity, nationhood and nationalism. English football hooligans forcefully invoked their own unique notion of English identity by their public displays of mindless violence, overt racism, and embittered nationalism during the Euro 2000 football championships. Although most English people would challenge and condemn this notion of English identity, competitive spectator sports have become an important social arena for the display and sometimes violent defence of national and local identity and difference (Giulianotti and Williams, 1994).

Many people and places utilize leisure as a vehicle for celebrating cultural difference and for reinforcing the notion of distinctive identity. In the wake of the decline of traditional manufacturing industries in MDCs, some former industrial localities have turned to the so-called 'heritage industry' in an attempt to lure visitors, jobs and inward investment to their area (Kearns and Philo, 1993; Hewison, 1989). In an increasingly competitive marketplace for capital investment, local authorities (as the political representatives of localities) have created distinctive identities for the places they represent in order to more effectively market themselves. Heritage has been an important part of this refashioning of place identities. Associations with local historical characters, legends and events are used to create distinctive identities for otherwise undistinguished places. Thus Nottinghamshire becomes 'Robin Hood Country', Durham 'the Land of the Prince Bishops' and Stirling is 'Braveheart Country' (Aitchison, 1999b).

Part of this remaking of local place identities is an attempt to cash in on the recent growth in the leisure industry by establishing the locality as a recognized 'tourist destination'. Visits to heritage sites by both tourists and day-trippers have increased significantly since the early 1980s (Williams, 1998). Heritage appears to make places distinctive and even authentic, and many tourists go not only to see but also to taste, smell, hear, and feel this 'authenticity' (Urry, 1999). Whether this authenticity is manufactured (staged) or real may be difficult to discern (see Figs 3.2a and b). The heritage of a place, though, is not the same as the history of a place. Heritage is a selective, partial, and repackaged version of the past, primarily one that people will want to buy into (see Fig. 3.3). Globalization offers one possible explanation for the popularity of heritage, as when the future is uncertain and the present subject to rapid change, people turn to the past for reassurance, stability and a reaffirmation or reinvention of a sense of identity (Hewison, 1987).

Thus, concepts of place and identity are crucial in the marketing of tourist destination areas, but likewise they are also important in the consumption of tourist experiences as they offer the consumer a sense of authenticity, uniqueness and thus social distinction (see Box 3.5).

Figure 3.3 *Recreating the past: Beamish Museum, Consett, County Durham, Britain's number one heritage attraction.*

or the informal actions of a group of like-minded individuals. Recent decades in Britian have witnessed the creation of many new leisure spaces. Several of these have sprung up Phoenix-like from the ashes of the redundant industrial spaces left in towns and cities in the aftermath of deindustrialization and the growth of new service industries (see Box 3.3). The Albert Dock in Liverpool, Newcastle upon Tyne's Quayside, Salford Quays, and the London Docklands are examples of these transformed urban spaces. The land use transition required to create these new leisure spaces was by no means inevitable or accidental; it required a particular set of economic conditions coupled with certain social and neo-liberal political priorities prevalent in most MDCs since the 1970s. In Britain, the creation of seven new Urban Development Corporations (UDCs) in 1987 by the Conservative government marked a change in urban regeneration priorities (see Fig. 3.4). The intention was to redevelop redundant spaces in Britain's major cities by creating new spaces in which private enterprise could thrive without being stifled by restrictive planning policies and local social and political priorities (Deakin and Edwards, 1993). Responsibility

Box 3.3 Changing social geography of pubs in the London Docklands

Gomostaeva and Campbell (1999) provide an analysis of how local processes of gentrification and social change in the London Docklands area, caused by global economic restructuring and property-led urban regeneration programmes (e.g. UDCs) have impacted upon the social character of established public leisure spaces such as pubs. The diagram below illustrates the processes of change occurring in the Docklands locality:

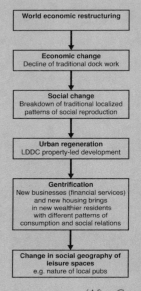

(After Gomostaeva and Campbell, 1999)

Pubs in the Docklands area were classified by Gomostaeva and Campbell (1999) according to the nature of their clientele: local, ethnic local, mixed and cosmopolitan. According to their research, the proportion of post-modern 'cosmopolitan' pubs in the area was increasing with the traditional local pubs declining in number.

Pubs are changing from places which cater traditionally for males, who are white, drink beer with working class 'mates' who share work in docks, live close together and marry their friend's sisters, to places which are for dining and early evening clubs, more often sexually (sic) and ethnically mixed with wine and selected beers, without loud music and satellite TV.

(Gomostaeva and Campbell, 1999:11)

These changes in the social character of pubs can be seen as either negative or positive. In a positive sense, racist and sexist forms of exclusion practised in the traditional white, male working-class, local pubs have become less dominant and the area could be described as having a more 'progressive sense of place' celebrating difference and diversity (Massey, 1994; Zukin, 1995). Viewed negatively, gentrification has simply replaced one form of social exclusion (gender and ethnicity) with another (class and income), leading to a loss of power and social control by the working class (N. Smith, 1996; Harvey, 1989a; see also Chapter 10).

THE LADY IS FOR TURNING

She's made her position clear—she wants to *turn* the Tyne and Wear into
the centres of *property* for which they were once renowned. The Tyne and Wear
Development Corporation was established to do just that.
    The private sector, the *people* of the North East and the Government are
working together to ensure that the new *opportunities* being created will be fully
exploited for the *benefit* of all.
    However, the ultimate *success* of our waterfronts could depend on the way
you *turn*.

LEADING THE GREAT WATERFRONT REVIVAL

Figure 3.4 *Newspaper advertisement promoting the work of the Tyne and Wear Urban Development Corporation. Source:* Newcastle Evening Chronicle, *13 March 1989.*

for redeveloping these areas was therefore taken out of the hands of local government and given over to the central government-appointed UDCs. Although it could be argued that the UDCs have dramatically transformed several urban landscapes (e.g. Newcastle's Quayside, London Docklands) their emphasis was heavily on property-led waterfront developments, particularly attractive to the financial and legal services, leisure- and tourism-related industries, and middle-class residential property developers (Mohan, 1999). The extent to which wider urban social problems have been addressed by these developments can therefore be questioned, as can the inclusiveness of these new spaces. The trendy bars and smart restaurants which now line Newcastle's quayside (see Figs 3.5a and b), then, are not simply a response to changing consumer tastes and lifestyles, they are a product of more deep-seated changes in the structure of the UK economy and a specific political response to these changes.

Similarly, the nineteenth-century public parks, baths, museums and libraries found in most British cities are also a product of a particular set of economic, political and social relations. During the Industrial Revolution, new forms of 'rational recreation' (Yeo and Yeo, 1981; Cunningham, 1980; Clarke and Critcher, 1985; Malcolmson, 1973) were introduced to replace pre-industrial forms of popular leisure (e.g. animal blood-sports, drinking, prize fighting, fairs, and wakes) that were perceived to pose a threat to industrial interests by undermining work-discipline and social decency and threatening social disorder (see Chapter 2, section 2.2). The rational recreation movement was encouraged by an alliance of philanthropic social reformers, the church, local government and industry, with the aim of raising both standards of health and the moral horizons of the new urban working classes. Traditional popular recreations were suppressed through punitive legislation and policing, whilst new recreations were encouraged through public provision and moral leadership. Again, we have an example of leisure spaces being

Figure 3.5a *Quayside, Newcastle upon Tyne, c. 1990. Credit: M. Barke.*

Figure 3.5b *Same quayside, 2000. Urban Development Corporation-inspired waterfront redevelopments have created new spaces for a thriving leisure and tourism industry. Credit: G. Mowl.*

constructed out of, and thus reflecting, a particular set of social relations. Our first point is that leisure spaces are socially constructed and that an understanding of change in leisure space provision necessitates an investigation of the processes involved in their construction. However, we should also recognize that individuals and their social actions and attitudes (human agency) construct leisure spaces. The railway station, for example, performs a dual function: for most it is a transit point. For train-spotters, though, the train station is a leisure space, a place to look out for particular trains and to make note of their numbers, a place to meet and exchange stories, photographs and rare train numbers! As we argued in section 3.1, leisure spaces (places) are not just created by capitalist developers or local authority planners, they are created by the actions and perceptions of individuals. In this sense, we can say that leisure spaces are the product of the interplay between structure and agency.

3.5.2 Leisure spaces, social relations and identities

Leisure spaces are also containers of social relations. At these sites individuals and groups interact, compete and conflict. While leisure is clearly one of the means by which we associate and identify with other people, thereby creating social groups, it is also at the same time used to distinguish, differentiate and distance ourselves from culturally constructed 'others'.

Any map of leisure space provision potentially tells us something about the way a particular society functions and about dominant ideas (or discourses) regarding who should do what, when, where and how. The social geographies of certain leisure settings will also vary over time: changes in use and users occur at different times of the day, week, year, and so on. Some of these changes may be associated with changes in the utility value of the space itself over time. For example, some city centres change from being a place to shop during the day to being a place to go out for a drink or something to eat at night. Other changes in usage, however, may be associated with the users themselves and their social behaviour. The specific actions of one group of individuals within a particular leisure space may have the effect of excluding others at certain times. The slightly sleazy, overt licentiousness of Amsterdam's notorious red light district can create feelings of discomfort and even disgust for the more 'conservative' reveller (see Figs 3.6a and b). Within the confines of this quite limited geographical area, gay sexuality, prostitution and recreational drug use are openly practised and promoted. For some, the area has become the ultimate international tourist attraction where they can select and sample from a cocktail of 'forbidden fruits'. For others, it is a den of vice to be avoided or critically gazed upon from a safe, detached distance.

While all social relations can potentially structure the use of leisure spaces, Boxes 3.4 and 3.5 look at the importance of gender and class relations specifically.

3.5.3 Leisure space conflicts

Although many of us associate leisure with feelings of relaxation, pleasure, sociability and freedom, leisure spaces have always been important sites of social conflict (Yeo and Yeo, 1981). For the reasons we discussed earlier, leisure in any society is rarely free from some form of social control. Social control comes in many forms and under several different guises. Parents, partners, siblings, friends, relatives, teachers, priests, publicans, park keepers, police, gamekeepers, gatekeepers and governments all control and regulate our use of leisure spaces in one way or another. Where we go, when we go, whom we go with and what we do when we get there are all subject to formal and informal rules and regulations. What books we read, what TV programmes we watch, at what age we can drink alcohol, smoke cigarettes and have sex are all subject to legislation. But just as leisure is an arena of social control, it is a site of popular resistance.

Some conflicts occur as a result of popular resistance against the social control and regulation of leisure spaces – for example, British ramblers deliberately trespassing on private land in an attempt to force improved rights of public access to mountain and

Figure 3.6a Amsterdam's 'red light' district. Credit: G. Mowl.

Figure 3.6b Amsterdam's 'coffee shop' district – leisure spaces of inclusion and exclusion. Credit: G. Mowl.

moorland in the 1930s, or the Countryside Alliance demonstrating against government proposals to outlaw fox hunting with hounds (see Chapter 9, section 9.5). Others result from the tensions between different users and uses of specific leisure spaces. For example, mass tourist destinations are often sites of cultural conflict between tourists and local populations, with local cultural practices, such as religious festivals, modified, re-staged and commodified for the purpose of touristic consumption resulting in a loss of original meaning and authenticity.

Box 3.4 Gender relations and leisure spaces

A significant amount of research by feminist geographers and other social scientists has focused on leisure spaces as important arenas for the expression, reaffirmation and challenging of dominant gender roles and relations (Dixey, 1988; Green, Hebron and Woodward, 1990; Hey, 1986; Hunt and Satterlee, 1987; Mowl and Towner, 1995; Scraton and Watson, 1998). In this work, the processes of social inclusion and exclusion within particular leisure spaces become particularly apparent when we contrast Dixey's (1988) analysis of the bingo club with that of either Hunt and Saterlee's (1987) or Hey's (1986) analysis of the pub. The bingo club is presented as being a predominantly 'feminine' space, one in which women can escape from the normal everyday constraints and responsibilities of patriarchal society (see Chapter 5). In the club, unlike other spaces within the local community, there is no direct social control of women's behaviour by male relatives and kin. There is social control within this leisure space (e.g. who can sit where and when) but this is carried out by other women. In contrast, the pubs studied by both Hey (1986) and Hunt and Satterlee (1987) are almost exclusively 'masculine' social spaces; ones in which 'normal' patriarchal beliefs and values are expressed and reaffirmed. Although the presence of women is tolerated, their behaviour is subject to informal regulation and subtle measures of social control are employed to discourage 'gender inappropriate behaviour'. Women rarely attended these pubs without a male partner, they were expected to drink in the lounge rather than the bar, and were not expected to go to the bar and buy drinks or to drink beer in pint glasses. The techniques used by men to enforce these social codes reportedly ranged from hostile silence and avoidance, to verbal abuses and ridicules (Hey, 1986; Hunt and Satterlee, 1987). The pub is not just a container of social relations but a space in which the processes of social exclusion and inclusion are apparent (see Box 3.3).

Box 3.5 Leisure and social class identity: 'it ain't what you do it's the way that you do it'

The French sociologist Pierre Bourdieu has carried out extensive research examining the relationship between leisure activity patterns and social class membership. He claims that a person's upbringing within a particular family and class has a powerful influence upon leisure choice. Bourdieu's concern is not just with leisure activities themselves but with the difference in 'styles', 'tastes' and 'dispositions' adopted by the social classes in their pursuit of particular leisure activities. So, although most leisure surveys indicate differences in participation rates between the different social classes, Bourdieu (1979) would argue that there is much more behind these variations than simply differences in income and the demands of employment. The participation in some leisure activities requires the acquisition or possession of 'cultural competencies'; certain skills, manners, codes of behaviour, together with a body of knowledge and expertise. For example, eating-out in a top class restaurant requires the 'proper attire', a familiarity with certain table manners, a knowledge of the correct use of silverware, and an ability to appreciate and select appropriate fine wines. These 'cultural competencies' however are not easily or rapidly acquired. Most require access to a certain type of education, training and upbringing. Individuals who have this background possess what Bourdieu calls 'cultural capital'; they have a wealth of knowledge, skills and competencies that give them access to a wider and more exclusive range of leisure opportunities. Bourdieu argues that we confirm our social class membership not only through our participation in certain activities but also through the manner or 'style' with which we participate. We use leisure spaces in order to express 'social class distinction'. Where we are is an expression of whom we are. There are leisure spaces where we want to be seen and others where we don't. Hence, there is a class system of leisure places, not just different tastes.

For example, most social classes take some sort of holiday, but what distinguishes between them is the type of holiday taken (e.g. independent or package; gîte or mobile home; high culture or the beach) and the choice of location. Certain destinations are considered 'fashionable', 'stylish' and 'exclusive' whilst others are considered 'popular', 'common' and 'mainstream'. There is a world of difference between the likes of Bellagio and Benidorm, Torremolinos and Tuscany. But these tastes change over time. In the 1950s Torremolinos (Spain) was a very fashionable resort, the place to be 'seen' for writers, film stars, and royalty. As the aspiring middle classes followed in these famous footsteps, the bourgeois moved on elsewhere. Today Torremolinos is regarded with general disdain by all but the British, German, and Spanish working classes.

Our use of leisure space(s) (and the 'style' of use) can also be a vehicle for either confirming or challenging identities related to our age (Pain, Mowl and Talbot, 2000; see Chapter 7), gender (Aitchison, 1999), ethnicity (Dwyer, 1998), ability (Butler, 1998) and sexuality (M. Lewis, 1994; Valentine, 1993).

The popularity of so-called 'rave culture' in the United States and Europe during the 1990s, and the response of national media and governments to this cultural phenomenon, provides an interesting contemporary example of leisure space conflicts and social control (see Box 3.6 and Fig. 3.7).

Box 3.6 Raves: moral panic, popular resistance and social control

Raves have been defined as:

> all-night dance events, held in abandoned warehouses and airplane hangers, open fields and clubs, where a predominantly young crowd (teens to mid-twenties) dances amid often elaborate lighting and visual displays to the hypnotic beats of techno, acid house, ambient house, brutal house, progressive house, trance, jungle, and related musics.

(Tomlinson, 1998:195)

Throughout Western Europe and North America, 'raves' became popular during the late 1980s and early 1990s. By the summer of 1993, a report by the Henley Centre reported that over a million young people a week in Britain were going to 'rave parties' (*Financial Times*, 26.10.1993). Annual spending at raves was estimated at between £1.5 and £2

Figure 3.7 *The underground rave scene of the late 1980s was an example of leisure transgressing the normal boundaries of social control and regulation. Source: Fleming, J. (1995)* What Kind of House Party is This? *Slough: Mind in You Publishing.*

billion (*Financial Times*, 30.10.1993). In Britain, initially the rave scene centred in the area around London's M25 motorway, with unlicensed events held in open fields and other disused spaces such as warehouses (Cloonan, 1996). Promoted mainly by word of mouth, they were sometimes funded communally by participants. But there was more to 'rave culture' than just dancing for hours on end to the 'hypnotic beats' of techno and house music. Reports suggested that up to a third of those at a rave will have taken drugs such as Ecstasy (*Financial Times*, 30.10.1993) and during 1990/91 there were seven deaths and 17 other cases of severe poisoning involving the drug (*Guardian*, 15.8.1992). The British tabloid press generated widespread public hysteria about the health dangers of this drug-fuelled 'Killer Cult', with much media attention focused on the tragic death of Leah Betts in 1995 (Thornton, 1994; Cloonan, 1996). By the 1990s the underground, informal nature of raves began to disappear as unlicensed events came under increasing pressure from government and residents, with police cracking down on those organized without local council permission. The first formal attempt by the government to control unlicensed raves came with the Entertainments (Increased Penalties) Act of July 1990 which enabled the courts to impose fines of up to £20,000 and prison sentences of up to six months for those guilty of organizing events in 'unsafe' venues. In February 1990 ravers demonstrated their opposition to the proposed Act with 2,000 of them attending the 'Freedom to Party' rally in Trafalgar Square (Cloonan, 1996).

To portray the rave phenomenon as purely mindless, drug-fuelled hedonism would be simplistic. Perhaps the most notorious group of rave organizers, Exodus, not only organize non-profit making raves in deserted warehouses and on patches of open land, but also squat in deserted buildings, setting up city farms for local children and hostels for the homeless (*Guardian*, 12.11.1993). Although the group's peaceful raves cheaply entertained thousands of young people each week, the collective suffered regular harassment from local police. The arrest of 36 members of the collective on 30th

Figure 3.2a *Big Thunder Mountain, Marne-le-Vallée, France. Credit: G. Mowl.*

Figure 3.2b *Big Thunder Mountain, Florida, USA. Theme parks like Disneyland create places with similar identities in different geographical locations. Credit: G. Mowl.*

3.5 The social geography of leisure spaces

No leisure experience is without spatial context. Most leisure activities and experiences occur in socially constructed leisure spaces. Some of these are exclusively designed and formally set aside for the purpose of leisure (e.g. swimming pools, pubs), others are annexed temporarily and perhaps even illegally for the purpose, such as derelict buildings, waste ground, and the urban street (Williams, 1995). Moreover, leisure spaces are containers of social relations, and thus important sites for social interaction, social conflict and the expression of power and control.

3.5.1 Social construction of leisure spaces

All leisure spaces have distinctive social geographies. Leisure spaces are socially constructed, whether they are the product of formal local government planning and decision making

January 1993 reportedly led to a five-hour demonstration by 4,000 local ravers outside the Luton police station where they were being held (*Guardian*, 12.11.1993).

But the pressure increased on the Conservative government to crack down on the rave scene. In October 1994 Michael Howard (then Home Secretary) introduced the controversial Criminal Justice and Public Order Act, giving the police increased public order powers particularly aimed at protecting rights of property and controlling the activities of squatters, new age travellers, all-night ravers, hunt saboteurs, illegal campers and mass trespassers. Under the Act it became a criminal offence for 'a group of 10 or more to gather to play loud music during the night and fail to comply with a police order to leave' (*Guardian*, 18.12.1993). Throughout 1994 the Act met with widespread and occasionally violent opposition from a coalition of groups whose lifestyles were threatened by the new legislation (see Fig. 3.8).

Figure 3.8 *Leisure and social conflict: throughout 1994 the Criminal Justice and Public Order Act met with widespread and occasionally violent opposition. Source: Fleming, J. (1995) What Kind of House Party is This?*

This legal crackdown did not, however, signal the end of 'rave culture'. Raves simply became organized events held in licensed premises. They became commercialized and legally controlled, subject to taxation (e.g. VAT) and attractive opportunities for private profit. Whilst the tabloid furore about the health dangers of Ecstasy died down, youth consumption of the drug continued unabated. It is also worth noting that legal and taxable drugs, such as alcohol and cigarettes, still cause far more deaths through excessive consumption than Ecstasy.

It is also interesting that the Henley Centre's report on raves in 1993 warned the leisure industry that raves threatened to undermine consumer spending for sectors such as licensed drinks retailers and producers, and that pub visits by young people had already fallen by 11 per cent between 1987 and 1991. In addition, they remarked on the time-consuming nature of raves, using up time and energy that could have been expended on other leisure activities (Henley Centre, 1993). Unlicensed raves were not just a challenge to private property rights through squatting and trespass, but also a potential threat to the commercial interests of the capitalist enterprises that dominate the leisure industry. Raves in their original 'underground' form can be seen as an unacceptable form of social deviancy that did not serve the interests of capital and were outside the boundaries of 'normal' social control, whereas in their reconstructed, licensed, commercial form they have become both socially and economically acceptable.

Summary

This chapter has noted the relative dearth of material by geographers on the subject of leisure, and has provided a theoretical framework for its study in social geography.

The position and relative importance of leisure in capitalist society have been discussed, with particular reference to the relationships between leisure and the spheres of work (production), reproduction and consumption.

Concepts of both place and space are central to our understanding of patterns of leisure behaviour. Leisure also plays an important role in fashioning and refashioning the identities of both people and places.

Leisure spaces must be studied as social constructions: the outcomes of social, cultural, economic and political changes. In most capitalist societies leisure is also an important site of social control and regulation, with leisure spaces often acting as arenas for social conflict and the reproduction of dominant power relations of class, gender, age, ability, sexuality and ethnicity.

Further reading

- Clarke, J. and Critcher, C. (1985) *The Devil Makes Work: Leisure in Capitalist Britain*. London: Macmillan.

- Green, E., Hebron, S. and Woodward, D. (1990) *Women's Leisure, What Leisure?* London: Macmillan.

- Hall, C.M. and Page, S.J. (1998) *The Geography of Tourism and Recreation: Environment, Place and Space*. London: Routledge.

- Haywood *et al.* (1995) *Understanding Leisure* (2nd edn). Cheltenham: Stanley Thornes.

- Williams, S. (1995) *Outdoor Recreation and the Urban Environment*. London: Routledge.

- Williams, S. (1998) *Tourism Geography*. London: Routledge.

4
Communities

The notion of community is an attractive, if often poorly defined one (Box 4.1). To planners, development agents, residents and would-be residents in a locality, the idea that there exists some organic, cohesive social structure that brings together individuals, households and businesses offers an organizing and supportive framework for everyday life and the management of change. That such social structures really exist in the form that popular conceptions would have us believe is contestable. This chapter begins with an attempt to define community; it is popularly associated with many social and cultural values, but in a geographical sense the added problems of defining 'where', as well as 'what', emerge. All too often community is taken as read, but in reality it is debated as an analytical category and is the source of much agonizing in political and religious circles. From an initial definition, the chapter will consider how previous and contemporary uses of the term community, in literature, politics, social practice and social analysis, have constructed and re-constructed the term in pursuit of particular outcomes or interpretations of the social world. We also examine how spaces and places, at different scales, are invoked in notions of community.

Box 4.1 Some common uses of the term 'community'

sense of community	European Community	pillar of the community
community action	care in the community	community spirit
community policing	community centre	community forest

4.1 The varied meanings of 'community'

There is a general consensus that 'community' is a good thing. Most of the images associated with the term tend to be positive. Politicians, religious leaders, the media, the police, social activists and many other interest groups all tend to use the term in this positive sense (especially if bemoaning the decline or lack of 'community spirit'). But it is clear that such groups may have widely differing versions of what they mean by community and what they expect from it. One of the reasons why community is perceived in this positive light is that it is usually viewed as the opposite of individualism, which has connotations of selfishness and isolation. Set against this, community appears to highlight belonging, co-operation, sharing and loyalty. This juxtaposition of

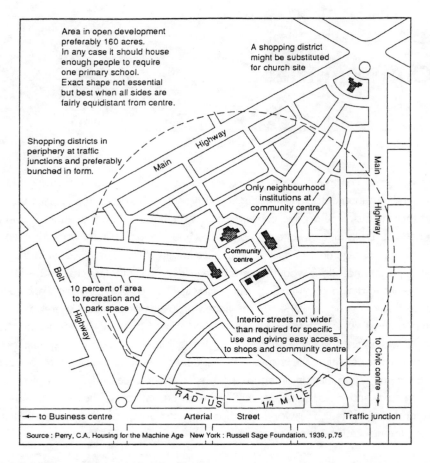

Area in open development preferably 160 acres.
In any case it should house enough people to require one primary school.
Exact shape not essential but best when all sides are fairly equidistant from centre.

A shopping district might be substituted for church site

Shopping districts in periphery at traffic junctions and preferably bunched in form.

Only neighbourhood institutions at community centre

Community centre

10 percent of area to recreation and park space

Interior streets not wider than required for specific use and giving easy access to shops and community centre

RADIUS — — 1/4 MILE

← to Business centre   Arterial   Street   Traffic junction

Source : Perry, C.A. Housing for the Machine Age   New York : Russell Sage Foundation, 1939, p.75

Figure 4.1 *Clarence Perry's neighbourhood layout.*

'community' and 'individualism' exposes one of the key tensions in modern life. Most of us live in what are usually called 'communities' of one sort or another, but many contemporary processes encourage a more fragmented and individualistic life-style. However, once we start to 'unpack' this notion of community we begin to see that, despite its common use, it is far from being a straightforward idea, let alone reality – it is a 'slippery concept'.

> *Communities are people who talk to one another.*
> (Bryden and Watson, 1995; cited in Watson, 1996)

This quotation is attributed to a community worker in Scotland. It is not presented here as a definitive statement of what communities are, but it offers the advantage of an easily remembered starting point for this discussion. At a very basic level the definition makes a great deal of sense, but Bryden and Watson further add that how and why people talk to each other is critical in understanding the underlying social structures; it is not simply enough to assume that communication makes community. In a rural context Newby has cast doubt on the relevance of the term community as a qualitative indicator of the level of contact and communication:

> because assessments of the spirit of community depend so much on highly variable subjective preferences and values, which may fluctuate according to the individual and the village concerned and even to the mood of the individual at a particular time, it is virtually impossible to generalize about whether there has or has not been a perceptible 'decline of community' in the English village.
>
> (Newby, 1985: 155)

Community may generally be seen as a good thing, but beneath the surface there may be very different reasoning (Box 4.2). For example, the idea of community appeals to the political left as it appears to emphasize notions of group solidarity, collective action and

---

Box 4.2 'Going for Growth': Newcastle upon Tyne, England

'Going for Growth' is an ambitious strategy put forward by Newcastle upon Tyne City Council in January 2000 relating to the future development of the West and East ends of the city, alongside and overlooking the River Tyne. With the decline of heavy industry on Tyneside these areas have seen a massive increase in unemployment levels, with consequent declines in the urban fabric and the whole spectrum of quality of life indicators. The 'Going for Growth' proposals are to:

- Demolish 6,600 existing properties
- Free up space for new investment
- Build 20,000 new houses
- Create 30,000 new jobs

- Improve the transport infrastructure
- Enhance access to urban green spaces
- Re-focus the provision of local facilities
- Improve access of health and education

While these objectives may appear positive, grave reservations have been expressed at a variety of levels about the viability of the policy, the top-down nature of the proposals, and the perception of the existing 'communities' that are essentially the subject of the masterplan. Nevertheless there are 111 references to 'community' and 69 to 'neighbourhood' in the 45-page draft masterplan (Newcastle City Council, 2000). At the time of writing the future of the plan is unclear, but the different perceptions of community are explored through the contrasting values and language of a resident writing in a local newspaper, and sections of the consultation document of the City Council, below. These indicate constrasting views of the links between society, space and planning.

contd.

Box 4.2 contd.

Letter from West End resident to *Newcastle Evening Chronicle* (30.8.2000)

It is with some sadness and great frustration that I write this letter and I feel sure it will not be the first you will receive on the issue of Newcastle's Going for Growth Policy.

The Labour council in this historic labour stronghold have embarked on a massive and largely unwanted programme of housing clearance that Newcastle has not seen since the days of T. Dan Smith ...

There is no doubt in my mind that, if these demolitions go ahead, this council ... will be instrumental in the destruction of two of the best and longest-established Tyneside communities.

Extracts from draft masterplan (Newcastle City Council, 2000)

There are housing areas near the riverside which have become very unpopular and population has dropped below levels that sustain communities.

We must accept that in certain areas the urban structure is broken and cannot be mended.

The local mix of people is changing and it is important that the masterplans respond to trends and draw mixed communities together whilst ensuring that minority groups have facilities.

Creation of a new urban village of 3,000 homes around a new neighbourhood centre ... These must be able to attract in families and younger professionals who would rebalance the area.

Healthy communities are dependent upon a range and choice of shops and facilities; health and childcare facilities; community provision, green spaces and recreation areas, schools and community safety.

responsibility, concepts that lie at the root of socialism. To the political right community has considerable appeal because it carries with it ideas of people taking responsibility for themselves, rather than relying on the state. The usually assumed territorial basis of community also has attractions for different groups for what may seem like contradictory reasons. Control is more easily exercised over an identifiable spatial unit and this may well be an important explanation for the State's continuing enthusiasm for the community ideal. Yet, others would see the territorially bounded community, with the possibility of organizing its own affairs, as a way of opposing or challenging the monolithic State. Furthermore, it would be naïve to accept the view that 'community' is always and unreservedly positive. As we see later in the chapter some tightly defined and restricted communities can express negative values such as bigotry, intolerance, aggression and violence (Keller, 1988). The idea of community is further complicated by considerations of scale (Box 4.1). Politicians especially talk about a national or even global community and there may be specific occasions when people feel that they belong to a community at that scale. Much more frequently, the idea of community is applied to a neighbourhood or residential area; at a smaller scale, it may be applied to a street, part of a street or even just one household.

In the past, most of these conceptions of community have been underpinned by the notion that they possess broadly identifiable boundaries. However, this is not a defining characteristic of all communities. As society is differentiated along lines of class, gender, race, age, ethnicity, sexual orientation and ability, communities develop that are not necessarily defined by spatial propinquity, although there is often a spatial expression to such divisions (see Part II of this book). But, in addition to these fundamental demarcations, other interest groups form communities of a sort, whether these be based on shared characteristics of employment or leisure pursuits, or social and political activism. Some of these may be non-place communities. It follows, therefore, that community could be viewed as a highly flexible phenomenon in the sense that most of us associate with several different types of community. A Sheffield University student, born and brought up in a Lincolnshire village where her parents still live may 'belong' to at least five such 'communities'. She may retain strong attachments to the community of her home village; more narrowly she may feel part of the community, probably more widespread spatially, of her local school; in Sheffield she may experience a strong attachment to her student residential area, be it a hall of residence, flat or house; she may feel part of her course community; and, finally, as the University hockey team's first choice goalkeeper, she may have a strong sense of belonging to that particular community. This brings home the extent to which 'community' is rarely a coherent entity that can exist without conflict and speak with one voice. Not only are there many different types of community, but many of us belong to several at the same time. 'Community' is also a cultural construct, the existence of which relies as much on symbols as on material practices, and the meaning attached to such symbols may well vary amongst group members.

The consideration of these issues leads to three important questions. First, given the problematic nature of both the concept and reality of community, what explains the continued enthusiasm for the notion? Second, given the complexity introduced above, what different types of community can we identify? Third, as ideas about community occur frequently in all sorts of policy initiatives, including education, housing and crime prevention (see Chapters 10 and 11 for the latter two), is it possible to 'measure' community? We shall discuss each of these questions in the next three sections.

4.2 A brief history of the concept of community

Academic community studies have resembled a roller-coaster ride. The death of community studies has been pronounced many times, but this diagnosis has been confounded by the resilience of the supposedly terminally ill patient. A brief historical consideration of the notion of community will help to make it clear why the idea becomes discredited and why it subsequently resurfaces (Box 4.3).

A number of authors have credited Tonnies (1887) with establishing the academic notion of community through his concept of *Gemeinschaft* (see Box 8.3). The latter was characterized as typical of 'folk' society where there was cooperation to achieve group

Box 4.3 Developing definitions of the term 'community'

The structural–functionalist approach

This was in many ways the theoretical starting point for community studies. The structuralist–functionalist approach saw societies as essentially well-functioning, coherent wholes. Accordingly, communities were defined as being relatively discrete in spatial terms, and relatively stable in both social and temporal terms. Tonnies' (1887) term *Gemeinschaft* was widely used as shorthand in this approach for 'a state of close positive interaction based on kinship, local proximity and mental connection' (Liepins, 2000, p. 24).

The ethnographic or essence approach

This approach did not contest the existence of community, but sought to investigate, through qualitative study, the diversity of the lived experiences and inter-personal and group relationships. The very existence of community as a social entity went unchallenged.

The minimalist approach

Community studies based in the previous approach were strongly critiqued during the 1980s, relegating both the academic field and the term of community to a backwater for much of the 1980s and 1990s. 'Locality studies' sidestepped the difficulties of the term, while maintaining a similar spatial focus. They embraced a spatially wider frame of reference by focusing on political and economic restructuring and local–global adjustment. In this literature the term community has been used, but in a very loose and infrequent way. Community, when used, has largely gone undefined and Liepins presents a critique of such work.

The symbolic construction approach

This shares with the ethnographic approach a concern with the meanings of community and the relationships and constructs which are seen to comprise it. Cohen (1985:98) summarizes the approach: 'in seeking to understand the phenomenon of "community" we have to regard its constituent social relations as repositories of meaning for its members, not a set of mechanical linkages'. Liepins (2000) has warned against an entirely uncritical focus on the cultural symbolism of community, noting the significance of 'material practices and physical elements' in generating such symbolic meanings; as they underpin the meanings, they cannot be hived off as a separate area of study.

(After Liepins, 2000; Harper, 1989; Murdoch and Marsden, 1994)

outcomes, and communal relationships were strong. In the early part of the twentieth century, particularly in North America, a group of urban scholars began to develop the idea that one of the social outcomes of urbanization was a loss of such characteristics. To writers such as Louis Wirth (1938), what characterized the modern city was competition rather than cooperation. Wirth and others noted the predominance of what they called 'secondary' relationships rather than the strong 'primary' relationships, often based on kinship, which had been argued to characterize 'folk' or pre-industrial societies. Wirth argued that the large size, high density and heterogeneity of cities were significant factors in preventing the growth of 'community'. In this sense, urbanization was perceived as a negative phenomenon. However, in the 1950s and 1960s a series of studies, mainly in rural or working-class urban areas, suggested that community was alive and well. The most influential were Gans's (1962) work on the west end of Boston in the USA, and that on Bethnal Green, London, by Young and Willmott (1957). Such longstanding working-class areas 'exhibit a sense of community … a feeling of solidarity between people who occupy the common territory, based on a strong local network of kinship, reinforced by localised patterns of employment, shopping and leisure activities' (Young and Willmott, 1957:89).

In Britain, a further dimension had been added to the notion of community with the adoption of a comprehensive town and country planning system in 1947. In a way that is now difficult for us to imagine, the post-war Labour government was elected because of a massive desire for change in the social order. In particular, the reduction in the significance of class and class barriers was seen as crucial. Along with the adoption of the 'Welfare State', planning and urban design were to be a means of achieving a more egalitarian society. The Dudley report of 1944 on post-war housing strongly recommended that the neighbourhood concept be adopted (Matless, 1998). Although the development of new towns in the 1940s and 1950s provided the most visible

Box 4.4 'Planning' for community development: some ambiguities

In the post-war period, and particularly in the New Towns then being built, there was considerable enthusiasm for the neighbourhood unit as a planning device. However, it is clear that different groups had rather different reasons for such enthusiasm. For many planners, the idea of the neighbourhood was nothing more than a pragmatic device to provide a certain number of people with a certain level of community facilities (see Fig. 4.1). For others it was primarily about segregating pedestrians from traffic and different types of vehicle flow such as local access, delivery and through traffic, from each other (see Fig. 4.2). But in the idealistic atmosphere of post-war Britain, the neighbourhood idea was expected to perform broader social functions. One of these was, indeed, to promote a sense of 'neighbourliness' amongst residents, to re-create the atmosphere of a traditional village community. Perhaps the most idealistic objective of all, however, was that neighbourhood planning could assist in the breaking down of barriers between different groups. The ideal that was sought was a 'balanced' community with a mixture of households of different ages and classes. Steps towards achieving these objectives could be made through physical design, through the detailed planning and placement of houses of different types, but these last two objectives were in fundamental conflict.

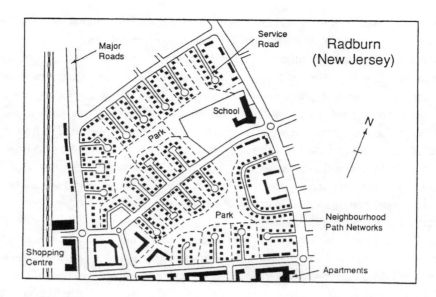

Figure 4.2 *Radburn layout of neighbourhood.*

examples of neighbourhood planning, pre-existing urban areas were also re-planned using the neighbourhood concept. Along with other objectives, the promotion of community life was a key feature of these planning efforts (see Box 4.4).

By the later 1960s, the community concept began to lose its appeal. Academics (for example, Stacey, 1969) argued that the idea was essentially a romantic one and that there was little evidence that a sense of belonging to a group within a defined geographical area existed in an increasingly mobile and fluid society. Some of the ambiguities in the practical application of community ideas, as outlined above, also began to be exposed, and even some of the pragmatic notions of providing a certain number of people with a specific number of services of different kinds began to be undermined by changes in mobility and the re-location of services. In the 1960s and 1970s there was also mounting concern over inner city decay and the process of urban renewal. Much of this concern was voiced in terms of community breakdown, for example, the dispersion of long-established communities with slum clearance (see Fig. 4.3).

Marsden *et al.* (1993:130) comment that by the late 1970s 'community studies had come to be characterized by functionalist methodologies and idealistic analyses that had left the concept indelibly tainted'. They favoured the structuralist–functionalist and ethnographic approaches described in Box 4.3. The new term 'locality', which carried far less baggage from previous usage was preferred. Yet the term community has lost none of its resonance in the media and for politicians. Most importantly, popular concerns often focus on community as something which exists and matters to people. For this reason the category retains significance. Day and Murdoch (1993:108) comment that 'if

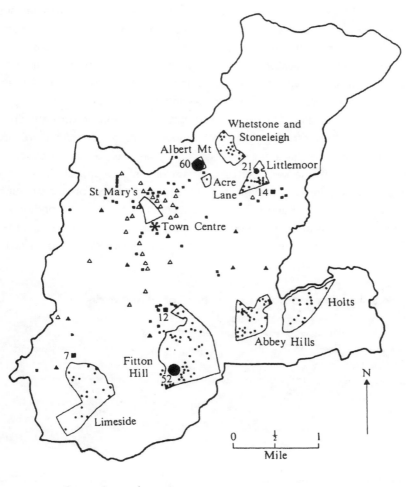

Respondents rehoused

- By the council in estates   △ Private owner-occupiers
- By the council others   ▲ Private tenants

Figure 4.3 *Displacement of St Mary's residents, Oldham, with redevelopment. Source: After MHLG (1970). Crown copyright is reproduced with the permission of the Controller of Her Majesty's Stationery Office.*

social researchers have a responsibility to follow the accounts of those actively involved in social processes then this would seem to argue for the reinstatement of "community" as a term at the centre of the study of social space'.

Gradually notions of community began to be revived and re-invigorated. Ironically, one of the ways in which this began was through a series of empirical findings, rather like those of the 1950s and early 1960s, but in very different areas. The former studies had demonstrated the existence of working class 'urban villages' but academics had argued that such 'community' features were largely lacking from middle income housing estates, growing through the rapid expansion of owner occupation from the 1960s onwards. Such areas 'represent a collective attempt to lead a private life. Suburbs ... are areas of loose-knit, secondary ties where life styles are focused squarely on the nuclear family's pursuit of money, status and consumer durables and the privacy in which to enjoy them' (Knox and Pinch, 2000:252). However, empirical studies began to reverse the previous understanding by demonstrating that, while various forms of community breakdown characterized some inner city areas, suburban middle-class areas actually displayed some community features. These were, perhaps, not as close, intense or spatially bounded as in the traditional working-class community, but they were a far cry from the stereotypical view of a highly privatized and individualistic suburban life style lived predominantly behind the net curtains or the privet hedge. Box 4.5 indicates some of the main reasons why suburban areas may actually help to promote social networks of various kinds.

Box 4.5 Factors promoting suburban social networks

- Suburbs (especially newly built estates) tend to be more homogeneous in social, economic and demographic terms than most other areas.
- Suburbs can possess a 'pioneer spirit', with people at similar stages in their life courses eager to make friends.
- Suburban residents of new developments are likely to be a self-selected group with similar preferences in social and leisure activities.
- Although car ownership levels are high, physical distance from other social contacts and facilities may encourage people to settle for local social contacts and networks.

It should be clear by now that, despite its varied history, the notion of community is one that refuses to go away. Some of its fiercest critics have failed to appreciate the subtlety and different levels of meaning attached to the notion. As noted at the outset, community is not necessarily defined solely in terms of spatial proximity. One of the most important features in re-conceptualizing 'community' is that, to some extent, all communities are 'imagined' (Anderson, 1991), in the sense that we can never really *know* all fellow members or *know* that they share the same sense of belonging to that community. This is particularly relevant in the light of the notion of identity. Many writers have argued that identity is essentially unstable and, given that part of identity is being part of larger groups, any sense of community is also likely to be flexible and mutating. This has implications for space and place. Until recently, these have been regarded as the essential 'containers' for community, defining its boundaries and its internal workings. As these boundaries become increasingly permeable, it is possible that a new and exciting phase for community studies will be opened up (Jeffers, Hoggett and Harrison, 1996).

4.3 Can 'community' be measured?

If community has any meaning it should be manifest in the interactions which take place between individuals. A number of attempts have been made to assess the cohesion and strength of communities, using attitudinal and behavioural indicators. While some theorists may dismiss the idea of attempting to 'measure' community as a fraught and even pointless exercise, assertions about the changing nature of community which are not empirically grounded are also problematic. Such research may also act as a necessary corrective to generalizations and stereotypes. One such example would be the widely accepted positive image of northern English, and especially north-eastern friendliness. Yet, a national survey of 80,000 households conducted by the Joseph Rowntree Foundation in 1998 found the country's unfriendliest neighbourhoods to be concentrated in the north-east, with Middlesbrough, Newcastle and Durham coming top of the 'nuisance neighbour league table' (*Guardian*, 28.10.1998). Moreover, many social policy initiatives have a community or neighbourhood basis (for example Box 4.2). It is therefore important to develop means of assessing community interaction.

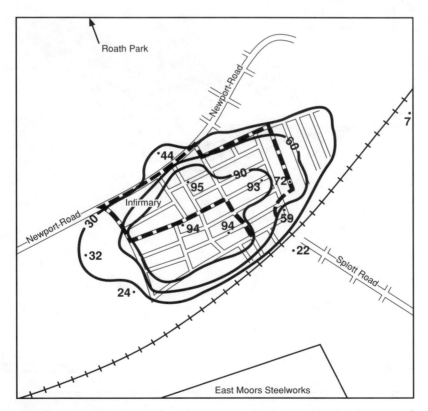

Figure 4.4 *Proportion of residents defining locations as within their neighbourhood, inner city Cardiff. Source: Herbert and Raine (1976).*

In attempting to measure community a common analysis has involved the construction of 'mental maps'. Figure 4.4 provides an illustration where residents of the Adamsdown area of Cardiff, Wales were asked to delineate the area they perceived to be their neighbourhood. In this predominantly working-class area there was a considerable degree of agreement over the 'core' area of the community. Such an exercise simply indicates the perceived territorial boundaries of a community. Rather more meaningful assessment of the nature of community demands analysis of the interactions that take place between individuals and groups. Social network analysis (Wellman, 1979) has been used to this end, by treating individuals as points in space and relationships as links between those points. This permits the examination of other features such as intensity, directionality and range of contacts (Figure 4.5). Clearly such features are likely to vary with factors such as social class, length of residence, and age.

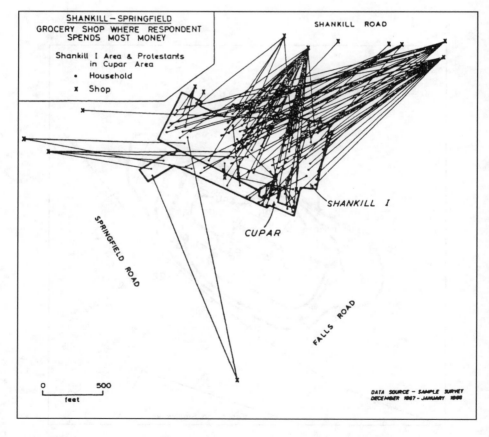

Figure 4.5a *Impact of community structure on grocery shopping patterns in West Belfast: Protestants. Source: Boal (1969).*

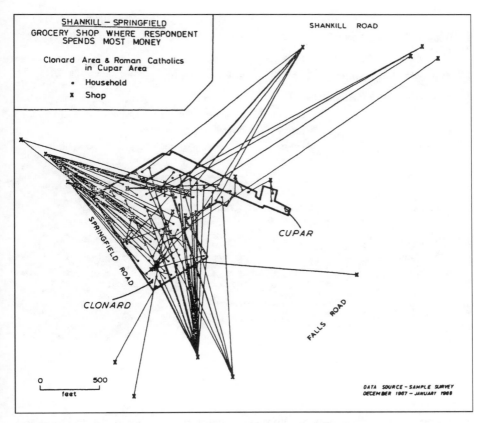

Figure 4.5b *Impact of community structure on grocery shopping patterns in West Belfast: Catholics. Source: Boal (1969).*

Another relevant dimension is the frequency and the nature of contacts between individuals. Box 4.6 indicates some of the ways in which these have been classified.

The degrees of interaction set out above represent a continuum. In broad terms, therefore, the strength of any community and its internal coherence might be reflected by such measures or some variation upon them. Some studies in the past have undertaken this task in a very mechanical and quantitative way, which is unlikely to shed a great deal of light on the subjective and perceptual category of community. On the other hand qualitative studies, for example involving intensive ethnographic methods, are able to give considerable, albeit different, insights. Further, as we now go on to explore, there are different types of community (Buckser, 2000; Jeffers, Hoggett and Harrison, 1996), and some of these might not be quite so easy to measure by the simple criteria in Box 4.6.

4.4 Types of community and their geographies

It is clear from the discussion so far that there are many types of community – as long ago as 1955, Hillary identified nearly 100 different definitions. This section will explore

Box. 4.6 Features of social interaction

Type of relationship	Type of social interaction
After Herbert and Raine (1976)	
1. Acquaintance	Pass 'time of day' if we meet, but never been in house
2. Quite friendly	Chat in street if we meet but rarely go in house
3. Friendly	Always chat in street if we meet; occasionally go in house (about once per month)
4. Very friendly	Chat regularly in street, frequently visit home (once or twice each week)
5. Very close friend	Chat daily, regularly visit home (at least four times each week)
After Bulmer (1986)	
1. Acquaintance	Aware of neighbours, make casual acknowledgement
2. Sociable	Chatting, visiting, shopping together
3. Communication	Exchange of information, gossiping regularly
4. Participation	Invited to family events
5. Collective involvement	Involved in local neighbourhood events

some ways in which the variety of communities, which differ in their social structures and their geographies, can be conceptualized. As Liepins (2000:30) observes, and as we have already suggested, different models of community are by no means mutually exclusive: 'people will be simultaneously participating in one "community" as a local network of interaction … whilst also being located in networks and 'stretched out communities' of many other kinds.'

4.4.1 The ideal type community

To begin with, it is useful to outline an 'ideal type' model of strong community, which may be expected to possess some of the features identified in Box 4.7. This ideal type has other features in addition to the internal interactions discussed in section 4.3, which are explored in the sections which follow – the influence of external processes and threats in stimulating the formation or assertion of community, the homogeneity of community, and the ways in which groups construct themselves and others as different and opposed ('us' and 'them').

There is also considerable variation in the strength of community adherence. For example, Warren and Warren (1977) identified three key determinants of this strength. First, there is the extent to which individuals feel they belong to the area. Second, there

Figure 4.6 *The headline of a local paper in the Scottish Highlands: in such communities, deviations from the 'norm' of any sort can be especially visible. Credit: R. MacFarlane.*

Box 4.7 Some features of the 'traditional' community

- Homogeneous social composition
- Fairly clearly defined and internally agreed spatial boundaries
- Numerous community organizations
- Considerable informal social interaction between individuals
- Considerable use of local facilities
- Relatively small in area
- Possibility of external 'threats', defining 'us' and 'them'

is the use that individuals make of the space within their community and the real contacts they have. Third, there is the extent to which individuals have links outside the community. These three dimensions define different stages within a continuum of community, and based on this notion Warren and Warren suggested a typology of communities (Box 4.8).

The ideal type model in Box 4.7 also carries certain assumptions which do not

Box 4.8 Community types based on three dimensions

Community types	Identity Sense of belonging	Interaction Active behaviour	Linkage External contacts
Localized community A strong homogeneous character, possibly based on ethnic or religious identity. Relatively self-contained and independent of the larger society.	✔	✔	✘
Integrated community Although residents are in close contact with each other and share concerns, they also participate in the larger society.	✔	✔	✔
Transitory community Population turnover means that there is little collective action or organization; there may be suspicion between the minority of long-established residents and the majority of new arrivals; residents' contacts may be stronger externally than internally.	✘	✘	✔
Stepping stone (short-term stay) As above, considerable turnover of population. But people make some effort to participate in 'community life'; however this is not because they identify with the neighbourhood in a social sense but because they see it as a stepping stone to something better and they wish to impress neighbours.	✘	✔	✔
Inactive community Stereotypical new middle-class estate where people identify with a locality address but, while they may have much in common, they do not interact with each other; this could be for a variety of reasons – physical design; privatized lifestyles; lack of facilities, etc.	✔	✘	✘

Community types	Identity *Sense of belonging*	Interaction *Active behaviour*	Linkage *External contacts*
Disorganized community Really a non-community with very little interaction between residents and no interest in creating community-based structures; equally, external contacts are weak.	✗	✗	✗

(Source: Warren and Warren, 1977)

necessarily apply for communities to be strong: for example, that communities must be geographically founded in concrete or 'real' spaces. In contrast, there are many communities which are not geographical at all, but are founded on shared interests or social characteristics. These are referred to as 'communities of interest' or 'communities of identity'. One example is lesbian communities, which are rarely visible through the presence of markers (e.g. concentrations of bars, clubs, shops or residential clusters), but often located in private or virtual spaces (this is discussed further in section 4 of Chapter 6).

Those communities which are geographically bounded may have important external ties and interactions, which often serve to strengthen sense of belonging. The next model falls into this category.

4.4.2 Community constituted by external threat

A sense of community may often be strengthened, or even form for the first time, when a group of people feel under some external threat. Frequently this involves a perceived risk to their identity, whether this is defined in economic, social or cultural terms. The response is to assert the difference of the group from external others, as well as the internal unity of the group, often by categorizing and homogenizing those who they perceive to be threatening them. An example of communities strengthening in an effort to exclude 'outsiders' is given in Box 4.9.

Some groups may quite deliberately resist change and increasingly look inwards: for example, the Hassidic Jewish community in New York (Belcove-Shalin, 1988). Other groups may seek to distance themselves from others and associate with those they regard as their peers through the mechanism of 'gated communities' (Fig. 4.7). Over half a million Californians live within these 'walled enclaves' (Luymes, 1997). These areas often develop for negative reasons – the exclusion of perceived inferiors, enhanced property values through excluding 'undesirables', the fear of crime (see Chapter 10) –

Box 4.9 Exclusive communities: a case study of nationalistic unity against 'white settlers' in 1980s Scotland

The rise of what has been termed counterstream migration in the late twentieth century has resulted in rural Scotland undergoing a slowdown and then reverse in the long-established decline of population. There have been a number of conflicting commentaries on this process. Incomers into rural areas have, in certain areas, been non-Scottish people, and in many cases English. The financial advantage by which such incomer groups, referred to in some contexts as 'white settlers', have been able to secure their desired properties has been well documented elsewhere (Shucksmith, Chapman and Clark, 1996), and there has been a widespread feeling in some areas that 'Scottish people are the victims of a new wave of clearances which are being carried out by the cheque book rather than the torch' (Jedrej and Nuttall, 1996:3). Jedrej and Nuttall go on to provide a critique of the social dynamics and cultural representations of the resulting conflicts. The debate over the 'Englishing' of parts of rural Scotland has been characterized by many labels, some supporting the 'indigenous' population and some which are highly pejorative of the new in-migrants. Terms such as 'locals', 'incomers', 'white settlers', 'absentee property holders' and 'Highland culture' are freely used to denote the erosion of communities, and the more general loss of community in rural Scotland; yet 'the reality to which they refer is elusive and contested' (p. 4). As an example of this, Stephenson (1984) reports from a sociological study in rural Argyll that the local population was divided into 'locals' and 'incomers', and that this was an accepted fact amongst those people. However, of the 59 heads of households in the research study area, only seven had been born in that locality. It is clear that the reality of migration histories is at odds with pervasive, subtle distinctions made on the basis of 'belonging'.

Incomers into rural areas can contribute to their positive development, and planners have long been happy to support the benefits of counterstream migration. But there are also well documented drawbacks of such an influx in terms of inflated house prices, dwindling services and the 'decline of community'; combined with the cultural boundaries that are drawn around groups that 'belong', these explain the relative success of anti-incomer groups such as Settler Watch and Scottish Watch. As Jedrej and Nuttall comment, 'the vocabulary of 'locals' and 'incomers' is a complex and deeply embedded metaphor providing the terms through which people express and give meaning to the experiences which constitute their lives' (p.12). The protest movements in Scotland have differed to those in Wales, where in the 1970s and 1980s there was a campaign of arson and property-related violence against the second homes of any English in-migrants and against estate agents that were actively marketing them (Jenkins, 1991).

but become a type of community. The enclave of Christianshavn in Copenhagen is a very different example. It originated in the 1970s as an extensive squatter settlement, which it still is, but is now better known amongst tourists as a faintly threatening, anarchic community where marijuana is freely available in spite of its illegal status in Denmark. To the visitor, it is accessible from only two narrow gates (Fig. 4.8), which symbolize very different motives to those of the wealthy Californians.

Figure 4.7 *Although not strictly a 'gated' community, the portals indicate a strong desire to privatize space and separate the locality from 'outside'. Credit: M. Barke.*

Figure 4.8 *The gated entrance to the Christianshavn commune in Copenhagen. Source: R. MacFarlane.*

In Belfast, working-class Protestant and Catholic communities have become more strongly defined and increasingly segregated from each other since the onset of the recent 'troubles' in 1969. This is largely in response to a perceived need for physical safety. Figures 4.5a and b (pp. 80–1) show the limited degree of community interaction which took place on the now notorious Shankill–Falls divide even before 1969 (Boal,

1969). In the centre of the area was a mixed community, Cupar Street, but communal violence and threats caused a 'retreat' of nearly 70 households from this street into the heartlands of each community. A physical defensive barrier now marks the Shankill–Falls divide. As violence continued in the 1970s, it is estimated that similar movements led to the relocation of between 35,000 and 60,000 people in Belfast, resulting in a reduction in the level of mixing of the two communities and a more marked pattern of segregation. The index of dissimilarity (a measure of the degree of segregation between two groups with 0 = no segregation and 100 = total segregation) for Catholics and Protestants increased from 67 to 80 between 1969 and 1977. In public sector housing in 1981 the index of dissimilarity was 92 (Boal, 1996). In one sense, therefore, 'community' areas have been strengthened in Belfast over the last three decades but the reasons for this can scarcely be celebrated as positive. Physical separation of residence reinforces division and reduces the likelihood of dilution of attitudes, beliefs and behaviour (Boal, 1982).

A contrasting example is of a community of interest, the British Countryside Alliance. This coalition of rural interests has expressed, especially to the Labour government that was elected in 1997, deep-rooted discontentment over a whole range of issues affecting rural Britain. Their demonstration on 1 March 1998 was the largest public protest in Britain since the Campaign for Nuclear Disarmament marches of the early 1980s. More than 200,000 people are understood to have joined the protest. Their protests in 1997–98 were stimulated by the Labour MP Mike Foster's Private Member's Bill which aimed to outlaw the hunting of wild animals with dogs. In addition, much public debate has been aroused by the likely impact of banning fox hunting on rural areas (see section 9.5 of Chapter 9). However, the publicity of the Countryside Alliance shows that a far wider array of 'rural' issues are being promoted. The objective of the precursor of the Countryside Alliance, the Countryside Movement, at the time of its establishment in the mid-1990s, was 'for the first time to offer the countryside the opportunity to speak with a single voice'. Milbourne (1997) has critically evaluated the Movement's ostensible aims of improving awareness and understanding of rural issues. He argues that 'within the Countryside Movement … we hear the voice of traditional power and privilege, of field sports, farming and landed property – a voice which is attempting to re-position and re-establish its vested interests within a rapidly changing rural Britain' (p.1). The message from the Countryside Alliance is somewhat different, however. The chief executive of the Alliance, a farmer, has argued:

> The credit for preserving what is left [of the countryside] must go to those who work on the land and take part in the activities which sustain it. Now is not the time for recriminations but for a determined effort to support those who still have the skill and the will to make the countryside work … although beleaguered by legislation, urbanization, pollution and prejudice, the country people of Britain are not doing a bad job.
>
> (Hanbury-Tenison, 1997:90)

Implicit in the message of the Countryside Alliance is that rural Britain does exist as a distinct geographical and social entity, which is seemingly founded on shared values and experience (an idea discussed in more detail in of Chapter 9). But does this uniformity of experience and agenda really exist? Who exactly are the 'country people' Hanbury-Tenison refers to, and might the definition actually *exclude* some or many rural dwellers? One of the defining characteristics of the countryside protests of 1997 and 1998 was the hostility expressed about the ingress and interference of 'townies' in rural affairs. The Countryside Alliance has quite explicitly supported this conception of a rural–urban divide, with the lines of separation based not so much on locational, as cultural factors. The community of interest around which the Countryside Alliance has developed has thus rejected the existence of cohesive, residential communities in rural areas. The long-running processes of social fragmentation in rural areas have been well documented (see Lowe et al., 1997) and the Countryside Alliance tapped into many of the tensions that arose. However, the Alliance quite explicitly proposed a model of rural community in which certain social values should dominate, certain practices should be promoted, and those with alternative values and interests should remain quiet, even if, as some opinion polls suggest, they are in the majority in opposing fox hunting.

These examples from Scotland, California, Belfast and England all demonstrate that homogeneity, or at least the illusion of homogeneity, can be an important component in the self-definition of community. The actual nature of the perceived threats identified (for example, the homogeneity in reality of 'other' groups) may be questionable. In the Scottish example, the English are defined as outsiders; for the English Countryside Alliance, it is town and city dwellers. In both cases, a false implication is given of the unity of the interests involved on both sides.

Thus the notion of community has been strongly criticized for its exclusivity, and for privileging one form of difference over another (Young, 1990b). As we discuss in section 4 of Chapter 6, work by geographers on gender and sexuality has also been central in challenging and redefining these exclusive concepts, and highlighting the multiple identities and positioning which we all experience.

4.4.3 Community and modernization

External forces may also have an eroding effect on communities. No communities in the MDCs exist in isolation from global processes, and both geographical and social communities may be undermined by uneven economic development, the high degree of mobility of production and people, and cultural internationalization and homogenization. Occupational mobility and rapid geographical employment shifts (see Chapter 2) increasingly disrupt the cohesion of communities, their collective identities and those of the individuals within them. Giddens (1991) has used the term 'high modernity' to capture some of the changes which would appear to undermine community. In the context of ethnic communities, Buckser (2000) writes:

> *The nature of identity becomes increasingly contingent and changeable; just as individuals switch jobs and families with increasing frequency, so too can they ... shift and redefine their understandings of self ... This increasingly fluid and contingent character of [personal] identity ... produces corresponding changes in ethnic identity ... Ethnicity as a feature of one's social position gives way to ... 'symbolic ethnicity', ethnicity as a dimension of self-perception. This style of ethnic affiliation militates against consensus within an ethnic community, since the individual supplants the group as the location where the nature of ethnic identity is determined.*
>
> (Buckser, 2000:714)

These processes are not limited to ethnic communities only, and may lead to the fragmentation or disintegration of communities of all kinds. However, it does not follow that any community is now impossible due to high modernity (Hirschmann, 1983). In contrast, communities sometimes form in reaction to these social changes, which might be interpreted as an attempt to find stability and to reassert the closely connected senses of place and identity when 'all that is solid melts into air'. As we have argued, 'community' often appears or strengthens when groups of people feel most threatened.

For individuals, the attraction of membership of a community can be seen as a reaction to the globalizing trend in many of the forces which shape everyday life, in combination with a range of other perceived threats to the social fabric (Scutt and Bonnett, 1996). The 1980s and 1990s saw a resurgence of nationalism across the world, right across the spectrum from violent resistance and civil war through to the gentler yet still politically charged debates around devolution and increased self-determination of the countries and regions which make up Britain. During this period, many governments have explicitly pursued a strategy of decentralization and regionalization of key administrative and planning functions. The recent devolution of power to Scotland is one example. There has been a set of movements which have sought to promote the significance of more distinctive regions over this period, and which have had variable success in gaining an increased power of self-determination.

Another response made by some communities to a changing world is to adapt, become more flexible and multi-versioned. A study of Copenhagen (Buckser, 2000) has demonstrated that despite considerable change taking place under such pressures, a strong Jewish community still persists, albeit one that is not necessarily defined in traditional, spatially bounded terms. Danish society is remarkably 'open', anti-Semitism is rare and barriers to the inclusion of Jewish people in the broader society are few. Box 4.10 indicates the negative consequences of this for the Jewish community but, conversely, some evidence which suggests that the community still survives.

Box 4.10 The Jewish 'community' in Copenhagen, Denmark

Processes potentially undermining Jewish ethnic community survival
- High rate of inter-marriage with non-Jews
- Disappearance of distinctively Jewish occupations
- Erosion of traditional Jewish life-styles
- Lack of concentration into a particular district
- Intensive interaction with non-Jewish culture
- Disappearance of use of Yiddish, limited knowledge of Hebrew
- Loss of consensus about the meaning of Judaism and Jewishness

The last element has resulted in at least three ways in which Copenhagen Jews define their identity:
- For some Judaism is primarily a religious identity
- For others, Judaism is not so much a religion, more a way of life, with specific rituals, patterns of thought and behaviour, distinctive food consumption, etc.
- For a further group, Jewishness is defined primarily in social terms, as a set of family, personal and business relationships.

Against this background, it might be anticipated that the 7,000 Jews in Copenhagen have ceased to function as anything resembling a 'community'. However, despite all of the above, the community persists with considerable vitality.

Evidence of community survival
- Attendance at services on Sabbath
- Flexible nature of worship allowing participation of those with different conceptions of Jewish identity:
  1. For those defining Jewishness in religious terms, the service is central to their identity
  2. Non-religious, 'cultural' Jews attend and appreciate services as they symbolize the 'difference' of Jewish from Gentile culture
  3. For social people, an opportunity to meet friends; the informal structure of the service allows conversation and movement
- High levels of membership of Jewish voluntary associations of all kinds
- Such associations also flexible in that they represent and cater for different conceptions of Jewish identity
- High levels of participation in community politics.

(Source: Buckser, 2000)

The elements outlined above provide a range of possibilities for involvement within the Copenhagen Jewish community. Box 4.10 does not advance a single model of ethnic identity: the community is, in effect, a 'symbolic' entity that provides a flexible framework upon which individuals can build their own identities and their relationship to the larger group. One may still belong to a community without withdrawing behind the barricades:

> *An ethnic group can become, like the Jewish community in Denmark, not an urban village, but a symbolic space, in which to be Jewish is not to hold any particular set of beliefs or practices, but rather to regard the Jewish world as the conceptual domain upon which one will draw for the construction of the primordial elements of one's own identity.*
>
> (Buckser, 2000:730)

Conclusion

Many technological trends in society and economy are permitting the coalescence of communities of interest that are increasingly far-flung. Whether such a diversification of community formation has weakened the internal ties of geographical communities is questionable, and it should never be assumed without question that geographically defined communities are unequivocally a good thing; processes of social control have changed since the demise of occupational communities, but neighbourhoods alone cannot define positive communities. Government policy remains keen on community as a form of social organization, yet many attempts to stimulate and develop community through interventionist strategies have failed to create the community ties that policy-makers and varied social commentators value. The failure of top-down approaches to defend and develop community will not be resolved overnight. The diffuse, differentiated and complex links that define communities will continue to attract research as long as the term retains its salience for politicians and those whom they seek to represent in society.

During the writing of this chapter one of the authors attended a conference which was concerned with the future of urban areas. Ideas about community came up in many of the papers presented at the conference; speakers from regeneration agencies pondered about how to rebuild communities, people discussed community safety, and others expressed regret at the loss of a sense of community in both urban and rural areas (Benson and Rowe, 2000). Many of the uses of 'community' listed in Box 4.1 came up. So the notion of community as a desirable element in social life is alive and well, but this goes hand in hand with a general consensus that it is increasingly scarce at the start of the twenty-first century. At the same time there is little consensus about exactly what communities are, or how they can be built and strengthened. It is this combination of being appealing to so many groups in society, and yet so elusive to define and develop, that explains the persistence of community studies by both academic and policy researchers over a number of decades.

Summary

- Community is a contested concept, frequently invoked in a variety of ways by different interest groups.

- Even in a contemporary world of fluid identities and the fragmentation of society, many people still associate with particular communities in specific localities, whether they be gang territories in Los Angeles or gay spaces.

- However, communities take many different forms, and equally their geographies are complex and various – they may be localized; exist at other distinct spatial scales; be imagined, private or virtual.

- Defining and measuring community is fraught with difficulty, but the strength of internal interactions is an important dimension.

- Communities are often formed or strengthened in relation to external processes and threats. Homogeneity is often assumed, and is an important means by which groups construct themselves and others as different and opposed.

Further reading

For older interpretations of 'traditional' communities:
- Frankenberg, R. (1966) *Communities in Britain: Social Life in Town and Country*. Harmondsworth: Penguin.

- Thorns, D. C. (1976) *The Quest for Community*. London: George Allen & Unwin.

For discussions and critiques of the notion of community in contemporary society:
- Knox, P. L. (2000) *Urban Social Geography: An Introduction*. Harlow: Pearson Education Ltd, 249–76.

For the issues and debates around rural communities:
- Murdoch, J. and Marsden, T. (1994) *Reconstituting Rurality*. London: UCL Press.
- Newby H. (1985) *Green and Pleasant Land? Social Change in Rural England*, 2nd edn. London: Wildwood.
- Simmons, M. (1997) *Landscapes of Poverty: Aspects of Rural England in the Late 1990s*. London: Lemos and Crane.

PART II

Power, identity and social geography

5
Race and ethnicity

5.1 Introduction

In popular discourse, the terms race and ethnicity are often used interchangeably. More precise definitions of these expressions are given in Box 5.1. In the nineteenth century, classifications of human beings based around aspects of physical appearance or biology became intertwined with 'value judgements about social status and social worth' (Jackson 2000: 669). Similarly, debates around social Darwinism, where the fittest survive, led to notions of competitive evolutionary and biological struggle being extended into the sociological realm, with different 'races' subsequently being seen as less or more superior. At the time, this appeared to lend support to imperialist notions of racial superiority.

We therefore begin by arguing that 'race' is a social construction through which groups of people are categorized on the basis of physical or biological criteria imposed from outside that social group. Ethnicity, on the other hand, should best be considered as 'a series of more or less self-conscious strategies employed by

---

Box 5.1 Race and ethnicity

Race is a controversial marker of human difference, usually based on biological distinctions or physical criteria such as skin colour and colour of hair (Jackson, 2000). The degree to which *discrete* 'races' may be identified by such criteria is highly questionable.

Ethnicity relates to the culture and lifestyle of a particular group linked by birth, which marks them out as being different from others. This encompasses both self-perception and social stratification (how society sees them, or how they 'fit' into wider societal structures as a result of this notion of their real or perceived origins). While the concept of ethnicity declined in usage during much of the twentieth century, in the 1980s interest in identity politics saw ethnicity return to the fore as ethnic nationalism became widespread in the post-Cold War era (Harvey, 2000a).

Racism may be defined as the practice of ascribing particular (usually negative) attributes to a 'racial' group who are erroneously believed to be biologically distinct: judgements of social worth are linked with presumed biological indicators.

subordinate groups to "handle" or contest their structural subordination' (Jackson, 1992: 152–3).

In the next section, we go on to examine the influence of important events at an international scale on the ways in which racial and ethnic groups have been labelled and subjugated in western societies. In sections 5.3 and 5.4, we examine and critique a large body of work in social geography which has attempted to measure and explain the spatial distribution of ethnic minority groups in North American and European societies. We then explore recent changes at different scales in the geographies of ethnic groups in European countries in sections 5.5 and 5.6. Finally, we conclude in section 5.7 by introducing recent perspectives in social geography which focus more explicitly on issues of racism, exclusion and whiteness.

5.2 The formation of racism at the international scale

The study of contemporary racism has come to occupy a central place in social geography. However, many of the processes through which racism has come to be embedded within western society operate on an international scale, and many are rooted in the past. For example, the period of mercantile capitalism of the European powers produced varied and distinctive forms of racial exploitation in different regions. The enslavement of black populations was an integral part of trade links between northern Europe, West Africa and the Americas, leading to the long-term inferior status of black people in the USA. British colonial rule in India involved the subjugation of indigenous peoples, but most extreme was the genocide practised on Indian and aboriginal peoples in the Americas and Australasia. Historical events have therefore shaped contemporary social relations between different groups, and these have been reinforced by the processes of industrial capitalism and the global division of labour. The populations of less developed countries (LDCs) are allotted a particular and subordinate role in that division of labour and this is reinforced by the organization and control exercised over immigration to MDCs. Specific immigrant groups have been recruited to perform specific functions at different times, reinforcing racial stereotyping and associated class relations.

One of Britain's leading trade unionists, Bill Morris, has strongly criticized the Labour government over its policies on immigration, accusing it of giving 'life to the racists' and accusing ministers of fostering a 'climate of fear and loathing' on asylum and immigration issues. This climate has been further cultivated by a national media whose reporting of asylum seekers often borders on the hysterical (see Box 5.2).

The existence of racism as a contemporary social problem cannot be denied and, in Britain, racist issues have been prominent since the murder of black teenager Stephen Lawrence. Sir William Macpherson's report into his death labelled London's police force 'institutionally racist', and instigated a government-funded £12m race equality programme. Yet, Metropolitan Police figures show a doubling of recorded racial incidents in London between 1999 and 2000, and a report by the Commission for Racial

Box 5.2 Challenging media myths about refugees

The Racial Harassment Support Group in Newcastle upon Tyne, England, has recently argued 'according to newspapers, the arrival of people fleeing terror in their home countries will cause house prices to tumble, crime to escalate and even compromise the virtue of local young women. It is time to give these attitudes their real name – racism – and start challenging the myths about asylum seekers with simple facts' (Newcastle City Council, 2000:1).

Examples of media comments

'Britain is seen as the softest of soft touches.' *Daily Mail*, 26 February, 2000
'Widespread concern about waves of asylum seekers arriving unchecked in the North East … but hundreds more are poised to set up home.' *Sunderland Echo*, 2 June, 2000
'The figures for asylum seekers, almost all of them bogus, are totally appalling.' *Sunday People*, 13 February, 2000
'Pensioners in particular are outraged that they have to scrape by while a few refugees receive huge benefits.' *Daily Mirror*, 15 March, 2000
'Refugees get flats with jacuzzi, sunbeds and … a sauna.' *The Daily Star*, 25 March 2000
'Clamp 'em at Calais.' *Sunday People*, 24 January 2000
'Time to kick the scroungers out.' *The Sun*, 15 March 2000

Myth 'Britain receives more than its share of refugees.'
Facts The UK receives less than 1 per cent of the world's refugee population. In 1998 the UK received 58,000 asylum seekers, and in application terms is second in Europe (15.3 per cent) behind Germany (18.5 per cent). In global terms, in 1998 Iran received 1.9 million refugees, Jordan 1.4 million, and Pakistan 1.2 million.

Myth 'Most asylum claims in the UK are bogus.'
Facts In 1999, of 74,000 applications, 54 per cent of the decisions resulted in protection being granted, a figure expected to increase on appeal. Most asylum seekers are refused not because their cases are bogus, but because they travelled through other countries on their way to Britain, or because of the lack of information and good legal advice.

Myth 'They come here to claim our generous benefits.'
Facts Asylum seekers are only entitled to 70 per cent of Income Support, a maximum of £36.54 a week. This takes the form of vouchers, which cannot be exchanged for cash. Asylum seekers are not allowed to work during the first six months after they arrive, and are not allowed to work if they are awaiting an appeal.

Myth 'Asylum seekers are a burden on the economy and taxpayer.'
Facts In 1998 the cost of supporting asylum seekers was £0.5 billion, or 0.33p out of income tax per week. Statistics on the number of asylum seekers who are working and contributing to the economy are not available. From fish and chips to the designer of the Mini, the UK economy has been greatly enriched by the contribution of refugees.

Myth 'Increased immigration leads to an increase in crime.'
Facts There is no established link between immigration and crime, and there is no evidence to suggest that the level of criminal behaviour of asylum seekers is above average. Many asylum seekers themselves become victims of crime. Supt Chris Eyre of Kent Constabulary estimates that racist assaults in Dover have cost his force £28,000 in overtime so far (*Police Review*, 28 January 2000)

(Adapted from *Challenging Media Myths about Refugees*, Newcastle City Council, 2000)

Equality stated that OFSTED, the body which monitors standards in England's schools, has been failing to inspect and identify the effects of racism and that the system was failing children from ethnic minority backgrounds. The list could go on.

5.3 Segregation, and the ghetto as an ethnic stereotype

Having discussed some of the key terms and established the contemporary significance of racism, we now consider how geographies of race and ethnicity have developed over time. Some of the language used sits uncomfortably in relation to contemporary understanding of these issues. For example, you will notice that Figure 5.3 refers to 'negroes'. The term was derived from the notion that there is a particular 'negroid' race; this has since been dismissed along with other ideas about the existence of distinct races.

5.3.1 Measuring segregation

The history of geographical work on issues of race and ethnicity derives in large part from the Chicago school of human ecology. A particular interest of this group, and its pioneer, Robert Park, lay in discerning the causes and consequences of urban ethnic segregation. The term segregation refers to the tendency for minority groups to be unevenly distributed in terms of where they live. However, as with most issues in geography the question of scale is of considerable significance in defining what segregation really means and how it may be measured. Figure 5.1 shows several hypothetical distributions for an ethnic minority group of exactly the same

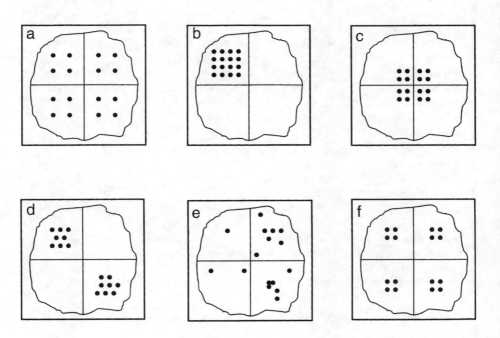

Figure 5.1 a–f Hypothetical segregation patterns.

size within an urban area. It is not too difficult to say which looks the most 'concentrated' population and which looks the most dispersed, but there are several variants in between. Clearly, segregation may be viewed as a continuum. The significance of this is that the scale at which segregation is measured can influence the apparent level of segregation. As the scale becomes smaller, the degree of concentration becomes greater. The most common measure of segregation used is the index of dissimilarity (ID) (see Box 5.3).

Box 5. 3 Measuring segregation

The index of dissimilarity (ID) measures the distribution of two different populations in the same sub-set of residential areas (e.g. wards, enumeration districts). A value of 0 indicates zero segregation while 100 indicates total segregation. The value represents the proportion of one group which would have to change its area of residence in order to be distributed exactly the same as the group to which it is being compared.

The spatial units which are used to measure segregation are fundamental in influencing the outcome. Ideally these units should be of approximately the same size and the location of the boundaries between units is also significant in interpreting apparent levels of segregation. For example, in Figure 5.1c the 'ethnic' population is clustered together just as much as in Figure 5.1b but because the ward boundaries divide the population into four, a different measure of segregation would be obtained.

Segregation levels of African-Americans in USA cities are extremely high and have remained so for many years. In Chicago in 1930 over 90 per cent of the black population lived in areas where they formed over 80 per cent of the population. By 1950 over half of the black population of Chicago were living in areas that were 100 per cent black. Taeuber and Taeuber (1965) measured segregation in 207 US cities from the 1960 census and found that only eight had an index of dissimilarity less than 70. Half had IDs over 87.8 and a quarter had IDs over 91.7. Massey and Denton (1993) demonstrated that for 1970 and 1980 (after over two decades of 'civil rights' legislation) for most large US cities IDs remained in the 80s.

5.3.2 The ghetto as an ethnic stereotype

The first ghetto appears to have been located in Venice and the term for many years was associated solely with areas of Jewish settlement (Wirth, 1928). The formal Jewish ghetto came to be defined by law as a place where Jews were forced to live (Figure 5.2). Even when such legal restrictions were lifted and physical barriers such as ghetto walls removed, an 'invisible wall' remained as demonstrated by Israel Zangwill (1921) in his bitter poem *The Goyim* (The Gentiles), which refers to persecution by 'beings of darkness/drunkards and bullies', the worst of whom are 'the creatures called Christians'.

These sentiments could perhaps be echoed by the residents of a multitude of other ethnic minority groups who live within highly segregated areas of large cities throughout the 'Christian' developed world. The term 'ghetto' is no longer limited in its application

Figure 5.2 *The Old Jewish Cemetery, Prague's former ghetto. Credit: M Barke.*

to Jewish people but is now used as a common term, applying to most segregated ethnic groups. It strictly applies to areas where not only just one ethnic group form the vast majority of residents, but also where the majority of that group is found in such areas (Peach and Rossiter, 1997). In more recent times our images of the ghetto have primarily developed from the segregation of North American blacks into such areas.

The formation of the black ghetto owes its existence to larger-scale processes, some of them international in scope. Between the sixteenth century and the mid-nineteenth, over eleven million slaves were transported from Africa, mainly to work in the plantations of America. Slavery was banned after the American Civil War in the mid-nineteenth century but the inferior social and economic status of black people remained. At the beginning of the twentieth century, 75 per cent of blacks were rural dwellers and 90 per cent lived in the south. By the 1960s over half lived in the north and west of the USA and 75 per cent were city dwellers. Of these, a large proportion lived in identifiable ghetto areas (H. M. Rose, 1971). Black people were perceived as a useful replacement labour force by northern industry and migration was also encouraged by black newspapers such as the Chicago based *Defender*, 'which painted a glowing picture of Northern living conditions and denounced Southern racism' (Meier and Rudwick, 1966:216). Chicago's black population increased from 44,000 to 110,000 between 1910 and 1920.

However, the reality of life in the northern cities turned out to be rather different from the image given by the Chicago *Defender*. Black ghettos were created through white exclusionary tactics adopted to 'protect' their own residential areas. These tactics included the widespread use of restrictive covenants: agreements amongst property owners that they would not sell to black people. More directly, beatings, stonings and arson were practised against black people who dared to 'invade' white areas. However, within and on the margins of the ghetto areas a common tactic used by real estate agents (usually white) to facilitate rapid turnover and subdivision of property was to move in a black family to induce panic selling by whites against the fear of depreciating property values. Figure 5.3a shows the expansion of black ghetto areas in Chicago between 1920 and 1950. The broad outlines of the ghetto areas were already established by 1920. Limited spatial expansion took place over the next 30 years, although the rapidity of turnover in some places should be noted. Districts with only 2 per cent black population in 1940 had over 90 per cent ten years later. The main feature of Figure 5.3 is the increasing density of black residents within the core areas. It has been suggested that this followed a consistent pattern (Duncan and Duncan, 1957): the influx of a limited number of black residents may initially be tolerated by existing residents; however, when a certain proportion is reached, termed the 'tipping point', a very rapid turnover of population ensues, with the minority population consolidating their colonization of the area. Empirical evidence suggests that the tipping point is only about 10 per cent of minority residents. Subsequently, an increase of already high densities will take place.

High levels of segregation were partly created through discrimination and hostile reactions from the majority population. But it has been argued that segregation can perform some positive functions. Even in the early stages of ghetto formation,

> *motivated by pride, habit, and the need for mutual protection from rejection, [black people] found a refuge within their own community. Furthermore, the institutional structure of the black community – the churches, clubs, fraternal orders – were centred in the ghettos, thus discouraging many from moving into distant white neighbourhoods. And the concentration of [blacks] in specific parts of a city proved beneficial to black politicians and businessmen who based their careers on the support and patronage of the [black] masses.*
>
> (Meier and Rudwick, 1966:218)

We can see in these processes – both negative and positive – significant components of the emerging North American urban black identity in the second half of the twentieth century (Box 5.4). Some related issues about ethnic communities are discussed in section 4.4 of Chapter 4.

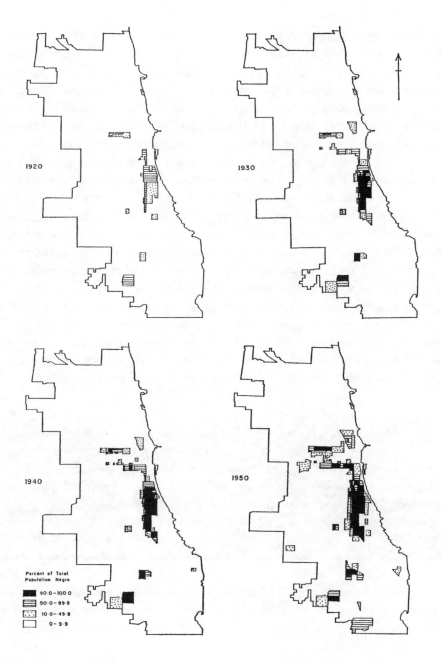

Figure 5.3a *Distribution of black populations in Chicago. Source: Duncan, O.D. and Duncan, B. (1957)* The Negro Population of Chicago. *Chicago: Chicago University Press.*

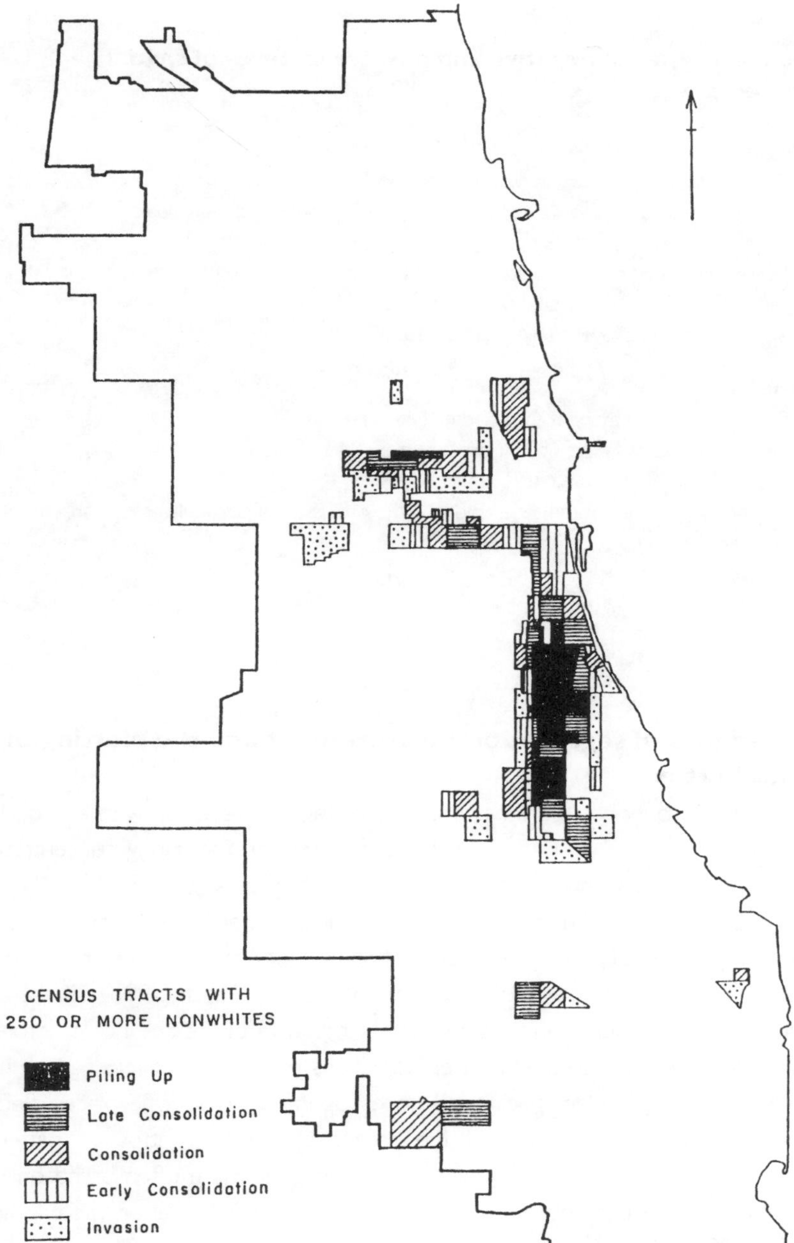
CENSUS TRACTS WITH
250 OR MORE NONWHITES
Piling Up
Late Consolidation
Consolidation
Early Consolidation
Invasion

Figure 5.3b *Classification of black residential areas in Chicago. The term 'negro' in the legend (as elsewhere in earlier literature) was used to denote a distinct racial group, a notion that has since been widely rejected. Source: Duncan, O.D. and Duncan, B. (1957)* The Negro Population of Chicago. *Chicago: Chicago University Press.s*

Box 5. 4 Alleged negative and positive features of spatial segregation

Negative

- By definition, segregation is a divisive phenomenon in society.
- Segregation reduces social interaction between groups and individuals.
- Segregation leads to mistrust.
- Segregation is often due to attempts by the 'privileged' to keep underprivileged ethnic minorities out of better-quality housing and environments.
- Segregation can prevent social and economic advancement.

Positive

- Segregation is a way of accommodating 'difference'.
- Segregation allows a group to maintain its social cohesion.
- Segregation reinforces cultural values.
- Segregation allows critical thresholds for the provision of culturally specific institutions and services to be reached.
- Segregation provides a defence from attack.

5. 4 Critiques of segregation measurement and the plotting of ethnic ghettos

From the 1970s onwards there has been increasing dissatisfaction with approaches to the geography of 'race' and ethnicity that simply rely on measuring concentration or plotting ethnic ghettos. Such critiques revolve around three key points.

First, the reasons behind the prevalence of such 'clusters' are unclear. As Box 5.4 highlights, high levels of geographical segregation are not necessarily the consequence of high levels of discrimination aimed at the segregated group. Peach (1996) has also argued that high levels of dispersal are not necessarily indicative of the absence of intolerance and prejudice. As such, abstract conceptualizations of ghetto formation are unhelpful, and we need to consider specific influences operating in specific places. Secondly, arguments remain centred around the means by which ghettos or patterns of segregation are plotted. Studies of patterns of segregation are often based on census data within which a person's ethnicity is defined by their national or 'racial' origin. As Harvey (2000: 237) argues, this can be a poor indicator of ethnic affiliation in that, for example, 'all those of Polish descent are lumped into the same category, whether or not they identify with that cultural heritage'. This approach also perpetuates the idea that distinct races exist, suggesting that the census itself is implicated in the racialization of minorities. The third criticism relates to the manner in which analysis of ghettos leads to a negation of difference within those populations: groups are wrongly assumed to be internally homogeneous and culturally fixed. For example, as black US ghetto areas grew, so internal differentiation emerged. Just as with the initial northward migration of blacks, this was due, in part, to changes in the USA space-economy. From the late 1950s onwards, black migration took on a new form, the main characteristic being the movement of higher skilled and better educated people *between* the cities of the north-east. In contrast with earlier patterns, the destinations of such migrants were not the 'core' inner-areas of the classic ghetto but the outer fringes. Table 5.1 shows the marked contrast in social and economic characteristics which had emerged through these processes within the 'Black Belt' in Chicago by the 1960s.

Table 5.1 *Socio-economic patterns in Chicago's Afro-American community (Zone 1 = innermost area; Zone 7 = outermost area)*

				Zone			
	1	2	3	4	5	6	7
Per cent illiterate(+)	13.4	4.6	3.2	2.3	3.3	2.9	2.7
Per cent males white collar	5.8	5.5	10.7	11.2	12.5	13.4	34.2
Per cent family heads born in the south	77.7	77.0	74.7	73.8	72.6	69.0	65.2
Per cent adult males single	38.6	38.1	35.9	32.0	30.7	27.3	24.7
Per cent families with female heads	22.0	23.1	20.8	20.4	20.5	15.2	11.9
Per cent house owners	0	1.2	6.2	7.2	8.3	11.4	29.8
Rate of family desertion (*)	2.5	2.6	2.1	1.5	1.1	0.4	0.2
Rate of juvenile delinquency (*)	42.8	31.4	30.0	28.8	15.7	9.6	1.4

(+) of persons aged over 10
(*) per 100 base population

Source: Frazier (1967)

The classic black ghetto therefore demonstrated considerable internal variation and provided the opportunity for a wide variety of identities to be formed. An approach that simply measures the concentration of a particular group ignores the fact that ethnic communities are obviously not homogeneous in terms of class, age, gender, and so on.

Furthermore, the example of the North American black ghetto is time- and space-specific. All other societies have ethnic minority immigrant groups, and in order to develop a more dynamic and contemporary perspective on ethnicity and social geography we need to examine outcomes in other places. Our aim in the next section is to illustrate how the presence of minority groups in 'alien' territories relates to various processes operating at national and international scales.

5. 5 The changing geography of ethnic minorities in Britain and other northern European countries

As the example of blacks in North America showed, the changing position of ethnic minority groups is highly contingent upon the nature of political and economic circumstances at various times. The post-Second World War migration of people of different ethnic origins into northern and western Europe reflected elements of the prevalent political economy which also influenced the distribution and location of ethnic minority groups. In the 1950s and 1960s movements related to former colonial linkages: from the Caribbean and South Asia to Britain, from North and West Africa to France and from Indonesia to the Netherlands. Somewhat later, in the 1970s, labour shortage at the core of industrial Europe and surpluses in the periphery led to the movement of 'guest workers' from Spain, Portugal and Turkey to France and especially Germany (Castles and Kosack, 1973). Yet, such groups have increasingly been represented as a 'problem' owing to racism in host societies, and have experienced various forms of exclusion.

The notion of ethnic minority groups functioning as a replacement labour force applies particularly to the history of post-war migration to Britain (Peach, 1968; 1998), and to the former West Germany at a later date. Ethnic minorities were recruited by the West German government to meet labour shortages in the 1960s but these shortages, as earlier in Britain, although in growth regions were not in growth industries. Labour import agreements were signed with eight different countries between 1955 and 1968. The number of foreign residents increased from only 170,000 in 1952 to 4.5 million in 1986. By far the largest proportion were Turks (31.8 per cent) (Friedrichs and Alpheis, 1991). As far as the West German government was concerned, residence in the territory was supposed to be temporary. As the economy slowed down in the early 1970s a 'recruitment stop' was initiated, banning further guest worker immigration apart from close family members. This slowed down but did not stop the rate of immigration and attempts at subsidized repatriation in 1983–4 had little impact. By default, therefore, and despite growing hostility from many in the 'host' population, the majority of guest workers have become virtually permanent immigrants. The government gradually ceased to return guest workers to their countries of origin, but application for citizenship became more difficult up until the early 1990s when re-unification of Germany prompted a relaxation of naturalization law and the possibility of the acquisition of citizenship on the basis of residence. At this time ethnic minorities constituted 7.4 per cent of the population of the former West Germany.

As in Britain, the immigrant groups have become a more significant component of the population of the large cities (Table 5.2), especially as those cities have declined in population. More recently the mismatch between the skill levels of the ethnic minority population and the requirements of new growth industries has increased, resulting in high levels of unemployment and welfare dependency for some ethnic minorities in the inner areas of many of these cities. This in turn has served to reinforce racial stereotypes.

Sweden represents another, if less spectacular, variant on the 'labour replacement' theme and is of particular interest because of its alleged liberality and several interesting policy changes. From the mid-nineteenth century to the First World War Sweden was a

Table 5.2 *Percentage of foreign population in West German cities of 500,000 or more, 1970 and 1986*

	Population		% Foreign born	
	Total 1986	% change 1980–86	1970	1986
Berlin	1,879,225	−6.0	3.5	13.7
Hamburg	1,571,267	−4.5	5.4	10.2
Munich	1,274,716	−1.9	14.0	17.3
Cologne	914,336	−6.4	9.1	15.0
Essen	615,421	−5.0	3.8	6.1
Frankfurt	592,411	−5.9	13.3	25.0
Dortmund	568,164	−6.6	3.7	8.9
Stuttgart	565,486	−2.6	13.1	18.1
Düsseldorf	560,572	−5.1	9.2	16.0
Bremen	521,976	−6.0	3.8	7.5
Duisburg	514,718	−7.8	6.2	13.0
Hannover	505,718	−5.4	6.1	9.7
FRG	61,140,500	−0.8	4.3	7.4

Source: Friedrichs and Alpheis (1991:121)

country of emigration (1.2 million Swedes left, mainly for North America). In the 1930s Sweden began to experience immigration, first of Swedes returning 'home', then of north European and Baltic State refugees during the Second World War and then a much greater volume and more varied influx to meet the post-war shortage of labour. Initially this took the form of a common Nordic labour market, the main movement being from Finland to Sweden. During the 1960s, however, a very different migration pattern emerged. The number of immigrants doubled and labour was sought from more distant countries, especially Greece and the former Yugoslavia, and settled in the main cities and industrial centres. By 1968, however, this replacement labour force had fulfilled its role and there was growing concern about the displacement of indigenous population from the labour market by foreigners because of economic slow-down (Lindén and Lindberg, 1991; see section 2.7 of Chapter 2). Immigrants now need to have a work permit and an actual job before entering Sweden, or to be accepted as political refugees, or have close personal ties with people already resident in the country. Reflecting political and economic changes at the global scale, the latter two categories are now the most common immigration types in Sweden and, as in other countries, led to a change in policy with regard to migrants.

From 1985, under pressure from politicians in the larger urban areas, policy was to direct new immigrants away from those areas. Between 1985 and 1995 more than 400,000 immigrants entered the country, the highest per capita in Europe. The 'All of Sweden' policy sought to spread immigrants through the country as part of their refugee reception programme, sometimes into municipalities whose governments were reluctant to accept them. Areas with high densities of immigrants in 1980 experienced relative loss by 1995 whereas those with few immigrants in 1980 showed relative gain. The policy appears to have been successful but, in reality, it has led to secondary migration, whereby on completion of the reception programme (usually about 18 months), immigrants tend to move towards existing spatial concentrations of their particular ethnic group: 'it was obvious to these secondary migrants that they were not appreciated by the authorities of the destination municipalities, and they therefore had to rely upon fellow countrymen, friends and sometimes relatives' (Andersson, 1998:406).

While quantitative studies of ethnic segregation declined from the 1970s onwards, these recent patterns and processes of immigration and policy manifestations led to a revival of interest amongst social geographers in the 1990s. One question was whether the ghetto concept could be applied outside the United States.

5. 6 Do ghettos exist in Britain and Europe?

Quantitative comparisons indicate that ethnic minorities in British cities are considerably less segregated than in North America. At enumeration district level the most concentrated group are Bangladeshis with one ward in Spitalfields, Greater London showing an ID of 90 (see Box 5.3 for explanation). But only one third of London Bangladeshis live in enumeration districts where they form over 30 per cent or more of the total population. Only one quarter of London Indians live in enumeration districts where they form over 30 per cent of the population. The highest level of black Caribbean concentration in any London enumeration district is 62 per cent, in Brent, and only 3 per cent of black Caribbean population in London live in enumeration districts

Table 5.3 *Indices of dissimilarity for main ethnic groups: London and Birmingham*

	White	Black Caribbean	Indian	Pakistani	Bangladeshi	Chinese
Greater London Wards						
White	0	49	51	54	65	30
Greater London enumeration districts						
White	0	54	56	66	77	52
Birmingham wards						
White	0	54	60	74	80	37
Birmingham enumeration districts						
White	0	58	68	82	88	70

Adapted from Peach (1996)

where they form 30 per cent or more of the population (Peach, 1996). Table 5.3 shows some indices of dissimilarity and segregation for the two British cities with the largest ethnic minority population, Greater London and Birmingham.

The index of dissimilarity is higher for the smaller spatial unit of enumeration districts than for wards, reinforcing the point that any discussion of segregation needs to be qualified by reference to the spatial units of measurement. Interestingly, the Chinese population of both cities, which appears to be only moderately segregated at ward level, is much more segregated at enumeration district level. The pattern appears to be one of overall fairly even distribution across the city but in a number of segregated groupings at a smaller scale. In both London and Birmingham and, indeed, in other large cities (Peach, 1996) Bangladeshis are confirmed as the most segregated of the minority groups, not only from the majority white population but also from other minority groups. Pakistanis are the next most segregated, followed by Indians and Black Caribbeans. However, in Birmingham, Chinese are more segregated at the enumeration district level than are either Indians or black Caribbeans. It would seem therefore that Britain's ethnic minority groups are behaving in rather different ways (see Figs 5.4a–c).

Peach used these data and other evidence to suggest that the North American ghetto model does not apply to Britain. At an empirical level this appears to be broadly the case but levels of segregation remain high. However, one further factor is important, this being the degree of change over time in levels of segregation of the different groups. The available evidence suggests that the early pattern of ethnic settlement has remained remarkably stable (Phillips, 1998). At the national scale, in fact, there has been growing metropolitan concentration (Rees and Phillips, 1997). Only just over one third of the white population of Britain lived in the nine metropolitan areas in 1981, between 54 and 83 per cent of these ethnic minorities lived there. Between 1981 and 1991 white people declined in these areas by 2 per cent, but all ethnic groups increased (black Caribbeans by 1.1 per cent, Indians by 1.8 per cent, Pakistanis by 1.1 per cent, Bangladeshis by 3 per cent and Chinese by 3.6 per cent). The main explanation for this trend is white decentralization. However, on a more localized scale the picture is somewhat different.

By the 1990s it appears that a small degree of dispersal from 'core' areas had taken place for some of the ethnic minority population of Britain. Indeed, empirical studies demonstrated limited black suburbanization in Birmingham in the 1970s (Ward and Sims, 1981), the decentralization of some Indian households from central Leicester to the high status suburb of Oadby in the early 1980s (Phillips, 1981), and an outward movement of Pakistanis in Manchester (Werbner, 1979). But there are substantial differences between the ethnic minority groups. The black Caribbean population (especially the British born) in particular shows fairly continuous reductions in levels of segregation from 1961 to 1991, and 'strong centrifugal movement towards the suburbs' (Peach, 1998:1667). In part, however, this is due to their increased movement into the council housing sector in the 1970s. The Indian population also shows a general tendency to decentralize, especially in Outer London which had a 64 per cent increase in Indian population

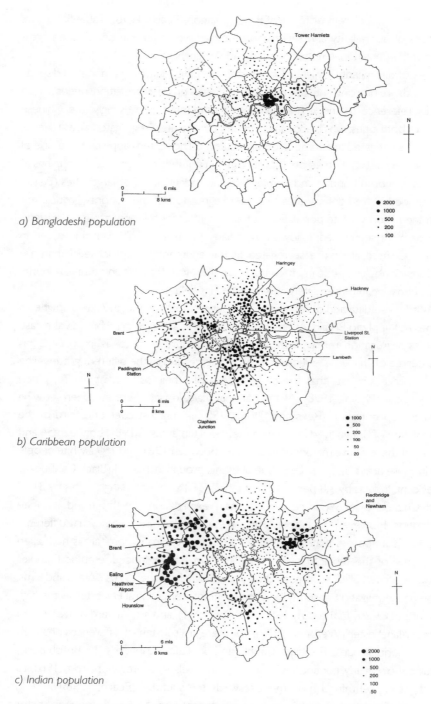

a) Bangladeshi population

b) Caribbean population

c) Indian population

Figure 5.4a–c Distribution of different ethnic groups in Greater London. Source: C. Peach, 1997: Pluralist and assimilationist models of ethnic divisions of ethnic settlement in London, 1991. Tijdschrift voor Economische en Sociale Geografie 88(2), Figure 3, p. 124, Figure 2, p. 125, Figure 4, p. 127.

between 1981 and 1991 (Phillips, 1998). For example, the Indian population of Redbridge and Harrow increased by more than 80 per cent in that decade (Fig. 5.4c). Whilst these trends support Peach's thesis of the non-applicability of the North American ghetto model in Britain, in terms of deconcentration 'Pakistanis and Bangladeshis are virtually absent. The rapid growth of the latter two predominantly Muslim minorities over the 1981–91 decade has been … characterized by a consolidation of their pattern of inner-city residence" (Phillips, 1998:1687). These spatial trends for the different ethnic groups are broadly confirmed by a study of the Leeds/Bradford conurbation (Rees, Phillips and Medway, 1995), and for Asians in Leicester and Bradford (Byrne, 1998).

One process which might explain these different trends is that as a minority group assimilates with the host population, particularly in terms of skill levels and employment opportunities, so the spatial distribution of the minority population will converge with that of the total population and be arranged on social class lines rather than ethnic lines. Table 5.4 indicates the male employment structure of different groups and it is clear that Indian men, for example, have a similar employment structure to white men. Yet, the other 'suburbanizing' group – black Caribbeans – are significantly under-represented in the managerial and professional categories. Pakistanis and Bangladeshis are relatively absent from the skilled manual categories, with the former over-represented as machine operators and the latter as personal service workers.

Although differences between ethnic groups in the changes in their occupation-related social class position may help to explain some of the desegregation or segregation tendencies we have noted, cultural factors – especially those relating to family and household size, marriage patterns, religion and community, and how these in turn relate to housing choices and availability – are also of considerable significance. Some have tried to argue that the extent to which different groups participate in, for example, small business formation may also be interpreted as a measure of assimilation and

Table 5.4 *Structure of male employment by ethnic group, Britain, 1991 (%)*

	White	Black Caribbean	Indian	Pakistani	Bangladeshi
Managerial	19.3	7.9	22.0	19.3	19.7
Professional	17.3	11.6	19.8	11.0	8.2
Clerical/secretarial	6.6	8.3	9.2	6.4	3.2
Skilled manual	23.4	26.2	16.4	13.1	8.6
Personal services	6.0	8.0	2.7	3.9	44.6
Sales	4.5	2.8	6.4	7.5	2.3
Machine operators	14.3	21.5	15.8	28.6	4.5
Unskilled manual	7.6	10.8	5.4	7.0	5.2
Other	1.0	2.9	2.2	3.3	3.6

Adapted from Phillips (1998)

desegregation, although Barrett, Jones and McEvoy (1996) argue that the reverse can often be the case.

Box 5.5 provides a summary of these recent changing locational tendencies and associated characteristics of the main ethnic minority groups in Britain.

Figure 5.5 *Indian restaurant in a converted Methodist chapel, Greater Manchester: an interesting manifestation of late twentieth-century cultural change in northern England. Credit: M. Barke.*

Box 5.5 Locational and related trends of British ethnic minority groups: a summary of the processes

Indians Increasingly white collar, increasingly suburbanized, living in semi-detached, owner occupied housing; family size larger than British average but declining.

Pakistanis Manual workers, living in inner-city areas, in owner-occupied, older terraced housing areas; large family size; strong traditional gender differences.

Bangladeshis Manual workers and personal service workers, living in inner-city terraced and flatted council property; large family size; strong traditional gender differences.

Black Caribbeans Manual workers also substantially present in council property but far less segregated than Bangladeshis and with a tendency to decentralize; whilst the majority of Indian, Pakistani and Bangladesh families are nuclear, over 50 per cent of Caribbean families are single-female headed.

Ethnic minority groups are significantly segregated from each other, often as much or more than from white populations.

(Based on Peach, 1998; Phillips, 1998; Robinson, 1997)

Figure 5.6 *Bank of Pakistan, Arthur's Hill, West Newcastle. A former corner shop replaced by a bank branch serving a different local community. Credit: M. Barke.*

Studies of other European cities suggest that similar patterns and processes are found there but that these are subject to local variation relating, for example, to local housing markets. For example, Amsterdam has a significant proportion of social housing while Brussels is dominated by privately rented housing. The latter city has much stronger concentrations of both Turks and Moroccans than does Amsterdam. In Brussels, immigrants are concentrated into the cheaper, residualized working-class private-rented housing stock to the west of the central area where they sometimes form up to 45 per cent of a neighbourhood's population. In Amsterdam, due to the greater availability of social housing, concentrations of Turks and Moroccans rarely rise above 25 per cent of a neighbourhood's population (Kesteloot and Cortie, 1998). However, different groups show different distribution patterns. The largest group are the Surinamese (69,000) whose presence is strongly related to the colonial past and who arrived in large numbers in the 1970s stimulated by the independence of Surinam in 1975 (Duerloo and Musterd, 1998). Migrants from Morocco (48,000) and Turkey (31,000) were consciously recruited to meet labour shortages in the Netherlands during the 1960s and, subsequently, their numbers were augmented through family reunion and family formation. More recently, a growing number of refugees and asylum seekers have come to live in the city.

The initial core area of the Surinamese was in the Bijlmermeer district in the south east of the city, in municipal housing units which had proved to be unpopular with indigenous Dutch residents, but they are now considerably more dispersed. The more recently arrived refugees are now well represented in this district. Moroccans are more concentrated into the early twentieth-century areas to the west of the city. However, both Turks and Moroccans showed quite high patterns of residential mobility over the

1981–95 period (Kesteloot and Cortie, 1998) and, while this had not resulted in high levels of suburbanization, it suggests that some constraints can be overcome.

The distribution of Turkish residents (at 138,000, the largest foreign group) in Berlin in 1996 (Kemper, 1998), six years after unification, was sharply divided between east and west: only 2 per cent of Turks were living in the east. This could suggest limited mobility and deconcentration on the part of the Turkish population. However, overall migration from Turkey to Germany declined considerably from the late 1980s, prior to unification, and may have reduced the demand for housing in 'new' areas. Although strong concentrations exist in inner-city areas, Turks are in fact present in every area of the city. There is evidence of slight decreases in the areas of main concentration over the 1991–96 period, but movement tends to take place in groups as 'Turks prefer residential areas with a social network and infrastructure of their own group and change residence with the support of familial and social contacts' (Kemper, 1998:1780; see Box 5.4). While foreigners of all nationalities do tend to be concentrated in inner-city areas of West Berlin, the index of dissimilarity declined from 32.1 (not particularly high by North American standards) to 30.1 between 1991 and 1996. Rather like Sweden's policy, although on an intra-urban scale, Berlin has sought to promote equality between districts with respect to housing refugees and this has led to a fairly even distribution of such people across the city. Nonetheless, as in other cities, it is clear that while different ethnic minority groups may overlap in some districts, they have their own detailed micro-geographies.

Overall, the evidence for British and several European cities suggest that ghetto-like areas, in the classic North American sense, have not developed and, if anything, some tendencies towards de-concentration may be discerned, although this is taking place at different rates between the various groups involved. These differences are largely explained by the socio-economic characteristics of the group concerned and the relative strength of their cultural ties. In other words, within the framework of externally determined, structural constraints, a degree (albeit limited) of choice may be exercised. The latter may, of course, involve the adoption of deliberate strategies to *avoid* certain residential areas through fear of rejection or harassment.

Perhaps a more important question than whether ghettos exist in any particular national territory surrounds the ways in which ethnic minority groups are perceived and treated by host societies. Residential segregation is just one measure, albeit an important one, of the relationship of ethnic minority groups to wider society.

5.7 Understanding the social geography of race and ethnicities: racism, exclusion and 'whiteness'

In some of the literature in social geography which has focused on ethnic segregation, there has been an unspoken assumption that assimilation, reflected in spatial and social patterns, is a good thing. While 'integration' refers to a situation where a minority group retains its cultural distinctiveness but participates fully in the wider society, 'assimilation' implies abandonment of 'difference', for example through full participation in the institutions of the wider society, changes in cultural patterns and intermarriage. Given that ethnic identities remain strong and, arguably, some have been strengthened through long-term processes of discrimination, most ethnic minority groups are not 'assimilated' in European societies. Indeed, it is questionable whether the goal of assimilation is a desirable one, and many would argue that difference should be celebrated rather than submerged or lost. As an objective, assimilation may be based on an agenda set by white majority groups.

Even if there is a tendency towards a lower incidence of segregation (Van Kempen and Özüekren, 1998), not all of those in an ethnic minority group may be able to engage in such mobility, and one consequence may be a marginalized sub-set of an ethnic minority group. In addition, a reduced concentration does not necessarily imply any reduction in either discrimination or racism being experienced. Racism and its continued manifestations are important ingredients in the internal changes within ethnic minority communities. Although, as we have shown, ghettos in the North American sense may not exist in north west European cities, ethnic residential areas are still commonly represented as spaces and places of the 'other', and reified as such in popular mythology as well as public policy initiatives. It is through such processes that social exclusion becomes manifest and some groups are problematized more than others.

In France, for example, discussions of immigration focus strongly on Algerians, despite the fact that there are actually more Portuguese living in France. This gives us an important insight into the social construction of difference – 'those who have been seen

---

Box 5.6 Four types of social exclusion affecting European ethnic minorities

- **Exclusion through legal mechanisms** – through the granting or denial of citizenship, 'difference' between the host population and the minority group is perpetuated in a highly formal way, and can impact upon political rights (the right to vote), personal mobility, and access to certain kinds of jobs (e.g. as civil servants).

- **Exclusion through the ideologies of 'othering'** – where 'everyday' attitudes (that is, not just those of extreme political groupings) within the majority population deny the rights of minority groups to live how and where they do.

- **Exclusion through denying minorities access to social capital** – where there is a failure to recognize group-specific needs in order to facilitate the reduction of inequalities and processes of social inclusion.

- **Exclusion through poverty and economic marginalization** – where patterns of economic disadvantage and exclusion are perpetuated from one generation to the next.

(Source: White, 1999)

as most significantly different are those from outside the social construction of Europe' (White, 1999), and hints at the racist basis of such perceptions. Even when groups do not experience overt forms of racism, they may be subject to more subtle forms which lead to social exclusion. Box 5.6 gives some examples of racist exclusion. National policies can clearly have considerable impact on each of these processes of exclusion in both a positive and negative sense. These various forms of social exclusion overlap and interact, sometimes in complex ways; for example, although many ethnic minority peoples hold citizenship in their country of residence they are still excluded from mainstream society.

While the concept of 'social exclusion' has several meanings (Byrne, 1999), it reflects a general shift in language and perspective in social geography and elsewhere which has refocused attention onto white majority groups and the processes by which minority groups are labelled as 'different'. Concentrating on processes of exclusion, rather than the measurement of segregation alone, highlights that a lack of integration has more to do with the majority group than the minority group. Increasingly, social geographers are focusing on the concept of whiteness and its relationship to issues of racism and nationalism, rather than on people of colour. Such work has analysed how boundaries are constructed between the 'self' and 'others', and how these are reflected in divisions and constructions of space (e.g. Anderson, 1991; Bonnett, 2000). Notions of colour are important, as different colours are labelled with positive and negative connotations, for example of superiority and inferiority, safety and danger. Whereas white is often thought of as representing purity, virtue, goodness, order, and rationality, black is often seen as the opposite (Sibley, 1995). In summary, then:

> Whiteness has developed, over the past two hundred years, into a taken-for-granted experience structured upon a varying set of supremacist assumptions ... Non-white identities, by contrast, have been denied the privileges of normativity and are marked within the West as marginal and inferior.
>
> (Bonnett, 2000:140)

This white supremacy is manifested in overt racism and prejudice as well as more subtle forms (Cone, 1992), promoting domination and subjugation as 'natural' outcomes. Increasingly, then, social geographers are becoming engaged with uncovering these processes and taking up explicit political positions against them.

Summary

- Race and ethnicity are socially constructed categories.
- Historical processes explain many deeply embedded notions of racial superiority.
- Early geographical studies of race and ethnicity were largely concerned with measuring levels of spatial concentration of different groups. The image of the North

American black ghetto came to represent the most extreme form of segregation of, and racism against, a particular ethnic group.

- There are significant differences within and between ethnic groups in their degree of segregation and in the way that housing market processes impact upon such patterns.
- Contemporary patterns of the international migration of different ethnic groups are explained partly by former colonial links and partly by the demands of the global economy.
- Rather than simply measuring segregation, the position of ethnic minorities is best approached through the concept of social exclusion, giving majority ethnic groups ownership of the problems of racism and nationalism.
- In taking 'whiteness' for granted as a 'natural' category, we risk legitimizing the labelling of other colours as different and problematic.

Further reading

For a general discussion of housing ethnic minority groups and particular case studies in both Europe and the USA see:
- Huttman, E. D. (ed.) (1991) *Urban Housing Segregation of Minorities in Western Europe and the United States.* Durham and London: Duke University Press.

More specific consideration of the role of the housing market in relation to segregation tendencies in Britain is found in:
- Smith, S. J. (1991) *The Politics of Race and Residence*, Cambridge: Polity Press.

For a discussion on the geography of different ethnic groups as represented in the 1991 census of Britain see:
- Ratcliffe, P. (ed.) *Social Geography and Ethnicity in Britain: Geographical Spread, Spatial Concentration and Internal Migration*, Vol. 3 of *Ethnicity in the 1991 Census*, 111–34. London: HMSO.

A wide-ranging overview of ethnic issues at the urban scale is found in:
- Moon, G. and Atkinson, R. (1997), Ethnicity. In Pacione, M. (ed.) *Britain's Cities: Geographies of Division in Urban Britain*, London: Routledge, pp. 262–76.

The social construction of 'race' and ethnicity and some of its geographical implications are dealt with in:
- Jackson, P. and Penrose, J. (eds) (1993) *Constructions of Race, Place and Nation*, London: UCL Press.

For a discussion of the debate on 'whiteness' see:
- Bonnett, A. (2000) *White Identities*. Harlow: Prentice Hall.

6
Geographies of gender and sexuality

6.1 Introduction

This chapter provides an introduction to work in social geography on gender and sexuality. The chapter has four main themes. First, it explores the connections between space, place, gender and sexuality at a number of different scales. Second, it emphasizes the importance of spatial divisions in establishing, maintaining and reshaping gender and sexual identities. Third, it highlights the multiplicity of gender and sexual identities, and the ways in which they relate to other identities of class, age, race, ability and so on. Finally, the chapter encourages you to think about positionality (introduced in section 1.3.2, Chapter 1), which has been central to both feminist and queer geographies.

In this introduction, we outline and define some of the important terms and issues around gender and sexuality. We introduce the perspectives of feminist and queer geographies, which have been the springboards for much of the work discussed in this chapter. In the sections which follow we examine some recent case studies of work on geographies of gender and sexuality.

6.2 Defining terms

6.2.1 Gender and sex

Gender is generally used to describe the socially constructed, rather than biologically fixed, aspects of being male or female. For a long time in feminist thought, sex was considered in opposition to gender. Sex described the characteristics you are born with as male or female; a different set of genitals and, for females, the ability to carry children, give birth and breastfeed. A key tenet of feminist thought is that most of the differences the sexes experience are determined by social influences rather than biological ones. These range from the way babies are dressed to discrimination in the workplace. Feminists have shown the ways in which gender differences are made to appear 'natural' or *naturalized* by being attributed to biology (cf. Chapter 5). Thus in the development of feminism in the twentieth century, gender became the preferred term, as 'one is not born but becomes a woman' (de Beauvoir, 1949:525).

But a neat distinction between gender and sex is problematic. Feminists have always understood that gender roles have been developed historically on the basis of biological sexual difference, even though the latter does not determine the former. Discussions about what men and women are capable of are likely to raise disagreements about the degree of social construction of gender. Are women and men equally capable of working as brain surgeons? How about as childcare workers, or building labourers? Recently new questions are being raised around sex/gender, as well as many other issues of 'nature or nurture?', including developments in genetics (as more research suggests that genes control at least some of our characteristics and behaviour), and transsexual and transgender identities. While still holding the belief that gender differences are socially constructed, social geographers are interested in the role of the body in these processes.

As Box 6.1 shows, gender inequality is a global problem. But the processes leading to gender inequality impact differently in different places, and these differences relate to social, economic and political contexts at different scales. Differentiation at local and household scales will be the main focus of this chapter.

> **Box 6.1 Gender difference at a global scale**
>
> In nearly every country, women work more hours than men – when paid and unpaid labour are taken into account.
>
> The global average wage for women is about three-fourths of the male wage – ranging from 92 per cent of the male wage in Tanzania to 75 per cent in Belgium, Germany and the US, to 42 per cent in Bangladesh.
>
> Of the 1.3 billion people living in extreme poverty, about 70 per cent are women.
>
> Although women constitute half the electorate, they hold only 13 per cent of the seats in the world's parliaments.
>
> (UNDP, 1995, 1997)

Gender is not simply about the different social roles of women and men: it is about the *relations* between them, and it is these relations which underlie the distinct roles. Hence this chapter is concerned with men's lives as well as women's, and our starting point is that patriarchy can be oppressive to all, although not equally.

It is important to be critical of discourses of inequality and the purposes they may serve. In Britain, for example, there have been many press reports and editorials in recent years suggesting that men are being excluded and left behind, as girls and women achieve more educationally and in the workforce (Box 6.2). Yet aggregate statistics on pay, women's and men's position in the workforce and the division of responsibilities in the home do not bear this out (see Boxes 6.7 and 6.9). Gender is a strongly political field.

6.2.2 Femininities and masculinities

Femininity and masculinity are social identities which are constructed by gender relations. They are defined as sets of social characteristics associated with those who are biologically defined as female or male. Some characteristics which are often associated with 'masculine' and 'feminine' are listed in Box 6.3. Many of these are commonly

Box 6.2 Men under pressure?

Under pressure

Last week Chris Woodhead, Chief Inspector of Schools, announced that girls are now more successful than boys in every subject except physics, and almost all ethnic minorities are achieving better examination results than white boys from poor inner-city schools.

(*Guardian*, 11 March 1996)

Women are the new men

Men are less intelligent, less self-confident and less articulate than women. They are also more likely to be criminal, unemployed and depressed. Or so the new female chauvinism would have us believe ... [but] it's time to throw out the old sexual stereotypes – not simply reverse them.

(*Guardian*, 1 July 1999)

situated in particular spaces – femininity has traditionally been associated with the home and with private activities, while masculinity has been associated with the public sphere and work-related activities (see Chapter 2, Box 2.1 and sections 2.2 and 2.7.2). So, for example, breastfeeding is considered private and unsuitable for the public domain in many western societies, creating problems for women who want to combine it with leisure, work or simply being in a public place.

Box 6.3 Some 'masculine' and 'feminine' characteristics

Masculine	Feminine
Public	Private
Outside	Inside
Work	Leisure
Rational	Emotional
Earning	Spending
Production	Consumption
Empowered	Disempowered
Freedom	Constraint

(Source: McDowell and Sharp, 1999)

Although the lists in Box 6.3 might imply that these characteristics are fixed, recent geographical work has drawn out the ways in which they differ across time, space and different cultures. Indeed, they may be variable in a given society at a particular time; for example, 'masculinity' may have different meanings on the football terraces, in the pub, in the workplace and in the home, even though these meanings are connected to each other (Connell, 1995). This is why it is usual to use the plural masculinities and femininities.

6.2.3 Sexuality

When geographers talk about sexuality they mean more than just individuals' sexual desire and behaviour. Sexuality is a social relation in the same way as class, gender and race. Geographers are interested in the social identities which are associated with sexual desires, and in the ways in which sexuality influences, and is influenced by, social, cultural, economic and political geographies.

Geographies of sexuality have largely examined 'dissident sexualities' – the lives of lesbians, gay men and bisexuals – but are also beginning to examine heterosexuality and heterosexual spaces. As concrete areas, heterosexual spaces are clearly more numerous, yet their social construction has not been examined or questioned until fairly recently. As a dominant spatial form, heterosexuality has tended to be seen as 'normal' and so not requiring any empirical or theoretical attention.

In many societies behaviour outside heterosexuality, and individuals associated with it, have been marginalized, ignored or persecuted. Homosexuality has often been portrayed as abnormal, despite evidence of widespread practice from an enormous number and variety of societies, from ancient Greece to modern Islamic Africa (Blasius and Phelan, 1997), suggesting that it is every bit as 'natural' as heterosexuality (Sullivan, 1995). In the contemporary MDCs, gay men, lesbians, bisexuals face contempt of their affections and sexual desires from family, neighbours, fellow workers and strangers, and have to fight not to internalize this ideology. They also face overt discrimination from physical violence and harassment, through discrimination by employers and housing providers, to legal inequalities (see Box 6.4).

Box 6.4 Homosexuality and legal inequality in Britain

Stonewall is one of the foremost organizations in Britain which works for legal equality and social justice for gay men, lesbians and bisexuals. Its campaigns centre around five challenges, all of which involve changing the law as well as social attitudes:

Equal at school: Homophobic bullying of young people is widespread, and Section 28, a notorious piece of legislation, was introduced in 1988 to prevent homosexuality being 'promoted' in schools, making support of these young people difficult.

Equal in love: There are still unequal ages of consent in many countries, and in Britain gay sex is criminalized (see introduction to Chapter 11).

Equal at work: There is no protection from dismissal or harassment in the workplace on the basis of sexuality.

Equal as partners: People in homosexual relationships have unequal rights to pensions, inheritance and housing.

Equal as parents: People in homosexual relationships have unequal rights as parents.

(Source: http://www.stonewall.org.uk/aoc/factshts.html)

6.2.4 Multiple and hybrid identities

The categories 'woman' or 'man' are not adequate by themselves to understand the position of each in society. Whether you live in the First World or the Third, whether you are black or white, rich or poor, able or disabled, old or young – all influence your social, economic and geographical position *at the same time* as gender relations. But in addition, these other social identities also *intersect* with gender to influence the impact of gender relations itself. In other words, they work together to produce particular outcomes in different places and times. For example, sexual behaviour is structured by many social processes, the most critical of which is gender; and the connections between gender and sexuality are crucial in understanding experiences of different spaces (Bondi, 1998; Duncan, 1996). This is why we consider issues of gender and of sexuality within the same chapter.

6.3 Radical perspectives on gender and sexuality

Most work on gender and sexuality in human geography has been carried out within feminist and queer frameworks. These are politicized approaches, and they have faced hostility from mainstream geography.

6.3.1 Feminist geographies

Feminist geographies are concerned with how gender relations influence and are influenced by the spaces around us. While twenty years ago the idea that 'gender' could be a subject of geographical study seemed radical, today the key ideas of feminism have had a fundamental impact on mainstream social geography.

Feminist geographies are diverse (McDowell, 1993a and 1993b, and Box 6.5), but share a belief in the existence of patriarchy. Patriarchy is a social, economic and political system in which men have more authority and control than women. Although most feminists view patriarchy as universal, it operates differently in different types of society. In advanced capitalist societies, for example, Walby (1990) has suggested that patriarchal control is exerted via six spheres: the household, waged work, the state, violence, sexuality and cultural institutions such as the media. But feminist geographers also focus on other forms of oppression, allowing voices from traditionally marginalized groups to speak for themselves. The days when feminist geography could be dismissed as 'just about women' are long gone (Longhurst, 2000).

Feminist geography has analysed rapid changes in gender relations in western societies in recent years. Identities of masculinity and femininity are constantly changing. For example, recent media images have portrayed a 'New Man' who is not afraid to cry and will look after the kids, and a tough, independent 'New Woman' who might look feminine but works, drinks and swears like a man. The fact that gender identities appear to be fracturing does not mean that the old structures which underpin gender inequalities have disappeared. Bondi (1992) has argued, for example, that postmodern

Box 6.5 Three strands of feminist geography

Historically, these strands were initiated in the order shown here, but all three are used in contemporary geography.

The geography of women

Topical focus	*Theoretical influences*	*Geographical focus*
Description of the effects of gender inequality	Welfare geography, liberal feminism	Constraints of distance and spatial separation

Socialist feminist geography

Topical focus	*Theoretical influences*	*Geographical focus*
Explanation of inequality and relations between capitalism and patriarchy	Marxism, socialism, feminism	Spatial separation, gender place, localities

Feminist geographies of difference

Topical focus	*Theoretical influences*	*Geographical focus*
Construction of gendered, hetero(sexed) identities; differences among women; gender and constructions of nature; heteropatriarchy and geopolitics	Cultural, poststructural, postcolonial, psychoanalytic theories, writings of women of colour, lesbian women, gay men, women from 'developing' countries	Micro-geographies of the body; mobile identities; distance, separation and place; imaginative geographies; colonialisms and postcolonialisms; environment/nature

(Source: Johnston *et al.*, 2000, p. 260)

(or contemporary) society merely refashions gender identities in such a way that a predominantly patriarchal culture remains stable.

Feminist geographers have argued that gender relations are central to the geography of society and vice versa. Some ways in which this is so are shown in Box 6.6.

Box 6.6 The mutual constitution of gender identities and geographies

1. Through place. The different ways in which gender identities are shaped within different countries, regions or local areas.
2. Through specific spaces, sites and networks. For example, different gender identities are forged through spaces such as the home, the workplace, or local neighbourhood networks.
3. Through discourses about gender. At different times, particular sets of meanings about gender are current. These ascribe meaning to particular places and spaces, such as the traditional idea of the home as feminine and public space as masculine.

(Source: Laurie *et al.*, 1999:12–14)

6.3.2 The masculinism of academic geography

Feminist geography has also criticized the spaces of academic learning and research. Chapter 1 introduced the idea of positionality, or how our social, economic, personal and political positions affect the geographies we create through reading, writing and research. Before the late 1980s, it was largely the powerful groups in society, especially white, middle-class, First World, ostensibly heterosexual men whose geographies were represented. Where they mapped the geographies of 'others', the conclusions often told us more about their own viewpoint than the subjects they were examining (Driver, 1992; Sidaway, 1992).

The masculinism of geography has been identified as a major source of bias. Rose (1993) argues that masculinism exists in all spheres of geographers' activities; from the nature of research that is carried out, to modes of teaching, the structure of geography as a career, the questions asked by interview panels, and exchanges in departmental meetings and the staffroom (see also McDowell, 1990). Perhaps not surprisingly, women are poorly represented in most academic geography departments, making up around one in five lecturers in Britain and still lower proportions of readers and professors, despite being well represented among undergraduates (Dumayne-Peaty and Wellens, 1998). Box 6.7 shows some of the ways in which female geography undergraduates and lecturers are disadvantaged in Britain.

Box 6.7 Gender discrimination in academia and beyond

Universities underpay women
Shock report warns that the cost of eliminating sex discrimination in salaries would be £400m a year.

Guardian, 4 May 1999

Graduates in gender pay gap, too
Women face a 'female forfeit' on pay regardless of their level of education ... The study puts paid to the myth that the incomes gap is down purely to motherhood, revealing that women are economically disadvantaged before having children, despite doing better at school than boys.

Guardian, 11 June 1999

It is still a common view among the geographical establishment that the remedy for women's non-involvement in the power structures and their lack of representation at senior levels is seen to lie *within their own hands* ... this argument denies the structures of male power that confront women and inhibit their participation. Until the nature of sex and power in academe is addressed and altered, women will remain marginal actors within the institutional structures of academic geography.

(Source: McDowell, 1990:324)

6.3.3 Queer geographies

Queer geographies, while diverse, are based on a view that society oppresses homosexuality and privileges heterosexuality, a system sometimes referred to as heterosexism. They developed partly from the spaces opened up by feminist geographies, and partly from the influence of queer theory elsewhere in the social sciences. Queer geographies in some ways have had a similar history to feminist geographies. They have moved from mapping the housing and social facilities used by lesbians and gay men to critical engagement with heterosexuality. They encompass micro-scale work on the body and performance, and macro-scale consideration of how sexuality influences social, cultural, economic and political change (Binnie and Valentine, 1999). Most work has focused on the lives of gay men, though lesbians, bisexuals and transgender people have received more attention recently (Valentine, 1993a; Bell, 1994; Namaste, 1996), as has the relationship between gender and sexuality in space. Again, intersections with other forms of oppression have become central, so that 'the whole notion of a [single] lesbian and gay identity and community has become untenable in both politics and theory' (Binnie and Valentine, 1999:181).

While this work is expanding rapidly, it is still marginal to mainstream geography. In a critique of a decade ago, Bell suggested that 'gay and lesbian geographies have remained largely outside squeamish academia, and have not been subject to the same depth of analysis as other marginalized groups' (Bell, 1991:327). Today, even as research progresses, the homophobia he identified within the discipline has changed little (see also Valentine, 1998); 'sexuality as an object of study has become assimilated into the discipline while homophobia remains deep-seated' (Binnie and Valentine, 1999:175).

We now move on to some selected examples of social geographers' wide-ranging work on gender and sexuality. Our examples centre on three sites, the home, the workplace and the community, highlighting their connections to each other. Other spaces are also important, for example women's and men's relation to streets and leisure spaces (Wilson, 1991; see also Chapter 3), national regimes of gender (Duncan, 1994), and the gendering of the relations of humans to nature (Rose et al., 1997), but we do not have space to discuss these here.

6.4 The household and home

6.4.1 The home/work split under patriarchy and capitalism

An important contribution of feminist geography has been to show that the household and home are as central to social and economic life as the public spaces on which geographers have traditionally focused. In Chapter 2 (section 2.2) we described how the distinction between the spaces of the home and waged work has evolved historically, and discussed the role of industrial capitalism in developing this separation. But this split is inseparable from gender relations. Before industrialism in Europe women had had the major responsibility for caring for household members; with the coming of industrialism this gender division was continued, but now women were to perform these tasks in distinct spaces from which men were absent much of the time. Waged work, on the other hand, has been dominated by men. Many women, particularly from poorer households, have performed wage work, and this is the norm in contemporary society; but, compared with men's jobs, women's have generally been lower paid, of less security and with fewer prospects. Gender roles have thus become strongly spatialized, with women expected to take responsibility for domestic space, and men having privileged access to the public spaces of production.

This gendering of the home/work split has evolved and been reproduced in complex ways (Seccombe, 1993). Women's ascribed role in caring work has constrained their forms of participation in waged work. Their lower pay and inferior job prospects have then made it 'natural' for them to take primary responsibility for domestic tasks, in a vicious circle. 'The division of urban space both reflects and influences the sexual division of labour [and] women's role in the family' (McDowell, 1983). Moreover, employers have found it convenient to have a female workforce whose socially defined norms of employment are low (see Chapter 2). In both sites women's subordination was sanctioned by legislation. At the level of ideology, women's 'place' was viewed as the home, an ideal reinforced by governments, social and 'moral' campaigners and male-dominated trade unions. But women, individually and collectively, have contested or found ways to bypass these restrictions.

Thus gender relations are constructed in the *relation between* home and work; and the public/private divide is a central way in which gender differences are created and maintained. These relations develop in distinct ways in different territories. Even within a small country like Britain, there were historically large differences in women's participation in the workforce (Lewis, 1984), and today there are still large regional and intra-urban variations created by a range of cultural and economic factors (S. Duncan, 1991; McDowell and Massey, 1984). These relations are dynamic. For example, in many communities where the home has been a feminine preserve, and men's work and leisure outside the home accorded them status and power within it, male unemployment has altered masculine identities (see Box 2.10). Similarly, we shall see in Chapter 7 (section 7.3.2, p. 157) that older men's retirement from paid work and increased use of the home can impact on gender roles.

In our account of the home/work relation, then, both capitalism (the separation of production from reproduction, firms' choice of labour force) and patriarchy (women's responsibility for caring work, men's privileges in employment) are important, and both class and gender conflicts are involved. This illustrates our view that patriarchy and capitalism are structures which are interdependent and continually transform each other; one is not clearly primary to the other (Foord and Gregson, 1986; cf. Box 2.2).

We now examine the two sides of the home/work divide in turn, though keeping in view their inter-relation.

6.4.2 Gender divisions of labour in the home

The home is an important site where gender identities are created, expressed and recreated. Despite women's role in waged work (Box 6.9), ideologies persist about women's (and especially mothers') place in the home, and the traditional family unit as the best place to bring up children (Gregson and Lowe, 1995). Thus although housework is gradually becoming more fairly shared in many European countries, women still hold primary responsibility (Box 6.9). Interestingly, this is true of the highest earning professional women who work alongside men and are often thought to be equal. Meanwhile, traditional male responsibility for tasks such as DIY and gardening have been reinforced by their repackaging as 'leisure'.

Box 6.9 Gendered divisions of domestic labour

In Britain, 85 per cent of men and 72 per cent of women now have waged employment, and 67 per cent of working women return to their jobs within the first year after becoming mothers. However, the 'new woman' in the workplace hasn't always been accompanied by a 'new man' at home ...

	Usually or always the man	Usually or always the woman
Shopping for groceries	5%	41%
Deciding what to have for dinner	4%	59%
Doing the washing and ironing	2%	79%
Doing small repairs	74%	5%

(Summerfield, 1998)

This pattern has been contested. During the Second World War in Britain, for example, there were some moves towards collective domestic work (canteens and nurseries), though these were closed after the war (Gregson and Lowe, 1995). In Israel's kibbutz system, meals and laundry are provided in collective facilities, and children are not only cared for during the day but also live away from their parents' houses after a certain age – an arrangement which was also partly a response to wartime insecurity. However, more recently there has been a move towards private household reproduction on many kibbutzim. Feminist planners and architects such as Hayden (1984) have outlined 'utopian' ideals of planning housing and community where domestic tasks are shared between households.

The sharing out of domestic work in Europe today largely either takes place within the extended family or is paid for by employing cleaners, nannies, childminders and nursery workers (see Fig. 6.1). It is a stereotype that working-class households depend upon extended family care, while middle-class households pay for help; the reality is more complicated with many households using both forms (Holloway, 1998; Jarvis, 1999). One constant is that the providers of paid domestic labour and childcare are overwhelmingly women, mainly working-class and, in many countries, include a high proportion of black women; so women are still largely responsible for domestic work, but this is especially true for certain class and ethnic groups.

There are some shifts in men's domestic roles. In Britain, for example, recent research has shown the continuing importance of the ideology of fathers as family providers, but also increasing diversity in the roles men take on in childcare and housework (Lewis, 2000). Men now form a significant minority of single parent families, and a growing, though still tiny, minority are 'house-husbands' looking after children full time. However, traditional masculine identities die hard. The provision by employers of paternity leave or career breaks for men is rare in Britain. Even in Scandinavian countries which have generous parental leave, allowing fathers to take several months off work to look after children without losing their jobs or pay, relatively few have taken up the opportunity. Both the 'New Man' and the 'New Woman' who are free to combine domestic work,

Figure 6.1a *Domestic work is now big business. Adverts are employing images of femininity to sell their product.*

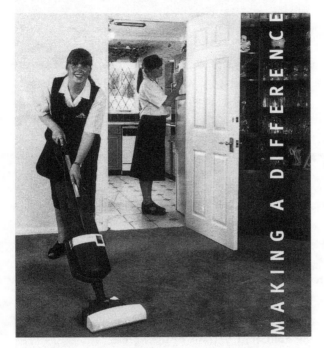

THE AFFORDABLE NECESSITY UNCONDITIONALLY GUARANTEED

Dependable home cleaning by a locally owned Franchise in an international network of 400 Franchise Business Owners.

Figure 6.1b *Another example of adverts employing images of femininity to sell their product to middle-class dual earner homes.*

paid work and parenting remain, for most people, little more than a media image (Jackson, 1991).

6.4.3 Sexual identities and the growth of alternative households

Until the late twentieth century, non-heterosexual relationships were excluded not only from public life, but from notions of 'family' and 'home'. Changing heterosexual practices and changing social attitudes have facilitated the formation and acceptance of gay and lesbian households. It is now usual for unmarried younger men and women to live in shared single- or mixed-sex households, whether they are in sexual relationships or not. In some places gay or lesbian households have become publicly legitimate, for example in Denmark, where gay men and lesbians may now marry their partners. To some extent the home and parenting are becoming increasingly judged as sites of consumption, witnessed by media interest in home décor and accessories for children, rather than judged 'morally' as a unit which must contain a married man and woman.

But there are still sharp constraints. As Box 6.4 shows, in Britain homosexuals are not equal in the home, either as parents or partners, in the eyes of the law; one statute refers to non-heterosexual households as 'pretended family relationships'. Norms about acceptable domestic arrangements for single women and non-heterosexuals are variable between localities. Within cities, suburbs have tended to reproduce feminine roles of domestic work and childcare (Saegert, 1980), with inner areas more likely to be accepting of non-heterosexuals. Thus concentrations of single women, gay men and lesbians have grown in some inner areas, sometimes, though not always, associated with gentrification (see Knopp, 1990 and Chapter 10).

6.4.4 Challenging dominant notions of the home

The home is most commonly viewed as a safe and comfortable place; not only a haven from the troubles of the world outside, but a site where women and men may find personal fulfilment in relationships with other adults and with children, where self-identity can be expressed and you can 'be yourself' (J. S. Duncan, 1981; Saunders, 1989). In contrast, for the reasons already outlined, much feminist work has analysed the home as an oppressive place for women. In Chapter 11 we highlight the commonness of domestic violence to women, children and older people. Such violence is often effectively sanctioned by the status of domestic space, where men's traditional power as head of household is reflected in modern-day responses to domestic violence by police, local communities and friends (N. Duncan, 1996). Equally, victims of domestic violence from partners of the same sex are also often ignored (Renzetti, 1988).

However, the notion of home primarily as a site of oppression has been criticized as a culturally and geographically specific one, which applies to white, middle-class women who have entered the labour force in large numbers from the mid twentieth century onwards. For other groups of women, the possibility of paid employment may not be a refuge from domestic labour. For some working-class women, domestic roles may provide relief from gender and class discrimination in the workplace, where they experience lower status and lower pay than middle-class women. Equally, for ethnic minority women the home may be a necessary haven from a racist society and a site of resistance (Hooks, 1991).

The home, then, can be very ambivalent. Johnston and Valentine (1995) make this point in discussing the conflicts between lesbians and heterosexual family life, be it the culture of suburbs or their own families. For many of their interviewees, their own home was important in expressing their identity. However, many lesbians in their homes or visiting others had their identities judged and policed by heterosexuals, whose reactions ranged from denial and embarrassment to harassment (Box 6.10).

Box 6.10 Lesbian identities and 'home'

'I mean, as much as I love my family I always feel I don't fit in. The only place I feel at ease is with gay people ... I feel I sit in a room full of my family and I feel I'm just not part of this, I don't fit in.' Jane, English lesbian

'When I came out to my parents, my mother said, "There's only one stipulation, you can bring your girlfriends home but they can't sleep in the same room with you" ... That was it. When I have taken a lover home there she has just been really different. It's felt really uncomfortable.' Julie, New Zealand lesbian

'There's a neighbour who's a bit of a worry ... I walked past them [neighbour and son] and they said "fucking dyke" ... I just ignored it and carried on walking. When they started giving Mike [another neighbour whom the two men have accused of being gay] trouble and wrecking his car and things [by pouring acid on it], I got more careful about kissing Emma goodbye at the door and whatever because I don't want to be victimized.' Jo, English lesbian

(Source: Johnston and Valentine, 1995)

6.5 The workplace

As we have seen, experiences of the home are inextricably bound up with wider relations, particularly to work. Recently, geographers have focused their attention on the 'social' as well as 'economic' relations of waged work. Much of this research has centred on gender cultures. Paid work is central to the construction of masculinities (Jackson, 1991), and the masculine cultures of many workplaces, historical and contemporary, have implications for women who enter them and for the femininities which are constructed in opposition to masculinities there. Moreover, in Section 2.7.2 of Chapter 2 we introduced the idea that gender and sexual relations in particular localities influence, and are influenced by, local working traditions and cultures. Two recent examples of geographers' work illustrate these processes.

Massey (1998) discusses the social relations of high technology industry in Cambridge, England. The subjects of her research are scientists and engineers, a largely male workforce who share a masculine working culture both in terms of the type of work they do (involving problem-solving, logic and rational thought), and the way they do it (very long hours which fit poorly with the responsibilities and demands of the domestic sphere). Massey suggests that this culture exists for three reasons; because of the competitive nature of the industry, because of competition within the labour market, and because male scientists choose it – they love their work. The culture is inevitably unfriendly to female employees who have family commitments, and impacts negatively on men in their roles as partners and fathers. Several respondents were dismissive and deprecating about domestic work and their own domestic abilities, and even where they prioritized their partners' or children's needs, this was a problematic choice (see Box 6.11).

Box 6.11 Reconciling home and work: high tech in Cambridge

'He is thinking about it [work] most of the time. He might be digging the garden but he is thinking about it. If he gets back at two in the morning he can go to sleep and just wake up in the middle of the night ... and he has solved a problem in his sleep, or he will...go and have a look at textbooks and things.' Female partner

Laundry? 'I shove it in the machine.' *Cleaning?* 'I do it when it gets too much.' *Shopping?* 'Tesco's, Friday or Saturday.' *Cooking?* 'I put something in the microwave. Nothing special. As long as it's quick and easy that's good enough for me.' *Gardening then?* 'When necessary.' Male scientist

'I feel frustrated ... when ... after this baby that's changed my life ... I go home early every other day (almost) and pick her up at 4.35, take her home, play with her until bedtime, and ... I find that sometimes that's quite frustrating, and keeps me away from work. I mean – it's fulfilling in its own right, but it's ... I'm conscious of the fact that ... I call it a half day, you know. I find it frustrating.' Male scientist

(Source: Massey, 1998)

Massey evaluates this opposition between the spheres of home and work, noting that much feminist work has been critical of such dualisms. However, the division and the dominance of work over home is clearly present in these workplaces and men's lives. Home is invaded by thoughts and activities of work, rather than vice versa. The workplaces made few concessions to domestic life, for example none provided crèches. The scientists' female partners had largely given up the struggle to defend domesticity from the incursion of work. Moreover, the goal of the scientists' work is the production of knowledge, which has been traditionally viewed as separated from the body and from reproductive activities. The boundaries between home and work are blurred by various strategies of daily negotiation and resistance by the scientists, but these strategies almost all involved personal, rather than institutional, action. Thus the home/work dualism is central to these gender relations, and it is interpreted and used both by individuals and their employers.

As we saw in Section 6.4.2, women are working outside the home in increasing numbers. However, in every country in the world, women are paid less than men for comparable hours of comparable work (see Boxes 6.11, and also 6.1 and 6.7); they are less likely to be promoted to senior positions; and even where they may appear to be working as equals, for example in professional careers, working cultures may militate against them and against men who do not fit in with stereotypes of heterosexual masculinity.

Box 6.11 Gender and pay in Britain, 2000

Women in full-time work in Britain earn on average 80 per cent of the male full-time wage. (http://www.eoc.org.uk/ValuingWomen/html/introduction.html)
Reasons include:

- Segregation of women into jobs involving what are traditionally seen as 'feminine' skills (e.g. cleaning, catering, childcare, nursing). These are lower-paid than jobs where men are over-represented, since historically women's paid work was poorly unionized and, as much of this work was previously carried out unpaid in the home, it was seen as having less 'value'.

- Direct and indirect discrimination in the workplace.

- Fewer women than men are in senior positions which are higher paid.

- Women are more likely to take career breaks than men.

McDowell's (1995) study of merchant bankers in the City of London illustrates this point. This workspace involves a specific form of masculinity which she describes as 'aggressive', and 'saturated with heterosexist imagery and behaviour'. The majority of employees are young men who present themselves as masculine socially and bodily. McDowell's interest was to examine how women bankers, as well as men from non-upper class backgrounds, had fitted in, given the gradually changing social profile of bankers and the equal opportunities policies of recent years.

McDowell argues that women's increasing presence in the industry may lead to the reinforcement of masculine working cultures, rather than breaking them down. The same is true of gay men, or those with the 'wrong' body image. These women and 'other' workers are seen as 'out of place' in the City, and reminded of this by daily harassment linked to bodily difference and codes (see Box 6.12). In response, some women tried to behave and dress more like men in order to fit in. McDowell concludes that here, as elsewhere, the strength of masculine working cultures means that equal opportunity policies have had very marginal impact.

Box 6.12 Doing gender in the City

'The young men here are very open about where they think a woman's place is – in the kitchen or in the bedroom … They think it's a man's prerogative to work at the bank and women shouldn't be here.'

'I guess I'd rather be the honorary male and not have all the comments than be on the other side.'

'We had a very nice chap in for interview but he was very overweight … the fact that he was very large was going to weigh on the client's mind.'

'Aggression from a woman is seen as trying to compete too well. It's not natural, certainly from a dealer's point of view.'

(Source: McDowell, 1995)

6.6 The neighbourhood and community

Gender relations are constituted also at the scale of the neighbourhood and 'community' (on this concept, see Chapter 4). The separation of home and work discussed in Section 6.2.1 was reflected in the way that cities grew, placing domestic life in neighbourhoods distanced from workplaces, and representing and perpetuating the traditional roles of women. Thus suburbanization has been viewed as the spatial reflection of the ideology of women's place being in the home (Saegert, 1980). In Britain the times of most rapid suburban development – the Victorian era and the 1950s – coincided with a strong ideology of female domesticity.

The layout of cities and their transport facilities severely constrain women's lives. Matrix (1984) give the example of the new town of Milton Keynes in England, which was planned assuming 100 per cent car ownership amongst its inhabitants. Here the land uses of home, work and leisure were segregated, ignoring differentiation among residents by class and gender, so that those without free use of cars had poor access to facilities. Urban structure, then, may reinforce existing inequalities between men and women, while women's role as carers and houseworkers in turn limits their mobility. Increasing car ownership has helped some women in better-off households. But many women now have a 'triple working day', including not only waged work and work within the home but the work of trips to schools, health facilities and shops; urban layout and transport are badly geared to the tight time constraints of this pattern of life (McDowell, 1983).

Masculinities and femininities are locally constructed, not just by differing built environments, but also by local social, economic and political histories. In the last section we mentioned that local gender relations are partly constructed by local work practices and traditions. They are also forged through changing social and community practices. Campbell's (1993) study of low-income urban neighbourhoods of Britain which experienced rioting in the late 1980s illustrates this point (also discussed in Chapter 11, section 11.2.4). She highlights the constructions of masculinity which were current in 'problem estates' during the late 1980s and early 1990s. While often labelled a 'war waged by young men', she notes that experts rarely ask what it is about young men in these localities which leads to their criminal behaviour.

Campbell starts from the economic and social transformation of these areas in recent years. The transition from almost full employment in heavy manual labour to mass unemployment has meant a crisis for working-class masculinity, which traditionally emphasized the strong, capable male breadwinner whose public life of work and leisure was separate from the feminine domain of the home. Men have therefore lost both income and public and family status. In response a new form of masculinity has evolved, being seen as 'mad and bad'. The adverse publicity given to petty crime and joy-riding, and negative labelling of the neighbourhoods involved, actually reinforce this identity. For Campbell, young men's involvement in rioting and crime represents the attempts of a new generation to maintain control in their localities; through dominating public space and restricting others' access to it through fear, and through resisting domestic space and their responsibilities to mothers, female partners and children. Thus behaviour which is often represented as a complete break with the past can be viewed as having much continuity with traditional working-class masculinity. Masculinities, then, may take specific and local forms, which are continually being remade (Connell, 1995).

Likewise, the construction of femininities has a local dimension beyond the influence of the economy alone, as Holloway's work on motherhood has demonstrated. As with other ideologies that surround what it is to be female, the ideas and practices perceived as 'good mothering' are historically, geographically and socially specific (Arnup, Levesque and Pierson, 1990). Holloway (1999:109) argues that 'moral geographies of mothering' exist. Ideologies about mothering (who should look after children, where and how) are structured by socio-economic changes at a national scale – the changing position in the global economy, the feminization of the workforce, national policies on maternity leave, and 'nationally hegemonic understandings of femininity which ... have been dominated in Britain by the association of women with the home'. However, motherhood and femininities are also constructed within local neighbourhoods.

She illustrates this point with a study of mothers' attitudes to paid employment. More mothers are in paid employment in areas where women have a stronger position in the job market, where there is better access to childcare, and where shared attitudes exist amongst a high proportion of mothers that combining work and motherhood is beneficial to both children and mothers. Women make decisions about paid work once they become mothers against a background of ideas about the 'morality' of different practices of mothering which are current among friends, relatives and neighbours. Class is of central importance in defining the local cultures which develop. Holloway describes how middle-class women's greater cultural and financial capital allows them greater access to relief care for their children, in the form of paid babysitters or local babysitting groups, 'thereby reinforcing the advantages enjoyed by middle-class women, and compounding the disadvantage experienced by working-class women' (Holloway,

1999:328). Her work demonstrates that both 'traditional' and 'new' femininities are constituted at different scales, from the home to the international. This geography can reflect traditional discourses of gender, but may also provide opportunities for some women to challenge them.

Thus for the majority of women whose lives are no longer reflected by patriarchal assumptions, communities of women are important in resisting these assumptions (Bondi and Peake, 1988; Holloway, 1999).

The large literature on 'gay communities' has taken varied perspectives. Unlike gender identities, the city has not been planned on the basis of differences between heterosexuality and homosexuality. Instead planners have largely assumed that urban inhabitants are 100 per cent heterosexual; it is only recently that the development of gay villages has been encouraged in some European cities, largely in order to cash in on the 'pink pound' (Binnie, 1995; Knopp, 1990).

Much early work on geographies of sexuality centred around the question of whether there are identifiable 'gay communities' in cities. Levine (1979) defined these as having four features; a concentration of gay institutions, a conspicuous and locally dominant gay culture, the isolation of social facilities from the wider community, and a mainly gay residential population. In these terms there are a few gay communities in North America and Australia but not in Europe. In Britain gay communities are most easily identified in terms of leisure spaces. There are few distinctive residential areas, although some neighbourhoods have a significantly higher proportion of lesbians and gay men. The existence of gay areas within cities can be viewed as both positive and negative (Knopp, 1995). It is potentially liberating in allowing the expression of otherwise marginalized identities, and potentially politically important in fostering group cohesion including, as for example in San Francisco, influencing mainstream local politics. But these areas also signify the exclusion of gay men and lesbians from areas which remain dominated by heterosexual culture.

However, descriptions of 'gay communities' can mask the enormous differences in the gay population – they are mainly male, white and middle-class. Much early work on 'gay' communities has been criticized for actually being about men. For lesbians, gender may be as or more important than sexuality in relating to urban space and politics, so that they have a 'double vision' (Adler and Brenner, 1992). As women they are more likely to be spatially restricted than gay men: they may suffer discrimination and have more restricted opportunities because they are female, they are likely to have less money than men, they are more likely than gay men to be living ostensibly heterosexual lifestyles or to have children. Because of these constraints they are less able than gay men to participate in public sexualized spaces and to pursue visible political activity (Valentine, 1993b). The 'pink pound' and its associations with particular neighbourhoods or leisure areas is therefore less relevant for women, as is evidenced in the much lower number of lesbian pubs and clubs in most European cities. The general pattern we have seen repeatedly in this chapter, that men have more access to public spaces than women, is as true for homosexuals as heterosexuals.

As we outlined in Chapter 4, there are competing notions of 'community'. Work on gender and sexuality has made a particular contribution to these debates in highlighting that some communities may be 'private' – either not located in public spaces, or not spatially rooted at all. Thus Wakeford (1998) charts virtual lesbian communities in California through a study of websites, e-mail lists and chatrooms. In Britain, lesbian communities in the form of residential enclaves, or even substantial concentrations of bars, are virtually non-existent (Valentine, 1993b). However, Valentine has argued that lesbian communities exist as private networks of varied scale, strongly based in people's homes, less publicly visible than male-dominated 'gay villages', and consequently more spatially fluid (see Box 6.13).

Box 6.13 Lesbians' informal spaces of community

Using in-depth interviews to explore the notion of community, on the grounds that statistical data are inadequate and only allow us to make inferences, Valentine argues that lesbians create their own informal spaces and achieve a sense of community through the following:

- Social networks between people living in different parts of a town.
- Appropriating 'heterosexual' spaces: recognizing other lesbians in workplaces or straight clubs through dress code or behaviour.
- Imagined spaces created by films, books, and so on.
- Celebrities and music, such as Martina Navratilova and kd lang.

These spaces of community are not fixed but shifting, and people move in and out of them. Lesbian culture is invisible to those who are not 'in the know'.

(Source: Valentine, 1993b)

Summary

- Gender and sexual orientation are important bases of inequality in modern western societies, and those inequalities are reflected in and reinforced by space and place.

- There is a multiplicity of gender and sexual identities, and these relate to other identities of class, age, race, ability and so on – they are mutually constitutive, continually reshaping each other in particular economic, social and cultural contexts.

- Work on gender and sexuality has criticized and reconceptualized many concepts in social geography, including 'home', 'work' and 'community'. The meanings and associations of particular spaces, and the cultures which operate within them, may be multiple and complex owing to the different groups who inhabit them. Each is fundamentally structured by dominant power relations, but each is also a site for resistance.

- Gender and sexuality have come to be seen as centrally important to many of the areas of interest of social geography. There has been resistance in social geography to ideas about gender and sexuality which still exists in some quarters. There is still a tendency for issues of sexuality in particular to be ghettoized, and for the issues of positioning raised by the study of sexuality and gender to be ignored in depersonalized practices and accounts of research.

Further reading

- Ainley, R. (1998) *New Frontiers of Space, Bodies and Gender.* London: Routledge.

- Bell, D. and Valentine, G. (eds) (1995) *Mapping Desire.* London: Routledge.

- Blunt, A. and Wills, J. (2000) *Dissident Geographies: An Introduction to Radical Ideas and Practice.* London: Prentice Hall.

- Duncan, N. (1996) *Bodyspace: Destabilizing Geographies of Gender and Sexuality.* London: Routledge.

- Laurie, N. *et al.* (1999) *Geographies of New Femininities.* Harlow: Longman.

- Women and Geography Study Group (1997) *Feminist Geographies: Explorations in Diversity and Difference.* Harlow: Longman.

7
Age, generation and lifecourse

7.1 Introduction

Our focus of this chapter is on the geographies of children and older people. We start from the position that different stages in the lifecourse are socially constructed, and that these constructions have significant implications for the use of space. We go on to show that space has an active role in the construction of identities of age and the geographical experiences of different groups. Throughout the chapter, we again emphasize the close inter-relationships and interdependence between different spatially constructed social identities.

7.1.1 Age: current political issues

As outlined in Chapter 5, 'race' is prominent in public discourses as a source and symbol of social disintegration and conflict. Some would argue that 'age' plays a similar role, as a focus for broader social concerns and a more acceptable public preoccupation in the twenty-first century. At opposite ends of the lifecourse, both older people and children are often constructed as 'problematic' groups who are outsiders to the spaces of mainstream social life.

Where children and young people are concerned, this is not just a recent tendency; for at least a century, recurrent moral panics or crises have been constructed around youth subcultures, particularly those in which working-class boys are involved (Pearson, 1983). Such crises focus on their behaviour in different spaces, whether crime and disorder, under-age sex, drinking and drug-taking, or just their presence in public space (which emerges as the key worry in many public surveys, and is discussed further on in this chapter). They are also linked to, and symbolic of, broader problems perceived by some groups of adults in particular places, including dramatically changed economic and cultural forms, the supposed decline of 'community' and 'family', and the loss of control and order in urban spaces. In some localities, children and young people have become a scapegoat for a range of problems which, it can also be argued, have the most serious implications for young people themselves.

Older people, too, are often portrayed in terms of a 'crisis'. The ageing of western populations is presented as a threat to the rest of society (see Fig. 7.1). Problems often cited include huge financial burdens on the welfare state in the provision of pensions, health and social care for these growing proportions of older people, and growing intergenerational conflict as a result of these problems.

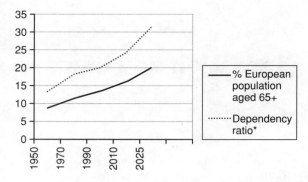

* Dependency ratio refers to the number of people aged 65+ per 100 persons aged 15–64.

Figure 7.1 Proportion of the European population aged 65 years or over, and elderly dependency ratio. Source: Adapted from Table 15.4 in Unwin (1998: 255).

While this tendency is common in media portrayals of the older population as well as in professional and academic literature, it is open to criticism on several fronts. Katz (1992) describes it as an 'alarmist demography' which unnecessarily constructs older people as threatening the living standards of others. In particular it masks the huge differences between older people, importantly those of income, gender and race, and some critics have suggested that the notion of a 'crisis' is unsupported by statistics in many countries which show that overall dependency ratios are declining rather than increasing, as there are fewer dependent children being born (Katz, 1992).

However, such images of older people, children and young people as essentially *problematic* for the rest of society are very powerful. There are widespread concerns over their dependency, but also condemnation if they appear to step out of place – for example, people in their eighties or nineties who take part in sport activities which are usually the preserve of the young are likely to be ridiculed or patronized (see Chapter 3). Box 7.1 gives examples of some common stereotypes about children and older people in western cultures, pointing out the similarities as well as differences in the ways they are commonly viewed. Some of these are contradictory – for example, children may be simultaneously viewed as innocent and barbaric, while constructions of older people as stupid and wise are both common. Of course, there are variations between and within different countries and cultures. Stereotypes also differ for different groups of young or older people. For example, common images of young people with disabilities may be similar to those of older people (Butler, 1998). But as general stereotypes they have profound implications for the use of space for these groups, the focus of this chapter.

Box 7.1 Social constructions of children and older people in western societies

Similarities

- occupy ends of lifecourse, outsiders
- economically dependent
- less physically and socially able
- heavy service users

Differences

Children	*Older people*
• growing mental and physical ability	• declining mental and physical ability
• gradually introduced to 'real life'	• withdrawing from 'real life'
• cute, lovable, innocent	• ugly, unloved, out of touch
• valuable, have potential	• useless, finished
• worth educating and investing in	• no point educating or investing in
• strong cultural precedent of family care	• weak cultural precedent of family care

but	*but*
• barbaric, in need of control	• harmless, no need to control
• stupid and incapable	• wise

In this chapter it is argued that such stereotypes and assumptions about appropriate activities and spaces for people in particular age groups are produced by *ageism*, a pervasive form of discrimination in western societies which is not widely recognized (see Box 7.2). The young and the old are acceptable targets for social concern and, importantly, because of their general lack of forms of social and economic power and access to representation, they have few opportunities to answer back. Those who set political agendas, write for newspapers and undertake academic research are predominantly from the middle age groups, whose experiences are assumed to be the norm. In this way, children and older people are inevitably constructed, in different ways, as 'other'.

Age, then, is a political issue. A second concern which forms the basis of this chapter is the difficulties which social scientists (including geographers) have had with defining and theorizing 'age'. These difficulties partly arise from the prominence of the two groups in popular moral crises and panics (above), and partly from major shifts in recent social theory which have changed our understanding of social identity. These include what is broadly termed the cultural turn and the effect of postmodernism (see Chapter 1, section 1.3.1).

Box 7.2 Ageism

Ageism describes culturally prescribed sets of norms about appropriate behaviour for certain stages in the life course.

Bytheway (1995) has suggested that:

- ageism assumes that people who share a chronological age have other things in common
- ageism is a wide-ranging and shifting ideology which can affect people of any chronological age
- ageism cannot be understood simply as a parallel to racism or sexism. As everyone has been younger, and most people can expect to grow older, ageism is the one form of discrimination which everyone suffers at certain times.

Ageism is an issue for geographical study, as it is both expressed in space and constructed by space. However, it is important to be aware, too, of ageism in the way that geographers approach and represent children and older people in their research (see Sibley, 1991; Pain, 1997).

7.1.2 What is age?

In social geography, 'age' is no longer viewed as a series of static categories into which individuals can be grouped, under the assumption that sharing a certain number of birthdays means they have specific experiences in common. Instead, it is recognized that we all live a changing life course, rather than a fixed *life cycle* associated with predictable changes in behaviour and perception at certain times. There may be generally recognized *life stages* in the life course, but these do not have clear beginnings and ends, nor are they experienced in the same ways by people sharing a biological age. Instead, different meanings of 'age' and associated 'life stages' such as childhood, middle age and old age are socially constructed and have varied meaning across time and space.

For example, the identities of old age available to (or imposed on) older people are held to be fracturing and increasing as a feature of postmodernity (Featherstone and Hepworth, 1989). Multiple cultures and identities of old age exist, and positive images of ageing are increasingly visible. To take one example, it has been argued that consumer culture is blurring the traditional distinctions between age groups, fashioning 'the adult child and the childlike adult' (Meyrowitz, 1984: 19) who no longer behave in predictable ways (though this is assuming that there was once a time when they did). One 'positive' and relatively recent identity of old age is of active and fulfilling retirement, or 'golden age', as many older people can expect to be physically fit and healthy by retirement and, if affluent, may pursue leisure activities which were traditionally the preserve of the young (Fig. 7.2). However, despite these changes and fracturing of the meaning of 'old age', it is still predominantly viewed as negative in western societies, and commonly associated with mental and physical decline, spatial withdrawal, social isolation and dependency.

October 2000 – April 2001 1st Edition

THOMSON
Young *at* Heart

Look after Nº1. Let Nº1 look after you.

Figure 7.2 Holiday companies increasingly sell specific products based on a discourse of active and 'youthful' retirement.

The most striking evidence that our understanding of age is culturally constructed comes from comparison with non-western societies (see Katz and Monk, 1993). In some traditional African cultures, for example, 'old age' is associated with social power and accumulated wisdom (and often refers to people who, in terms of years lived, might be considered relatively young in the west). On the other hand, childhood is not the prolonged mixture of dependency and freedom that it is in the west, but children may be economically productive early. Within western countries, cultural constructions of childhood exist which are varied and contradictory. For example, Valentine (1996) discusses how, in Britain, parents simultaneously voice concerns about their own 'innocent' children's safety, and the dangerous, 'out of control' children of other people, a trend she dates from the highly publicized murder of the toddler Jamie Bulger by two young boys in 1992.

Because of these variations, Bytheway (1995) has suggested that 'age' can only be spoken about in *relative* rather than *absolute* terms. In fact, some suggest giving up the language of age altogether, as even to talk about older people and children is to identify them as groups with common experiences, and imply that these experiences are shaped by a 'master identity' of age. This solution would make a chapter on age and ageism difficult! – and so with these problems of representation in mind, we use the term 'older people' in this chapter to describe those over retirement age (in preference to 'the elderly' or 'the aged'), 'children' to include those under the age of 16 and 'young people' those aged 16–21.

7.1.3 Identifying and labelling age

As Laws suggested in one of the earliest discussions of the geographical construction of age, 'we wear labels that *other* people assign us, with or without our knowledge and/or our consent' (Laws, 1994: 789). To understand what lies behind the social construction of age, it is useful to examine the basis on which people are labelled 'old' or 'young'. Three such grounds are explored below.

Chronological age

The first basis is chronological age, or the number of years lived. Every country has statutory age barriers which delimit our identification of age groups: for example, ages for starting school, for sexual consent, becoming criminally responsible, getting married and so on. Perhaps the most important of these rules governs who is able to participate in the cash economy as a worker. While in western countries child labour, which was common until the late nineteenth century, is now considered exploitation, vast numbers of older people are excluded from earning simply because of their chronological age. Thus, as Walker (1987) has suggested, their dependency is socially and economically created by artificial retirement from production, and retirement is the first common identifier of becoming 'old'. The low status of retired people reflects the low value given to non-workers in capitalist societies (another important example is women who look after children unpaid and full-time). It has been suggested that in pre-modern societies, with no distinct cut-off point between work and retirement, 'old age' did not exist as an independent phase of life, and older people were accorded higher rather than lower status and respect. Their knowledge also tended to be valued more, whereas under capitalism, knowledge is owned and deployed by capital. Alongside these constraints on economic participation, modern western forms of the family no longer involve a cultural expectation that adult children will support their ageing parents. On the other hand it is still expected that children before the age of 16 will be dependent on their parents.

The low status accorded to older people because of retirement from paid work is also gendered. The concept of retirement as a time entailing redundancy and decline is influenced by a traditional masculine construction of what 'work' is (Phillipson, 1993; see Chapter 2). For women and increasing numbers of men, domestic work continues after retirement, and new duties such as grandparenting and voluntary work may be taken up.

Physiological age

Physiological age involves the health, fitness and visible appearance of the body. We frequently judge and label others on this basis, whether we know their chronological age or not. For example children who look older than they are may be subject to different expectations about their behaviour and the spaces they are permitted to use. Likewise older people who look 'young' are generally well received; there is a growing pressure to defy or alter the bodily signs of ageing (Fig. 7.3). This is because stereotypes about older people as intellectually, socially and economically redundant are *embodied* or closely associated with declining mental and physical health. This association with all older people is misplaced; the health of many people improves immediately after retirement, only around a third of people aged 60 and over have

Figure 7.3 *Appearing more youthful is big business.*

some form of disability, and a small minority ever need any level of social care (McGlone, 1992). Yet, the association is pervasive and affects our own and others' perceptions of our identities (see Box 7.3).

Box 7.3 Ageing, self-identity and labelling through the eyes of older people

Do you think there's a particular age when people become old?
'Oh not really no – until some of these younger generations say "Oh, here's an old man coming in" – then you start to think.' (Male, 65)

Do you think of yourself as old?
'Not really, no, no, I still think youngish. I mean em like when you look in the mirror you'll say to yourself "You look old" or you'll say – you might never think but if you see yourself on video you'll think "Godstrewth, I didn't think I looked like that".' (Male, 64)

When do you think a person becomes old?
'Never.'

Never, why would they never become old?
'I think in your mind you never, you can't. I don't know, er, it's just an age, it's not old, you're not old in your mind.' (Female, 70)

Are you old?
'How do you mean *old*?'

Well this is the problem isn't it? Do you think of yourself as old?
'Well, I don't feel any different you see. You see that's where people don't realize that you, I mean people might have an old body but you don't feel any different inside.' (Female, 83)

(Source: Mowl, Pain and Talbot, 2000)

The labelling of the ageing body has been described as central to ageism and experiences of old age as a distinct and different stage of life (Harper, 1997). Harper (1997:183) suggests that notions about the physical body, especially its finality, have become replaced with the cultural notion of frailty; the idea that death and decline can be controlled, 'somehow transcended by science'. Thus old age is no longer seen as inevitable, and those older people who do not avoid becoming frail are distanced from other life-stages and the spaces associated with them. Harper argues that:

Only when we are able to accept the changing and declining body as part of the normal experience of humanity [and] return it spatially and metaphorically to centre-stage within human experience, will the inclusion of all adults within the mainstream occur.

(Harper, 1997:191)

The degree and speed at which individuals show signs of physiological ageing is not just a genetic lottery; it is influenced by income and class, and ethnicity and gender (Pain, Mowl and Talbot, 2000). Increasingly, some people can resist physiological ageing, but it is also *read* differently by others – consider the different implications for men and women of acquiring the first facial wrinkles and white hairs.

Social age

Social age involves generally held beliefs and attitudes about the capability of people of different ages and the social and spatial behaviour which is appropriate for them (ageism). These attitudes have a considerable impact on the opportunities of older and younger people and also on how they view themselves (see Box 7.3).

7.2 Geographies of age: from spatial patterns to spatial constructions

These developments in how we understand 'age' have implications for the issues which are studied and the ways they are approached by social geographers. Earlier work, which focused on spatial patterns of residence, welfare and service provision, tended to be in the positivist, empiricist tradition (see Chapter 1, section 1.3.1) – for example, see the collection edited by Warnes (1982). In such research, 'age' tends to be taken for granted as a category of analysis and is rarely questioned; instead the aim has been to make suggestions for policies which impact on either older people or children. While such work clearly has a place in geography as well as a broader role to play, a growing critique has emphasized what it has left out; in particular that the spatial construction of age, generation and lifecourse has been relatively little explored compared with identities of race, ethnicity, gender and sexuality (see Chapters 5 and 6).

In recent years geographers have begun to redress this balance, often adopting new theoretical and methodological positions. Boxes 7.4 and 7.5 summarize some important contributions to debates over how best to explore the interrelationships between space and different age identities. As you can see, there are a number of parallel issues in how geographers have recently approached research on older people and children. However, it is worth noting that there is still a far larger literature on children in geography than on older people, and that this work has always been more diverse, including humanistic approaches (e.g. Hart, 1979) and radical perspectives (e.g. Bunge, 1973).

These shifts in perspective have been accompanied by new epistemological and methodological positions. The problems of representing these groups are obvious, as academic geographers largely belong to the middle age groups. Research using qualitative and ethnographic methods has helped to elucidate geographies of age and ageing, allowing children and older people to speak for themselves and interpret their own lives. As Matthews and Limb (1999) have recently argued, geographical research should entail and encourage participation. For example, to get round some of the

Box 7.4 Rethinking the geography of ageing

In a review of work on geographies of ageing and older people, Harper and Laws (1995) made a number of suggestions. They argued that recent theoretical advances in the social sciences have been neglected in much geographical work on ageing, and that the following perspectives should contribute to the theoretical basis of geographers' work in order to make it more critical, challenging and relevant:

- political economy theory, which highlights the institutionally created status of old age.

- feminist theory, which informs accounts of older women's experiences, the 'feminization' of old age, and epistemological issues in researching 'old age'.

- postmodernism, which emphasizes the geographical and cultural variability in meanings of 'old age', points to a diversity of 'elderly' identities, and to the need for exploration of how relations of age, race, gender, class and sexuality are constructed and lived out differently over time and space.

They also argued for further use of qualitative methodologies in order to explore the geographies of older people through their own eyes and voices.

(Source: Harper and Laws, 1995)

Box 7.5 The geography of children

A debate in the journal *Area* in the early 1990s raised some of the issues and contradictions inherent in studying children's geographies. Importantly,

- the relationship between structure and agency: it is important to examine the influence of adults' control over children's spaces, but also to acknowledge that children create their own spaces, as well as profoundly influencing the geographies of their parents and other carers.

- social difference: the experience of childhood and children's geographies differ greatly between children of different ages, classes, gender, ethnicity, places and times.

- methodology: achieving a perspective that is truly 'through children's eyes' means not just doing research 'on' children, but adopting appropriate methodologies which allow children to speak for themselves.

(See James, 1990; Sibley, 1991; Winchester, 1991)

problems of accessing and representing children in an intensive account of children's streetlives, McKendrick (1997) has focused on one local street and one child (the street where he lived, and his own daughter). This gave him the benefit of being a participant observer, but at the same time complicated his involvement because as well as researcher he was, as a parent, directly positioned in the power relations which structured the children's spatial lives.

7.3 Space, identity and age

The emphasis of geographical research has shifted, then, from spatial patterns to an interest in the spatial construction of age. In the first part of this chapter we outlined some of the ways in which age may be *socially* constructed – for example, through limits on labour market participation, or through common ideologies about bodily appearance and function. In the remainder of the chapter, drawing on examples of geographical research, we illustrate how age is also *spatially* constructed, and suggest that this is an important dimension of age which cannot be separated from its social construction. Just as social geographers consider particular places and spaces to have particular gendered identities,

> *The material spaces and places in which we live, work and engage in leisure activities are age-graded and, in turn, age is associated with particular places and spaces. Our metaphorical social position also varies with increasing age as old age is peripheralized (its immense disadvantage) into discrete locations, while 'youth is everywhere'.*
>
> (Laws, 1997: 91)

Whether youth is 'everywhere' is perhaps arguable; while it may generally be true of popular culture, there are many other spaces and avenues of power where children and young people are denied access or a voice. However, Laws' point is that '*where* we are says a lot about who we are … aged identities are not only the product of particular spatialities but … they also constitute spaces and places' (Laws, 1997: 93). If we conceptualize 'age' in terms of an identity which is socially constructed, rather than a category which is static, then space and place have a number of interrelated roles. For example:

- People have different access to and experiences of space and place on the basis of their age.
- Spaces have their own age identities, which have implications for those who use them.
- People may actively create and resist particular age identities through their use of space and place.

In the rest of this chapter we examine these themes in more detail, illustrating them with recent examples of geographical research on young people, children and older people.

7.3.1 People have different access to and experiences of space and place on the basis of their age

The most obvious and visible social geography of age is the different access to space which people have on the basis of their chronological (or apparent) age. In most societies, people are segregated on the basis of age. While there are parallels with differential use of space on the basis of ethnicity and gender, age segregation is perhaps the most profound form, yet is less remarkable and most widely accepted. Some of the 'rules' which govern this segregation are formal age bans (such as those on workplaces or schools), but others are deeply embedded cultural norms which are equally effective. This is the case in many arenas of leisure (see Chapter 3) – think of clubbing, predominantly a 'young' site (though legislation limits the access of children and young teenagers). The activities which take place in clubs – dancing, drinking, drug-taking and sexual courtship – are not beyond the bodily ability of most older people, but their participation and even presence would be considered inappropriate. Space, then, is 'age-graded' through a mixture of formal bans, people's own choices about their use of space, and various exertions of control from others.

Children's freedom in public space

A sizeable body of geographical work has focused on the geographical constraints placed upon children's lives. There are many cultural codes concerning appropriate behaviour and locations for children, and young children in particular are under the jurisdiction of their parents. James (1990: 282) has suggested that 'children's places and spaces (like women's) are an artificial device created by adults (those who dominate and control the space) to keep the young in their place'. Katz (1993), writing about girls' geographical knowledge and experience in rural Sudan and urban United States, illustrates the differences between places in these cultural codes. In the Sudanese village, boys and girls in early and middle childhood shared a wider environmental range and richer geographical knowledge than children in the United States. However, girls' access to space became much more controlled and closer to home after puberty. Girls' and women's spaces were equally constrained in the United States, by the threat of violent crime rather than purdah – in both cases, codes about access to the female body circumscribed their mobility.

In the west, geographers have focused on the restrictions which are increasingly placed on children's access to public space because of parents' worries about strangers and traffic. Along with the growth in domestic-based popular culture and the erosion of outdoor playspaces for children, this means that children explore the outside world far less, and many do not have freedom to do so at all until a significantly later age than in the past. A number of implications have been noted (e.g. Hart, 1979; Hillman, Adams and Whitelegg, 1990; Moore, 1986; Valentine and McKendrick, 1997). Children are considered to have less environmental knowledge, competence and confidence as a result. Their movements are becoming increasingly restricted, with consequences for physical development and health as fewer walk or cycle, and for their social and emotional progress as it is argued they are losing the chance to develop coping skills, a sense of responsibility for themselves, and to use their minds creatively.

The social class, gender and age of children, as well as the separate responsibilities and time constraints of their parents, have a bearing on the degree to which their activities are restricted. Valentine and McKendrick (1997) showed in their study of north-west England that higher incomes and private transport allow some parents more opportunity to protect children from public space than others. When children are very young they are rarely out of their parents' sight. As they get a little older and begin to want autonomy and the freedom to explore on their own, parents begin to impose more rules. Constraints imposed on boys' activities tend to lessen once they become teenagers because of the traditional notion that boys can or should be able to look after themselves by this age. However, once girls become adolescents, restrictions governing people, places and times may tighten, as parents anticipate greater sexual danger (Burt and Estep, 1981). Teenage girls begin to learn about appropriate social behaviour as well as which spaces to avoid; adults' rules about dress, behaviour, lifestyle and sexual conduct are partly affected by concerns that they do not 'attract' assault or rape (Stanko, 1990a; Valentine, 1992; see also Chapter 11).

Children do not accept parental rules without rebellion, but evidence suggests that by the time they are allowed autonomous mobility, adolescents have learnt powerful lessons about safe places and spaces and safe times to be outside the home. Anderson et al. (1990) found that many of the children in their study had taken on their parents' ideas about danger, and that girls in particular would comply with their parents' rules after a certain age and begin to regulate their own exposure to the places they had learnt were dangerous.

Ironically, most accidents and most of the violence which children suffer take place in the home, so warnings about danger which revolve around public space are spatially inappropriate. Yet media reports of crimes against children, and advice from formal agencies such as police forces and governments, tend to legitimate the location of these concerns (Fig. 7.4a and b).

Children as a threat in public space
Public space, then, is a site where adults fear for and regulate children. It is also a site in which 'youth' has been constructed as a threat and where intergenerational conflicts over space are played out. Many children and young people resist the rules which govern their use of space referred to above. This illustrates some of the complexity of geographies of age and ageism – rather than space being divided into 'old' and 'young', every space has multiple uses. In addition, the experiences of different age groups of particular places are interrelated and contingent. Just as it is not possible to understand the spatial experiences of children without reference to their parents and other carers, older people's use of space is influenced by discourses around youth and the behaviour and attitudes of younger people. So age relations across generations are the key to understanding the geographical experiences of both children and older people (as well as those in other age groups, who are not considered in this chapter).

The presence of children and young people 'hanging around' in public places such as

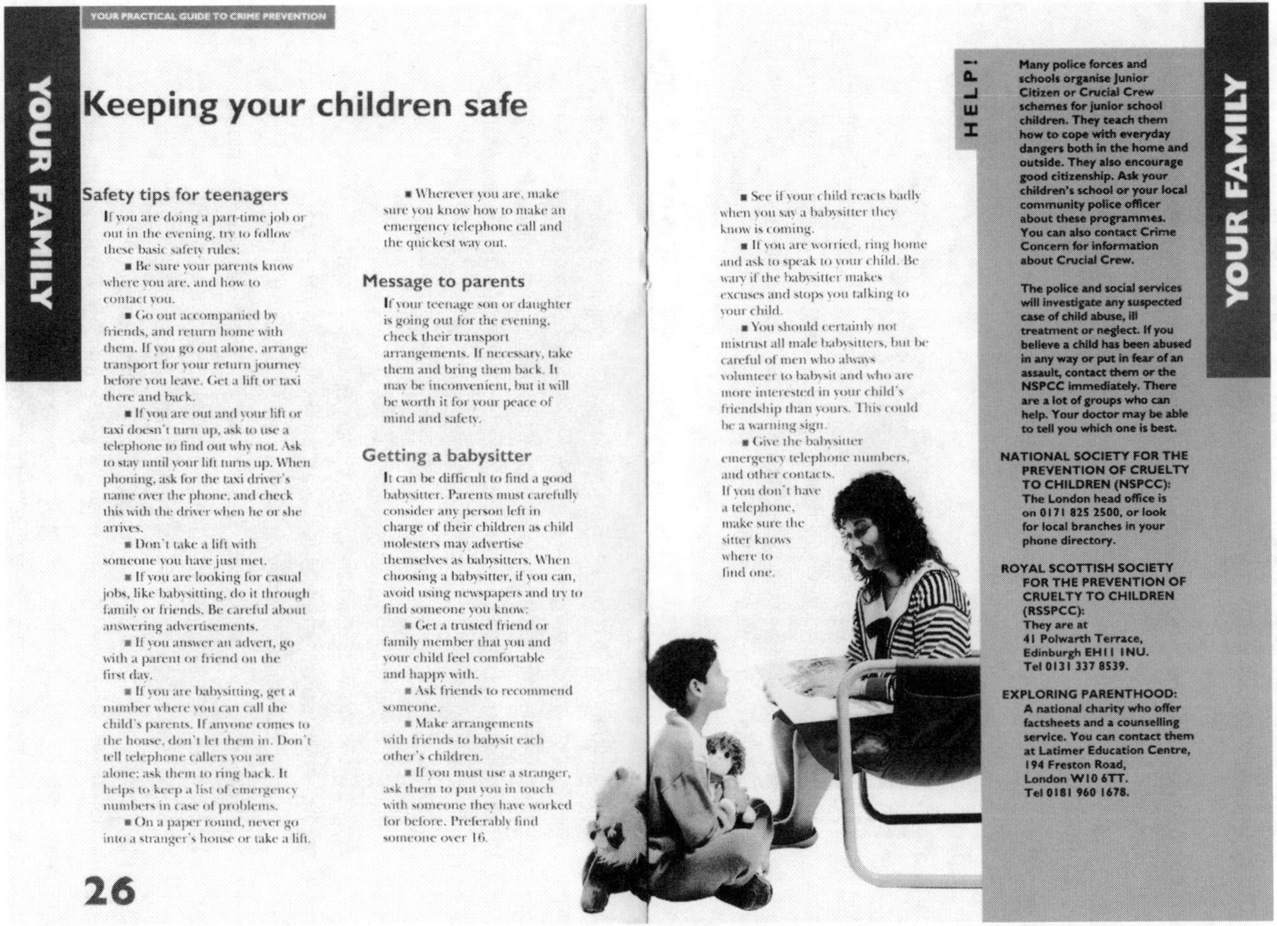

YOUR FAMILY

Keeping your children safe

Safety tips for teenagers

If you are doing a part-time job or out in the evening, try to follow these basic safety rules:

■ Be sure your parents know where you are, and how to contact you.

■ Go out accompanied by friends, and return home with them. If you go out alone, arrange transport for your return journey before you leave. Get a lift or taxi there and back.

■ If you are out and your lift or taxi doesn't turn up, ask to use a telephone to find out why not. Ask to stay until your lift turns up. When phoning, ask for the taxi driver's name over the phone, and check this with the driver when he or she arrives.

■ Don't take a lift with someone you have just met.

■ If you are looking for casual jobs, like babysitting, do it through family or friends. Be careful about answering advertisements.

■ If you answer an advert, go with a parent or friend on the first day.

■ If you are babysitting, get a number where you can call the child's parents. If anyone comes to the house, don't let them in. Don't tell telephone callers you are alone; ask them to ring back. It helps to keep a list of emergency numbers in case of problems.

■ On a paper round, never go into a stranger's house or take a lift.

■ Wherever you are, make sure you know how to make an emergency telephone call and the quickest way out.

Message to parents

If your teenage son or daughter is going out for the evening, check their transport arrangements. If necessary, take them and bring them back. It may be inconvenient, but it will be worth it for your peace of mind and safety.

Getting a babysitter

It can be difficult to find a good babysitter. Parents must carefully consider any person left in charge of their children as child molesters may advertise themselves as babysitters. When choosing a babysitter, if you can, avoid using newspapers and try to find someone you know:

■ Get a trusted friend or family member that you and your child feel comfortable and happy with.

■ Ask friends to recommend someone.

■ Make arrangements with friends to babysit each other's children.

■ If you must use a stranger, ask them to put you in touch with someone they have worked for before. Preferably find someone over 16.

■ See if your child reacts badly when you say a babysitter they know is coming.

■ If you are worried, ring home and ask to speak to your child. Be wary if the babysitter makes excuses and stops you talking to your child.

■ You should certainly not mistrust all male babysitters, but be careful of men who always volunteer to babysit and who are more interested in your child's friendship than yours. This could be a warning sign.

■ Give the babysitter emergency telephone numbers, and other contacts. If you don't have a telephone, make sure the sitter knows where to find one.

HELP!

Many police forces and schools organise Junior Citizen or Crucial Crew schemes for junior school children. They teach them how to cope with everyday dangers both in the home and outside. They also encourage good citizenship. Ask your children's school or your local community police officer about these programmes. You can also contact Crime Concern for information about Crucial Crew.

The police and social services will investigate any suspected case of child abuse, ill treatment or neglect. If you believe a child has been abused in any way or put in fear of an assault, contact them or the NSPCC immediately. There are a lot of groups who can help. Your doctor may be able to tell you which one is best.

NATIONAL SOCIETY FOR THE PREVENTION OF CRUELTY TO CHILDREN (NSPCC): The London head office is on 0171 825 2500, or look for local branches in your phone directory.

ROYAL SCOTTISH SOCIETY FOR THE PREVENTION OF CRUELTY TO CHILDREN (RSSPCC): They are at 41 Polwarth Terrace, Edinburgh EH11 1NU. Tel 0131 337 8539.

EXPLORING PARENTHOOD: A national charity who offer factsheets and a counselling service. You can contact them at Latimer Education Centre, 194 Freston Road, London W10 6TT. Tel 0181 960 1678.

Figure 7.4a *Crime prevention advice from the British government: the strong message is that children are most at risk outside the family. Credit: Home Office, 1994*

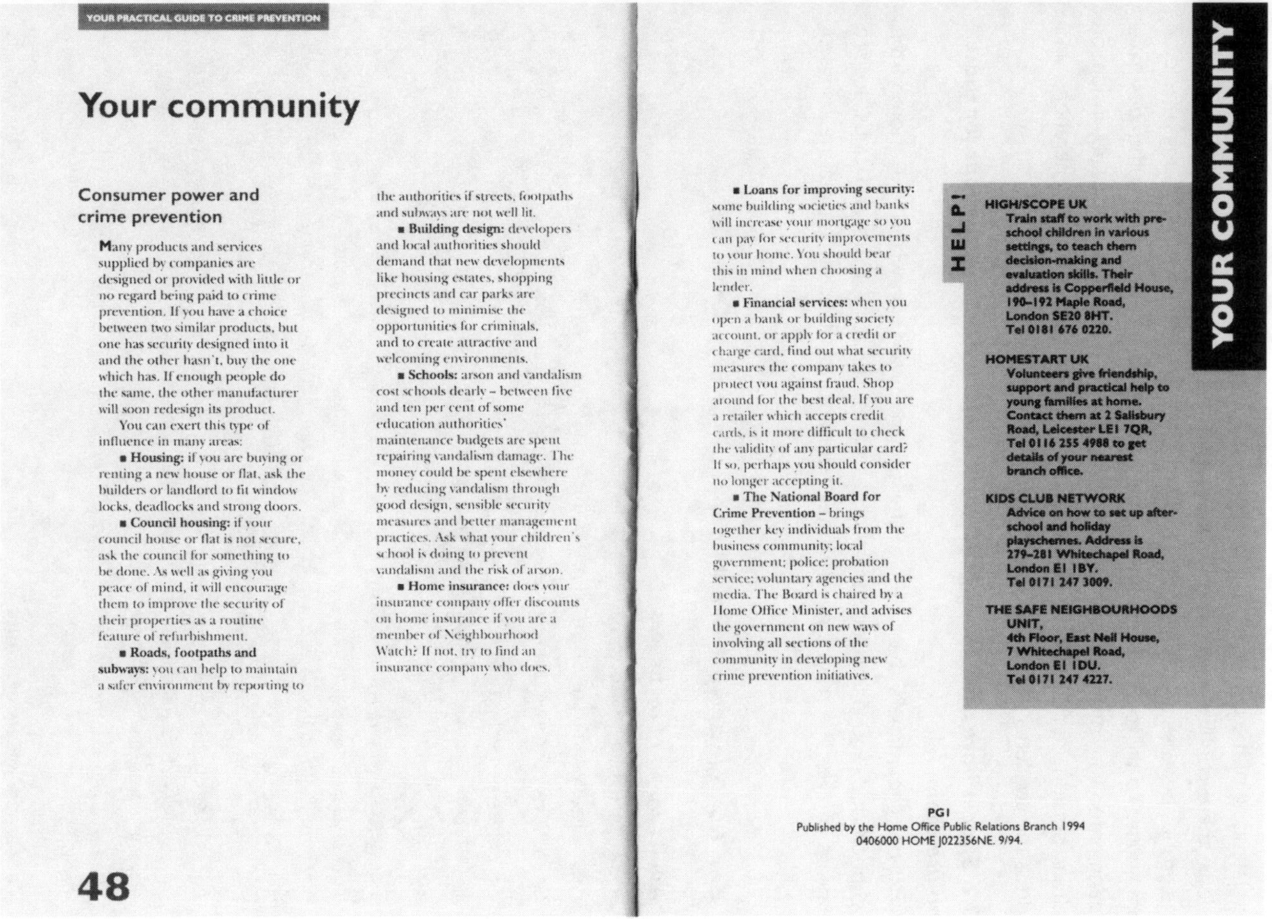

YOUR PRACTICAL GUIDE TO CRIME PREVENTION

Your community

Consumer power and crime prevention

Many products and services supplied by companies are designed or provided with little or no regard being paid to crime prevention. If you have a choice between two similar products, but one has security designed into it and the other hasn't, buy the one which has. If enough people do the same, the other manufacturer will soon redesign its product.

You can exert this type of influence in many areas:

■ **Housing:** if you are buying or renting a new house or flat, ask the builders or landlord to fit window locks, deadlocks and strong doors.

■ **Council housing:** if your council house or flat is not secure, ask the council for something to be done. As well as giving you peace of mind, it will encourage them to improve the security of their properties as a routine feature of refurbishment.

■ **Roads, footpaths and subways:** you can help to maintain a safer environment by reporting to the authorities if streets, footpaths and subways are not well lit.

■ **Building design:** developers and local authorities should demand that new developments like housing estates, shopping precincts and car parks are designed to minimise the opportunities for criminals, and to create attractive and welcoming environments.

■ **Schools:** arson and vandalism cost schools dearly – between five and ten per cent of some education authorities' maintenance budgets are spent repairing vandalism damage. The money could be spent elsewhere by reducing vandalism through good design, sensible security measures and better management practices. Ask what your children's school is doing to prevent vandalism and the risk of arson.

■ **Home insurance:** does your insurance company offer discounts on home insurance if you are a member of Neighbourhood Watch? If not, try to find an insurance company who does.

■ **Loans for improving security:** some building societies and banks will increase your mortgage so you can pay for security improvements to your home. You should bear this in mind when choosing a lender.

■ **Financial services:** when you open a bank or building society account, or apply for a credit or charge card, find out what security measures the company takes to protect you against fraud. Shop around for the best deal. If you are a retailer which accepts credit cards, is it more difficult to check the validity of any particular card? If so, perhaps you should consider no longer accepting it.

■ **The National Board for Crime Prevention** – brings together key individuals from the business community; local government; police; probation service; voluntary agencies and the media. The Board is chaired by a Home Office Minister, and advises the government on new ways of involving all sections of the community in developing new crime prevention initiatives.

HELP!

HIGH/SCOPE UK
Train staff to work with pre-school children in various settings, to teach them decision-making and evaluation skills. Their address is Copperfield House, 190–192 Maple Road, London SE20 8HT. Tel 0181 676 0220.

HOMESTART UK
Volunteers give friendship, support and practical help to young families at home. Contact them at 2 Salisbury Road, Leicester LE1 7QR, Tel 0116 255 4988 to get details of your nearest branch office.

KIDS CLUB NETWORK
Advice on how to set up after-school and holiday playschemes. Address is 279–281 Whitechapel Road, London E1 1BY. Tel 0171 247 3009.

THE SAFE NEIGHBOURHOODS UNIT,
4th Floor, East Neil House, 7 Whitechapel Road, London E1 1DU. Tel 0171 247 4227.

YOUR COMMUNITY

48

PG1
Published by the Home Office Public Relations Branch 1994
0406000 HOME J022356NE. 9/94.

Figure 7.4b *Again, crime prevention advice tends to focus on crimes outside the family, and emphasizes the responsibility of individuals and businesses to tackle it. Credit: Home Office, 1994.*

streets, parks and shopping malls provides one of the most salient 'age crises' in western societies (Loader, Girling and Sparks, 1998). Box 7.6, containing quotes from discussion groups carried out in two areas of north-east England, emphasizes the mutual lack of understanding of the behaviour and concerns of those in other age groups which often underlie these conflicts over space. For example, some young people choose to be in large groups because they feel in danger themselves, either from other young people or from adults. To try to alleviate some of the conflicts this creates, local authorities have experimented with providing teenagers with their own spaces (whether clubs inside, or shelters outside), and projects to foster communication between generations and address the concerns of both.

7.3.2 Spaces have their own age identities, which have implications for those who use them

Work by geographers has also examined the ways in which the home, the neighbourhood, and particular sites such as parks, shopping malls and clubs acquire meanings of age. The meanings such sites hold are not static, as societal meanings of

---

Box 7.6 Age and use of public space on North Tyneside

Adults' views of teenagers

'Well, you get abused by the children and threatened.' (Older women)

'You're frightened to tell them off really.' (Mothers)

Do you think people around here are worried to approach teenagers?

General agreement.
'In case they get their windows broke or something like that you know.'
'You don't know if they're full of drink.' (Mothers)

Teenagers' views of teenagers

'I mean all of us have probably done it as well, hang around on, because there was nowhere to go and nothing to do, and so you just hung around.' (Young women)

'The people who are standing round in groups are just as scared of getting mugged by the other groups as anyone else is.' (Young men)

'Nine times out of ten you'll walk past a big group and nothing will happen, and nothing will be said, but you're still just as scared as that one time when something does happen. You can never tell.' (Young women)

'The first thing you think when you see a massive group of people is trouble.' (Young men)

Teenagers' views of adults

'Everybody up on Finton Park who lived there used to phone the police, even if you were just sitting on the wall. And they'd be like, "Will you move them, they make the

---

place look bad." … Just the fact that you're sitting there, everybody feels like "Oh God what are they going to do, break the windows and stuff." It's stupid. Nobody understands.' (Young women)

'That's when you start getting a bad reputation, even when you're not doing anything because people just assume, because you're a teenager that you're horrible.' (Young women)

'I think the older ones need more awareness that it's going on, because it never happened in their generation so they don't understand. And maybe if they did, then they'd get something sorted out.'

'I think people should have awareness to be able to do something about it.'

'My Grandma's like, "Why don't you go down Spanish City [local amusement park]? You and your friends go down." And I'm thinking, "I wouldn't dare do that." That's where they used to go when they were little.' (Young women)

(Source: Pain and Williams, 2000)

'childhood' and 'old age' are always fluctuating and are modified by contemporary economic and social changes. In Britain, for example, working men's clubs are associated with a certain type of production (involving manual work), and a particular set of social relations around class, race and gender which were historically predominant in certain regions. While in the past these clubs were a source of pride to the skilled working class, under changed economic conditions today they are associated with redundancy, which has implications for the older men who still use them as a site of leisure. Below, related work is discussed which has focused on the meanings associated with particular built environments and domestic spaces, and how these influence older people's use of space.

Built environments for older people

The domestic separation of older people from younger people in western societies is a relatively recent phenomenon, as over most of history and across most cultures older people have lived in extended family units. The work of Laws (1994, 1995, 1997) focuses on the impact of domestic segregation on identities of old age, suggesting that the separation reflects the economic and social marginalization of older people. Although most older people stay in their own homes as they age, there is increasing provision of very different types of age-segregated residential environments. What this process of separation has meant is that particular spaces acquire their own age identities, although these may be perceived differently by different people. However, where their associations are with old age, Laws has argued that they have predominantly negative connotations for those who use them.

Sheltered housing for older people provides one example. In studying environmental planning processes in Toronto when new sheltered housing schemes were being planned for low-income older residents, Laws (1994) identified a number of ageist assumptions made about the inhabitants and their physical and mental condition. These included assumptions about disability owing to their age, and about their competence to negotiate the built environment (for example, one suggestion was that housing should not be situated near a busy road onto which they might wander). Thus housing provision may be a site where ageist identities are created and sustained. However, it can also be a site where they are challenged – elsewhere Laws identified recognition amongst policy-makers of the diversity amongst older people, and efforts to keep older people in their own homes or in mixed age blocks.

She has drawn a related argument about 'retirement communities' in the United States, whole 'designer' settlements which have a minimum age of 50 (Laws, 1995). These have developed in recent years, partly in response to the so-called 'white flight' from large cities in the second part of the twentieth century which led to growing segregation on the basis of class and race. The settlements which have developed place particular emphasis on defensibility of self from 'other', particularly the threat of crime and disorder from groups of people unlike the middle class and largely white residents, and now, if only for a minority of affluent older people, age is following suit. The businesses promoting retirement communities are seeking to capitalize on the growing number of affluent retirees who are seeking a certain lifestyle (see Fig. 7.2); so their success is dependent on the construction of a particular identity of old age, as well as an assumption that age segregation is desirable. Promotional material avoids the negative connotations of ageing, such as bodily change, and even the language of retirement, seeking instead to appeal to a new brand of 'active retiree', people who are affluent, physically active and sporty – a more positive image of ageing than that constructed by the sheltered housing facilities.

These two examples illustrate the centrality of social class and income to the construction of the age identities attached to certain places. Laws suggests that in both cases the identities are based on ageist stereotypes. Neither identity is unequivocally negative or positive; rather the meanings of 'old age' attached to each environment are a product of changing wider social and economic conditions in particular places.

Conflicting meanings of the home in old age

It is a popular stereotype that the home is an appropriate place for older people, with a general expectation that we will spend more time there as we age (Laws, 1994; Rowles, 1983). The idea of progressive 'disengagement' from spaces commonly frequented by younger people, or 'natural' spatial withdrawal, formed the basis of an influential early theory about older people's use of space (Cumming and Henry, 1961). However, this perspective has been criticized, as it fails to recognize the historical and cultural specificity of disengagement, the wide diversity amongst older people in their use of space, and the many different meanings which spaces such as 'the home' may have.

For example, for some people, spending a lot of time in the home in old age is viewed as an identifier of old age and therefore something to be avoided. In Mowl, Pain and Talbot's (2000) qualitative study of older people, the prospect of spending more time at home on retirement was resisted by men, as they considered it to accelerate 'old age' and even death (see Box 7.7). This association of the homespace with bodily decline is linked to redundancy and the loss of a productive economic role in a working-class area where for most older men's lives the norm was for their work and leisure to be located outside the home, while the home was a feminine preserve. Clearly, then, the meaning of the home is influenced by ideas not only of certain age but gender and class too. The women in the study felt more positive about retirement and had fewer problems negotiating the changes it brought (Box 7.7). Because 'a woman's moral standing and status may be judged by the way in which she keeps her house and, by implication, her family' (Roberts, 1991: 104), the home is more likely to be an important symbol both of a positive feminine identity and of resistance to negative old age identities.

Box 7.7 Ageing and the meaning of the homespace

'I think that's deadly that me, staying in. I believe in getting out when I can.'

Why's that?

'Oh – I, I've known too many that didn't come out and they die in the house – I've known too many of them. Well this fella next door here, he retired just before me. This is Mr Brown and he retired just before me and he wouldn't go out – he didn't go out. The farthest he got was sitting in the back garden.'

Yeah.

'And he only lived 'til he was 69. He retired at 65 – works hard all his life at Parsons [local engineering firm] you know and then he dies at 69 – well it's not a lot is it? Four years.' (Male, 74)

'I do think nowadays old age is probably a misnomer because a lot of old people, especially women, although they're getting older, they keep themselves smart – they go out. [. . .] I mean I must admit my mother – my mother was a home bird, she never went out you know and I think probably that was a mistake. Em, I think my mother probably got old before her time because she allowed herself to, you know.' (Male, 68)

'A woman can take retirement better than a man because a woman can keep busy and do things whereas men, well, I think they miss work. ' (Female, 77)

'Women are more used to being at home, used to being in the house and working in the house and finding things to keep them occupied whereas men aren't.' (Female, 70)

'I mean I like to go out every day. I'm not one you know for sitting in all the time. Em, I mean I'm lucky – I keep in good health, I look after myself. You know I like to keep me place nice and so on.' (Female, 78)

(Source: Mowl, Pain and Talbot, 2000)

The home is also viewed, by some, as a site of resistance to ageing in that it is a place in which independence can be maintained in the face of ill health or disability. Given the choice, most people prefer to remain in their own homes in later life, and community care policy in the UK is increasingly encouraging this (Milligan, 2000). Indeed, attachment to the homespace can be a source of relief from ageist, sexist or racist prejudice, and one way of strengthening self-identity amid the changes of old age (Rubinstein and Parmalee, 1992). The home may promote independence in old age, by giving people space to do what they want and freeing them of dependence on others, though 'there may only be a fine distinction between being independent and being disengaged' (Sixsmith, 1986: 346). Thus for some older people, being 'old' is defined not as spending a lot of time in their own homes, but as moving on to residential care institutions or sheltered housing. As discussed in the context of Laws' work above, institutional domestic spaces are more likely to be associated with negative characteristics of old age, tending to be viewed as being designed for less capable people who are withdrawn and isolated from mainstream society and lifestyles. However, as Milligan (2000) notes in a recent commentary on changing geographies of caring, the differences between these spaces are becoming blurred – again, the age identities of spaces and their implications for those who use them are never static.

7.3.3 People may actively create and resist particular age identities through their use of space and place

> If we accept that we all (to a lesser or greater extent) have the ability to present ourselves in different ways in different places and at different times, then the spaces or contexts of social interactions become key factors in terms of our opportunities to refashion ourselves and identify with others.
>
> (Malbon, 1998: 277)

As the examples discussed so far illustrate, space and place may be implicated in the regulation, labelling, and oppression of certain age groups. However, our identities are not simply fixed and determined for us by more powerful groups. Geographers have highlighted the ways in which dominant meanings of age are constantly challenged, reshaped or subverted through the use of space. This section considers how people of different ages may create their own spaces in an environment dominated by others, and actively resist their labelling with particular identities. This form of interaction between space and identity is an example of 'Third Space' (see Chapter 1, Box 1.4) where space may be used to resist oppression or a safe arena in which marginalized groups can determine their own lives.

Detailed case studies of children resisting adults' meanings and rules illustrate the complexity both of uses of space and the age identities involved. McKendrick (1997) builds a portrait of children's streetlife in an account of a cul-de-sac known as 'the Close' where he lived for several years with his young children. Resident and neighbouring adults and children all used the space of the street differently. Despite the constraints placed on their activities by adults, and attempts to contain them within the Close, children adapted the particular form of the built environment for their play. Road defects and a discontinuous path around the Close were the focus for games on bikes and foot; a play den was created in an abandoned site domesticated by the children; another popular game was to stand next to a large pool of water which collected on the road in order to get splashed by cars passing by. All these environmental features were viewed by most of the adults as problematic, unsafe or undesirable for children. Yet the attempts of adults at regulation, such as removing 'defects', or the erection of fences and bushes to contain small children or keep out older ones from a neighbouring estate, were resisted and subverted by children.

Underlying conflicts within the locality over the development of the relatively newly built and privately owned Close on what was previously part of a council estate help to explain the behaviour of children from neighbouring streets. McKendrick describes the incursion and use of the Close of these 'other children', sometimes causing conflict with resident children and frequently a source of trouble in the eyes of the adult residents, as an expression of their previous use of the space and their relative economic marginalization.

Recent geographical interest in youth subcultures has highlighted some of the ways in which young people create new spaces and new identities (see Skelton and Valentine, 1998). Fewer studies have examined how older people negotiate ageist discourses by using space. Pain, Mowl and Talbot (2000) make such a case with reference to older people's use of leisure clubs in different areas of Newcastle upon Tyne. As we mentioned earlier, certain leisure spaces (such as working men's social clubs, women's tea clubs, and bingo halls) may hold negative associations of ageing – as being for less able people who are disengaged from wider society. As such, they are avoided by some older people, largely those who have access to other forms of leisure which they view as superior and are able to distance themselves both from the particular spaces and from certain ideas about old age. However, our ability to create and benefit from spaces and identities of resistance may depend on other forms of social and economic power. The success of older people in distancing themselves from negative old age identities through their use of particular leisure spaces was contingent on their financial position, gender or display of physical ability. In the study, middle-class men and women tended to view their own clubs as having fewer of the negative associations of old age than working-class clubs, while men felt their clubs to be superior to women's (Box 7.8).

Box 7.8 Negotiating old age through gendered and class-based use of leisure spaces

'Well now, there's a definite definite stigma in this area on bingo – ha! There's an awful lot of friends, my friends wouldn't.'
Why's that, what is it?
'Oh they think it's, you know, beneath them. It's not intelligent enough, you know, it's too simple. Oh no, there's friends of mine wouldn't. I mean occasionally we go to places where you have to play a little bingo you know on an outing, but they play with you know disgust, you know they don't want to play. They think the bingo's for the working classes ha!' (Female, 83, West Deneside)

Have you ever come across anybody who's had that attitude in the Senior Men's group – sort of felt 'Oh what am I doing here – it must be that I'm old', you know?
'No. I don't – no I don't see that at all – that doesn't – I think you would find that in the Ladies' Tea Club. See what you find in the Men's Club is that never seems to arise [...] It's not just sitting round drinking cups of tea. It is listening every week to intelligent talks and thinking about them you know [...] As far as I know it's just a chat club [the Ladies' Tea Club] – it's a tea club is what it sets out to be – "Come in and have a cup of tea and meet your friends and we'll have a speaker on – how to make fish cakes" and that sort of thing, you know.' (Male, 80, West Deneside)

(Source: Pain, Mowl and Talbot, 2000)

Summary

- In this chapter, we have illustrated some of the ways in which space, identity and age are closely intertwined. Divisions of age and generation may sometimes be less visible than those of gender or race; they are less often publicly challenged and debated, and less well represented in human geography. However they also underpin social and spatial life.

- Not only do people have different access to and experiences of space and place on the basis of their age, but spaces acquire their own age identities, which have implications for those who use them. This makes it possible for some people to actively create and resist particular age identities through their use of space and place.

- Importantly, this process is dependent upon the other social identities which construct space and place, including gender, race, ethnicity, sexuality and ability.

- Many textbooks in social or cultural geography have chapters on gender, sexuality and race, but age is rarely given the same status. Although in this collection we have devoted separate chapters to race, gender, age and ability, we have emphasized the point that different forms of discrimination work together. They are 'inextricably intertwined in social life; each can only be fully understood with reference to the other' (Arber and Ginn, 1995: 1).

Further reading

- Bytheway, B. (1995) *Ageism*. Buckingham: Open University Press.

- Harper, S. and Laws, G. (1995) Rethinking the geography of ageing. *Progress in Human Geography* 19 (2), 199–221.

- Holloway, S. and Valentine, G. (2000) *Children's Geographies: Playing, Living, Learning*. London: Routledge.

- Katz, C. and Monk, J. (1993) *Full Circles: Geographies of Women over the Lifecourse*. London: Routledge.

- Matthews, H. and Limb, M. (1999) Defining an agenda for the geography of children: review and prospect. *Progress in Human Geography* 13(1), 61–90.

- Skelton, T. and Valentine, G. (1998) *Cool Places: Geographies of Youth Cultures*. London: Routledge.

8
Geographies of disability

8.1 Introduction

January 1999 witnessed one of the more bizarre recent episodes of British sporting history. Referred to since as the 'Hodgate' incident, the then England football team manager, Glenn Hoddle, was quoted in the *Times* newspaper as saying that people were reincarnated 'to learn and face some of the things you have done – good and bad'. He continued; 'You and I have been physically given two hands and two legs and half-decent brains. Some people have not been born like that for a reason.' The comment was taken to mean that disability is a divine punishment for sins committed in a previous life. Hoddle was forced to resign as condemnation became widespread: the chairman of the British Paralympic Association suggested that Hoddle's claim was 'as nonsensical as it is unhelpful', and, the *Guardian* quipped, 'It is hard to imagine what sins Glenn Hoddle committed in an earlier life to have been saddled with such a disabled intellect in this one.' Hoddle's comments had the effect of putting the issue of disability on the front pages of the British press, and stimulating debate about the position of disabled people within British society as a whole.

However, such powerful verbal condemnation sits uncomfortably when we consider the lack of public action in addressing the discriminatory practices that affect the lives of disabled people within modern society. As Kitchin (1999: 223) has argued:

> Disabled people have long been labelled as Other. Across the globe, ableist prejudice, ignorance and institutional discrimination is rife. ... As a consequence, disabled people generally occupy inferior positions within society, marginalized to the peripheries. Disabled people are more likely to be unemployed, occupy poorer housing, and have restricted access to education and transport than their non-disabled counterparts.

In terms of actively attempting to counter what can be viewed as 'the disabilities which are imposed on top of our ... impairments by the way society is organized to exclude us' (Union of Physically Impaired People Against Segregation (UPIAS), 1976: 4–5), action rarely speaks as loudly as words.

Social geographers have only relatively recently begun to research and write about the experiences of disabled people (e.g. Chouinard, 1997; Golledge, 1993; Gleeson, 1996,

1999; Imrie, 1996a, 1996b; Kitchin, 1998), lagging significantly behind other social sciences. As Gleeson (1996: 388) argues, 'human geographers have, in the main, overlooked the fact that disability is a profoundly socio-spatial issue'. Many reasons have been suggested for this lack of attention (Imrie, 1996b; Park, Radford and Vickers, 1998). On a general level, and as is the case with other 'minority' groups, people with disabilities are under-represented in academia. This is true also of student numbers, which raises the question of how far 'degree programmes facilitate disabled people's involvement; for instance, are field courses designed with the needs of vision-impaired or wheelchair users in mind and how accessible is the lecture theatre?' (Imrie, 2000a: 180). It is unsurprising, then, that this area of study has remained 'hidden' from the gaze of a profession which is not only male-dominated (see Chapter 6, section 6.3.2), but predominantly able-bodied, especially given the relatively powerless status of disabled people in society more generally. Further, Imrie blames the invisibility of the disabled in academia on the general portrayal of disabled people in western society as inferior, abnormal, dependent, and of little or no economic and social value. This relates to notions of geography as inherently *'ableist'*, placed within a wider context of *disableism* (see Box 8.1).

Box 8.1 Ableism and disableism

Ableism is a term used to describe the attitudes of those who view disability primarily as a problematic medical condition that requires some form of treatment or cure. Ableism emphasizes the difference between the able-bodied and the disabled, for example in the use of terms such as 'normal' and 'ordinary' to describe able-bodied people, and pejorative terms such as 'abnormal', 'subnormal' and 'deficient' to describe disabled people (Imrie, 1996). Ableist concepts of disability also fail to recognize and celebrate the variety and differences in the human condition, intimating that the goal of society should be to return disabled people back to a 'normal' state. Consequently, we need to, *'recognize the ways in which conventional geography has been and is 'ableist' in practices and subject-matter'* (Chouinard and Grant, 1995: 159) in order to develop more empowering and non-ableist geographies.

Disableism, on a personal level, describes assumptions made about another individual's behaviour, capabilities and interests purely on the basis of a visible impairment. At a broader societal level, disablism describes the socio-political processes that marginalize and oppress disabled people (discussed in some detail in the rest of this chapter). The exclusion of disabled people from academic literature, and the manner in which, 'writings about disabled people are usually aspatial or lack geographical frames of reference' (Imrie, 2000b: 5) is part of the wider social process of 'disablism'.

We will begin by discussing the problems of defining disablement and the different theoretical positions which have been adopted by geographers and other social scientists in the past. We then examine the importance of disability as a source of social and spatial inequality and oppression in contemporary society, illustrating how social, economic and political processes produce and reproduce spaces which disable certain members of society.

8.2 Defining disability

Definitions of disability can be grouped into two broad approaches or models which have been viewed as oppositional until quite recently. The first model is variously described as the 'functional-limitations', 'individualistic' or (our preference) 'medical' model of disability. It conceptualizes disability as an individual medical or physiological condition, purely related to bodily impairment. The second, 'social' model identifies disability as societally – or attitudinally – based. One example of this distinction is found in the use of language. We use the term 'disabled people' throughout this chapter, reflecting our belief that people with impairments are disabled by society. In contrast, the phrase 'people with disabilities', infers individual ownership of the impairment. However, as we will note, use of the term 'impairments' is not a straightforward issue either.

8.2.1 The medical model

Until relatively recently much of the dominant theory on disability tended to individualize the nature and experiences of the disabled. Disability was treated as a 'personal tragedy' (Oliver, 1990) amounting to a series of medical impairments that needed treatment or care. Disability represents some functionality (for example, vision, hearing, use of limbs) that some people lack and others in society have; compared to other 'normal' (sic) people, disabled people are functionally limited. Consequently the negative experiences disabled people encounter, for example in moving around a city, are conceptualized as resulting from their individual impairment (mental or physical) rather than discrimination from others. Conceptualized in this way, disability is seen as the property or even fault of the individual concerned.

The definition of disability used by the British government in drafting the Disability Rights Commission Bill (1998) is typical of this approach:

> The term 'disabled person' ... means a person who has a physical or mental impairment which has a substantial and long-term adverse effect on his [sic] ability to carry out normal day-to-day activities. (Emphasis added)

Such conceptions of disability are however now subject to a growing critique (e.g. Oliver, 1990; Imrie, 1996a; Gleeson, 1996). Studies adopting this approach fail to take account of how societal values, attitudes and structures may be conditioning the experiences and opportunities of disabled people (Imrie, 1996a; Gleeson, 1996). Critiques have also been based around the notion that the medical model emphasizes the 'normality' of able-bodiedness, alongside the idea that the goal of society should be to make disabled people 'normal'. Box 8.2 displays the binary and oppositional nature of such social stereotyping.

Box 8.2 Social stereotyping and construction of the 'able-bodied' and 'disabled' as unequal and opposites

Able-bodied	Disabled
Normal	Abnormal
Good	Bad
Clean	Unclean
Fit	Unfit
Able	Unable
Independent	Dependent

(Source: Imrie, 1996a: 37)

We discuss the notion of normality further in Section 8.6, where we consider how conceptions of difference play key roles in the articulation of disabled people as Other. However, at this stage we can at least strongly question the extent to which any of us are really 'perfectly normal'. Very few of us are without any impairment whatsoever when we consider conditions such as short-sightedness, asthma, hayfever, premature baldness and obesity. There is no natural distinction between 'normal' and 'abnormal'; they are purely social constructs. Further, it is also worth considering what would happen if the world were turned upside down, with the 'able-bodied' becoming 'disabled', and vice versa (see Finkelstein, 1980).

A related critique of the medical model concerns the manner in which it tends to treat disabled people as a homogeneous group, further reinforcing the notion that there are two human 'conditions', able-bodied/normal and disabled. This simplistic dualism fails to take account of the fact that 'disabled' is a very broad categorization covering people with a range of impairments, abilities, needs and social backgrounds (for example, see Fig. 8.4). Further, academic literature on disability has sometimes been guilty of the same failings as work on other oppressed groups such as women, older people, and members of ethnic minorities (see earlier chapters), with a tendency to generalize, and a failure to recognize both diversity within the group and the intersections between different aspects of identity.

In sum therefore, the medical model 'conserves the notion of impairment as abnormality in function, disability as not being able to perform an activity considered normal for a human being, and handicap as the inability to perform a normal social role' (Oliver, 1990: 4). Such critiques led to the development of a second set of definitions.

8.2.2 The social model
Advocates of this second approach argue that disability does not just result from an individual's impairment, but importantly, stems from 'societal and/or attitudinal or

environmental restrictions placed upon people with physical and/or mental impairments to the point whereby they are 'disabled' or prevented from exercising their civil liberties' (Imrie, 2000a: 179). In other words, society has created a world with social, political, and/or environmental structures that disable some individuals and not others; disabling environments are not natural, they are socially constructed, and as such, the 'problem' is the 'fault' of society, not disabled people themselves.

By placing the emphasis on society, this approach to disability not only brings politics to the fore, but allows for the development of a geography of disability which goes beyond simply plotting the distribution of places where individuals with a specific impairment can and cannot go (e.g. Golledge, 1993; Matthews and Vujakovic, 1995) (see Box 8.3). If society is key in determining the extent of disablement, then in different societies, the nature and experience of disablement will vary. Indeed, as social and political structures change over time so does the nature and experience of disablement, so at different times as well as in different places disability is conceived of in quite different ways (Imrie, 1996b; Gleeson, 1999). Imrie (1996b) therefore suggests that the geography of disability should be about the description, theorization, and analysis of variations in the social reproduction of disability in different places. This approach, in contrast to the medical model, gives disability a spatial and temporal dynamism.

8.2.3 Approaching disability in geography

As you may already have considered from the above discussion, how we define disability has a fundamental affect on how we approach the study of disability and, more importantly, how we begin to tackle the social inequalities associated with disability. There are a range of ways in which the issue of disability has been approached. These can be sited along a continuum from the more medical to the more socially focused (see Box 8.3).

Box 8.3 Approaches to studying geographies of disability

(Bio)medical models
Traditionally found in medical geography, in this approach interest in disability is limited to mapping disease and impairment patterns and the analysis of demographic characteristics of disabled people. Criticized for their descriptive and reductionist content (see Foster, 1988).

Behavioural perspectives
Characterized by the work of Golledge (1993), who analysed the spatial cognition, mobility and spatial competencies of visually-impaired and blind populations. Similarly, criticized for their descriptive and reductionist content.

Geography of psychiatric impairments
Characterized by their positivist style (see Introduction), these approaches have focused on the spatial variations in the incidence of psychiatric conditions, and the location of

---

mental health-care facilities (Giggs, 1973; Hunter, 1987). More recent work has focused on the reaction of society, and the resultant exclusionary processes, as they affect people with mental impairments (Dear and Wolch, 1987).

Socio-political (materialist) perspectives

These emphasize the significance of historical, geographical and material conditions in the definition, categorization, and experiences of disabled people. They view the spatiality of capitalist development as a constitutive part of disabled people's oppression and marginalization in society (Imrie, 2000a).

Bio-sociological approaches

A developing theme within disability research, that seeks to meld the main, oppositional, medical and social approaches in order to 'recognize the complex interactions between physiology, culture, and wider socio-economic and political relationships' (ibid.) (see Dyck, 1995; Butler and Parr, 1999).

(Adapted from Imrie, 2000a and Park, Radford and Vickers, 1998)

This chapter adopts a broadly socio-political model of disability. We begin by highlighting the role played by the rise of capitalism in the late eighteenth and early nineteenth century in drawing a distinction between the 'able-bodied' and the 'disabled'. We then consider the political reproduction of disability – the type of policies and the nature of provision that different societies make for disabled people, using Britain as a case study. The economic position of disabled people in the wake of such policy developments is discussed, together with the manner in which people with impairments continue to be disabled by economic forces. Finally, we consider a range of social and cultural discriminatory processes and their manifestations in space, with particular reference to the built environment, housing, mobility and the generalized and subtle forms of discrimination which have come to be termed 'othering'.

8.3 Disability and the rise of capitalism (or 'capitalism and the rise of disability'?)

It is argued by historical materialist or Marxist writers on disability (Barnes, 1991; Finkelstein, 1980; Oliver, 1990; Gleeson, 1999; Imrie, 1996b) that the emergence of capitalist waged-labour relations in Western Europe, in particular the factory mode of industrial production during the late eighteenth and early nineteenth century (see Chapter 2), greatly exaggerated (or even produced) the social distinction between the 'able-bodied' and the 'disabled'. The enforcement of factory discipline, with its production norms and strict constraints on work-time and -space, initiated the social and spatial exclusion of mentally and physically impaired people from the economic sphere as they were increasingly defined as unproductive. This economic marginalization of disabled people led to them being seen as a social and educational 'problem', with the solution generally being their segregation from the rest of society into various institutions (Oliver, 1990). This situation contrasted sharply with the slower-paced, more self-determined and flexible methods of work that were common in pre-capitalist society (Ryan and Thomas, 1980), and which were less likely to preclude the involvement of the great majority of disabled people or lead to their social segregation:

> The blind and the deaf growing up in slowly changing scattered rural communities had more easily been absorbed into the work and life of those societies without special provision. Deafness, while working alone at agricultural tasks that all children learned by observation with little formal schooling, did not limit the capacity for employment too severely. Blindness was less of a hazard in uncongested familiar rural surroundings, and routine tasks involving repetitive tactile skills could be learned and practised by many of the blind without special training.
>
> **(Topliss, 1979:11)**

However, while these fundamental changes undoubtedly impacted upon the nature of all social relations, historical materialists have been criticized for oversimplifying the situation. It would be naive to assume that people with disabilities were treated altogether favourably by the rest of society prior to the development of industrial capitalism. The few historical records which exist suggest that disabled people, although not necessarily spatially segregated, were often physically persecuted and socially rejected (see Barnes, 1991). In medieval Europe disability was associated with evil and witchcraft. Deformed and disabled children were regarded as the Devil's substitutes for human children, the result of their parents' involvement with black arts and sorcery, or as a form of divine judgement for wrongdoing (Barnes, 1991). Martin Luther (1483–1546), leader of the German Protestant Reformation, even stated that he saw the Devil in severely disabled children and therefore approved of killing them. According to Barnes (1991) disabled people were also primary targets for amusement and ridicule during the Middle Ages, with some members of the aristocracy keeping 'idiots' as objects of entertainment.

Consequently, materialist (Marxist) explanations for the origins of discrimination against disabled people in western society are inadequate alone, and cultural factors also need to be considered (Barnes, 1991; Kitchin, 1998). Nevertheless, it is clear that the institutionalization (that is, the use of workhouses, prisons, asylums, hospitals, and colonies) of disabled people (and others also considered 'non-productive') coincided with the spatial separation between work and home that accompanied the rise of industrial capitalism in most western economies (see Chapters 2 and 6). The factory-based work regime meant that some poorer families no longer had the opportunity or resources within the home to care for their elderly, sick or disabled relatives. Further, the opportunity for these groups to contribute to the household economy, through informal home working, became limited under the factory-based production system. In Britain after the 1834 amendments to the Poor Law, which proclaimed that all 'objects of charity' be placed in a new national system of work houses, the institutionalization and segregation of people with disabilities intensified (Gleeson, 1999). A distinct social geography of disability emerged as new spaces, often on the fringes of towns and cities, were created to segregate the mentally and physically disabled from the rest of society (Philo, 1989; Parr, 1997). It was not until the 1950s that the numbers of individuals in institutions started to fall (Barnes, 1991; Imrie, 1996a).

More recently, the development of a comprehensive welfare state in Britain from the mid twentieth century onwards brought significant changes in both policies and attitudes regarding people with disabilities. However, it can still be argued that the political reproduction of disability continues in Britain today. As the following sections suggest, state policy continues to play an important role in the ongoing economic and social marginalization of disabled people.

8.4 The political reproduction of disability

As Oliver (1990) stresses, the state plays an important role in defining, categorizing and legislating for disabled people, and in particular state policy is significant in sustaining their marginal and dependent status. In this section we consider the political reproduction of disability in the context of policy developments that have occurred in Britain since the 1940s. This takes the form of three main sections; post-war interventionism, 1980s and 1990s neo-liberalism, and most recently the Labour government's 'new deal' for disabled people.

8.4.1 Post-war: welfare state interventionism

Prior to the 1940s and the establishment of the welfare state in Britain, state policy regarding disabled people still revolved around segregation and institutionalization. The need to provide for the large numbers of people who had suffered impairments during the two world wars gave impetus for a new direction in policy. There was a growing belief that disabled people should be 'cared for' by society and within society. Several significant acts of parliament were introduced which signalled this move towards integrationalist policy (Barnes, 1991) (see Box 8.4).

Despite these improvements in specialist service provision for disabled people, some authors have been critical of this 'welfarist' approach. Imrie contends that this approach was still underpinned by paternalist, ableist social values and tended to reproduce the assumption that having a disability was 'synonymous with needing help and social support' (1996:54). It created a dependency culture; people with impairments became objects to be treated, changed, improved and made 'normal' (Barnes, 1991). In other words, while the approach was sympathetic, it failed to acknowledge or even celebrate the positive aspects of a diverse society, based on wider and more inclusive conceptions of bodily perfection and performance.

Box 8.4 Post-war: welfare state interventionism in Britain – Acts of Parliament

Disabled Persons Act (Employment) (1944)

This represents the first legislation to seriously address the question of disabled people's employment. It established disabled people's legal right to employment and attempted to ensure them jobs by introducing a quota scheme that compelled employers to employ a proportion of disabled people. All employers with more than twenty employees were required to employ 3 per cent of registered disabled people on their workforce. The 1944 act also enabled the setting up of sheltered workshops which were run as non-profit-making companies and subsidized by public money.

The Education Act (1944)

This introduced free secondary education for all and had a stated commitment to equality of opportunity in education. However, the introduction of a two-tier secondary system (Grammar schools and Secondary Moderns) was accompanied by a selection test (the 'Eleven Plus') designed to sort out the 'academically able' from the less able, and Local Education Authorities were instructed to make separate provision for children with an impairment of 'body or mind'. This led to the development of 'special schools' for children with impairments, and, despite the inclusionary rhetoric of the Act, the continued social and spatial segregation of disabled people from an early age. Furthermore some children who were designated 'severely subnormal' were considered 'ineducable', and this group did not obtain the right to even a specialist education until the Education (Handicapped Children) Act of 1970. Under the 1976 Education Act an attempt was made to remove selectivity from the state secondary sector and provide for the needs of all children (including disabled children) within the mainstream school environment. However, the streaming of ability ranges and the use of separate remedial classes helped retain an element of segregation within the new inclusive comprehensive schools.

Local Authorities and Disabled Persons Act (1970)

This Act lead to the establishment of a number of social services departments to deal with the needs of disabled people as perceived by the state. The range of state services available to disabled people proliferated to the extent that as many as 23 different helpers could be involved in the life of one disabled person.

(Source: Barnes, 1991)

8.4.2 The 1980s and 1990s: 'neo-liberalism' and the move towards voluntaristic policy and provision

Since the 1980s the influence of 'neo-liberal' ideology on British central government thinking has led to the widespread reform of state welfare policy and provision, including much of that which pertains to the lives of disabled people. Under the Conservative government (1979–97) there was a move away from blanket public provision of welfare services in an attempt to reduce costs and improve 'value for money' by introducing the efficacy of the market through privatization. This restructuring of welfare provision was accompanied by a programme of de-institutionalization and the movement towards a system of 'care in the community', a policy direction favoured by most neo-liberal western governments at the time (for example, US, New Zealand, Australia) (see Gleeson, 1999).

Community care programmes were intended to tackle the socio-spatial exclusion of disabled people in remote, often dehumanizing, institutional settings by reintegrating them into the broader community in dispersed, small-scale residential settings. However, despite the government rhetoric of progressive social policy it has been argued that the main motivating force behind community care was simply to reduce public welfare spending and to shift the 'burden of care' from the state to individuals, families and the local communities (Gleeson, 1999; Eyles, 1988). Community care programmes were also criticized because the de-institutionalization of disabled people generally occurred without the simultaneous development of adequate, publicly funded, community care infrastructure (Gleeson, 1999). This situation, rather than enabling and empowering disabled people, has led to their increasing dependency on families and inadequately funded informal carers, or for some socio-spatial exclusion in inadequate, residual social housing in stigmatized problem neighbourhoods.

At the same time, many state services were privatized in order to reduce public spending and supposedly improve their efficiency by introducing the discipline of market forces. Voluntary and for-profit agencies became involved in the delivery of community care support services, with disabled people becoming (in the eyes of government at least) 'the customers' who were now empowered to freely choose which services they required according to their own specific needs.

The Disability Discrimination Act of 1995 was a reaction to a sustained period of pressure from disability rights activists. The Act made it illegal for employers to discriminate against disabled people, although there were exemptions for firms employing fewer than twenty people. Further, discrimination by employers can only be tackled after it has actually occurred, which puts the onus on disabled employees to take discriminatory employers to court. The Act also claims to ensure disabled peoples' rights of access to public buildings, places of work and public transportation systems, but there is an underlying 'voluntarism' to the Act that weakens its power and only requires some service providers to provide access 'where reasonable' (Imrie, 1996a).

The Disability Discrimination Act has therefore been criticized by disability activists for its failure to secure full and equal access rights for disabled people. Indeed, from one perspective it can be argued that the reason the Act fails to enshrine the access rights of disabled people relates to the unwillingness of the neo-liberal, Conservative government to threaten the interests of capital by insisting that employers, developers and service providers bear the costs of access improvements. The underlying motivation was neatly illustrated by the words of the Minister for Local Government, David Curry in 1993:

'Whilst committed to creating an environment more accessible to people with disabilities we must ensure that any additional costs do not bear unreasonably heavy on those who provide and use buildings or on the community which ultimately pays the price for goods and services.'

(cited in Imrie, 1996a:67)

8.4.3 New Labour and welfare reform: a 'New Deal' for disabled people?

Welfare reform has been a key policy initiative of the Labour government since their election in 1997. While they have been keen to publicly distance themselves from their Conservative predecessors' neo-liberal reforms of social welfare policy, some disability activists have been quick to point out the similarities between the policies of the two governments (Roulstone, 2000).

The language of the government is positive and inclusive, making claims to be committed to both a move to 'introduce effective civil rights for disabled people' and to 'remove barriers to work and give active help to disabled people who wish to work' (Department of Social Security, 1998). These aims are both welcome and ambitious, with several policy measures designed to help in their achievement.

However, the so called 'New Deal for Disabled People' can be seen as representing a clever combination of 'carrot and stick' measures, in that while it contains a number of initiatives designed to help disabled people into work, it also contains several measures aimed at tightening up the procedures for determining entitlement for Incapacity Benefit and the Disability Living Allowance. According to Department of Social Security annual statistics, Incapacity Benefit alone is now almost one tenth of the total social security budget, with just over one and a half million people receiving it in 1999 – about three times as many as in 1979. Regular and more rigorous assessments of claimants are consequently being introduced in order to determine their capacity for work as opposed to their 'incapacity'. Some disability activists are therefore very critical of the Labour government's approach. Roulstone (2000: 435) points to a clear attempt by government to separate the 'work able' from the 'severely disabled' in terms of social policy, and there are clear echoes here from the past (see section 8.3):

The rhetoric of barriers, barrier reduction and unused abilities seems to be less in evidence than a punitive sifting process and a return to Draconian social policy.

(Roulstone, 2000: 435)

8.5 Economic marginalization, and the economic reproduction of disability

Despite the range of policy measures apparently intended to ameliorate the marginal position of disabled people in European societies, the economic marginality of disabled people has been an ongoing and persistent concern throughout the post-war period. In Britain, Harris, Cox and Smith's (1971) survey uncovered disproportionately high rates of unemployment amongst disabled people. Townsend's (1979) work highlighted that even when employed, disabled people were more likely to be lower paid and lacking assets such as savings, consumer durables and personal possessions than non-disabled people. The Office of Population Censuses and Surveys (OPCS, 1987) noted the similarities in income levels between disabled people and pensioners, with the former likely to have higher levels of expenditure on essential items such as disability aids. Similarly, Dalley (1991) found that unemployment rates amongst disabled people were around double the national average. What these findings suggest is the economic as well as political reproduction of disability, with many authors viewing the discrimination that disabled people face in the capitalist labour market as the principal reason for their economic marginalization and social exclusion.

As Box 8.5 shows, the economic marginalization of disabled people has not been alleviated in recent years.

Tables 8.1–8.3 contain information relating to labour market status and benefit receipt of disabled people (8.1), employment and unemployment rates by the type of main disability (8.2), and employment and unemployment rates by Government Office region (8.3). These tables illustrate that in Great Britain there are over 6.4 million disabled people of working age, with a broad range of impairments, who account for nearly a fifth of the working age population. Of this population, disability levels increase with age: only 9 per cent of those aged 16–17 years have a current

---

Box 8.5 The economic marginalization of disabled people in Britain

- Disabled people are up to seven times more likely to be without a job than non-disabled people, are more likely to be long-term unemployed, and are six times more likely to face discrimination when applying for a job than their able-bodied counterparts.

- Only 13 per cent of disabled workers earn more than £20,000, compared to the national average of 39 per cent. Of those looking for work, 62 per cent felt that they had been refused a job or interview because of their disability and 85 per cent thought that employers were reluctant to offer them jobs because of their disability.

- Disabled people are twice as likely as non-disabled people to have no qualifications. This difference is consistent across all age groups.

- Employment rates vary greatly between types of disability. They are lowest for people with mental illness and learning disabilities.

(Source: Scope, 2000; Disability Rights Commission, 2000)

long-term disability compared with 33 per cent of those aged 50 to state pension age, whilst Pakistani/Bangladeshi people and older people from ethnic minorities more generally have higher disability rates than the white population. Further, there are intriguing regional variations in the incidence of disability. Although the Disability Rights Commission suggest that these variations may be as a consequence of differences in the age profile of local populations, it is possible that different industrial backgrounds may also contribute to the construction of a regional geography of disablement. Perhaps significantly, higher than average proportions of disabled people are found in the former heavy industrial regions such as the North East and Wales whilst there are lower proportions in the South East and Outer London.

Beresford (1996) takes a holistic approach to the factors discriminating against disabled people. Whilst his focus remains on issues of economic marginalization and poverty (discussed in Chapter 12), and measures to counter their effects on disabled people, he situates these within a broader framework of tackling the wider social, economic and political causes of disability. As such, and having considered the main aspects of economic and political reproduction of disability, we turn in the final section of this chapter to a range of aspects of the social and cultural reproduction of disabled people.

Table 8.1 *Labour market status and benefit receipt in Britain 1999/2000*

	Long-term disabled (6.4 million) (%)	Rest of working-age population (29 million) (%)
In work		
Total number	46	80
Not on state benefits	40	77
Receiving state benefits	6	3
Receiving sickness/disability benefits	3	*
Receiving incapacity benefit	1	*
Out of work		
Total number	54	20
Not on state benefits	13	13
Receiving state benefits	41	6
Receiving sickness/disability benefits	30	1
Receiving incapacity benefit	21	*

* = fewer than 10,000/less than 0.5 per cent; estimate not shown.
Base: All people of working age (men 16–64, women 16–59).

Source: Disability Rights Commission (2000)

Table 8.2 Employment and unemployment rates by the type of main disability 1999/2000

	Percentage with this main disability (% of all disabled)	Percentage in employment (% of total with this disability)	Percentage on state benefits and not in work (% of total with this disability)
Problems with:			
arms, hands	6	47	40
legs, feet	11	42	46
back, neck	19	47	43
Difficulty in seeing	2	51	42
Difficulty in hearing	2	65	22
Speech impediment	*	*	*
Skin conditions, allergies	2	62	25
Chest, breathing problems	14	60	24
Heart, blood pressure	11	45	40
Stomach, liver, kidney, digestion	5	48	36
Diabetes	4	65	22
Mental illness	8	16	73
Epilepsy	2	42	47
Learning difficulties	2	29	63
Progressive illness n.e.c.	4	35	54
Other problems, disabilities	7	51	34
Total number of all long-term disabled in GB	*6,449,000*	*2,996,000*	*2,626,000*

* = fewer than 10,000/less than 0.5%; estimate not shown.
Base: All people of working age (men 16–64, women 16–59).

Source: Disability Rights Commission (2000)

8.6 Stares and stairs: the social reproduction of disability

We have already noted that a number of authors have rejected the notion that disability is solely determined by political economies. Some argue that class is only one 'axis of oppression', one of a multiplicity of interacting fields of power (Pile, 1997) including disability, gender, race, sexuality and so on, which 'provide the context in which other power relations operate' (Kitchin, 1998:345). We have also noted the work of Young (1990) and Beresford (1996) who argue for more holistic and combinatorial thinking with regards to the causes and manifestations of disability within society. Such thinking is reflected in the work of Kitchin (1998), who argues that:

It is increasingly clear that the relationships between disability and society cannot be framed within either strict economic and political terms or purely socio-cultural processes, but must encompass a mixture of the two. In a mixed approach, disabled people are excluded not only because of capitalist modes of production, but also because of socially constructed modes of thought and expression enshrined in cultural representations and cultural myths.

(Kitchin, 1998: 345)

Table 8.3 *Employment and unemployment rates by government office region*

	Total number of long-term disabled in govemment office regions (% of local population)	Percentage of total number in region disabled and in employment	Percentage of total number in region disabled and on state benefits and not in work
All long-term disabled in	*(6,449,000)*	*(2,996,000)*	*(2,626,000)*
Great Britain	*18*	*46*	*41*
North East	23	34	53
North West & Merseyside	20	39	49
Yorks. and the Humberside	19	46	41
East Midlands	17	51	35
West Midlands	20	48	39
East of England	17	54	32
London	16	45	40
Inner London	18	39	48
Outer London	15	50	34
South East	15	61	27
South West	18	55	32
Wales	23	35	53
Scotland	20	37	52

Base: All people of working age (men 16–64, women 16–59).

Source: Disability Rights Commission (2000)

From this viewpoint, space is viewed as an active constituent of social relations – the spaces which disabled people inhabit are shaped and given meaning by people. Kitchin argues that space is socially reproduced to exclude disabled people in two main ways; first, space is organized to keep disabled people *'in their place'*; and secondly, spaces can be seen as 'social texts', carrying messages that disabled people are *'out of place'*. In the remainder of this chapter we illustrate these processes using four examples – the built environment, mobility, housing, and the role of culture.

8.6.1 A disabling built environment

Many disabled people have to confront hostile and exclusionary built environments in their everyday lives. As Imrie argues, 'it is popularly assumed that … it is the responsibility of the minority to cope by overcoming their handicaps and/or compensating for them' (Imrie, 1996a: 12). However, the built environment is not a 'natural' construction, but is rather reflective of a range of socio-institutional relations. As Kitchin suggests, 'current planning practice is underlain by modernist concerns for aesthetics and form over building use with environments and buildings designed as if all people are the same – able-bodied' (Kitchin, 1998: 346).

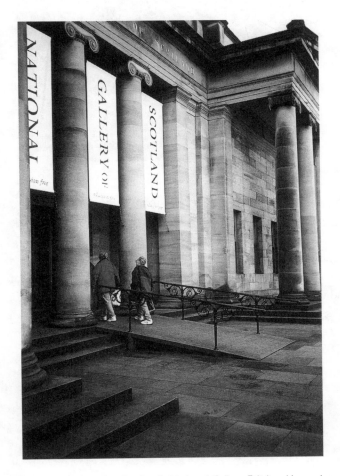

Figure 8.1 *Many public buildings (e.g. Scotland's National Gallery, Edinburgh) now have generally good access for wheelchair users. Credit: G. Mowl.*

Figure 8.2 *'Reasonable access?' Credit: G. Mowl.*

Examples of this 'design apartheid' (Imrie, 1996a: 16) are all around us, specifically in terms of 'access'. The problems faced by disabled people obviously vary widely depending on the nature of their disability. The presence of steps and the inappropriate design of doorways may make access to many public buildings difficult or impossible, and even those buildings that enable entry through the use of ramps and automatic doors (Figs 8.1 and 8.2) may still be inaccessible inside because of their ableist interior design (such as stairs, and the height of door handles, light switches and so on). These problems are highlighted in the following quotations by disabled people (taken from Mowl and Edwards, 1995):

> 'Things have improved but the situation is still far from ideal. Access into Boots and Woolies (Woolworths) is now no problem as they've got ramps and automatic doors but the majority of the shops are no-go areas. A lot have got very narrow doorways and there's a lot with steps at the entrance too.' (Fiona)
> 'A principal problem in pubs is the toilets. If there isn't an accessible toilet then you're obviously strongly restricted to how much you can drink or how long you can stay.' (Robert)

In general terms, the effects of such ableist environments are either increased dependency on others to facilitate involvement in 'normal' spaces (vastly decreasing taken-for granted spontaneity in action or social relations), or the effective segregation of disabled people into spaces in which they 'should belong', or are comfortable in.

Box 8.6 Disability Discrimination Act and accessible public service provision in Britain

At the time of writing, a three-month period of consultation has just ended in Britain, which seeks to build upon the duties placed by the Disability Discrimination Act 1995 on those providing goods, facilities or services to the public and those selling, letting or managing premises. The Act made it unlawful for service providers, landlords and other persons to discriminate against disabled people in certain circumstances, with the duties being introduced in three stages. Since December 1996 it has been unlawful for service providers to treat disabled people less favourably for a reason related to their disability; since October 1999, service providers have had to make 'reasonable adjustments' for disabled people, such as providing extra help or making changes to the way they provide their services. The new code of practice on access rights means that from 1 October 2004, service providers may have to make other 'reasonable adjustments' in relation to the physical features of their premises to overcome physical barriers to access. The question of what is 'reasonable' will remain.

Figure 8.3 *Independent mobility is sometimes a problem for disabled people. Credit: G. Mowl.*

8.6.2 Mobility

Mobility issues, which are intrinsically related to the discussion above, range from access to transport through to uneven surfaces of pavements and walkways. Partly due to their economic marginalization, disabled people are more likely to be reliant on public or local authority transport. However the design of most public transport systems can make access difficult or impossible. Consequently disabled people's movement and use of space is considerably restricted, not just because of impairments, but because of the design of public transport infrastructures and the physical layout of many cities, constructed with the limited needs of able-bodied people in mind.

Mobility difficulties may also limit disabled people's social and employment opportunities; for example even those who manage to overcome the discriminatory barriers to gaining employment may still experience difficulty in actually getting to their place of work (see Box 8.7)

Box 8.7 Improving accessibility in Britain?

The 1995 Disability Discrimination Act was designed to improve accessibility of transport system. However, according to Scope (2000):

- Disabled people will have to wait until 2020 for all buses/coaches to be accessible.

- Only 40 per cent of disabled people have access to a household car compared with 67 per cent of all households in GB.

- Trains are used by only 25 per cent of disabled people compared with 40 per cent of non-disabled people.

- 60 per cent of all train stations in the network are inaccessible to wheelchair users and people with severe mobility impairments without assistance.

Away from the public provision of transport, private sources remain just as problematic. The costs of obtaining and running specially adapted private cars are considerable:

'I stopped [learning to drive] as I got a bit frightened. I had difficulty in finding a company that had a suitable car. Some places don't have specially adapted cars and seats are never high enough. I had to sit on cushions. I didn't like the instructor. He was a bit insensitive so in the end I just stopped.' (Kate, quoted in Mowl and Edwards, 1995)

As the contrasting quotations below illustrate, whilst taxis offer both independence and assistance, they are costly and not always reliable:

'The taxi drivers have all got to know me. It's no problem. They just come into the pub and collect me when I'm ready. The taxi service has helped me to maintain my independence more.' (Kate, quoted in Mowl and Edwards, 1995)

'I prefer to avoid taxis. I've had a couple of bad experiences in the past, waiting outside in the cold or rain, which is not good for the nature of my particular disability. I also found that not all taxi drivers were accommodating.' (Jeffrey, quoted in Mowl and Edwards, 1995)

Clearly therefore, issues of mobility, access, and the disabling built environment, 'constitute "a denial of place" to those who, through no fault of their own, are penalized by oppressive socio-institutional structures and practices from exercising choices over how to utilize space' (Imrie, 1996a: 22).

8.6.3 Housing

Disabled people also experience discrimination and exclusion within residential spaces, and the private space of the home. Despite numbering a considerable presence in society, very few houses are built with disabled people's needs in mind, meaning that even within their own homes disabled people may experience considerable mobility problems which constrain independent living and restrict personal freedom. In addition, as a consequence of their marginal economic position, many disabled people are reliant on public sources of housing. This situation, according to Scope (2000), effectively restricts disabled people's freedom of movement from one area to another, as access to such housing usually relies on being resident in the local authority area in the first place. In Britain, 45 per cent of disabled adults are tenants of local authorities or registered social landlords, compared with 31 per cent of the general population (Scope, 2000).

Very few private-rented or owner-occupied homes are adapted for the needs of disabled people and the costs of adaptation are often prohibitive for those able to own their own homes. Younger disabled people often end up continuing to live with their parents because of the difficulties and costs involved in obtaining a suitable home of their own (Scope, 2000). Such a lifestyle restricts their ability to live an independent social life and reinforces the commonly held view of disabled people as dependent and vulnerable. Even for those who have their own accessible homes, the problem of visiting others (particularly those without impairments or adapted housing) can remain a problem to contend with. Effectively disabled people can become 'prisoners' in their own homes (see quotations below), or at least ghettoized into limited forms of spatial behaviour which revolve around the homes of similarly impaired people and the limited number of adapted facilities which exist.

'I've sometimes had to turn down invitations to dinner. I know very few of my friends have got downstairs toilets and I know I wouldn't have felt comfortable and relaxed, just in case I had to go!' (Katiya, quoted in Mowl and Edwards, 1995)

'We usually entertain here in our home as I'd have a job to get into most friends' houses in my wheelchair.' (Jeffrey, quoted in Mowl and Edwards, 1995)

8.6.4 Cultural imperialism and processes of Othering

People with impairments are not only disabled by such forms of material discrimination, but also by prejudice (Shakespeare, 1994), which is 'implicit in cultural representation, in language and in socialization' (Barnes, 1996: 48). This has been variously termed cultural imperialism or processes of 'othering'. In drawing on work from psychoanalysis, social constructivism, and social anthropology, both Kitchin (1998) and Barnes (1996) highlight the way in which such prejudice marks disabled people out as 'deviant', as 'different' from 'normal' or 'perfect' conceptualizations of the human body.

Barnes (1996) draws on the work of Mary Douglas on 'primitive societies' in which she highlights the manner in which a range of anomalies (such as 'impairments') are reacted to in a number of ways; by the reduction of ambiguity, by physically controlling it, by avoiding it, by labelling it as dangerous, or adopting it as 'ritual'. Such ideas have been developed by Sibley (1995), who stresses the importance of ideas around dirt and pollution. These are popularly manifested in discourses of colour (see, for instance, Chapter 5 on the notion of 'whiteness'), and also nature and disease, in considering the socio-spatial categorization of certain groups as 'out of place', and those identified as different from 'the norm'.

In a similar manner, Kitchin considers the ideological meanings behind spaces and places, which shape whether or not we feel as if we belong in them, and which ultimately lead to:

distinct spatialities with the creation of landscapes of exclusion, the boundaries of which are reinforced through a combination of the popularizing of cultural representations and the creation of myths. ... Disabled people are 'freaks of nature' deemed to be abnormal, unproductive, unattractive, anti-social and tainted by disease/ill health. They are 'non-human', 'burdens on charity' and 'diseased organisms' (Cocks and Cockram, 1995), labelled with monster images and their ability to carry out the most mundane of tasks questioned (Hahn, 1988). Disabled people, regardless of impairment, are often labelled 'retarded', unable to cope on their own. They are the charity cases, reliant on hand-outs and hand-ups; the hangers-on (from death), ungodly and unsightly.

(Kitchin, 1998: 351)

Figure 8.4 *Out of place? Positive images of disabled people are rarely displayed in the media.*
Source: Fleming, J. (1995) What Kind of House Party Is This? *Slough: Mind in You Publishing.*

In this way, and based on a medical definition of disability, society is 'absolved of blame and guilt for disablist practices' (ibid.). For example, consider the prevalent view in society that disabled people are asexual (Morris, 1989). To what extent is this accurate? To what extent is it unacceptable for the disabled body to be seen as sexual, and to what extent is this view reinforced by the passive, helpless images (and lack of positive images, such as Fig. 8.4) of disabled people that are portrayed in literature and the media (Barnes, 1991)?

Summary
- Disability is a social construct rather than simply a medical condition.
- Geographies of disability reflect differences in political ideologies, economic development, social policies and cultural attitudes.
- A wide range of historical and contemporary processes have led to and help to maintain discriminatory practices against mentally and physically impaired people.

- Economic (materialist) explanations of disablement are by themselves inadequate, and we need to examine the influence of social and cultural factors in constructing geographies of disability.

Further reading

- Barnes, C. (1991) *Disabled People in Britain and Discrimination: A Case for Anti-Discrimination*. London: Hurst & Co., in association with the British Council of Organizations of Disabled People.

- Barton, L. (ed.) (1996) *Disability and Society: Emerging Issues and Insights*. London: Longman.

- Gleeson, B. (1999) *Geographies of Disability*. London: Routledge.

- Imrie, R. (1996) *Disability and the City: International Perspectives*. London: Paul Chapman.

- The Disability Rights Commission website at www.drc-gb.org/drc and the Scope website at www.scope.org.uk are very useful sources of up-to-date information on disability issues in the UK.

PART III

Social geography and social problems

9
Society, nature and landscape

9.1 Introduction

This chapter concerns peoples' perception of, attitudes towards and management of their local environments. Underpinning all the material is a recognition that concepts such as nature and landscape are social constructs, and as such they are *seen* to have an objective reality, but our understanding of their form, importance and desirability is often highly subjective and conditioned by our own personal economic and socio-cultural circumstances. The aim of the chapter is not just to explore theoretical issues but also for you to develop an appreciation of how these theories can inform our understanding of, and effective management of, local environments. Because society is so diverse, social constructs form, and are formed, at the individual and group level, as well as the level of society as a whole. Rural areas, countryside, nature and landscapes all have objective and tangible realities, but as humans we tend to see them in the light of our own situation and background; that is they have, for us as individuals, a subjective reality. We all see situations ranging from global warming to a proposed social housing development in an 'exclusive' village, in a subjective fashion, whether we are uninvolved individuals, analysts, managers, planners or policy makers. Thus, all our personal, human, social and political-economic characteristics bear on our environmental behaviour because they influence both our perception of the environment and how we react to perceived changes and

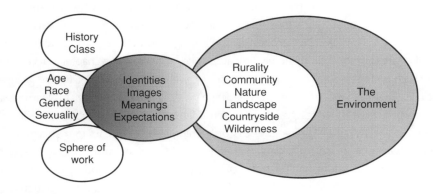

Figure 9.1 *Social constructions and environmental realities.*

threats (Harrison and Burgess, 1994; Harrison, Burgess and Clark, 1998; Kong *et al.*, 1999). The social construction of environments and environmental problems underpins everything from NIMBYism (Not In My Back Yard) to saving the whale.

Figure 9.1 presents the environmental orientation of individuals as a function of intersecting influences from their past and present characteristics, experiences and situations. It is neither fruitful nor appropriate to over-engage in generalizations about how particular groups in society are oriented relative to various environmental debates and issues, but patterns do exist and these may reflect particular groups' experiences of relative advantage and disadvantage, or discrimination and privilege in society more broadly. All of us as individuals have complex identities, images and expectations of the world around us, and we attribute meanings to aspects of that world in an equally complex manner. Through such complex and socially contested meanings, terms such as 'nature', 'the countryside' and 'wilderness' come to have resonance and an identifiable reality for individuals and groups in society. It is these socially contested spaces which provide the interface between people and their wider environment, between the reality of environmental conditions and change and people's perceptions of the significance, urgency and relevance of those conditions. Our experience of the environment from our place in advanced societies is filtered and mediated by values and perceptions which arise through the complex interaction of dominant and alternative social values, through the media, through our personal and group histories and through our personal fears and expectations of the future.

9.2 Nature: what is it and what do we want it to be?

Ideas about nature abound in everyday life. Buses and television carry adverts about 'natural' products, and about products that are 'more natural' than the previous version. Nature and the natural carry connotations of goodness, health and balance, which explains the popularity of the term for health, beauty and food product manufacturers. People who are commenting on a wide variety of issues, from human sexuality to animal welfare, can often be heard saying 'Well, it's just not natural', and countryside designations in the UK include National Nature Reserves and Areas of Outstanding Natural Beauty. So, the terms nature and natural are widespread, yet when people are pressed to think about what they really mean, they often fall back on very vague terms, and definitions vary widely from the all embracing (the Natural World) to the highly specific (areas untouched by human impact). A key aspect of this chapter is to examine how such understandings may be shared, or not, within and between different groups in society. As Urry (1995) has argued, 'Reading nature … is something that is learned; and the learning process varies greatly between different societies and between different groups in society' (p.174). That process of learning may be in part formal, and in part through wider processes of socialization and value formation, but it is argued here that understandings of nature, and related social constructions such as landscape, countryside, wilderness and the rural are critical in understanding human–environment relations from a social geographical perspective.

9.2.1 The nature of Nature

The attraction of the term nature and the label natural is largely premised on its perceived separation from the human; to take another example from health and beauty and food products, you may have noticed that many items contain spring water, not just any old water. This carries with it an image of purity and, perhaps more importantly, a distinct separation from water that may have been industrially recycled in any way; the purity is natural, not the result of a human process. This separation of the natural and the cultural spheres is highly pervasive (and Whatmore (1999) points out that geography itself crudely reflects this division, with physical geographers and their human counterparts). The separation is worth placing in a historical context, through the work of Dickens (1996).

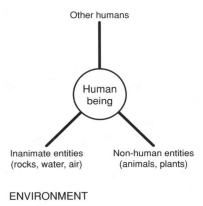

Figure 9.2 *The place of nature in pre-modern societies. Source: Dickens, 1996 (Figure 1.1, p. 6).*

In pre-modern societies there is little distinction made between 'society' and 'nature'. Usually the perception is of one world, containing all the components shown in Figure 9.2. Knowledge of that world is gained through dwelling in it and interacting with it. In modern societies we tend to distinguish between two worlds: human society and nature. In reality this division is clearly false and humans, as living organisms, are inescapably part of a natural order, yet our knowledge, as humans, is dominantly about human society, as we have little direct interaction with the environment (with some clear exceptions, e.g. breathing!) that is not somehow 'filtered'. Figure 9.3, also from Dickens (1996), illustrates this latterday separation between human society and nature. Social relations and interpersonal relationships are often perceived as having a reality that is far more concrete than individuals' relationships with the natural world. Although the media and environmental pressure groups bring geographically remote and exotic species and their problems into our living rooms through TV, the internet and fundraising mailshots, those resources and associated problems lack any real sense of immediacy, proximity or deeply personal significance to many people in 'advanced' societies.

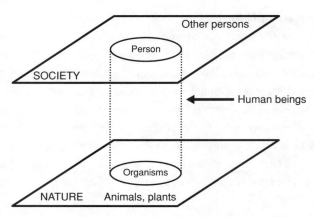

Figure 9.3 *The place of nature in 'modern' societies. Source: Dickens, 1996 (Figure 1.1, p. 6).*

In spite of the pervasiveness of the divide between the human and the natural worlds, which is reflected in other categories, such as the rural and the urban or the wild and the cultivated, human impacts on the environment are proliferating and understood to be accelerating with uncertain implications for the planet as a whole. Against this backdrop, how should we view the natural world? Dickens (1997:84) describes the process of alienation by which humans have become increasingly 'detached' from nature at the level of local environments through the processes of urbanization, industrialization, specialization and consequent spatial divisions of labour. With the move from the land that has accompanied industrialization, the direct link to the land that was based in food and fibre production has been lost for most people in the developed world.

> *In modern societies, therefore, relationships with nature that were at one time visible have been drastically displaced to other parts of the world. . . . In short, modernity has entailed a systematic detachment from our local environment.* (Dickens, 1997:84)

Notwithstanding the vagaries of gardening, or managing an allotment, most of us should be only too aware of the distance, both literal and cultural, that stands between us and the origin of our food. The spaces of production and consumption have been separated, sometimes within the region, but commonly at a global scale, with many people's supermarket shopping trolleys representing a global catch of fruit, vegetables and other commodities. Dickens argues that the alienation from nature that has followed this occupational and geographical separation is dangerous, as we have little of the instinctive knowledge of sustainability or environmental degradation that 'primitive' societies commonly exhibit. The spatial division of so many of the spheres of production and consumption has engendered something of an 'out of sight, out of mind' mentality.

9.2.2 Nature, humanity and the 'problematization' of environmental change

So, Dickens (1996, 1997) has argued that we have lost much of our instinctive knowledge of environmental systems and nature, but this is not immediately easy to reconcile with the rapid increase in environmental concern during the 1980s; if we have little instinctive knowledge, what has modern environmentalism taken root in? Environmental concern and protests over environmental degradation date back to the 1960s counter-culture and far beyond (Pepper, 1984), but it has been argued (Macnaghten and Urry, 1998) that the coalescence of a number of factors alongside environmental issues lent that movement a gravity that it might not have exerted independently. These coinciding debates and concerns included a critique of the globalizing of society and a widespread unease with 'a highly technocratic and unresponsive political culture' (Macnaghten and Urry, 1998). This unease has been paralleled by growing public concern over the relevance, reliability and accountability of science, illustrated in the outcry over Bovine Spongiform Encephalopathy (BSE) in Europe, and the inability of scientists to reassure the public and politicians over the stability of so-called terminator genes in genetically modified (GM) food crops. In particular, the relationship between science and the political sphere, both the government and opposition, has been seen as extremely problematic. The environmental movement has frequently and very visibly exercised itself in opposition to developments and processes of degradation. However, it is useful to question to what degree there really is a single social force that can be described as 'the' environmental movement. Young (1993:23) asserts that:

> The idea of an environmental movement is misleading. It implies common aims, coherence and co-ordinated activity. The reality is different. Environmental groups have some views in common and a shared sense of what has gone wrong. There is often some agreement about what to oppose. But there is a lot of disagreement over solutions. (Original emphasis)

McCormick (1991) describes how concern over the countryside was a central issue in the growth of environmental concern during the 1970s and the 1980s in particular, and Marsden et al. (1993:14) draw attention to the significance of social relations in rural areas as a key dynamic in defining when a problem becomes a problem:

> what counts locally as unwanted development has become a matter of growing contention. Social and cultural tensions arise from the different visions and expectations people have about the same place, reflecting their separate lifestyles and livelihoods.

The centrality of countryside issues has been displaced by global environmental issues such as climate change, the ozone layer and declines in global biodiversity. Concern over the British countryside is still on a par with wilderness in the US and forests in Germany, but public concern now has to be shared with worries over food safety and ethics, in addition to the wider and longer-term uncertainties which climate change and other globalized problems threaten (Wilson and Bryant, 1997). Hinchcliffe (1996) has argued that environmental policy has had to accommodate a multiplication of foci in recent years, whilst simultaneously dealing with a shift in the representation of environmental issues through the media away from narratives and images of catastrophe (which characterized the mid to late 1980s) to a rather more low-key, but relatively constant level of coverage. So, broadly defined environmental issues have been socially constructed as problems, in spite of a limited backlash from within the environmental movement, which has sought to discredit negative forecasts (Easterbrook, 1995; North, 1995), and also from industry, which has attempted to counter the environmental agenda by promoting concerns about employment structures, social welfare and the all-embracing term of 'progress' in addition to more direct-action anti-environmentalism, for example, in North America where old growth forest conservation groups have come into sometimes violent conflict with logging interests (Rowell, 1996).

Evans' comment that 'conservation is seen by some as protecting the Nature we like, from the Nature we don't' (1996:8) is provocative, and many environmentalists would strongly object to the notion that their concern is biased, preferential or otherwise uneven in favour of certain species. Certainly many species are officially designated as rare at a national or a global level, but these selections are made on the basis of the scientific research that established the current knowledge basis about the prevalence and decline of particular species. However, leaving aside debates over the relevance of science in such an exercise, ask yourself why the World Wide Fund for Nature (WWF) sports a panda as its emblem? It is the sheer attractiveness (albeit at an almost virtual, far-removed-from-reality level) of the animal that makes it so valuable to the WWF as a symbol of the natural world? Put simply, the WWF panda logo is portrayed as big, cuddly and threatened, but not very threatening. In the same way that cuddly toys for small children are highly stylized (is Pooh really a bear?), they are also highly selective from the bewildering diversity of the animal world. Tigers, rabbits, bears, lions and monkeys form the staples of the cuddly toy department, but where are the leeches, the ants or the nematodes? Values about the environment are inculcated from an early age, and the role of the media in portraying a particular image of the wider natural world has been critiqued by Jeffries (2000:71), who asserts that 'Natural history television presents nature as an ideal. The natural world, perceived as Nature, is presented as possessing an essential perfection separate from humanity.'

So, environmental change has often been constructed as a set of environmental problems that are problems because they are deviations from 'the natural', yet widely accepted visions of nature are at times myopic, highly selective and often fundamentally flawed. Issues that are of scientific importance are often lost on the vast majority of people; human significance is premised in a wider variety of reference points than scientists utlilize, 'Is it cuddly enough?' being only one of them. All this is very cynical, but the point we are getting to is does it really matter, and what frames of reference dominate in making judgements about different environmental futures? At this point the focus shifts from nature to an equally widely used, but perhaps more concretely understood term, landscape.

9.3 The development of landscapes and 'landscape'

Landscape is a term that has been widely appropriated by different areas of academic research, which has taken the term beyond that which is most widely understood as meaning a view over a relatively extensive tract of land. Landscapes of poverty, of accumulation and of despair have all been written about, using the term to import a sense of a shared and pervasive characteristic over a particular area. When questioned about the meaning of landscape, people tend to report a highly value-laden concept, which for some people, includes a definition of what actually constitutes an attractive landscape. Strictly speaking, the term is really just that which is seen by the eye. However, as Preece (1991) notes, terms such as 'to detract from the landscape' do have a strong qualitative dimension. Just as the term natural has been assimilated into everyday language and has gained connotations of appropriateness and belonging, terms such as 'a blot on the landscape' carry a very strong and judgemental message. But such judgements are situated in specific social contexts, which often reflect underlying patterns of power and relative advantage, such as those between a travellers' encampment and the exclusive settlement from which, both visually and socially, the encampment constitutes a blot on the landscape. It is the accessibility of landscape as a lived reality that makes it so important as an environmental entity around which management or protest groups may emerge. The loss of rare species, however cuddly, in Sumatra or Rwanda, will always remain a relatively abstract idea to most people. Their experience of creatures such as orangutans or gorillas is mediated by television or the internet and lacks the immediacy and the personal relevance of a proposed new development on a green space close to home. The green space may have little to commend it from an ecological perspective, and such spaces may be replicated across metropolitan areas the world over, but it is green, it exists in one's immediate landscape and it is threatened. There is no specialist knowledge required to attach value or a rationale for protection to such spaces where their loss would constitute a deterioration in one's quality of life, whether the threatened landscape belongs to the everyday, less frequently visited leisure spaces, or perhaps landscapes that have value from personal, yet historical memories. The value of landscape is constructed relative to personal values, which reflect past and present use and anticipated future use as well as deeper ethical positions and cultural associations. The next sections consider a number of factors which are critically formative in this respect.

Figure 9.4 *The marginalization of nature in cities often increases the social value of local green spaces, however 'ordinary' they may be. Credit: R. MacFarlane.*

9.3.1 Cultural values

Mills (1997) refers to landscapes as having multiple 'layers of meaning'. What constitutes an ugly landscape to people may still have considerable value due to some personal or social meaning (perhaps forged by childhood memories or the role of the media). It is also necessary to consider the cultural values which may have served to explicitly drive landscape change through human intervention over time (Nassauer, 1997). Wiltshire chalk carvings, Cambridgeshire iron age forts and Stonehenge are all expressions of past cultures which have had a major influence both on the English physical landscape and people's appreciation of it. 'Capability' Brown and other landscape architects have had considerable and lasting impacts on relatively small areas across Britain, as have their employers, and the significance of class relations in the formation and perception of landscape is dealt with in some detail in section 9.4.1.

> *It is these very images [of landscape] that not only reflect contemporary attitudes, but help to influence further involvement with the physical world. The image 'in here' comes to leave its traces in our impact 'out there'.*
>
> (Mills, 1997:7)

Belonging and appropriateness are ideas that will be raised again later in the chapter and the issues are far from simple. What elements can and should be considered as negative intrusions in the landscape? For example, Fylingdales Early Warning Radar station on the North York Moors (intended to provide a four-minute warning of impending nuclear strike) was initially opposed by local residents and environmental groups but became seen as an integral part of the landscape with time, and there were actually protests when the UK Ministry of Defence came to remove 'the golf balls' to make way for a new installation. Preece (1991:77) suggests that it is often not the actual character of the 'intrusion' that inspires positive or negative feelings in people, but the 'power of symbolism ... the associations, the train of thought which it induces'. Examples of this include steam trains, the pit head winding gear above deep coal mines and even country houses, which are seen by some commentators as symbols of social inequality and injustice in times past. The American landscape forms an interesting comparison in this respect as, with the clear exception of native Americans, the history of the dominant society is much shorter than that of the Old World. Nelson (1989) argues that 'wilderness' areas were found by the settlers of the New World who were looking for something distinctively American 'which would rival the great cities and civilizations of the Old World'. The notion of countryside, and its representation and idealization as a pastoral ideal, was very much something of the Old World, and perhaps England in particular. However, 'in the States scenery is often thought of as something contrived and [hu]man-influenced, as of course in Britain it mostly is' (Preece, 1991:81). Wilderness, in contrast, has had a powerful symbolic status for Americans, especially in their self-portrayal to other cultures. Mills (1997:69) describes this iconographic landscape as it was portrayed in American film:

> *Spectacular scenery made more than just a convenient backdrop for the emerging movie industry: it established the movies as peculiarly American.*

That such areas were wrested from the native populations, whose subsequent treatment has been well documented, is something that Americans are less comfortable with. However, the derivation of value in American wilderness is firmly associated with the process of conquering a hostile environment and until some decades into the twentieth century, the subject of that conquest explicitly included these indigenous people.

9.4 Axes of division in access and control

There are many axes of division and disadvantage in society, and a number of these have been researched in a geographical context, from a landscape perspective. Only class and race are reviewed in detail here, for reasons of space, but see Bell and Valentine (1995), Cloke and Little (1997), Milbourne (1997) and Simmons (1997) for a wider review of 'others' in the rural landscape and society.

9.4.1 Class

Class relations structure both the material reality of landscape and peoples' perception of nature, the countryside and wilderness. Class divisions in society have historically shaped the physical structure of landscape through de-population, enclosure and landscape gardening, and the dominant social values attributed to different landscapes at different periods in history. Although the overt significance of landowners in the rural environment has diminished over the course of the last few decades, and class relations in rural settlements have shifted dramatically away from those associated with strongly hierarchical, occupational communities (see Chapter 4), it would be naïve to assume that class divisions in access to and control over rural landscapes no longer constitute a major divide in society, both urban and rural.

The rural idyll

The rural idyll is a pervasive theme in the literature. The central plank of the idyll was that rural inhabitants (as distinct from the leisure classes in the past and the incomers of the present) were happy folk, and if there were some that were disadvantaged, that was somehow part of nature and the organic rural scene. 'The sentimentalized portrayal of country folk and village life became a central element of the mid-Victorian idyll' (Bunce, 1994:53) and such sentimental visions have proved highly resistant since that time.

Just as urban conservation initiatives became linked to wider social and community development initiatives, 'the conservation of the countryside' has also become linked to the agendas of other social groupings (Frouws, 1998). However, these agendas are commonly exclusive in a social sense, as the environmental values and amenity interests of what may be termed elite groupings conflict with the more basic requirements, such as employment and housing, of less privileged groups in society. Halfacree (1995) reviews ideas that have been presented relatively uncritically so far; that a largely uniform rural idyll exists in our minds, and that this set of imagery exerts a significant pull in drawing people to the countryside and influencing their behaviour once they have arrived. His research into these ideas is rather inconclusive, but he argues that middle class incomers do have ideas of the countryside that are characterized by tradition and preconceived notions about landscape. It is these ideas that the middle classes seek to preserve, however tenuous they may be in reality. Hoggart (1997) has argued that there are three ways in which rural England is dominantly middle-class. First, there is the issue of 'countrysides of the mind'. The middle classes show a strong disposition towards 'the rural idyll', and although they were not instrumental in constructing this dominant image, the maintenance of that idyll in the face of development and change tends to be of greater significance than for other classes (Cloke, Phillips and Thrift, 1995). To a large degree this is a function of access to resources which elevates their perspective away from processes such as declining local services, and the fact that their employment opportunities rarely hinge directly on the economic fortunes of where they have chosen to live. Second, middle-class incomers have a demonstrated capacity to influence or control local institutions that influence rural change, such as environmental pressure groups or parish councils. This is a reflection of what are (clearly at the aggregate level) middle-class conceptions of what is appropriate, and inappropriate, for certain rural areas. Finally, rural areas are increasingly dominated by middle-class incomers, both as a result of greenfield development and their greater financial ability to bid for existing housing over and above existing rural residents.

So, it would be wrong to regard class relations in the countryside as a historical hangover of times past, when lords of the manor and country squires were afforded respect both due to their position in society and as vast landlords. In reality the nature of class relations in rural areas has changed as the social composition of these areas has evolved over time. The next section brings us back to the role of tradition in land-use, landownership and landscape, but provides an example to make the point that tradition itself can be extremely malleable as a cultural resource, and indeed as a commodity.

The 'Balmoralization' of the Highlands

The interest of Queen Victoria in the Highlands of north-east Scotland had a significant influence on developments there, both objectively in the realm of landownership and land-use, and also in the wider construction of images of Scotland. The 'romantic gaze' on the Highlands has long been focused through the paintings of Landseer, the writings of the nineteenth-century writer and poet Sir Walter Scott, and images of tartan and the clans:

> These are circulated and consumed globally through the tourist gaze and also, crucially, through more recent estate owners and stalkers who are drawn by this version of the Highlands, often from outside of Scotland, and who enact this discourse and reproduce the social relations, landscapes and nature in roughly the same way as their historic counterparts did.
>
> (Toogood, 1995:104)

Queen Victoria is reported as being a fan of Sir Walter Scott, and she purchased a highland estate at Balmoral which was subsequently developed into the pseudo-gothic castle it now is. Short (1991) describes how the Queen ordered all her new staff to wear kilts in a tartan of her own design, which is of interest if only because monarchs in previous centuries had banned the wearing of kilts in an attempt to bring the lawless and rebellious Highlands to the English heel. As Short comments: 'Balmoral became a Disneyland for the monarchy, a place of make-believe, a never-never land, a tartanized Scotland emptied by clearances' (p.74). This was written before the faded pop icon Michael Jackson made his own exploratory foray into Highland estate ownership, but you might suspect that his sentiments were similar. The rise of interest, both economic and cultural, in the land and landscape of Scotland has been subject to a counter-reaction against the threat, it is argued, to the right to self-determination, culture and the very essence of Scottish Highland landscapes. This theme is returned to in the next section.

9.4.2 Race and ethnicity

It is not our aim to elaborate the documented landscape preferences of Finns, Afro-Americans, Scots, Indonesians and British-Asians, although a partial body of literature on this subject does exist (Wypijewski, 1997). Rather we aim to describe the way in which strands of nationalism and environmental activism have come together in the definition of landscapes that are appropriate in particular geographical and cultural contexts. In this narrative of belonging and appropriateness, ideas about the natural are explicitly mapped onto ideas about what is native (Agyeman and Spooner, 1997). Such narratives have been criticized for adopting a particular period of history to legitimize claims about what should be present and what should be excluded, a particularly bounded view of the past that has even been termed ecological fascism.

Barker (1996:19) examines the sometimes thorny issue of what is native and what is alien, and what is judged to be appropriate in any given place. He comments that 'there is little in ecological science with which to defend any arbitrary point set to separate organisms into groups based on length of residency under the circumstances which hold in Britain'. Although the circumstances to which Barker refers are dominated by the last glaciation which essentially 'wiped the slate clean', a more cultural interpretation of the environment begs the question of the 'rightness' of particular species, habitats, micro-landscapes and environments. This is especially true in metropolitan areas, where the ethnic mix is drawn from many different parts of the world.

Dominant discourses of nature and the natural, landscape, belonging and the appropriateness of certain environmental management strategies are being increasingly contested by a wide range of interest groups in British society. How people are defined by, constrained by, and react against landscapes that are reflections of a dominant culture is an area of growing significance, perhaps most notably in urban conservation circles, but it is important to trace this back to what may be seen as the heart of the conservation movement, the countryside. For example, the place of landscape in the definition of Englishness, both as a source for self-definition and also as a point of distinction for the non-English, has been widely discussed (for a key review see Matless, 1999), and the enduring power of images such as church steeples, thatched roofs and cricket on the village green, however isolated in reality and hackneyed in popular use, remains considerable. Indeed dominant narratives of the English countryside have, both explicitly and implicitly, 'naturalized' the landscape and the socio-economic, political and cultural forces that have shaped it.

However, certain groups in society are 'excluded from popular images of the countryside' (Scutt and Bonnett, 1996:1) and as such have limited power to contribute to the development of the English national identity which, Scutt and Bonnett argue, is situated in rural life and rural landscape. The centrality of the rural landscape to the self-definition of the English seems long established, and this is indeed part of the appeal, but Lowenthal (1991:213) points to the critical role of the enclosure movement in the creation of an 'idealised medieval vision'. Short's (1991) coining of the phrase a 'perfect past to an imperfect future' has been widely cited in explanations of the landscape aesthetic and cultural attachment for the English. However, Scutt and Bonnett (1996:12) assert that part of the perceived uncertainty and imperfection of the future is due to the growth of non-White elements of the English population:

> *contemporary ideologies of Englishness are firmly fixed within the White space of the countryside. Indeed, it may be argued that the exclusion of ethnic minorities from the rural has been intrinsic to the survival of the countryside as the visual foundation of Englishness (p.12).*

That foundation is illusory in many respects, and perhaps most significant is the selective 'naturalization', with overtones of nationalism (see also Toogood, 1995), or appropriation, of elements of the physical and cultural landscape to represent the essence of Englishness.

> *If landscape is a site of value, it is also a site of anger, at buildings, against authorities, developers, different pleasures. Statements which might at first appear to be taken-for-granted as to the architectural character of a place rest upon cultural judgements as to what and who belongs there.*
>
> (Matless, 1999:10)

Lowenthal (1991), Paxman (1998) and a number of other commentators have described the mixed ethnic origins of the British as a whole, which is overlooked in the myopia of much of the nationalistic analysis of the all-important heritage landscapes. Further to this, Muir (1999:43) observes that the coherence and historical continuity of those landscapes are in fact the result of different episodes over history, some quite recent, 'which have endured for different lengths of time for different reasons'. It is clear that the cultural context from which landscape conservation stems is heavily constructed around ideals and histories that are variously selective and muddled.

Returning to the Balmoralization of the Highlands, underlining the fact that axes of division in society such as class, gender, age, race and sexuality rarely operate in isolation from each other, but intersect and can reinforce patterns of relative advantage, Toogood (1995) describes the construction of Highland imagery by different groups in society, for different purposes. Conservationists and estate owners alike evoke images which are not representative of much of the country, and are rooted in different perceptions of the past. The process of Balmoralization has been fuelled by the estate owners, with their reliance on red deer as a source of income and identity.

In essence, the debate is fairly straightforward, and is anchored in the fact that deer eat trees. Red deer numbers in the Highlands are maintained at artificially high numbers through supplementary feeding and selective culling. As a result, it has been estimated that there are between two and six times too many red deer to permit the natural (here meaning unassisted) regeneration of native pinewood forests, dominated by Scots pine. The truly natural landscape of the Highlands would be dominated by such pinewoods in the glens and lower mountain slopes, but only small, fenced-off, patches of ancient pinewood exist today. However, the landscape of Scotland that has been represented in films, advertising and consumed through the purchase of Highland estates by non-Scots is almost entirely at odds with the 'natural' state. Management of red deer herds is implicated in the perpetuation of treeless moors outside of remnant ancient woodland and twentieth-century industrial non-native spruce, larch or fir plantations. It has been in the estates' interests to present their parcelled-up version of the Highlands as the 'natural' one, but conservation groups have challenged their view of history and naturalness.

> An important dimension to the nature conservationists' discourse is the idea of a national past, of a national heritage, which is more natural, more appropriate for environmental conditions, and therefore more sustainable than many of the existing land-uses in the Highlands.
>
> (Muir, 1999:107)

There is a clear cultural dimension to this, one that has been fuelled by high levels of absentee and overseas ownership of Highland estates, but images such as Figure 9.5 are iconic of a landscape that has passed away through the emergence of powerful social interests that some Scots see as alien and to blame for the loss of a national landscape. Reclaiming the Highlands in this respect is driven by a clear socio-cultural agenda, which has strong parallels with the growth of Settler Watch and similar elsewhere in the country (see Chapter 4).

> The debate is seen as ... about ... the discourses of nature and society that are implicit within the differing representations of ecology, tradition and space in and between the social groups involved. ... Thus the dispute is not merely about trees or deer, even though they are very important, but about how the ecology and tradition of the Highlands is represented simultaneously in different social worlds. ... Moreover, this dispute can be related to constructs of nation and national identity tied to landscape and the legitimation of what constitutes national heritage.
>
> (Muir, 1999:103)

Figure 9.5 *The lone Scots pine in a landscape denuded of native trees is evocative of a lost heritage to some Scots. Credit: R. MacFarlane.*

Race and ethnicity are critical factors in defining what is held to be important, attractive, relevant and appropriate in local environments. Ideas of Englishness, Scottishness and the alien have been briefly reviewed here. These are emotive issues, and disentangling debates over conservation value (science) and national value (culture) may not always be all that helpful, in that conservation as an activity is becoming increasingly absorbed with understanding and managing cultural landscapes which have resonance for a wider range of social groupings than has historically been the case (Adams, 1996; Sheail, Treweek and Mountford, 1997).

9.5 Studies of rural Britain: image and reality

The recent 'politicization' of the British countryside as a geographical, environmental and social category, focusing most recently on fox hunting in particular, requires that we understand what people from different social groupings mean by 'the countryside' and 'rural' areas. Although categories such as 'townies' and 'the urban majority' are seemingly used in a rather careless fashion by 'activists for rural Britain' they are usually underpinned by a very clear conception of what the countryside should be, what it should look like, who should live there and what their rights should be (also see Chapter 4 for a section on imagined and exclusive communities).

An often vast gulf has developed, and continues to exist, between popular conceptions of 'rural' and the highly differentiated nature of rural reality. Mormont (1990:9), has argued that 'the rural is a category of thought'. Similarly, a journalist covering the Countryside March in London in 1998 stated that 'the countryside is not a place, it is an idea'. The point of these commentators is that in spite of the fact that individual rural areas are places in their own right, with a tangible reality in relation to local services, land-uses and employment structures, the British countryside means different things to different people, and different groups have markedly different opinions of what constitute legitimate activities and appropriate ways of life in rural Britain.

The next three sections elaborate the existence of these social divides within the countryside, using two case studies from farming and then further developing the case of fox hunting in the third.

9.5.1 Farm pollution and the new rural whistle blowers

Lowe et al. (1997), in their detailed case study of farm pollution in England, describe how, until the mid 1980s, pollution of surface and ground water from farm waste and agro-chemical applications was viewed as a non-problem. Next to no data on the problem existed, so there was negligible public interest and, in turn, minimal pressure on policy-makers to do anything. In spite of early evidence of the impact of agro-chemicals on wildlife (Carson, 1962), it was only in the mid-1980s that pressure groups in Britain began to mount publicity drives and lobbies to alert policy-makers to the environmental and health dangers. Until this time farm pollution had been viewed by farmers as a normal side-effect of rural land-use, and certainly nothing to get worked up about. The scientific evidence strongly suggested otherwise, and the growth of data on farm pollution in rural areas was facilitated by a network of whistle blowers, in part co-ordinated by Friends of the Earth local groups. Rather than watch birds or ramble at weekends, middle-class residents mounted pollution patrols and riverbank walks to monitor the situation and inform the National Rivers Authority (now part of the Environment Agency) of possible incidents. Given that many of these, primarily 'new' residents lived in close proximity to the polluters themselves, the social strain in such 'communities' can be imagined. For instance, during the 1980s in East Devon alone some 700 farm buildings were converted into residences, the vast majority of which would have been sold in a highly competitive housing market to become executive homes. Through such a process of change, marked by the decline of the occupational dominance of farming in rural areas and the substantial in-migration of new and well-heeled residents into these 'communities' (see Chapter 4), traditionally accepted environmental practices and standards have been challenged. Although such challenges have placed additional financial burdens on farmers and introduced further strains into local social relations, 'traditional' ideas about acceptable environmental practices have been shown to be damaging.

9.5.2 BSE: Yuk, they do that on farms ...

One of the things that the British BSE (Bovine Spongiform Encephalopathy) or mad cow disease crisis of 1996 did was to shatter many residual, cosy images of farming as a natural, organic activity that took place in green fields and stone-built barns. The intensity of the media interest was generated in part by the potentially vast and rapidly unravelling health crisis and the clumsy and inept handling of the whole affair by the government and civil service, but also by the gruesome details of many practices that are commonplace on agro-industrial farm units. Many authors have written about 'wholesome' images of the countryside; these were undoubtedly challenged by the news, new to most people, that reconstituted spinal material and cattle brains were part of cattle diets. This was the pathway which permitted BSE to spread. Public revulsion was coupled with a sense of anger that 'their' countryside could have been the scene of such a process. As with previous ethical conflicts over animal rights, this issue sparked widespread calls for change. What the issue had in common with water pollution was the differing conceptions of what constituted acceptable practice among agro-businessmen, many farmers, incomer ruralites and 'the urban majority'. Furthermore, links can be drawn between the work of Macnaghten and Urry (1998) and that of Dickens (1996, 1997) in respect of how visions of mad cow disease on the television were hard to relate to personal concepts of risk from the disease. As Macnaghten and Urry comment (1998:263), 'bad beef cannot be sensed as bad and hence people are hugely dependent upon expert systems which have to provide guarantees across space and time'. This dependency is a condition of the modernity which has de-connected people from their local environments, and yet such expert systems have proven highly fallible in regulating practices and the safety of those practices, as the BSE issue has clearly illustrated. Thus, regulatory systems relating to the environment and human welfare are distrusted by many people, yet the systems of production and consumption are so globalized that most people have no alternative than to follow state guidance on safety and health.

9.5.3 Fox hunting: us and them

The issue of fox hunting revolves more centrally about the notion of socially acceptable practices than the BSE crisis. The pro-hunting lobby bases the acceptability of fox hunting on a range of factors, including the rural economy, habitat and landscape management, and its ethical superiority as a method of pest control. However, once the more superficial (and arguably, unsubstantiated) arguments such as population control are discounted, notions of tradition can be seen to underpin most of the arguments of the pro-hunting lobby. At one level, 'the hunting set' are often satirized, especially in the left-wing press. As MacKenzie (1988:1) notes:

> *The phrase 'hunting, shooting and fishing' was transformed long ago from a conventional description of recreations in Who's Who into a joke. It was emblematic of a particular class at a particular time, a class whose interests and pastimes soon seemed eminently satirizable.*

Fox hunting has a very long history in Britain, but those supporting present attempts to have it outlawed argue that tradition is no answer to changing social values in society at large and rural society in particular. Animal welfare issues (along with environmental concerns in general) have become increasingly mainstream in recent years, as evidenced in the protests over live veal calf exports to France during the early 1990s. What does this tell us? Is fox hunting a class issue, an animal rights issue or part of a wider environmental movement? Can these aspects be disentangled at all?

One way in which the pro-hunting lobby has tried to circumvent the latter argument is to recast the debate as being about the future of the countryside as a whole, as 'we' like it. More accurately, the debate is about the countryside as 'they' like it, but organizations such as the Countryside Alliance have been established to lobby against the bill in the name of the future of rural Britain (see *also* Chapter 4). An explicit conceptualization of 'them and us' was engendered, arguably to paper over the cracks within rural Britain on this and other issues. In a very skilful campaign to draw together diverse groups with a shared concern for the various aspects of rural life and landscape, the Countryside Movement, precursor to the Countryside Alliance, put out a leaflet in 1995 to try to recruit members. On the cover of this leaflet was an almost startlingly green landscape, complete with stone walls, traditional barn and those most English of trees, the oak. Below this undoubtedly beautiful rural scene there was the question 'Do you care about the countryside?'. By such means the Countryside Alliance has engineered a much wider protest movement than the issue of fox hunting alone could ever have managed (MacFarlane, 1998a, 1998b). Whatever the outcome of the legislative attempt to ban fox hunting, the campaign on both sides will stand as an excellent example of the socially contested values that underpin protest and change in rural areas.

Summary

* This chapter has attempted to place dominant and competing values about environmental resources into a context which has emphasized the significance of society, geography and history – at the personal level, at the level of communities of interest, and up to and beyond the level of nation states. Ideas about value, worth and belonging are formed and contested across these different levels, in a dynamic that undermines the idea of any coherent, single environmental movement, but instead reflects and reinforces the diversity of society.

- Geographical space has a changeable contribution to landscape quality, the conservation of rare species and recreational potential. Social spaces, too, are not uniform in respect of different individuals' and communities' perceptions of the everyday, the valuable, the threatened, and the scope for effecting change that might have a positive outcome for them.

- Socially constructed facets of the environment, such as nature, landscape, countryside and wilderness are interpreted and used in ways that are often highly flexible. Such approaches and values are rooted in the cultural history, relative advantage and aspirations of those making claims about the past (e.g. the Balmoralization of the Scottish Highlands) and the future (e.g. fox hunting and rural Britain). As such, ideas about social order and appropriateness can cross over with attributes of the environment in conflicts about what should be in the countryside, how landscapes should appear and what aspects of nature are the most important in negotiating change and development into the future.

- This chapter has not attempted to resolve such tensions for you, and indeed it may have raised more questions in your mind than it has settled uncertainties – that reflects the highly contested nature of these issues which lie at the interface of our social lives with the wider environment.

Further reading

- Adams, W. M. (1996) *Future Nature: A Vision for Conservation*. London: Earthscan.

- Atkins, P., Simmons, I. and Roberts, B. (1998) *People, Land and Time: An Historical Introduction to the Relations between Landscape, Culture and Environment*. London: Arnold.

- Bunce, M. (1994) *The Countryside Ideal: Anglo-American Images of Landscape*. London: Routledge.

- Cloke, P. and Little, J. (eds) (1997) *Contested Countryside Cultures: Otherness, Marginalization and Rurality*. London: Routledge.

- Macnaghten, P. and Urry, J. (1998) *Contested Natures*. London: Sage.

- Muir, R. (1999) *Approaches to Landscape*. Basingstoke: Macmillan.

10
Housing, space and society

10.1 Introduction

Housing is both a physical and social phenomenon, and one that is of profound geographical significance. While the concepts of the household and home are clearly social, the dwelling is a tangible, physical entity. In this chapter we are concerned with both elements, with the interactions between housing and society, with the spatial outcomes from these processes and with the role of space in mediating them.

The relationships between housing and society are complex and mutually interdependent; they affect each other in many ways. For example, a society in which there is a strong sense of collective welfare may be expected to be favourably disposed towards the provision (possibly through generous state or other subsidies) of public sector housing for rent or for gradual purchase by the occupiers. Conversely, a society which is focused much more on the individual or the household unit, and which emphasizes the accumulation of personal wealth and capital, may be expected to favour the ownership of private housing, access to which is achieved through a system of competitive purchasing. However, as we shall see, the structure of tenure in a country may also be influenced by other factors, especially historical factors and different interpretations of the prevailing political economy. A society that is predominantly family-oriented may be expected to produce (or demand) housing and a housing environment which promotes 'family values' (e.g. suburban, detached or semi-detached housing with gardens in 'safe', green environments with access to good schools), whereas a society that is more career- or consumer-oriented, or where alternatives to heterosexual marriage as the dominant form of household are more common, may produce or demand a very different type of residential environment (flats and apartments near to central city employment and leisure/entertainment opportunities).

The nature of housing and residential environments may also have some impact upon various aspects of society, for example, the alleged negative impact of high-rise flats (Fig. 10.1) on children's development (Gittus, 1976) and their association with some psychological disorders (Kearns and Smith, 1993). Other residential environments have been claimed to be 'criminogenic' (see section 11.2.1 of Chapter 11) in the sense that aspects of their layout appear to induce a greater probability of criminal activity than others (Newman, 1972; Coleman, 1985; Evans and Oulds, 1984). It has also been argued that various types of housing and housing layout may be interpreted as a form of 'social control' or, at least, 'social engineering', with the objective of changing the ways of life and perhaps values and standards of the recipients. As we shall see in the next section, housing is one of the most important mechanisms of social reproduction (*see also* Chapter 2), with important spatial implications. Finally, the housing market is the fundamental process through which social areas are formed and change, and where we live and the kind of house we live in are amongst the most important signifiers of identity in contemporary society.

Figure 10.1 *High rise development, Red Road flats, Glasgow. At the time of building believed to be the tallest flats in Europe, they were never popular with families. Allocations came increasingly to be made to single people, including students and former offenders. Credit: M. Barke.*

We illustrate the role of housing in social reproduction in the next section, with reference to some historical examples, the manifestations of which can still be seen in the built environment around us. We then go on to examine the processes of tenure change and their socio-spatial significance in twentieth-century Britain. Some contrasts and similarities with other societies will be noted. The emergence of a spatially and socially polarized housing market and set of housing environments will be emphasized, and the chapter will conclude with a discussion of the issues of homelessness and alternative housing strategies.

10.2. Housing, ways of life and ideology

10.2.1 Ideological expressions in the built environment

The nature and design of housing is of obvious importance to the ways our cities, towns and villages look. Yet, it would be naïve to assume that the design of individual dwellings and residential layouts is simply a consequence of changes in architectural trends and fashions. The nature of the residential built environment is also strongly influenced by economic factors (national, regional and local) and by public policy (the nature of subsidies for housing, land use planning policy, etc.). However, over and above these factors, the nature of housing provision is a product of the belief systems of governments, urban managers and the rich and powerful, reflecting their views of the functions that different (usually social class) areas are meant to perform. Of course, at different periods and in different countries, architects themselves have been an important part of this decision-making elite.

A historical example illustrates the centrality of housing in social reproduction. For employers (especially nineteenth-century industrial employers) the character and costs of their workforce were likely to be directly related to the character and costs of housing.

Box 10.1 Change in the working-class residential built environment in the later nineteenth century

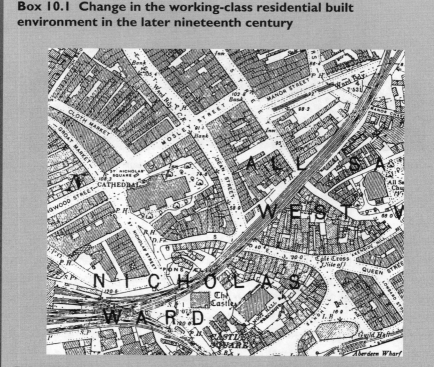

Figure 10.2a shows a haphazard, 'cellular' type of urban form, consisting of closes, courtyards and alleyways; a series of small 'self-enclosed' social worlds, difficult to provide with services such as water, sewerage and street lighting but also difficult to police and regulate. The boundary between 'public' space and 'private' space is unclear. Source: Ordnance Survey, Newcastle upon Tyne, 2nd edn at 1:2500 scale, 1898.

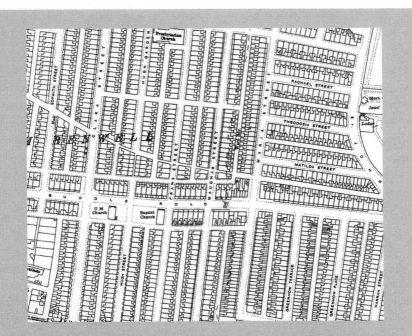

Figure 10.2b shows a much more regular and geometric layout, the grid pattern of housing produced through by-law regulation of street widths, housing densities and heights. This is an urban environment which was much easier to provide with services and to police. Instead of the confusion of public and private space, the distinction is clear and is marked by the front door or the gate. Such a built environment was likely to promote a more private and family-oriented lifestyle, reflecting the dominant Victorian middle-class ideology (Daunton, 1983). Source: Ordnance Survey, Newcastle upon Tyne, 2nd edn at 1:2500 scale, 1898.

After all, workers themselves were produced (or re-produced!) in the home and, more importantly, the home and neighbourhood were where the next generation of workers were socialized into the community. Therefore, the dwelling and its surroundings played, and still play, a major part in the process of 'reproducing' society (see Chapter 2). This is where the norms, mores and disciplines of society are inculcated and learnt (or, in some cases, rejected!). In the nineteenth-century context, it was to the advantage of mainstream capitalist society and economy to produce a built environment for at least part of the workforce that was conducive to this process – its future stability depended on it. Thus it became necessary to make some quite fundamental changes to the nature of some working-class residential built environments in the last third of the nineteenth century and, indeed, to segregate different components of the working class from each other. These changes are encapsulated in the contrasts between the two examples of urban morphology shown in Figures 10.2a and b, a change which produced the long rows of small terraced houses which we have come to associate with nineteenth-century working-class residential areas in Britain (Box 10.1). Up until the 1860s most additional working-class housing simply took the form of sub-dividing existing space. This produced tenement style housing with massive overcrowding, with families sharing houses and even rooms, and the indiscriminate mixing of people seeking accommodation. After this, by-law housing for some members of the working class predominated, consisting of small but, most significantly, separate family houses. At the same time, the increasing physical separation of home from work reflected ideas about women's role in society (see section 6.2 of Chapter 6).

In contrast to the type of housing discussed above, the municipal 'garden suburbs' were built with state subsidy after the First World War (Fig. 10.3). Swenarton (1981) has demonstrated how, in these 'homes fit for heroes', we can see ideology operating through design. The provision of state-subsidized housing was specifically aimed at maintaining social cohesion after the sacrifices of the First World War and in the face of the potential threat to other European ruling elites represented by the Russian Revolution of 1917. The war-time prime minister, Lloyd George, told the Cabinet in 1918, 'In a short time we might have three-quarters of Europe converted to Bolshevism. ... Britain would hold out, but only if the people were given a sense of confidence' (quoted in Swenarton, 1981:78). That confidence was to come from a new form of housing provision. As we saw in Chapter 4, ideological commitment, albeit of a different nature, also influenced the design of neighbourhood areas in the British New Towns programme after the Second World War. Here again, the nature of the residential built environment was shaped in an attempt to achieve specific social outcomes. If we are to fully understand the nature of our housing environments, therefore, we must comprehend that 'design – the silent testimony of

Figure 10.3 *Inter-war council housing, Newcastle upon Tyne, attempting to create the atmosphere and 'cottage' building styles of rural England. Credit: M. Barke.*

inarticulate objects – is one of the ways in which "suitable" ideas are propagated and reinforced' (Swenarton, 1981:196).

10.2.2. Home-making

Having considered some aspects of the dwelling as a physical entity, we now turn to some more explicitly social considerations of housing. Paramount amongst these is the question of home-making. While this has always been important, many commentators have noted the development of what appears to be a more home-centred, 'privatized', culture in most western societies (Saunders, 1990). Improvements in domestic technology have made the home a much more comfortable and welcoming place in which to spend leisure time. The growth of mass consumption, fuelled by more easily available credit, has allowed the purchase of consumer goods and a more home-centred life-style. Some have argued that an increase in home-centredness is also a natural response to increasing alienation in the workplace. As the world of work becomes increasingly impersonal, bureaucratic, routinized and demanding, so greater emphasis is placed upon one's own time and space. The spread of suburbanization may also be a contributory factor, with its distinctive physical form, which is both a product of and a promoter of a distinctive way of life, one that is essentially 'private' behind the front door, garden gate and privet hedge, but which also has elements of competition over domestic symbols of success and security. Others have argued that a sense of community emerges most strongly in circumstances of adversity, but as relative affluence has increased for many so the need for close-knit ties for community support recede into the background.

The home has also been viewed as a site of emotional security. Some authors argue that this sense of security is enhanced by ownership of the dwelling (Saunders, 1990). This, however, is a function of national cultures where private domestic property is emphasized, a particular feature of the English-speaking countries. Psychological security may be enhanced through private ownership but emotional security may also be related to a sense of freedom from surveillance, where external social roles may be abandoned and where one can truly be 'oneself' (Sixsmith, 1986b). The warmth and security of the home is also often related to the significance of the family, a factor which is not restricted to owners only.

The process of home-making also has symbolic significance. The type, size and location of the dwelling is an important signifier of position in society, and is indicated by the lengths that people go to to personalize their dwellings. The late twentieth-century boom in 'do it yourself' is indicative of this trend. The location and character of the local area are also important signifiers: even place names for newly built suburban estates are central in image creation (and marketability), and carry messages about social status (Eyles, 1987).

However, different social groups have different perspectives on and relationships with the home. For example, many feminists would argue that the home may represent a sanctuary for men but a place of subordination and thankless work for

Figure 10.4 *Personalizing the exterior of the home, Meadowell Estate, North Shields. An unexpected but joyously defiant statement made by at least one resident of one of the most deprived estates of northern England. Credit: M. Barke.*

Figure 10.5 *Rather a banal attempt to create a rustic environment in new build housing on the edge of the village of Acomb near Hexham. Credit: M. Barke.*

many women as domestic divisions of labour persist (see section 6.2, Chapter 6). Watson (1986:5) suggests that home ownership represents, in fact, a significant perpetuation of patriarchy:

> *The promotion of home ownership by the state acts to perpetuate patriarchal and capitalist relations and women's subordinate position: first by enabling an idealization of privatized home life and women's domestic role within it; second by locking women into dependence on men for access to a ... subsidized commodity.*

10.3 Changing tenure structure and its significance

10.3.1. Variations in tenure structure

Tenure is a fundamental variable in social structure, one that is strongly geographically expressed and which has profound social and geographical consequences. It is influenced by the prevailing political economy of the state and, just as much as built form, has been the object of policies aimed at influencing society. However, tenure varies from country to country and by historical period. Table 10.1 shows the variation in tenure structure between some European countries at the end of the twentieth century.

Table 10.1 Tenure structure in twelve European countries, c. 1990 (%)

	Owner-occupied	Privately rented	Social rented	Co-ownership or co-operatives	Other
Denmark	52	18	17	7	6
Sweden	43	21	21	15	–
Norway	60	18	4	18	–
West Germany	38	43	15	–	4
Netherlands	45	17	36	–	1
Belgium	65	28	6	–	1
France	54	20	17	–	9
Switzerland	30	66	4	–	–
Austria	50	18	21	–	11
Spain	78	18	2	–	2
Greece	77	23	–	–	–
United Kingdom*	66	9	24	–	–
(Scotland)	54	6	40	–	–

* including Scotland

Source: McCrone and Stephens (1995:18)

Although home ownership has increased in most European countries since the Second World War, it varies widely and in ways that are not explicable by variations in national wealth. Britain and Belgium have extremely high levels of owner-occupation, but even higher are three of Europe's poorest countries – Ireland, Spain and Greece. Former West Germany and Switzerland, despite being two of the wealthiest European countries, have relatively low levels of owner-occupation. Similarly, the significance of the social rented sector cannot be explained by differences in national wealth. The Netherlands, Sweden and Austria have relatively large social rented sectors whilst Greece and Spain have very few dwellings in that sector. Various co-operative forms of ownership are particularly important in Scandinavia. These differences in tenure structure, which have existed over long periods, are part of the 'national settlements' discussed in Chapter 2.

10.3.2 Implications of tenure structure

The structure of tenure varies widely across geographical space. We will examine some of the processes that have led to this situation in Britain in the next section, but here we briefly outline some of the problems and advantages associated with each main tenure form.

Renting from a private landlord is in many ways the most flexible tenure form, as entry does not require large amounts of capital or long-term indebtedness. The general absence of rules for entry also facilitates geographical mobility for employment or for those who wish to adjust the type of housing needed through their life course. However, security of tenure can be a problem and the absence of long-term commitment to the property by those living in it may have negative implications for fixed investments and improvements.

In the second half of the twentieth century home ownership has permitted the accumulation of capital gains through the increase in the equity value of property. In the long term, inflation of house prices has been higher than general inflation. Before the Second World War, people purchasing their dwelling usually expected to live in that house for the rest of their lives. From the 1960s onwards, however, the demands of a more mobile labour market and the possibility of long-term capital gains through selling the present house and 'trading up' have greatly increased the number of housing transactions. Owner-occupied housing has become a source of personal wealth for the majority of the population and has major implications for the inheritance of wealth by the next generation (Hamnett, Harmer and Williams, 1991). Equally significantly, it has opened up a divide between the majority of households who own property and the substantial minority who do not. Owner-occupation is also a source of symbolic security. However, the sector is inherently inflationary as the system depends on continually increasing property values and prices. This exerts significant upward pressure on wages. As personal circumstances or the nature of the economy change, individuals may find themselves unable to pay and, as in the early 1990s (Box. 10.2), negative equity may result.

Social housing caters for those who cannot afford market rents or are not able to buy their own homes. However, the state may, from time to time, seek to economize on the costs of providing such subsidized accommodation and may seek to control the lives of tenants. Bureaucratic entry rules may serve to exclude certain groups and have a negative impact on mobility at the inter-regional scale.

10.3.3 Changing tenure structure in Britain

At the beginning of the twentieth century the vast majority of British households (90 per cent), including many of the wealthy, rented their homes from a private landlord. By the end of the century the tenure structure was entirely different (Table 10.2). The last two decades saw Britain abandon a model of housing provision with a strong role for subsidized housing for rent (council housing), and adopt one predominantly based on market forces through the stronger encouragement of owner-occupation.

Table 10.2 *Changing tenure structure in Britain, 1950–91 (%)*

	Owner-occupied	Housing associations	Local authority rented	Private rented
1950	29.0	–	18.0	53.0
1961	42.3	–	25.8	31.9
1971	50.6	–	30.6	18.9
1981	56.6	2.2	30.3	10.9
1991	66.0	3.2	21.3	9.5
1996	67.0	4.6	17.9	10.5

Source: Office for National Statistics (2000), *Annual Abstract of Statistics, 1999*. London: The Stationery Office.

Although the provision of state-subsidized municipal housing has been particularly important at specific periods, for example, in the inter-war period and after the Second World War, the broad trend towards higher levels of owner-occupation is unmistakable (Fig. 10.6). The post-First World War rhetoric of 'homes fit for heroes' had barely died away when Neville Chamberlain justified the 1923 Housing Act's support for private builders with the words, 'Every spadeful of manure dug in, every fruit tree planted … converts a potential revolutionary into a peaceful citizen', and signalled the Conservative party's long-term aim of creating a property-owning citizenry. Here too, then, we see housing policy attempting to shape society. However, there have been important changes in the nature of owner-occupation over the century. In the 1930s increases in real wages for those in employment, low interest rates and changes in the nature of building societies encouraged this growth. The latter included substantial growth of funds, allowing them to advance money on more favourable terms and to more people, and the granting of mortgages over 20 or 25 years instead of the previous 15 years. Building societies began to compete with each other for business and to associate with builders and developers. Marketing became more aggressive and with quite specific iconography, using images of sunlight, health, privacy and, above all the security of the family (Fig. 10.7) – often represented by the image of a small girl playing safely in the garden (Gold and Gold, 1994). Improved transport, and ease of development of land on the urban periphery in the absence of effective planning controls, also assisted the supply of middle-income, owner-occupied housing. The suburban middle-class housing area and its residents became a fundamental part of the social structure, allegedly representative of 'middle England' and the target for politicians and consumer marketing.

From the mid 1950s, government policy has increasingly favoured owner-occupation, through granting generous tax relief on mortgages and, since 1979, encouraging the sale of council houses (Figure 10.8). The de-regulation of financial services relaxed some of the constraints on home purchase. In 1990–91, tax relief on mortgages for owner-occupiers amounted to £7,500 million whilst subsidy for council housing was only £900 million (Balchin, 1995). This rather artificially enlarged owner-occupied sector has had

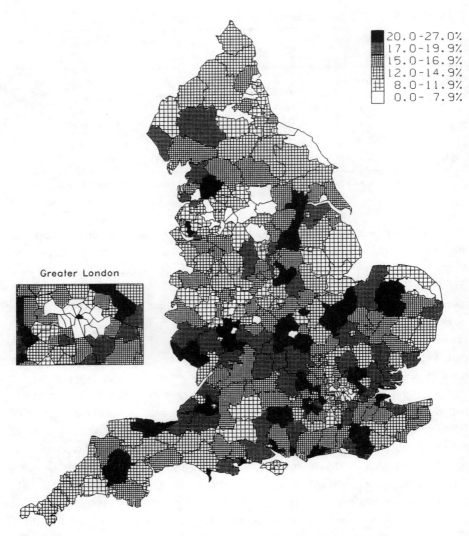

20.0-27.0%
17.0-19.9%
15.0-16.9%
12.0-14.9%
8.0-11.9%
0.0- 7.9%

Greater London

Figure 10.6 *Pattern of sales under RTB. Source: Dunn, R., Forest, R. and Murie, A. (1987), The geography of council house sales in England, 1979–1985. Urban Studies 24, 47–59 (Figure 2, p. 51).*

some negative implications. These were experienced in the late 1980s and early 1990s when economic recession, rising unemployment and increases in interest rates prompted the inter-related problems of mortgage arrears, repossessions and 'negative equity' (see Box 10.2).

As owner-occupation increased during the course of the twentieth century, private renting decreased from 90 per cent in 1900 to less than 10 per cent in 1991. As a sector, it has provided relatively poor returns on investment. One of the reasons often cited for this is the introduction of rent controls in 1915 in response to militant working-class

Figure 10.7 *Advertisement from the 1930s for Hearts of Oak building society. Source: Gold and Gold, 1994:76.*

campaigns, originally intended to deal with profiteering landlords in war time. Governments have been reluctant to totally remove rent control ever since through fear of electoral unpopularity but, from time to time, have sought to reduce the amount of control. Particularly significant was the 1957 Rent Act which decontrolled rents on 2.5 million dwellings, with more expensive houses being decontrolled at once and less expensive houses being decontrolled when the sitting tenant left. The latter became open to substantial abuse as, in a situation of continued housing shortage, it became advantageous to landlords to get rid of sitting tenants and substantially increase the rent

Box 10.2 Repayment arrears and negative equity

- In 1992, 350,000 households were in mortgage arrears of more than six months and 68,000 houses were repossessed (Bank of England, 1992).

- By 1992, 21 per cent of all UK households and over 40 per cent in London and the South East were caught in the negative equity trap (their home being worth less on the current market than the outstanding amount of their mortgage).

- By 1996, over three million households were unable to move because of negative equity.

- People buying their property between 1988 and 1991 were more likely to have negative equity.

- Negative equity was disproportionately held by those on lower incomes, by younger borrowers in every region and those purchasing properties at the lower end of the market (less than £40,000).

(Source: Dorling and Cornford, 1995)

for new tenants. This was particularly the case in areas of high immigrant demand where this process, known as Rachmanism after a notorious slum landlord in London's Notting Hill, also led to overcrowding, illegal sub-letting and unsanitary conditions and was a contributory cause of racially based riots in the late 1950s (Kemp, 1997). The policy also led to many landlords quitting the private rent sector by selling to owner-occupiers. Also in the late 1950s and in the 1960s, large-scale slum clearance led to a decline in the number of houses for private rent. Many of these houses were nineteenth-century dwellings with inadequate facilities. Between 1951 and 1961 the number of privately rented dwellings fell from 45 per cent to 25 per cent of the stock. In the later 1960s and early 1970s area-based grants, intended to prolong the life of older housing, had the effect of encouraging landlords to displace tenants and sell an 'improved' house for owner-occupation, one of the processes of 'gentrification' discussed below (section 10.4).

The decline in private renting has impacted on those groups who are not permanent residents of an area, who do not fit the conventional household image and structure, and who cannot afford to buy their own home or who do not qualify for access to council housing. Ideally, private renting should be able to meet the need for shelter for groups such as those just described. Yet it has declined drastically. Ironically, when there is a need for a mobile labour force, one of the means of enabling it cheaply has all but disappeared.

The decline of private rented housing was one factor behind the continued support for municipal housing, built for those who could not afford to buy their own home, up until the 1970s. However, the nature and quality of that stock varied considerably over time. From 1919 to the early 1930s most council housing built was of a very high standard, conventional two-storey housing with gardens and built with 'garden city' layouts (Fig. 10.3). From the 1930s, however, priority swung in favour of slum clearance housing, built with less generous subsidies on smaller, often inner-city sites. Spatial and social differentiation within the council sector was therefore introduced and has subsequently been significant in estate popularity and reputation. After the Second World War Britain had a massive housing shortage, and policy initially favoured local authority house building. Continued household formation increased the pressure on housing stock through to the 1960s, and the main political parties vied with each other in their electoral promises of how many houses they would build. At the behest of the large building companies, this led to experimentation with different methods of mass-producing housing in 'industrialized' systems (Power, 1993) (Fig. 10.1). But problems of damp, condensation, waste disposal and poor insulation soon became apparent. As in the inter-war period, this housing compared unfavourably with the conventional two-storey council housing built in the 1940s and 1950s.

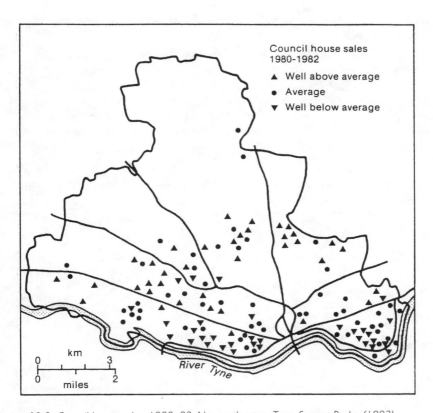

Figure 10.8 Council house sales, 1980–82, Newcastle upon Tyne. Source: Barke (1992).

In 1979, the incoming Conservative government was ideologically tied to a policy of privatization. The sale of council houses to sitting tenants was an important part of this policy. However, the geographical pattern of sales inevitably reflected the historically created structure of council house provision. The more affluent tenants have purchased the best housing, leaving a residue of the least popular houses and areas, and the poorest tenants (Williams, Sewel and Twine, 1988; Forrest and Murie, 1991). Sales have led to a greater concentration of problems within the public sector at a time when that sector has been increasingly deprived of resources to deal with them (Hoggart, 1995). An increasing proportion of tenants is dependent upon state benefits for their income (Box 10.3). Up until the 1970s council housing served to break the connection between low incomes and poor housing, but since then that link has been reinforced and geographical segregation has increased.

Although the British public sector has effectively ceased to play a role in meeting general housing needs it still plays an important role for 'special' groups (Smith, 1993) who need specific forms of care or domestic adaptations. This includes sheltered housing

Box 10.3 Council house sales and residualization in Tyne and Wear, Britain

Table 10.3 below shows the changing socio-economic structure of local authority tenants in the Tyne and Wear area (the Districts of Gateshead, Sunderland, South Tyneside, North Tyneside and Newcastle combined). Although the changes in socio-economic structure could theoretically be due to extreme variations in the mobility of different socio-economic groups, in reality they are explained far more by the in situ purchase of dwellings by those in employment and the inability of the remainder to exercise their 'right to buy'.

Table 10.3 Socio-economic structure of Local Authority tenants in Tyne and Wear, 1981 and 1991

Socio-economic group	% 1981	% 1991	Percentage point change, 1981–91
Professional, managers and employers	3.2	1.5	−1.7
Intermediate and junior non-manual	7.3	5.2	−2.1
Skilled manual and own account non-professional	20.1	12.0	−8.1
Semi-skilled and personal service	18.2	9.9	−8.3
Unskilled manual	9.6	5.4	−4.2
Economically inactive	31.5	66.0	+36.5

Source: Barke (1997)

for older people, and for those with mental health problems or mobility problems. At one level such provision may be regarded as beneficial, but we should not overlook the fact that governmental enthusiasm for such developments owes much to a wish to 'pigeon hole' and target particular groups, and to ration resources (Clapham and Smith, 1990). Some forms of special housing provision carry with them a sense of control and containment. In Sweden for example, the idea of segregation as a policy to deal with HIV/AIDS patients who are regarded as promiscuous has been adopted (Smith, 1993).

With the decline in council housing the importance of housing associations in meeting social housing need has increased. Their traditional role was in meeting the needs of particular groups, such as seamen, people with mental problems or who had recently been discharged from prison or institutions, young single people and, especially, older people. But from 1988 they were expected to become the main providers of new build social housing and to take control of some former council housing estates. Yet, financial controls have tended to compromise quality just as they did in the council sector, and housing associations are required to seek funding from the private sector and charge market rents. Ironically, those on state benefits could afford such rents through housing benefit payments, while those with low wages could not. The poor are therefore faced with a choice: no job but a house, or get a job but lose the house.

It is clear that the tenure structure in Britain has changed dramatically in the last twenty years. In many ways it has become more complex. Figure 10.9 shows how many recent housing initiatives cut across conventional public/private divides. Under the name of diversification, collectivized provision has been systematically eroded (Clarke and Bradford, 1998). The net effect has been to more deeply entrench social and spatial polarization.

10.4 The processes of gentrification

Gentrification is the process by which run-down, usually inner-city, residential environments have their residents displaced by middle-class professionals. A variety of theoretical explanations have been suggested to explain the phenomenon. These can be initially divided into explanations focusing on the supply of and demand for housing respectively.

The main concepts on the supply side are the rent gap (Smith, 1979) and value gap (Hamnett and Randolph, 1986) theories. The former seeks to explain why capital is reinvested in inner-city locations after a period of disinvestment, arguing that a key factor is the gap that emerges between the return from land under its present use and that which could be obtained from converting that use to a higher-yielding function. This gap is likely to stimulate investment, such as in high-quality housing, necessitating the replacement of poorer populations by wealthier. The rent gap theory attempts to explain physical change and why capital returns to disinvested areas. The value gap is concerned with the conversion from one tenure to another (Hamnett and Randolph, 1988). The gap in this case occurs when a property's value is greater under owner occupation than under rental. This relates to the long-term change in the structure of

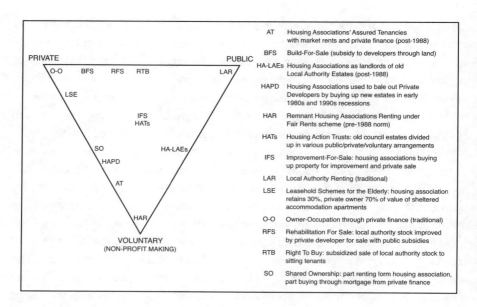

Figure 10.9 *Blurring of housing provision in the UK in 1980s and 1990s. Source: Clarke and Bradford (1998) (Figure 1, p. 882).*

tenure discussed in section 10.3 and can be produced by state interventions such as tax relief for owner-occupiers and rent control. The gap may stimulate a conversion of tenure from rented to owner-occupation and may lead to gentrification as lower-income households are excluded from the latter. A third supply side theory is concerned with the role of institutions and argues that the process of gentrification is often set in motion by the designation by the state of special areas for upgrading. Hamnett (1973) has shown how, in some London boroughs, the availability of grants for prolonging the life of older houses was used by property owners to get rid of sitting tenants, upgrade and sell the dwelling to wealthier inhabitants. This, then, is related to the rent-gap and value-gap models, but greater emphasis is placed on the roles of state and quasi-state institutions (see, for example, Brownill, 1994).

The second major group of theories suggest that the main explanatory factors lie with the changing demands of households (Ley, 1986). First, a higher proportion are better educated and are in middle-class occupations. This ties into a range of factors associated with culture and life-styles. The nuclear family has declined in significance and a much broader variety of household structures is now apparent. Many professional workers work irregular hours, seek to live close to their work in the central city, and carry their working relations into their social lives, thus blurring the boundaries between 'home' and 'work' (see section 2.2 of Chapter 2 and section 6.3 of Chapter 6). Leisure activities have become important, especially for relatively younger adults without children. More people therefore search for socially and physically distinct residential communities that provide for these life styles and opportunities for self-expression. These may include the formation of specifically gay or lesbian communities (Lauria and Knopp, 1985; Rothenberg, 1995; see section 6.4 of Chapter 6). Bondi (1991; 1999) has stressed the role of gender and changing gender relations in specific locations, for example the Stockbridge and Leith areas of Edinburgh where 'gentrification is associated with a professional strand of the middle class, within which a substantial proportion of women have become strongly career-oriented' (Bondi, 1999:277). The structure of the local economy and job market are obviously significant in this context, and economic forces may also play some part in encouraging households at a particular stage in their life course to seek inner-city locations. Commuter costs, including the hidden costs of congestion and delay, have increased in all large cities, making a suburban-commuter life style less attractive. Relatively higher house prices in suburban locations may also encourage younger people to turn to central-city housing opportunities. Finally, it has also been argued that improvements in domestic technology and their fall in costs relative to the costs of property have been significant in allowing gentrification to take place through permitting comfortable use of old buildings (Redfern, 1997).

Rather than being in opposition, these various explanations of gentrification are complementary to each other. Changes in demand may stimulate rent gaps and value gaps. Moreover, processes vary in their importance. For example, in Stockholm gentrification has taken place without the accompanying tenure change assumed under the value-gap explanation. 'Gentrified' properties have remained in the rented sector rather than being converted to owner-occupation (Millard-Ball, 2000). Gentrification in some inner areas of Edinburgh is particularly associated with the emergence of financially independent, career-oriented, childless women. Such examples alert us to the importance of socio-spatial circumstances that give more or less importance to particular models (Lees, 1994). Again, place and spatial variations are important in shaping local outcomes.

10.5 Homelessness

Homelessness is probably the most extreme form of social exclusion in that one of the most fundamental of human needs is being denied. However, homelessness is difficult to define, partly because for an individual it may be subject to temporal variation, and partly because there are many different varieties of homelessness. For example, street sleepers, those living in institutions because they have nowhere else to go (but with variations in their length of stay), those who have accommodation but it is insecure (e.g. squatting), and those living in substandard accommodation, all represent variations of homelessness.

It is difficult to make cross-national comparisons on homelessness because of the lack of comparable data sources and, in some countries, the absence of data. However, Box 10.4 provides some relevant data.

There are many competing interpretations of homelessness and policies have

Box. 10.4 Some European homelessness data

- 1.6 million people are subject to eviction procedures each year and are 'at risk' of homelessness.

- 400,000 people are physically evicted from their homes each year.

- 1.8 million people are known to be dependent on public and voluntary services for homeless people.

- A further 2.7 million people rotate between friends, relatives and rented furnished accommodation.

- 15 million people live in severely substandard and overcrowded dwellings.

- The highest numbers of homeless are found in Germany (876,450), United Kingdom (460,000) and France (346,000).

(Source: Harvey, 1999)

reflected these different interpretations (Jacobs, Kemeny and Manzi, 1999; Somerville, 1999). In the past, homelessness was thought to be a consequence of personal inadequacy, but even if this is a factor, it is only one of many. Rather than explanations for the growth of homelessness lying with personal pathologies, structural changes are now widely recognized as playing a major part. Amongst these are: increasing unemployment, increase in divorce rate, increase in one-parent families, changing home-leaving patterns for young adults, increase in mortgage default and re-possessions, the discharge of ill homeless people onto the streets, low or absent income support systems, and the deinstitutionalization of psychiatric units with often only limited provision of community care facilities (see Chapters 2 and 8). Among the most important factors, however, is the gradual withdrawal of the state from providing affordable housing for low-income households. Successive British governments have encouraged the growth of home ownership but this is not an option for the latter, and Ford (1999) has demonstrated that many who were drawn into this tenure have ended up having their homes repossessed and, in some cases, being made homeless. Access to council housing has been severely limited due to the decline in this tenure and, in any case, single homeless people generally have low priority in its allocation. Where they are accommodated it is often in the most problematic and least popular dwellings and estates (Fitzpatrick and Stephens, 1999), an example of 'segregation and containment'.

Homeless people also often have distinctive medical problems (Bines, 1994), resulting from the life style they are forced to adopt and their limited access to health care for lack of a permanent address. Ironically and, in some cases, tragically, some of the very health problems that homeless people suffer from are used to exclude them from public sector housing (Shanks and Smith, 1991), almost certainly with the consequence of exacerbating those problems.

The state takes responsibility for alleviating homelessness to some extent, although this varies between countries. In Britain, for example, local authorities have responsibility for providing long-term accommodation for households who are 'unintentionally' homeless as long as they are in a 'priority' group of families with children or pregnant women. Most single homeless people are excluded from even temporary accommodation. Across the EU voluntary agencies provide about two-thirds of services and the state one third, although the proportion varies considerably by country. In general, the states of Europe have failed to care for homeless people, leaving their needs to be met by charitable organizations (Fitzpatrick, 1998).

10.6 Alternative housing strategies

In Britain in the recent past, various alternative forms of housing provision have emerged which involve a greater popular participation in housing than the mainstream. These range through squatting, shared ownership, self-build, 'staircasing' (part purchase, part rental arrangements), to tenant self-management. The growing range of these alternative housing strategies could be interpreted as an indication of the extent of dissatisfaction with or even failure of mainstream housing provision. Some of these alternative housing strategies also illustrate some of the tensions between structure and human agency, and have specific local outcomes.

In several European countries, particularly in southern Europe with its less well-developed credit systems and relatively easier access to available land, self-build is a favoured option. In some rural areas of northern Europe, however, it has also received considerable support in recent years. As a result, in the 1980s it accounted for over 60 per cent of housing output in Belgium, and over 40 per cent in Italy, Ireland, France, Austria, West Germany and Norway. In Britain, it was less than 10 per cent (Duncan and Rowe, 1993) although a number of self-build schemes have benefited from serviced or cheap land being sold to them by local authorities where the authority could no longer afford to build itself (Shucksmith, 1990). However, such schemes are really only possible where a number of energetic individuals with appropriate skills coincide in one location. In Britain, unlike much of the rest of Europe, the dominance of large construction firms, the concentration of land ownership and established planning policies have negative effects on the self-build option.

Squatting is a common response to the plight of homelessness. It is estimated that there are between 30,000 and 50,000 squatters in England (Bailey, 1997). Large-scale squatting began immediately after the Second World War when there was an acute housing shortage, combined with large numbers of empty properties in seaside resorts, large cities and former military camps. This gradually became a social movement which changed the law – a good example of popular action changing housing structures. In the late 1960s ugly events at Ilford in Redbridge Borough Council produced a significant legal change. A large number of council dwellings were standing empty and scheduled for redevelopment, but not for at least five years. An organized squat took place in

December 1968 and the furious council responded by deliberately attempting to smash up the dwellings and make them uninhabitable, and then subsequently resorted to hiring thugs to physically remove the squatters. The police were forced to intervene to prevent further violence and, with governmental approval, by the early 1970s licensed squatting or 'short-life arrangements' for homeless people to occupy unoccupied property had become a feature of many London boroughs (Bailey, 1997).

Within the social-rented sector in Britain, various forms of tenant participation or self-management have been attempted as an alternative way of attempting to tackle some of the perceived problems. This development has gone through several phases. From 1919 to the mid 1960s the relations between councils and their tenants was highly paternalistic (Clapham, 1997), characterized by a close relationship between housing, social work and moral improvement and leading to practices such as grading tenants on their 'housekeeping standards'. Tenants were largely passive, and tenants' organizations were usually a response to specific, localized, issues. From the mid 1960s to the early 1970s, however, there were increasing pressures for more real tenant participation. Attempts to restructure and increase council rents by national governments led to resistance and demands for tenant participation. At the same time, mounting concern over the social consequences of large-scale slum-clearance and redevelopment in urban areas led to measures for public participation in planning matters. This was stimulated by the discovery in 1974 that 50 per cent of the most 'difficult to let' estates had been built in the last ten years. The huge problems and cost of maintaining unpopular 'industrialized systems' estates (Fig. 10.1) began to worry the government. One response was to encourage the development of tenant co-operatives in the hope that this would lead to more effective management. As Box 10.5 indicates, participation was seen as a way of 'educating' the public and making them more aware of the problems of management. In other words, the response was to attempt to incorporate the opposition.

From the 1980s governments have sought to end public ownership of housing altogether, not only through sale to individual tenants but through transfer of estates to social or private landlords. The Housing Act of 1988 empowered local authority tenants to enter into discussions with potential new landlords approved by central government agencies. These could be housing associations, co-operatives or private sector landlords. A number of local authorities, mainly Conservative-controlled and in rural areas or the south, took advantage of this policy to undertake 'large-scale voluntary transfers' (LSVTs). A specific variant of this policy was the imposition of Housing Action Trusts (HATs) on run-down estates, where the intention was to undertake wholesale transfer of the properties to selected landlords. Initially there was no requirement for a ballot of tenants before this could take place but opposition from the House of Lords caused the Secretary of State for the Environment, Nicholas Ridley, reluctantly to change his mind. It appears that two levels of 'participation' were envisaged for different kinds of council tenant, with those on 'problem estates' being told who their new landlord was going to be.

Box. 10.5 The Morris Committee (1975): advantages of tenant participation

To the community
- Less apathy
- More local control over environment
- More sensitive management practices

To local authorities
- Better information on tenants
- Greater awareness of need for co-ordinated service delivery
- Consumers better informed about conflicting demands on scarce local authority resources

Variations on the theme of removing housing from the control of local authorities have continued in the 1996 Housing Act, which permits local housing companies to be established in former council estates as non-profit-making social landlords. A requirement is that their boards should consist of elected councillors, representatives from the local community and, importantly, tenants themselves. It seems inevitable that the continued shortage of public funding for municipal housing will ensure that various alternative forms of managing this stock will continue to develop.

One alternative with, as yet, only limited growth in England, although it is rather more popular in Scotland, is housing co-operatives. However, in all Scandinavian states apart from Finland housing co-operatives are a popular tenure form. Although varying in details of finance and organization, they reflect the broadly consensual 'national settlement' of those states in the post-Second World war era that has favoured collectivist rather than privatized welfare promotion, housing being one

Box 10.6 Housing co-operatives in Sweden

Housing co-operatives account for about 16 per cent of the total housing stock in Sweden. They are mainly associated with multi-apartment dwellings. The incomes of households in this tenure form tend to be higher than even those in owner-occupation (Turner, 1996) and members are mainly adults without children (85 per cent). This trend is likely to grow as elderly people are increasingly selling homes they own in order to move into co-operatively owned accommodation with additional services, such as nursing facilities, catering and recreational provision.

Membership is acquired by payment of an initial fee. There is full security of tenure and when the member leaves the right to occupy the dwelling is sold for the market price. Members may take out loans to finance the entrance fee and make payments to cover common services and repairs. Co-operatives in Sweden therefore are something of a hybrid between owner-occupation and renting. They involve an investment which can appreciate with house values generally. However, they also represent a commitment to communal values and responsibilities and are one way of resolving some of the problems associated with managing multi-occupied apartments.

manifestation of this. Box 10.6 describes some of the features of housing co-operatives in Sweden.

Mainstream forms of house building, ownership and management are often taken for granted. But they are formed by particular economic, social and political conditions. Movements for alternative forms may, then, be able to mould housing in ways that offer better forms of control to individuals and communities.

Summary

- The relation of society and housing is multi-faceted.

- Housing directly influences households' quality of life and access to employment.

- Housing is an important signifier of social status, segregation and inequality as it closely reflects income, class, culture and aspirations, as well as social power relations involving age, race, gender and sexuality.

- The structure of tenure varies geographically and confers different combinations of advantages and disadvantages.

- Housing outcomes are profoundly influenced by policy considerations.

Further reading

- Balchin, P. (1995) *Housing Policy: an Introduction*, 3rd edn. London and New York: Routledge.

- Malpass, P. and Murie, A. (1994) *Housing Policy and Practice*, 4th edn. London: Macmillan.

- McCrone, G. and Stephens, M. (1995) *Housing Policy in Britain and Europe*. London: UCL Press.

- Shucksmith, M. (1990) *Housebuilding in Britain's Countryside*. London and New York: Routledge.

- Williams, P. (ed.) (1997) *Directions in Housing Policy*. London: Paul Chapman.

11
Crime, space and inequality

11.1 Introduction
Since the late twentieth century, crime has become one of the foremost social problems of the western world, achieving a high profile in the media and political agendas as well as in many people's everyday lives. Today, it is not an unusual event but an ordinary experience, which is embedded in and shapes our routine expectations and experiences of space and place. Crime and the fear of crime are of long-standing interest in social geography, as a number of dimensions of space and place are involved in their causation and the way they are experienced. As we will demonstrate in this chapter, crime, fear and their impacts are unevenly distributed between geographical areas and social groups; there are geographical patterns to where offenders and victims live, as well as where they are perceived to live; people tend to fear particular places at certain times; and the spatial behaviour and identities of social groups are shaped by fear of crime.

11.1.1 Defining crime
The term 'crime' is contested terrain. Standard dictionary definitions usually refer to 'an offence punishable by law', or 'a violation of criminal law', the law itself supposedly being based on what 'society' feels is unacceptable behaviour. However, 'shared' values represent only the views of some people. In particular it has been argued that official definitions of which behaviours are criminal most often reflect the interests of powerful groups (Peet, 1975). This means that legal definitions of crime vary between places at a variety of scales. Ideologies about particular social groups, often emplaced in certain spatial contexts, also result in unequal access to the law, as the following examples show.

- *The criminalization of homosexuality* The age of consent for gay men varies across Europe from 14 in San Marino to 18 in Austria.

- *The criminalization of homophobic violence* In recent years some US states have developed 'hate crime laws' (see Fig. 11.1, which shows variations between states), some of which encompass homophobic violence, which is discussed in section 11.4.

- *The legalization of hard and soft drugs* Compare the relaxed laws on drugs in Holland with those of other European countries.

- **Blood sports** Some have been illegal in Britain since 1835 (e.g. bear-baiting and cock-fighting), while others (e.g. fox-hunting) are still legal. Within Europe laws vary widely – for example, bull-fighting is legal in Spain.

- **Middle-class crime** In most countries of the world, 'white collar' crimes in the workplace, such as fraud, are never punished as harshly as minor thefts by the less affluent (Langan, 1996).

- **Violence against women** This has been widely viewed as less acceptable between strangers in public space, than within the family in private space. Only after a long struggle led by feminists to change attitudes and statutes have domestic forms of violence begun to be treated by law enforcement agencies as criminal.

- **The redefinition of activities of those who occupy marginal or contested spaces** The Criminal Justice and Public Order Bill (1994) in Britain newly defined as 'criminal' the activities of new age travellers, hunt saboteurs, those attending raves and mass trespasses – groups perceived as threatening the interests of the right-wing Conservative government and its traditional supporters (see Chapter 3).

11.1.2 Methods and approaches

Until relatively recently, geographical research tended to focus upon quite a narrowly defined range of criminal acts. Part of the reason has been the data which are available for analysis. Official crime statistics are notoriously misleading, as only an estimated 44 per cent of all UK crimes are reported to the police, and personal/violent crimes are particularly unlikely to be represented (Mirrlees-Black et al., 1998). Geographers' earliest contributions to the study of crime involved the analysis of the better documented property crimes in cities, often using quantitative techniques such as computer mapping and statistics. In recent years social geographers have also examined the spatial patterns of violent crime, as previously 'hidden' crimes such as racial, sexual and homophobic violence have come to light.

Much research on fear of crime has been criticized for using data from questionnaire surveys in which respondents are asked to choose from pre-set lists of responses to crime, without also using qualitative or subjective data to suggest what labels such as 'fear' actually mean (see section 11.3.1). More recently a range of alternative methods have been applied to study fear and its effects on individuals and communities, including in depth interviews, focus groups and local ethnographies. The philosophical approaches taken to the study of crime and fear of crime have also diversified, from early welfarist and positivist spatial science to recent work influenced by the humanistic tradition and more radical standpoints such as feminism (see Chapter 1, section 3.1).

11.1.3 Outline of chapter

Section 11.2 is concerned with geographical theories about 'crime areas', and mainly concentrates on the environmental correlates of property crime and fear of crime. Section

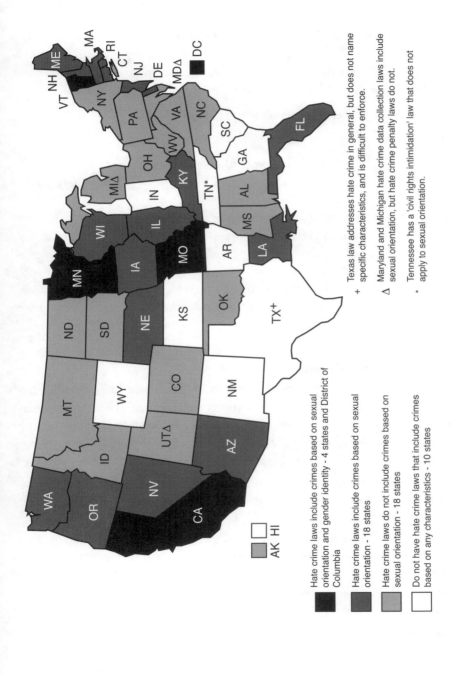

Figure 11.1 *Hate crime laws in the United States, December 1999. Source: National Gay and Lesbian Task Force.*

Hate crime laws include crimes based on sexual orientation and gender identity - 4 states and District of Columbia

Hate crime laws include crimes based on sexual orientation - 18 states

Hate crime laws do not include crimes based on sexual orientation - 18 states

Do not have hate crime laws that include crimes based on any characteristics - 10 states

AK HI

+ Texas law addresses hate crime in general, but does not name specific characteristics, and is difficult to enforce.

Δ Maryland and Michigan hate crime data collection laws include sexual orientation, but hate crime penalty laws do not.

* Tennessee has a 'civil rights intimidation' law that does not apply to sexual orientation.

11.3 introduces the spatial patterns of fear of crime, and their geographical relationship with crime. Section 11.4 deals more specifically with geographies of violent crime, their implications for the geographical experiences of individuals and social groups, and the ways in which space and place are involved in violence and resistance to violence.

11.2 'Crime areas' and geographies of inequality

According to official statistics, the greatest predictor of becoming a victim of crime is where you live. The distribution of crime has three basic characteristics which have remained and, some evidence shows, deepened, in recent years:

- A small number of offenders commit a large number of crimes

- A small number of victims suffer a large number of crimes

- A small number of areas suffer a disproportionate amount of crime

(Trickett et al., 1995)

These three characteristics tend to coincide, as the most deprived areas of cities typically experience the highest levels of property crime. These frequently lie in or close to city centres in the USA, while patterns of public housing provision in Europe often means there are additional high crime areas on urban peripheries. These spatial patterns are not universal, but have been fairly prevalent and persistent across space and over time. Geographers and those working in related disciplines have interpreted these areal patterns in a number of ways.

11.2.1 The built environment

At a fine spatial scale, a large body of work has noted an association between the incidence of crime and particular built environments, and theorized a causal link between design and crime. This literature grew from the influential critique of post-war housing estates in the USA by Newman (1972), who identified four important housing design features which he suggested directly influenced the number of opportunities for crime:

- **Territorial influence:** 'mechanisms for the subdivision of and articulation of areas of the residential environment intended to reinforce inhabitants in their ability to assume territorial attitudes and prerogatives'

- **Surveillance opportunities:** 'mechanisms for improving the capacity of residents to casually and continually survey the non-private areas of their living environment, indoor and out'

- **Perception:** 'mechanisms which neutralize the symbolic stigma of the form of housing projects, reducing the image of isolation, and the apparent vulnerability of inhabitants'

- **Juxtaposition:** 'the effect of location of a residential environment within a particular urban setting or adjacent to a "safe" or "unsafe" activity area'

(Newman, 1972:50)

Although Newman's work has been heavily criticized for environmental determinism (the assumption that the built environment *creates* crime), the social nature of space and its use and perception by the people who live there is central to his thesis. In Britain, Coleman (1985) followed up these ideas with large-scale studies of high rise housing estates. She too found positive correlations between design features – such as the density and size of estates, the number of storeys in blocks, the length of corridors, entrance positions and the layout of grounds – and signs of social decay, such as crime, vandalism, delinquency, graffiti and litter. In another well known study Newman's ideas were applied to areas of housing on the borders of identifiable neighbourhoods (Brantingham and Brantingham, 1975). Here it was suggested that a lesser sense of belonging and identity allowed burglars anonymity and led to higher rates of crime.

Figure 11.2 *West Granton Gardens, Edinburgh: the open-access upper walkways meant easy access for burglars, with the public stairways providing easy escape. Credit: R. Pain.*

Figure 11.3 *West Granton Crescent, Edinburgh: local people were afraid of being mugged or attacked using this tunnel on their way to the bus stop. Credit: R. Pain.*

These ideas quickly gained currency among planners and architects, and the push to 'design out crime' which began in the late 1970s is still popular today. A large body of research has been hailed as supporting the association (Clarke, 1992). The notion that fear of crime can also be 'designed out', by removing or altering those aspects of the environment which people find frightening, has been equally popular. As Newman and Coleman showed, the absence of protective features is often most marked in poorer, marginalized areas. Figures 11.2 and 11.3 show some of the fear-provoking features of the built environment in West Granton, a 'hard-to-let' estate in Edinburgh, Scotland which was demolished in the early 1990s. The design of this estate provided many opportunities for burglars, muggers and vandals to commit crimes unseen and with ease of escape, and as a result some local residents were reluctant to leave their homes or use local tunnels and stairways (see Box 11.1).

As these women suggest, however, it is not just the design of the area that worries them – they would not have felt safe walking there even if it had been well designed and well lit. This illustrates one of the major flaws of the defensible space hypothesis: poor building design may simply coincide in space with a range of social and economic problems, which have a far more important role in the causation of crime (Mawby 1977). For example, Box 11.2 describes the problematic findings of one set of studies which sought to link environmental changes to patterns of crime and fear.

Box 11.1 Women's fear of crime in public space, West Granton

Are there any places round here which would worry you?
'Well, quite a lot of it actually. The park, for example, that's never safe. And down at the shops here, especially at night. And *The Gunner* [pub] – that should be closed down completely. There are places you sortae feel safe, like Davidson Mains [nearby village], but then you've got to get a taxi there and back if you can afford to.'

Are there any areas you avoid?
'Er, I think Muirhouse, West Granton [local council estates], because of the tunnels. There's drug addicts, weird drug addicts and everything. You see them if you go across the street to the shops, you see them having their fights.'

'I think there should be better lighting in some places but that said, the places that aren't properly lit are really places where I wouldn't consider walking anyway.'

'The stair's revolting, that, revolting. The lighting's really bad on the stairs as well. The archways, the tunnels is terrible, you ken. But I'm no too happy walking anywhere to be honest.'

(Source: Koskela and Pain, 2000)

Box 11.2 The story of the British streetlighting research

The streetlighting research of the early 1990s is significant as one of the largest experimental programmes aiming to reduce crime and fear of crime in built environments. One of the first to report success was Painter (1992), who found that better lighting reduced levels of crime and fear in a number of London schemes. Herbert and Davidson (1994) reported on initiatives in Hull and Cardiff, where better streetlighting not only appeared to reduce residents' fear of crime, but improved neighbourhood satisfaction. In an Amsterdam study, Vrij and Winkel (1991) found similar improvements.

However, other research has shown mixed results or contradiction. One study of Wandsworth in London found no effect on feelings of safety (Atkins, Husain and Storey, 1991), while for some respondents in a Glasgow study, worries about crime actually grew (Nair, Ditton and Phillips, 1993). The suggestion that brighter streetlighting will improve feelings of safety assumes that people feel safer if not only potential assailants, but they themselves, can be seen – less of an advantage if assailants are the only people watching. The presence of passers-by, and their willingness to help, are important factors. There also exists a possibility that better lighting might increase fear if it makes signs of disorder, and the presence of drunks or young men on the street, more visible (Herbert and Davidson, 1994).

The range of findings arising in different places suggest that reactions are more complex than experimental studies allow for. Many of the methodological issues in this debate are also relevant to other 'designing out crime' schemes, including questions over the appropriateness of before and after surveys to measure changes in fear, the possible short term nature of benefits, and the intervening effects of other factors.

Despite these criticisms, crime and fear reduction through environmental design remain popular in Europe and North America, especially where political ideology has sought to shift the focus away from the social and political causes of crime (Gilling, 1997). However, even proponents have suggested the effects of such schemes are only ever local or partial, and may displace crime elsewhere (Herbert and Davidson, 1994). Such initiatives may have a range of other benefits, including satisfaction with the local community and neighbourhood.

11.2.2 The journey to crime

As some of the earliest critiques of the defensible space thesis suggested, the spatial concentration of crime in certain areas can be alternatively interpreted simply as proximity to criminals. Studies in the 1970s and 1980s showed the very localized nature of much property crime, with offenders generally not travelling far to commit crimes (Baldwin and Bottoms, 1976; Davidson, 1981; Herbert and Hyde, 1985). It is now widely acknowledged that property crime – at least as defined in this particular discussion – is largely committed and suffered by people living in poorer areas. The reasons why burglars and car thieves have traditionally offended close to home are bound up with their perceptions of space (Herbert, 1982), including knowledge of the area and of escape routes, more poorly protected property, and the easier disposal of stolen goods. Figure 11.4 illustrates this trend, showing the location of residence and the location of offending for a sample of offenders in Swansea, Wales.

However, this truism was subject to some change during the 1990s, as at least some criminals became more mobile, and crime spread to suburbs and rural areas in many countries. This has occurred partly as a result of some inner urban areas becoming better protected against crime. It is important to bear in mind that while recorded crime rates may be increasing in some more affluent areas, the impacts of crime on victims, and the vulnerability of residents to fear of crime, are usually less than in poorer areas. Greater affluence cushions the blow of crime with insurance and crime prevention measures, while a sense of common interest with neighbours, and the ability to distance criminals as outsiders to the community, may reduce feelings of insecurity (Pain, 1995).

11.2.3 The economic and social marginalization of 'problem areas'

One danger of focusing too closely on local environments and the journeys of burglars is to ignore the class conflicts and inequalities which lie at the root of crime (Herbert, 1982). Structural explanations take into account economic and social history and change in order to understand particular problems of crime in particular places.

In Britain, 'problem areas' with the highest rates of crime have persisted since before the 1970s; typically they are public housing estates in peripheral urban locations. Public housing policy during this period often led to the 'dumping' of tenants with adverse characteristics in concentrated areas (Baldwin, 1975; Herbert, 1982). Such marginalized areas, often stereotyped as 'difficult to let, difficult to live in, and difficult to get out of

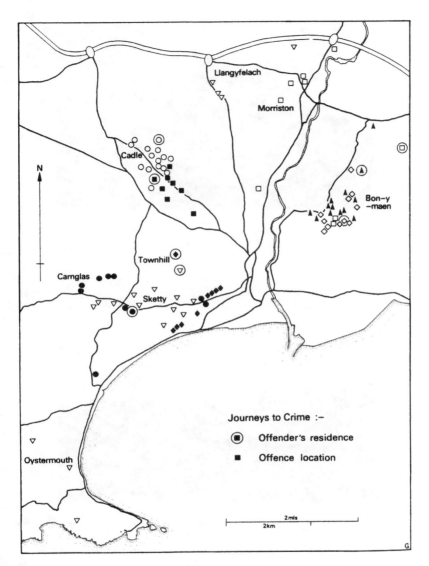

Figure 11.4 *Journeys to crime for a sample of known offenders. (Each symbol represents an individual offender's crime locations; where the symbol is circled the location is the offender's residence.) Source: Herbert and Hyde (1985) (Figure 2, p. 266).*

(Berry and Jones, 1995), suffer a range of other social and economic problems or 'urban clustering': high rates of unemployment, poverty, family break-up and drug abuse, and poor housing and access to services such as health and education. Thus social geographical processes create conditions which, coupled with local criminal subcultures which develop over a period of time (see next section), make crime a likely occurrence. Such areas acquire a reputation for crime, a self-fulfilling label as they become further stigmatized (see Barke and Turnbull, 1992; *also* Chapter 4).

Figure 11.5a *'The Terraces', Benwell, Newcastle upon Tyne. To the consternation of the local community, the council are now considering demolition as the only solution to high crime rates in this area. Credit: R. Pain.*

Figure 11.5b *A CCTV camera dominates the landscape in Benwell, Newcastle upon Tyne. Credit: R. Pain.*

Moreover, victims are most likely to be certain types of people who tend to be concentrated in marginalized areas. Many of the social indicators associated with poverty (see Chapter 12) are highly correlated with a greater chance of burglary victimization (Table 11.1). What is more, those who have been victimized once are far more likely to be victimized again. This 'multiple victimization' (Genn, 1988), which is more common in areas with high crime rates, is an important facet underlying geographical concentrations of crime (Duncan, 1997). Multiple victimization is also unequally distributed within high crime areas, as Table 11.1 suggests. Such inequalities in victimization risk for particular social groups are, as we suggested above, compounded by inequalities in access to forms of crime control – private transport, crime prevention devices such as alarms and

Table 11.1 *Proportion of households victims of burglary in 1997, by selected characteristics*

	% victims once or more	% of victims victimized more than once
All households	5.6	19.5
Head of household aged 16–24	15.2	n/a
Single adult and children	11.2	36.6
Unemployed	10.0	n/a
Income < £5,000 per annum	8.3	22.9
Social renters	8.0	25.8
Private renters	9.7	17.6
Inner-city area	8.5	25.5
Council estate area	8.1	25.0

Source: *1998 British Crime Survey* (Mirrlees-Black et al., 1998)

expensive locks – which might reduce those risks or at least allay the fear of crime. There may also be poorer community spirit in marginalized areas, as high levels of crime can divide communities and create suspicion and mistrust (although on the other hand, alternative community structures can provide protection from crime and fear, as the next section suggests). Poorer areas and groups who suffer the highest rates of victimization are also more poorly served by policing and criminal justice.

11.2.4 Crime and local subcultures

Other research has investigated the criminal subcultures which exist in particular localities, often employing qualitative methods. The idea of subculture emphasizes that sets of values and customs, shared amongst local social networks, underlie particular patterns of crime in different places. So, not only do individual criminals follow 'criminal careers' (Hobbs, 1995), but shared trajectories of socio-economic change and the relationships between people within places mean that localities can be described as having 'community crime careers' (Bottoms and Wiles, 1997). If crime is part of everyday local cultures, it is harder to tackle than the explanations discussed so far would suggest. Environments can be changed, and with far more effort social and economic stresses can be alleviated, but culture itself is seen by many as far less movable. Studies in this area are relatively few, partly because of the difficulties of access to the criminal world faced by researchers, and the need for long-term and intensive methods, such as ethnography.

Wright and Decker's (1994) study of burglars' perspectives on the process of committing burglaries provides a useful insight into the motivations behind this type of crime and the ways in which targets are chosen. It is set in deprived inner-city areas in St Louis, Missouri, in the USA, which have seen deindustrialization, population loss, the concentration of poverty and high crime rates. The chief motivation of the burglars interviewed in their research was the need for money, for basic survival but also for clothes and drugs to help individuals gain status within street cultures. The houses they targeted were frequently identified either during the course of daily activities and movements through local areas, or else from intelligence passed on from others, and were watched over a long period before the crime was committed (Box 11.3). The implications for crime prevention are profound, as although some environmental cues were relevant, both the decision to offend and the choice of target were far from 'opportunistic'. The authors comment that only tackling low pay and drug dependency are viable long-term solutions.

Box 11.3 Burglars' choice of targets

'I never go into a house where I don't know nothing about it or who's [living] there. You got to at least know something.'

'In my everyday routine, I can see things. Like, I work for a interior decorator company, so I travels a lot and I sees a lot … When [the company] calls me … to go set up panelling or something, I look around. [The occupants] got money; they buyin' from that company, they got some money.'

'I know a lot of people, and they know my game, so they put me up on certain people: "so and so's leavin' town next week." I don't like nobody in the house … Say, for instance, a friend of theirs might be going out of town and they want something out of the deal, they ain't going to do it for nothing. They scared to go do it, so they tell [me] about it.'

(Source: Wright and Decker, 1994:63–74)

In a British study of rioting and disorder amongst young men in Cardiff, Oxford and Tyneside, Campbell (1993) places a different emphasis. In analysing local cultures of criminality she highlights the constructions of masculinity which were current in high crime, inner-city 'problem estates' during the late 1980s and early 1990s. While it has been known for hundreds of years that most of those who commit crime in western Europe are young white males, criminologists have only recently begin to examine how masculinities relate to offending behaviour (Newburn and Stanko, 1994). For Campbell (1993), the British riots were an extreme manifestation of a longer-term malaise of petty crime and disorder, burglary and car theft experienced daily on marginalized council estates. She argues that economic and social changes have necessitated the reformulation of masculine identities for young men (her work is discussed further in Chapter 6, section 4).

Such local subcultures tend to be viewed negatively. But in some places, while appearing to threaten the established social order, they can provide some protection, support and resistance for local people. In an ethnographic study of two high-crime, inner-city areas of Salford in Britain, Evans, Fraser and Walklate (1996) examined how residents managed the daily threat of crime in localities which are geographically and socially isolated, and where residents did not feel their interests or concerns were supported by mainstream crime prevention agencies such as the police and criminal justice system. The authors identify different levels and meanings of 'community' here: 'in Oldtown your place in relation to crime places you in a community of belonging and exclusion' (Evans, Fraser and Walklate, 1996:379). Other residents, local families and for some, the 'Salford Firm', an influential local gang, were seen to protect residents; 'moreover, it is the absence of confidence in the formal agencies which creates the space for these other forces to come into play'.

While providing sometimes fascinating insights into the causes and mechanisms underlying the social geographies of crime, such work has tended to focus on low-income, marginalized places and people, reproducing a particular definition of 'crime' and sometimes further stigmatizing these groups. Domestic crimes, middle-class crimes and the crimes of organizations and governments are more difficult to detect and research, but are also enmeshed in place-specific cultural practices.

11.3 Geographies of crime and fear

We have already made reference to fear of crime in several of the studies we have discussed. A growing body of work in social geography focuses on the problem of fear in its own right.

11.3.1 Defining fear of crime

The meaning of fear of crime is different to different people, and is dependent on spatial, temporal and social context. It refers not just to an emotional reaction to the idea of victimization, but the impacts which the threat of crime has on broader aspects of people's lives. So it describes the sudden dread which you might feel on waking up in the night and hearing an intruder downstairs; but also the longer-lived and much lower-key anxiety which means you lock doors carefully each night, think about how you relate to people on a night out and how you will get home, and have evasive strategies planned in case of danger. Box 11.4 gives examples of the ways in which fear of crime is manifested in common behavioural adaptations and spatial strategies. Fear of crime is of interest to social geographers beyond its effect on individuals, as 'its effects reach beyond the prudent management of risk to impinge on public morale, individual well-being and the quality of social life' (S. J. Smith, 1989).

11.3.2 The geographical coincidence of crime and fear

Like crime itself, fear of crime tends to be higher in certain areas and affects certain groups more than others. Successive sweeps of the British Crime Survey have directly compared levels of victimization and levels of fear amongst particular social groups. Early on, it was suggested that because fear appeared to be greater than victimization amongst certain groups, particularly women and older people, these fears were irrational (Hough

> ## Box 11.4 The impacts of fear of crime on use of space
>
> **Avoidance**
> Staying indoors at night
> Seeking alternative routes
> Avoiding particular places
> Taking a taxi instead of walking or
> taking bus
>
> **Resistance**
> Carrying a rape alarm or weapon
> Adopting 'fearless' behaviour
> Meeting and moving around in pairs or
> groups
>
> **Precaution**
> Fitting locks, burglar alarms, car
> immobilizers
> Dressing 'modestly'
> Not making eye contact or talking to
> strangers
>
> **Communal**
> Increased suspicion
> Less social contact
> Lower levels of peopling of public space

and Mayhew, 1983). Despite being heavily criticized, this has been an influential conclusion. However, the spatial match of crime and fear is complicated (Herbert and Darwood, 1992), and local crime rates only partly explain geographies of fear. There are a number of problems with 'mapping and matching' crime and fear locally, as follows:

- Both fear of crime, and the crimes which concern people the most (notably violence), are notoriously difficult to measure in a way which allows comparison. Reliable data for rates of violence are difficult to acquire, and unlikely to be at the necessary scale, unit of aggregation or with the necessary coverage for comparison with data gathered on fear.

- People's perceptions of crime in their local area differ from their personal levels of concern about crime, yet surveys have frequently confused or obscured the two. For example, you may know that a certain area is 'bad' for muggings, but may feel the chances of it happening to you are very small.

- Individuals' fear of crime is affected by events that have taken place over their lives. For women, minor forms of intimidating behaviour such as harassment create concern about more serious attacks (Stanko, 1987), while other life experiences and circumstances can make people feel vulnerable to crime and more fearful, such as bereavement, divorce and moving house (Hollway and Jefferson, 1997).

- Localities have many aspects other than crime rates which influence fear of crime. These include population profiles in different areas; different environments and the reputations they acquire; different experiences of policy-making; economic histories and change; and the social and cultural identities of places (see Brown, 1995; Evans, Fraser and Walklate, 1995; Loader, Girling and Sparks, 1998; Taylor 1995). Box 11.5 suggests some of the reasons why rural areas have lower rates of fear of crime than urban areas, regardless of crime rates.

Box 11.5 Fear of crime in rural areas

Although crime rates are rising in many rural areas, and policing tends to be less concentrated and less able to respond rapidly because of distance, fear of crime tends to be lower in rural areas.

Research has shown how specific cultural contexts and local meanings of 'community' can make a difference in rural as well as urban locations. Well developed local knowledge and social networks promote greater feelings of security in some rural areas (Shapland and Vagg, 1988). Equally, where rural residents are able to distance criminals from the local community, assuming that they come from urban areas (Anderson, 1998), this provides a sense of common interest and greater safety.

In a study of rural Worcestershire in England, Yarwood and Gardner (2000) demonstrate that fear of crime is related to cultural constructions of rurality and the changing nature and use of the countryside. Acts by outsiders such as trespass, leaving gates open, disturbing livestock, and the presence of groups of teenagers and travellers were linked to the fear of crime by their respondents. These outsiders, who may not have been doing anything illegal, were viewed as a threat to dominant rural culture – 'their presence was seen to disrupt the countryside and to intrude on both the environment and economy of the locality' (Yarwood and Gardner, 2000).

Fear of crime involves a complex set of emotions and cognitions, and to label it with simple opposites such as 'rational' or 'irrational' has little meaning (Sparks, 1992). Fear is certainly higher in most high-risk areas, and amongst those who have been victimized (Mirrlees-Black et al., 1998), but it also exists outside high-crime areas and high-risk populations. Place and locality influence both the patterning and construction of crime and fear. Individuals are positioned within these local contexts in different ways, influenced by their class, race, gender, age and so on. The next section goes on to examine how the social identities and spatial behaviour of certain social groups are influenced by fear of crime.

11.4 Systemic violence: space, power and fear

In recent years social geographers have begun to focus on the relationships between violence, fear and the distribution of social, economic and political power. Evidence has grown over the last two decades of forms of violent crime which are specific to certain gender, sexual, age and ethnic groups. These forms of violence, which have been labelled 'systemic violence' (Young, 1990a) or 'hate crimes' (Herek and Berrill, 1992), are discriminatory: they are targeted on the basis of social and/or political identity. They tend to be explained in terms of power relations and the vulnerable social and economic status of those at risk. The main forms of systemic violence are outlined in Box 11.6.

All these forms of systemic violence are seriously under-reported and, as Box 11.6 shows, this is partly because many are more common within the home and family than outside it. The structure of domestic space and the power relations commonly exercised there create conditions where the rights traditionally held by men of authority and privacy have been legally enshrined (see Chapter 6, section 6.2). This not only makes

Box 11.6 Systemic violence

Sexual violence

- More than 1 in 10 women experience rape over their lifetime.
- 3 per cent of men have been raped as adults or subjected to a sexual experience they did not want.
- The majority of these attacks are carried out by someone known to their victims, often in a domestic environment.
- In the 1998 British Crime Survey, 23 per cent of women and 15 per cent of men reported having been assaulted by a partner at some time in their lives, with women more likely to be seriously injured than men.

Child abuse

- Estimated to affect one in four or five children.
- Only a small minority of cases involve strangers; most take place within the home.

Racist violence

- Racist violence and harassment are endemic and widespread in European countries. In Britain, Asians are almost twice as likely to be a victim of street violence as white people.

Homophobic violence

- 34 per cent of men and 24 per cent of women reported experiencing violence because of their sexual orientation to a recent British study of 4000 lesbian, gay and bisexual respondents, and the majority had experienced homophobic harassment.

Elder abuse

- 1 in 10 older people experience physical, sexual, psychological or financial abuse each year in Britain.
- Most incidents take place in a domestic or institutional context.

violence against women and children more likely to happen, but also means that it has been less likely to be policed and prosecuted than violence outside the home until relatively recently (N. Duncan, 1996). Likewise, in instances of elder abuse, the nature of the family home and care institutions, and the ways in which social relations are structured there may provide conditions in which older people experience a lack of power, where they are dependent on younger carers with more social and economic capital, where intervention from outside is difficult, and where abuse goes unpoliced (Penhale, 1993).

11.4.1 Violence and socio-spatial exclusion

It has been widely argued that systemic violence, harassment, and fear which results, act to marginalize and exclude certain groups from mainstream social and political life in various ways.

- *Exclusion through violence* Systemic violence is a significant dimension of the oppression of marginalized groups (Young, 1990a). For example, feminists have suggested that sexual violence against women is the 'structural underpinning of hierarchical relations; the ultimate sanction buttressing other forms of social control' (Hanmer, 1978:229).

- *Exclusion through low level abuses such as racist, sexist, homophobic or ageist harassment* Many forms of harassment are not officially criminal but, especially when experienced frequently, these minor abuses too may lead to restrictions or exclusions from public spaces, workplaces and leisure spaces (Pain, 1991).

- *Exclusion through fear of violence and precautionary behaviour* (see Box 11.4 and Table 11.2). As Table 11.2 shows, it is often those already socially or economically disadvantaged who are affected most by fear of crime, which has the effect of reinforcing their disadvantage. While women and older people are popularly viewed as most affected by fear, the indicators of income, disability, single parenthood, being a council renter and living in an inner-city area are significantly more associated in the British Crime Survey. Davis' (1992) 'ecology of fear' (Fig. 11.6) illustrates that these exclusions are not only expressed in individual restrictions, but also in the social and planned geographies of the city, in this case Los Angeles, USA.

Table 11.2 *Social groups whose quality of life is most affected by fear of crime*

	% 'greatly affected' by fear of crime
All	8
Women	10
Older people (60+)	10
Single parents	14
People on low income (less than £5,000 per annum)	16
Disabled people	15
Council/Housing Association tenants	14
People in council areas	13
People in inner-city areas	12
People in areas with signs of physical disorder	16

Source: *1998 British Crime Survey* (Mirrlees-Black and Allen, 1998)

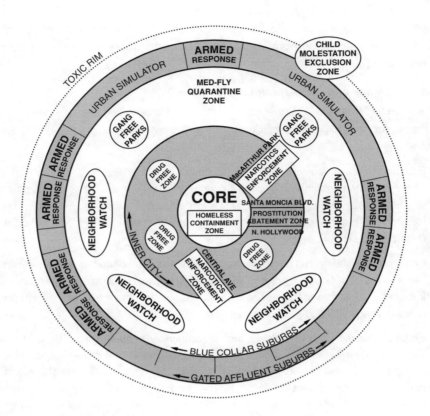

Figure 11.6 *An ecology of fear. Adapted from: Davis (1992:10).*

- *Exclusion through being constructed as a threat* Many people tend to fear stereotypical 'others', identified by their colour, class or other 'impurity', whose presence threatens disorder to mainstream life and values (Sibley, 1995; *see also* Box 11.5, and section 5.7 of Chapter 5). In reality, the groups and places frequently demonized as a threat to law and order may themselves be at the highest risk of violence and abuse – social 'others' such as children, young men, people who are homeless or have mental health problems may be simultaneously feared and fearful.

- *Exclusion through criminal justice and community safety policies* Policies which aim to improve the safety of some groups do so at the expense of others. As Garland (1996: 461) has outlined, the association of danger with 'the threatening outcast, the fearsome stranger, the excluded and the embittered' is often invoked at the level of governance in order to excite fear and promote support for punitive strategies. Equally, Davis (1992) argues that planning tactics to create 'safe spaces' (see Fig. 11.7) lead to greater fear, isolation and social exclusion, rather than less, and that the disbenefits of planning urban space in this way are fewest for the rich and greatest for those already marginalized from urban life. Yet paradoxically, many who suffer violence do so at the hands of people with whom they are intimate rather than from the strangers on the street who are the focus of so many crime prevention and community safety strategies (see Figs 7.4a and b, Chapter 7).

11.4.2 Fear of violence and identity

The various forms of exclusion discussed above have implications not only for the behaviour of particular social groups and the opportunities available to them, but also for social identity. The rest of this section uses the example of gendered fear to illustrate the ways in which violence leads to the reinforcement of, and resistance to, particular social identities. The ways in which space is labelled and used play an important role in these processes. Related arguments have been made about homophobic violence and its effect on sexual expression in public and private space, the sexual abuse of children (see Chapter 7, section 7.3), and elder abuse, racist violence and violence against people with disabilities (Pain, 2000).

Femininity, masculinity and fear of violence
Almost every survey of fear of crime finds that women report being more fearful of crime than men. Women's fear of sexual violence and harassment underpins this (Valentine, 1989). A growing body of feminist research has highlighted that given the high rates of violence against women (not always reported to crime surveys) this fear is well-founded (see Stanko, 1987). In feminist social control theory, women's fear is viewed as a manifestation of gender oppression and a damaging form of control of women's lives (Hanmer and Saunders, 1984).

Geographers have focused on the spatial outcomes of this control, particularly the well-documented effects of coping strategies which many women employ to avoid harassment and violence (Pain, 1997b). Arguing that the precautions which women commonly take constitute a 'spatial expression of patriarchy', Valentine (1989) has demonstrated how fear reproduces traditional notions about women's roles and the 'places' which are considered appropriate for them to use. Ideologies and images of sexual danger, supported by the media, rumour, first-hand experience and warnings from others, have a role in constructing fear in public space, although private space is actually more dangerous (Stanko, 1990a; Valentine, 1992). Sexual harassment, which polices 'bodies out of place' in masculinist, heterosexual environments, has also been implicated in contributing to fear (Junger, 1987; McDowell, 1995; see Chapter 6, section 3). While earlier commentators suggested that a 'conspiracy of silence' on domestic assault is also partly to blame (Hanmer and Saunders, 1984), recent research suggests that women are now more aware of the relative risks of different spaces (Pawson and Banks, 1993). However, this commonsense knowledge does not necessarily affect deep-rooted public space fears, because of the forms of socialization into fear mentioned above, and because of the tendency we all have to distance victimization from ourselves and the areas we live in, where this is possible (Pain, 1997b).

It has been argued that in some feminist writings on fear of crime, the emphasis on 'fear' and its negative consequences reproduced notions about feminine weakness

(Segal, 1990). It has also been suggested that responses to the newly identified problem of women's fear from police forces and government departments tend to entrench stereotypes further, rather than challenge them (Stanko, 1990b). However, social geographers' accounts of marginalized social groups are increasingly focusing on their resistance as well as their oppression, and the literature on gendered fear is no exception. Koskela's (1997) analysis of women's fear of attack in Finland emphasizes that women respond to the threat of crime with 'boldness' as well as fear, and 'spatial confidence' as well as spatial avoidance (see Box 11.6). Different notions of femininity, then, are entwined with different constructions of the fear of crime.

Box 11.6 Boldness and spatial confidence – Koskela on women's fear

Koskela's work (1997, 1999) on women's fear of violence in urban spaces in Finland makes an interesting contrast to similar research by geographers elsewhere, as many previous studies emphasized the negative impacts of fear and the oppression of women through male violence.

Koskela highlights the influence of the particular cultural and geographical context of Finland, which has a better record on gender equality than many other European or North American countries. She highlights the stories of those women who are not afraid but respond to the threat of violence with boldness and defiance rather than fear, and the fact that just as some women become fearful at certain times, others lose the 'space of fearfulness' through certain life experiences. In so doing she challenges the unintentional portrayal of previous research of fearfulness as an essentially female quality.

'It has been pointed out in this study that women do not passively experience space but actively produce, define and reclaim it. Many women in Finland reclaim space for themselves through consciously routinized use, and are able to "tame" space by various expressions of courage. They have several ways of negotiating danger, reading the signs of danger, taking possession of space, and using power on urban space: women show "spatial expertise". This demonstrates that women's everyday spatial practices can be practices of resistance. By their presence in urban space women produce space that is more available not only for themselves but also for other women. Women's spatial confidence can be interpreted as a manifestation of power. Hence, at the level of the whole society, women's safety in public is arguably improved more by women going out than by them staying inside.'

(Koskela, 1999: Epilogue p.3)

In contrast to women, men's low reported fear of crime has always seemed anomalous when, as a group, they experience high rates of violence, particularly from strangers in public places but also from partners and acquaintances (Mirrlees-Black et al., 1998). Part of the problem is methodological – male respondents seem reluctant to give answers to surveys where this might challenge the image of male invulnerability, meaning that their fear of crime is often hidden. However, where men have been the subject of qualitative research, this suggests that, for some, the effects of fear may be just as great (Gilchrist et al., 1998; Stanko and Hobdell, 1993). Goodey (1997) suggests that other social identities such as age, race, sexuality and class structure men's fear. While young boys may admit to concern about crime, as they grow up male fearfulness 'is progressively downplayed as normative adult identities are adopted' (Goodey, 1997:402). The dominant culture of heterosexual masculinity makes 'fear' a less acceptable response for men, but at the same time means that those perceived as being outside it, for example gay men, are more at risk from violence. As a result men too may be 'fearful', but this may be expressed in different types of coping strategies and constraints (Walklate, 1995). Box 11.8 illustrates some of these issues. Despite the usual stereotypes about young men as offenders rather than victims, there are numerous ways in which young men are positioned in relation to crime, risk and fear.

Box 11.8 Young men and fear of violence in Newcastle city centre, England

A recent study suggested that young men took more precautions against crime than any other group while using the city centre. They dealt with fear differently to other groups, in particular by trying to appear confident when in public space:

'If you walk past a group of lads and you're there with your head down and you try to walk past as fast as you can, then they're bound to say something. But if you walk past them, as if you couldn't care less whether they were there or not – they wouldn't say anything to ye.'

With most first- and second-hand knowledge of crime and hassle, and most likely to be in the city centre at 'dangerous' times, young men were the most aware of danger and most careful. However, young men perceive and deal with 'risk' in particular ways. Walklate (1997:41) has described this conception of risk as arising from a masculinity 'which values excitement, adventure, power and control as what men do. This is a masculinity to which all men relate to a greater or lesser degree'. Risk-taking behaviour is part of the attraction of the city centre at less safe times for some young men (and increasingly, some young women).

However, the differences between young men were as important as the commonalities: respondents identified the risks associated with being a football fan, of student bashing, and of having an accent from other parts of Britain:

'They get absolutely tanked up [drunk] and then it's like, "Oh, there's a bunch of students, we'll go an' harass them for a laugh!" '

'I think it's your accent as well, like, em, when you've got a foreign accent it's alright, but em variations of the English accent. People who are, like, from down south are getting picked on.'

Some of the young men had experience of being viewed as potentially dangerous or criminal themselves because of their age and gender. Some had been harassed by the police, and others were aware of how they might be perceived by older people.

'If you're in a group of, like, eight lads, the police always come over and ask what you're doin'. And, like, yer, just goin' for a drink – but they automatically assume that you're killin' somebody!'

'I think with old people it's what they read in the papers as well. I mean, they seem to think that everybody that's young's got [...] a drug habit.'

'They think that we all go to nightclubs and take ten 'Es' [ecstasy] every night.'

(Source: Pain and Townshend, forthcoming)

Summary

- A diverse literature can inform our understanding of social geographies of crime. Approaches vary dramatically, from focusing on the built environment in which crime takes place, to highlighting the subcultures operating in high crime areas, to investigating the relationships between fear and the geographies and identities of individuals, social groups, towns, cities and rural areas.

- A recurrent theme is that the geographies of crime and fear must be understood not just in terms of impacts upon individuals, but as sharply focused on particular social groups in particular places, frequently following (and reinforcing) social, economic and political divisions.

- Social geography has a contribution to make to debates over crime prevention and community safety policy. There are very good reasons to suggest that such policies should be place-centred and place-specific, that is, tailored to local problems and conditions.

- However, as we saw in section 11.2, while environments can be changed, the patterns and processes involved in crime relate far more strongly to social, economic and cultural factors which are not so easily resolved. Situational strategies such as environmental improvements, and in particular, CCTV (close-circuit television), are as popular as ever with policy-makers. The material presented in this chapter would suggest that they may tackle the symptoms of crime and fear – although there is evidence that they do not do either particularly well – but not the causes.

- Instead, social crime prevention, which emphasizes the root causes of crime, is more complex and costly but perhaps the only realistic long-term solution (Gilling, 1997; Young, 1999). Crime and fear remain endemic while many of the other social problems dealt with in this book, such as racial and sexual inequality, poor housing and poverty, remain entrenched in western societies.

Further reading

- Crawford, A. (1998) *Crime Prevention and Community Safety*. London: Longman.

- Evans, D. J., Fyfe, N. R. and Herbert, D. T. (eds) (1992) *Crime, Policing and Place*. London: Routledge.

- Muncie, J. and McLaughlin, E. (eds) (1996) *The Problem of Crime*. London: Sage.

- Pain, R. (2000) Place, social relations and the fear of crime: a review. *Progress in Human Geography* 24(3).

- Yarwood, R. and Gardner, G. (2000) Fear of crime, cultural threat and the countryside. *Area* 32(4), 403–12.

12
Geographies of poverty

The subjects which have been dealt with in preceding chapters have related to social inequality: the forms that it takes, who suffers it, where it is concentrated and how it is reproduced in space. In this final chapter we bring these themes together, by focusing on a topic which is central to the concerns of social geography.

12.1 Introduction

Poverty has been a long-standing interest in social geography. Most early geographical work on poverty focused on mapping indicators across space (for example Brunhes, 1920; Watson, 1951), and this was also an important strand in the social geography of the 1960s (see Chapter 1, Box 1.1). From the 1970s onwards, radical work attempted more political and socially concerned analysis. Geographers began to 'think more conceptually about the connections between welfare, (in)justice, poverty and place' (Philo, 1995:628) in order to *explain* the continued existence of poverty. The inter-relationship between poverty and wealth has been of central concern, with Marxist geographers in particular arguing that capitalist societies actively produce these opposites.

However, 'poverty' was missing from the third edition of the *Dictionary of Human Geography* (Johnston *et al.*, 1994). In a commentary (1995:1022), Leyshon expressed surprise and concern at its omission, given that during the time since the publication of the first edition of the *Dictionary* in 1981 the growth of poverty on a global scale had become 'one of the most observable socio-economic phenomena of the period'. Leyshon argues that poverty has been a victim of the recent 'cultural turn' in social geography (introduced in Chapter 1) and the associated decline in materially based radical geographies. There has thus been little recent geographical work on poverty as a concept and as an overall condition.

However, over the last few years there has been a large amount of work on *aspects* of poverty by geographers, or from a geographical perspective. Further, the inclusion of 'poverty' as an entry in the 2000 edition of the *Dictionary* also suggests a re-engagement with the geographies of poverty. It states that poverty is 'a condition experienced by many people who have a shortage of financial and other resources, and it means that they are likely to face difficulties in obtaining and maintaining sufficient nutrition, adequate accommodation and long-term good health' (Philo, 2000: 627). Taken in isolation however, this statement belies the extent to which poverty is a contested concept:

> [Poverty] conjures up powerful and shocking images: of emaciated bodies in Ethiopia or Somalia; of violence and riots in American inner cities or on 'problem' estates in this country; of ragged Victorian children like Oliver Twist, who are punished because he dared to ask for 'more'; of homeless families today, living, cooking and washing in one small room in a miserable bed and breakfast hostel ... (Family Policy Studies Centre, 1992: 5).

In other words, 'poverty' can mean different things to different people. Like many key concepts within social geography, because of its political nature there is no one correct, scientific, or agreed definition of poverty. In the first part of this chapter (section 2) we therefore examine different ways of defining poverty, and argue that these are dependent on time and geography.

This lays the basis for discussing the causes of poverty and its geographies, which are as controversial as its definition. The geographical patterns of poverty are complex. For the case of Britain, Philo (1995: 4) writes:

> The geography [of poverty] can be described in terms of nameable places and particular types of settlements, environments and regions, some of which are weighed down with poverty (complete with industrial decline, unemployment, bad housing, deficient services and social problems) and some of which are currently more fortunate. It can also be thought of at differing spatial scales, with a pattern of poverty and wealth at the regional level (e.g. the South-East or the North-West) being cross-cut by other patterns which operate along specific axes (town as opposed to country, factory district to farmland, lowlands to uplands) or which are more local in their extent (inner-city contrasted with neighbouring suburb, private estate with adjacent council estate, rural town with sparsely-populated surrounding hills and vales). In addition, at the most local of spatial scales poverty and wealth are sometimes closely intermixed, almost touching, and yet still remain separated by minute distances (think of the plush office block towering above a 'cardboard city') which keep poor and rich strangers to one another.

How can we begin to understand these patterns? A major concern in looking at causes of poverty is to tease out the extent to which, and the senses in which, geography constructs poverty. Many popular views of poverty, many political discourses and much academic work portray poverty as in some sense caused by place. For instance, the physical geography of the place is sometimes invoked. In nineteenth-century Britain a popular discourse attributed the relative poverty of Mediterranean countries to their climates, soils and vegetation, and the 'character' of the people which was supposed to follow from these. In the last hundred years, however, place-based explanations have focused on durable social aspects of places, on 'second nature'. Thus in the 1970s in

Britain, poverty was seen as *specific* to inner-city areas, and as substantially *caused* by those areas through their decayed built environments, their unfavourable location for modern industry, the longstanding culture of their inhabitants, and various forms of 'social dysfunction' that are supposed to be incubated by big cities. We, too, shall argue that place is important in constructing poverty, but we shall see that geography in itself does not cause poverty, but only as an aspect of social relations and processes.

A variety of theories of poverty have been developed in social science. One of the key differences in these theories is the spatial scale on which they focus. One set of theories focuses on the smallest scale, that of the individual; poverty is explained as the result of characteristics of particular people. Another type of theory focuses on communities of the poor, which are seen as generating their own poverty. Yet other theories, sometimes described as 'structural', seek the causes of poverty in society as a whole, and are therefore concerned with all spatial scales from the individual to the global. In section 12.3 we discuss the individual and community theories of poverty, and in the three subsequent sections examine structural theories.

There are, then, powerful and deeply embedded causes of poverty. However, these have been contested, particularly by the poor themselves, who are far from being passive victims; in the final section we consider the political activity of the poor.

12.2 Questions of definition

Approaches to defining poverty are intrinsically related to the times and places from which definitions have originated. As Philo has noted, 'it is not so much poverty that disappears and reappears as its acceptability or relevance to the agendas set by the most influential shapers of public opinion' (1995:2). In Britain, systematic work on poverty was pioneered by Booth (1889; 1892; 1894) and Rowntree (1901; 1937; 1941; Rowntree and Laver, 1951) in the late nineteenth and early twentieth centuries, but since then poverty research has been used, interpreted or simply ignored in varying ways at different times (Silburn, 1998). Two broad approaches to the definition of poverty have dominated discussion over a long period, 'absolute poverty' and 'relative poverty'. We first consider these, and then discuss a possible synthesis of them.

12.2.1 Absolute poverty

Notions of absolute poverty are based on definable minimum requirements needed for physical survival, or 'subsistence'. The prevalence of absolute poverty can then be measured and compared over time, normally through the notion of a 'poverty line' based on some form of survival criteria such as specified minimum daily caloric intake (Lipton, 1983), proportion of income spent on food (Rao, 1982), or income levels required to purchase a defined minimum basket of consumption goods (MacPherson and Silburn, 1998). Thus the concept of absolute poverty aims for objective, scientific measurement.

However, absolute measures have been strongly criticized for ignoring geographical variations in life requirements:

> *For instance, what is adequate shelter depends on the ambient climate and the availability of materials for construction – even the homeless poor living in London's 'Cardboard City' in the 1990s arguably are only able to survive because of the availability of cardboard. Adequate fuel for warmth also depends on the climate, the time of year, the condition of someone's dwelling and their state of health. Adequate diet depends on the availability of types of food, the ability to cook food, the nature of the work for which sustenance is required and – according to Rowntree, who allowed more in his basic diet for men than for women – on gender. Diet might also depend on taste – Rowntree included tea in his basic British diet, although it is of negligible nutritional value.*
>
> (Alcock, 1997:70)

Therefore, what is required for physical survival can differ over time and space, undermining its utility and basis for comparison and measurement. As a consequence, many approaches to poverty definition have taken a more relativistic stance.

12.2.2 Relative poverty

Notions of 'relative poverty' situate poverty in relation to the prevailing living standards of the society or community in question. The 1960s saw both the 'rediscovery' and redefinition of poverty in Britain, triggered by the work of Abel-Smith and Townsend (1965). They redefined poverty as representing levels below the means-tested assistance offered by the social security system, 'a useful and defensible benchmark to start a debate grounded in commonly encountered, real-life circumstances' (Silburn, 1998:207). Like Rowntree before him (Rowntree, 1941), Townsend subsequently further broadened his own definition of poverty to incorporate the notion of social participation, where 'individuals, families and groups in the population can be said to be in poverty when they lack the resources to obtain the types of diet, participate in the activities and have the living conditions and amenities *which are customary ... in the societies to which they belong'* (Townsend, 1979:31, emphasis added). Such a definition is more sensitive than 'absolute poverty' to territorial difference.

However, the concept of relative poverty has been criticized on both practical and theoretical grounds. First, up-to-date and accurate information on these factors is rarely available. Secondly, there have been disagreements concerning the definition of 'social participation', so that the incorporation of non-necessities is contentious. Third, critics have argued that relative notions of poverty merely express inequalities that exist in any society, and do not necessarily mean that anyone is poor.

We can see, then, that both absolute and relative approaches to poverty definition have their pros and cons. Recent attempts at poverty definition sought to incorporate the strong aspects of each approach to produce more 'hybrid' definitions.

12.2.3 Hybrid definitions

Amartya Sen (1983) has suggested that it is possible to consider certain features of human nature as being universal. These universal 'needs' and 'capabilities' exist in every society, but the means to achieve and express them differ from society to society. Poverty exists when such universal needs are not met. This approach thus shares with the 'absolute poverty' theory a belief that universal features of human beings should enter into defining poverty; but it shares with the 'relative poverty' approach a belief that the circumstances of particular societies need to be taken into account.

Sen illustrates these ideas by referring to a child's need for education, a need considered to be universal and absolute. However, the means to achieve this need differ between societies. For example, the assumed availability of computers in school lessons in one society means that a child is poor in that society if they lack access to these facilities, but this would not necessarily be the case elsewhere. In another example, Sen argues that dignity is a universal human need, but that what is dignified varies between societies. Drawing on Adam Smith's reference to the 'need' for labourers to possess a linen shirt in a particular society, Sen then argues that *lack* of a shirt in such a society makes someone poor as it destroys their dignity.

Criticisms of this approach have centred on the existence and measurement of universal needs. On the one hand the list of needs, such as education, defined as universal may vary from society to society, whilst Piachaud (1987) has suggested that a list of universally accepted activities would be so general in nature that only the relative differences at societal level would have any use.

Despite these critiques, there is now fairly broad agreement among academics and policy-makers on a hybrid approach, within which poverty has many dimensions beyond subsistence and include minimum standards of well-being as perceived by the particular society. For instance, Figure 12.1 shows an example of a wide-ranging interpretation of poverty encompassing 'the most important dimensions of deprivation' (Development Assistance Committee (DAC), 2000:10). In a similar manner, the United Nations Development Programme definition includes not only economic provisioning but deprivation in health, life-spans, knowledge, and participation in communities, and sees overcoming poverty as bound up with 'human development' – enhancing people's freedom, self-respect and social status. As in Sen's work, questions arise as to how many of these dimensions of poverty can be measured. Poverty studies, then, face a 'trade off' in that '[t]he more complex and multidimensional the measures are, the more adequate they are for understanding a context-specific situation and intervening in it effectively – but the less convenient for comparisons' (DAC, 2000:13).

Perhaps the strongest justification for adopting a multi-dimensional definition of poverty comes from the views of poor people themselves. Box 12.1 contains a selection of quotes from a research project undertaken by the Child Poverty Action Group (Beresford et al., 1999). The aim of this project was to include 'people on low income and with first-hand experience of poverty [who] have had little voice in this discussion'. Indeed, you might wish to consider whether these definitions are of more value than the academic arguments so far considered.

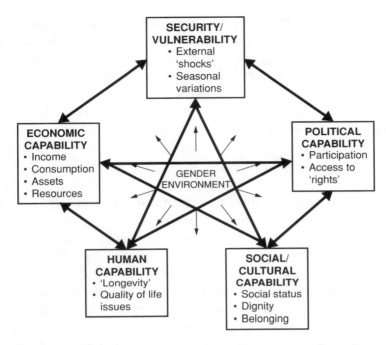

Figure 12.1 *A definition of poverty. Source: adapted from OECD Development Assistance Committee, 2000.*

Box 12.1 People's own definitions of poverty

'When you live week by week you're poor and being poor is just not having enough to pay for what you need for that week, everything that you'll need bills, food, clothes. If you haven't got enough for that then you're poor.' (Lone parents group, Yorkshire)

'Poverty is somebody that's not got a lot of things and there's no hope for them. I mean some people you class as 'poverty stricken' wouldn't see themselves as poverty stricken because they've got enough to get by with and there's always a light at the end of the tunnel, that one of these days it might change. Then there's people that are absolutely poverty stricken, people that are that far down there's no way out. (Group for low income families)

'I would define poverty as not being able to do the things that you want to do in life.' (Group of unemployed people, London)

'Poverty is a state of mind because on the one hand you can have very rich people who still fell [sic] inadequate about themselves, about the fact that they don't have certain things in life and they still feel they're not happy in life, so they still feel poverty of thought, poverty of knowledge and poverty of spirit'. (Mental health service users group)

(Source: Beresford et al., 1999)

Just as there are many definitions of poverty, so there are many different approaches to explaining it. Indeed, Figure 12.1 goes beyond mere definition. As the Development Assistance Committee itself argues, to be an adequate definition 'it should also recognize their causal interrelations. … All the boxes … are necessary in order to take into account the core elements of well-being and poverty as perceived in different societies' (DAC, 2000:13). In the next four sections, we consider these causal factors and interrelations. We first discuss analyses which focus on the individual or community (12.3), and then approaches which understand poverty in terms of wider social or 'structural' processes (12.4–12.6).

12.3 Individual and community explanations of poverty

Individualistic explanations of the causes of poverty concentrate on aspects of particular people rather than wider social processes. There are three main sets of explanations – pathological, genetic, and psychological. From the pathological perspective, poverty is suffered by individuals as a consequence of their own weaknesses or failures, such as indolence or fecklessness. The genetic model relates social status to apparently inherited characteristics such as intelligence, while the psychological model relates poverty to acquired or developed personality traits. In Britain these kinds of approaches have a long ancestry. In the early years of the industrial revolution poverty was said to be 'caused by idleness, by improvidence and insobriety, which were defects which could be overcome by discipline and new attitudes' (Townsend, 1993: 97). Reflecting these views, the 1834 Poor Law was established to attempt to encourage the poor to seek employment rather than be dependent on state support. While many studies (including Booth and Rowntree) have found that such causes play, at the very most, a very minor role in the causes of poverty, a focus on the individual has been persistent.

Other theorizations of poverty have strong similarities to individualistic explanations though they incorporate some social processes. An important example is the theory of the 'culture of poverty' or 'cycle of poverty' developed by Oscar Lewis (1969). Lewis argued that the 'culture' or way of life of the poor, resulting partly from their low incomes, undermines their ability to obtain jobs, and so perpetuates their poverty in a series of vicious circles (Fig. 12.2). We shall see shortly that there is some truth in this idea. However, in focusing solely on social processes *internal* to the communities of poor people themselves, such cycles neglect wider spatial and social processes which make people poor. Like the individualistic theories, the culture of poverty theory implies that poverty is the fault of the poor and should be tackled by policies which are purely internal to poor communities.

The culture of poverty approach has been popular in political discourse. In the 1970s, Sir Keith Joseph, then UK Secretary of State for Health and Social Security, referred to the cycle of deprivation, in which both poverty and deprivation were assumed to pass from generation to generation as a consequence of weaknesses in family mores and conventions. More recently, such ideas have appeared in writing on the 'underclass'

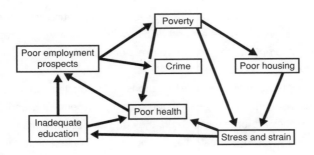

Figure 12.2 *The cycle of poverty. Source: Johnston et al. (2000).*

(W. J. Wilson, 1987; Murray, 1990, 1994): 'multiply deprived individuals – typically members of visible minority groups, and women and children in single-parent families – who experience a form of poverty from which there is virtually no escape' (Harvey, 2000b:863). In using this term, conservative theorists such as Charles Murray have concentrated on individuals as prime causes of their own misfortune, evoking longstanding distinctions between deserving and undeserving poor (for critiques see Townsend, 1993 and Harvey, 2000b).

As Townsend notes, however, 'in the last 20 years in Europe those working within the traditions of neo-Keynesian economic thought, development theory, the sociology of social policy, and feminism, and representatives of pressure groups acting for various social minorities, have been changing the nature of the analysis of poverty' (1993: 99). There has been a focus on social forces which affect everyone and make some people poor. We shall call these 'structural' approaches to analysing poverty. These generally understand poverty to be 'hybrid' and multi-dimensional (section 12.2.3). In the next three sections we examine these approaches, drawing on the earlier chapters of this book. We discuss the role of production organization, employment relations and wages in creating poverty, and the geography of poverty that these create (section 12.4). We then consider how the social life of the poor and the organization of housing and consumer services tend to further deepen poverty, including their effects on the jobs people are able to obtain (section 12.5). Finally, we analyse how these processes are bound up with particular forms of power – of gender, racism, age and disability – which make poverty worse for particular social groups (section 12.6).

12.4 Employment, wages and their geography

Wages and conditions of work are central to the creation of poverty. There are important sections of the poor who are not wage earners or whose current income does not come from wages, such as the unemployed, retired people, and people with disabilities which exclude them from wage work. However, the incomes of retired people are usually strongly related to their wages before retirement, and most state benefits are set at levels which are around or below the lowest wage rates. Wages and the organization of employment are therefore our starting point in considering the origins of poverty.

We saw in Chapter 2 that the social relations of production and their geography create enormous disparities in wages, security of employment, skill, and conditions of work. These disparities are precisely *created*: they do not occur by chance. In particular, poor jobs in the MDCs are created by a number of linked features of capitalist production. Jobs of low skill – which have often been *designed* by employers to have low skill – give workers weak bargaining power since they are easily replaced, and these jobs therefore tend to be low-quality. Moreover, these jobs often have no promotion prospects, as there are no mechanisms for training for higher-skilled work, and so the workers occupying them are often in poor jobs for their whole working lives. In industries where firms compete strongly on the basis of price rather than quality, employers tend to force down wages and force up the intensity of work; this is true in particular of most industries facing competition from lower-wage countries, such as clothing manufacture, and of many consumer service industries, such as catering. These pressures are particularly intense in labour-intensive industries where wages are the main direct cost. In low-skill, cost-competitive and labour-intensive occupations, employers often casualize the workforce, taking on workers at times of strong demand and laying them off when work is slack. Many industries also make use of the 'segmentation' of the labour force (Chapter 2, section 2.7), employing predominantly people from social groups who are constrained in their employment choices; thus industries, occupations and workplaces which employ primarily women, members of ethnic minorities or the young tend to provide inferior jobs (Peck, 1996). These processes mean that there is constant creation and recreation of jobs with low wages, high work intensity, no promotion prospects, long or unsocial hours, and providing casualized and unpredictable periods of work interspersed with unemployment.

These jobs create poverty not only in the low wages they provide but in the wider aspects of poverty discussed in section 12.2. They withhold training and deprive people of economically associated knowledge and culture. The job tasks, intensity and daily hours are often exhausting, leaving little energy for domestic work and for leisure pursuits. Many poor jobs undermine people's health. Daily interactions with management may be demeaning and humiliating, undermining people's self-respect and autonomy.

The system of capitalist production also systematically, though unevenly, creates unemployment, one of the major sources of poverty. During 'long waves of stagnation' such as the present period, rates of unemployment rise (Chapter 2, section 2.9). Moreover, competition between territorial units of production is generally weakly regulated within capitalism, and the units which are relatively uncompetitive therefore tend to suffer from high unemployment. Thus unregulated competition leads to some countries, regions and localities suffering chronically high rates of unemployment.

Shrinkage of employment can occur in sectors with both good and poor jobs. But medium- and long-term unemployment falls most heavily on those with the least skills or the least relevant experience. This is partly because in times of high unemployment those with substantial skills or work experience take jobs of lower skill, pushing the least qualified to the end of the queue; and partly it is because employers usually prefer workers with a steady and recent employment record. Moreover, those who experience long periods of unemployment are likely to occupy the worst and most insecure jobs when they (re-)enter employment. In fact, the employers providing these jobs make use of the pool of unemployed to hold down the conditions of employment. The result is that there is a very large overlap between the social groups and individuals who staff poor jobs and the social groups and individuals who have long periods of unemployment (Rodgers and Rodgers, 1989). The organization of jobs and of unemployment thus reinforce each other in creating poverty.

These processes contribute strongly to the geography of poverty. There is large variation between countries, and between regions and localities within countries, in the composition of employment with regard to wages, skill, security and promotion prospects. This is due to the dynamic interplay between the economic relations internal to territories and the economic flows between them, which produce very spatially uneven outcomes (Chapter 2, section 2.5). These create large differences in job- and unemployment-related poverty; for example, both these elements are larger in the north of England than the south, and larger in Spain than in England (compare Box 2.7, Chapter 2).

The geography of production-associated poverty, then, is constructed by processes at every scale: the relations between employers and workers within workplaces; local, regional and national labour markets; relations between firms and institutions within regions and countries; and flows of production, investment money and commodities at scales from the local to the global. This shows the major omissions in the theories discussed in section 12.3, which attempt to explain poverty by the characteristics of individuals or communities.

Box 12.2 Class and underclass

We can relate the argument so far to the discussion of class in Chapter 2, section 2.4. As noted in the last section, the poor are sometimes described as an 'underclass'. This can imply that they are a group with distinct individual characteristics, an example of 'class as personal attribute'. Alternatively, an 'underclass' can be taken to mean that the poor have completely different relations to the economy than 'ordinary' workers. But the discussion in this section suggests that both these approaches are misleading: unemployment and poor jobs arise from people's relation to *mainstream* processes of the economy. Thus a strongly relational approach to class is needed to explain poverty. *Ordinary* class relations create 'the underclass'.

Employment-associated poverty can be affected by state and other regulation at the national level, and in some countries at the regional level. Thus 'national settlements' (Chapter 2, section 2.7.1) include particular ways of regulating, or failing to regulate, production which can have major impacts on poverty. Wages, conditions of work, job security and unemployment benefits are regulated partly by national agreements between business and trade unions and partly by the nation state. Due partly to these mechanisms, low wages are *less* of a problem in corporatist Japan and social democratic Scandinavia than they are in the economically liberal US and Britain, and the incomes of unemployed people are much higher in Scandinavia than most other MDCs (see Figure 12.3). Moreover, state regulation can influence levels of unemployment over long periods (Therborn, 1986). Note, however, that these national settlements do not come out of thin air: they are created by social conflicts in which the organizations of business and labour are particularly important.

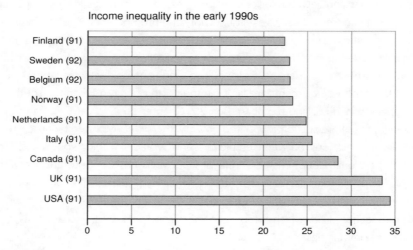

Figure 12.3 *Income inequality in various countries in the early 1990s. Source: adapted from Hills (1998).*

12.5 Social life, residential areas, and the creation of poverty

These geographies of production affect the residential geography of poverty, and the latter in turn can perpetuate and deepen poverty, partly through exacerbating poverty within the residential sphere, and partly by their impact on poor people's access to jobs. We now examine how such interactions between the production and reproduction spheres create poverty. (You might like to look again at the general arguments on their interaction in Chapter 2, sections 2.4–2.6.)

The residential geography of poverty is partly created by the national, regional and local geographies of production already discussed. The great majority of residents across whole regions of MDCs may be poor, producing territorial social life marked by poverty. However, in most regions the economy produces a wide spectrum of incomes; spatial differentiation of poverty then takes place at a smaller scale, that of the locality or the neighbourhood. The main processes constructing these local differences are the interaction of housing markets with people's economic and social resources (see Chapters 4 and 10). The poor tend to be concentrated into particular areas in the first place through their inability to afford either better-quality housing or a better-quality environment. This entrapment may be due not only to a household's income at that moment but to its security over time: people who have difficulty in keeping up rent payments often can access only the worst quality housing; paradoxically, this may be quite expensive, as landlords exploit people's lack of options. Some of the poor become homeless as a result (Dear and Wolch, 1987). Moreover, better-off people often use their influence in local government to ensure that cheap housing, whether private or social, is kept out of better-off neighbourhoods. Poor black people tend to be further concentrated into poor neighbourhoods by the racism of residents in predominantly white areas (see Chapter 5, section 5.3).

Poverty in poor neighbourhoods is further reinforced by the poor quality of their environments and of local services. Low quality of housing harms well-being and health. Poor localities may be badly polluted, whether by proximity to factories or by political decisions on the siting of polluting facilities, such as incinerators or major roads. Private-sector service firms make low investment in poor neighbourhoods; some services may be completely absent, as is increasingly the case with bank branches in Britain (with the effect, amongst other things, of raising the costs and time of paying bills). Paradoxically, this means that poor places often have expensive services since services providers have local monopolies. Utilities are often more expensive – public phones cost more than private, metered power more than billed – and access to the cheaper alternative is often denied people on the basis of their address alone (Speak and Graham, 1999). Public-sector services, such as primary and secondary education and health facilities, are often of lower quality than in better-off neighbourhoods. This is due to complex interactions of factors: the greater demands placed on these services by poor people; poor knowledge about their effective use; and political decisions biased against poor neighbourhoods. Furthermore, in countries such as the US where public services are mainly financed by local taxation, the low tax base of poor localities means low per capita finance and, hence, low quality services. Finally, the rate of crimes of property and violence committed by residents in poor neighbourhoods on others is often high (section 2, Chapter 11). There are, then, usually strong 'neighbourhood effects' in poverty: a person or household of a given income will experience more aspects of poverty when living in a poor neighbourhood or town than if they were somehow able to afford to live in a higher-income residential area (see the example in Figure 12.4a and b).

The nature and impacts of poverty in the residential sphere in turn disadvantage the

Figure 12.4a and b The withdrawal of services, sometimes by multinational corporations, damages lives in poor neighbourhoods. Credit: D. Fuller.

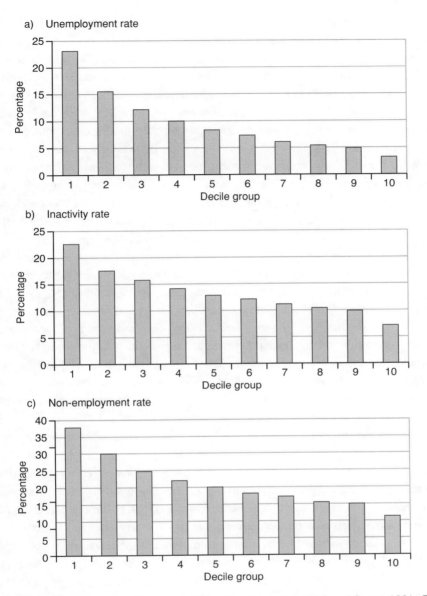

a) Unemployment rate

b) Inactivity rate

c) Non-employment rate

Figure 12.5 *Unemployment, sickness and disability by average income of ward, Britain, 1991. The horizontal axes show decile groups of wards (small neighbourhoods) in Britain ranked by average income. (a) gives the official unemployment rate, (b) those not working due to sickness, and (c) those not working due to disability. Source: adapted from Hills, 1998.*

poor in the labour market. Access to jobs is harmed by poor health, lack of private space within the home, lack of easy access to the telephone, and poor nursery and transport facilities. Children from poor homes and neighbourhoods are likely to end up in poor jobs through lack of resources in the home and poor education. Adults and, especially, young people may pick up attitudes to work such as low expectations, low commitment, and indifference to acquiring new skills; while these attitudes are rationally based on the experience of their families and neighbours, they produce further disadvantage in the labour market. Employers' attitudes to the labour of the poor exacerbate these problems. Many firms discriminate against people with addresses in poor areas, questioning not only their skills but their work discipline and honesty (Mee, 1994). On the other hand, firms using low-paid and casualized labour sometimes deliberately locate in a poor locality or residential area to tap its captive workforce, thereby further reinforcing the population's pattern of inferior employment (Waldinger, 1986).

Can geographical mobility help poor people to escape from these constraints of poor residential areas? Norman Tebbit, a British government minister in the 1980s, notoriously claimed that the solution to unemployment and poverty was for people to 'get on their bikes'. But the geographical differentiation of residential areas can prevent poor people having access to areas where jobs are plentiful. Within cities and regions, public transport is often inadequate and too expensive for people living in poor neighbourhoods to commute to the main employment districts. Migration from regions of high unemployment to growth regions is often impossible for poor people because of housing markets: private renting or ownership tend to be far more expensive in the better-off regions, and social housing in them falls short of demand. Once again, we see the impact of the residential sphere on the labour market, once again to the detriment of the poor.

These social roots of poverty may also be affected by national or regional settlements. The latter can strongly affect the provision of social housing, spending on public services, the spatial distribution and forms of public services, and local government land use and zoning policies, which all impact on poverty. Territorial regimes can also directly affect the access of poor people to jobs, via the form and funding of training programmes, equal opportunities legislation, the segmentation or opening up of jobs by business–union agreements, and government steering of the location of jobs. Thus poverty is influenced by territorial settlements not only through the latter's economic aspects, as we saw in the last section, but also through their social aspects.

Poverty varies not only over space but also over time. The last 30 years or so in the MDCs have seen a slow-down of the economy and the widespread adoption of neoliberal strategies by business and governments (see Chapter 2, section 2.9). The result has been an increase in relative, and in some cases absolute, poverty in most of the MDCs: in Britain, for example, the proportion of households living in poverty increased from 14 per cent in 1983 to 24 per cent in 1999; in the latter year 14.5 million people were too poor to afford some essentials, and 4 million were underfed (Gordon *et al.*,

2000). Unemployment levels in the MDCs have increased. Especially in the lowest-level jobs, wages have been held down, contracts have been casualized, and the protection afforded by trade unions has been weakened. Benefits and pensions have stagnated or been reduced, and criteria for unemployment benefits have been increasingly used to force people into poor jobs (see Fig. 12.6). Reductions in spending on public services, and increasing charges for many of them, have especially hit the poor. As public services and urban policies have become increasingly fragmented and made to compete with each other, the poorest areas have often been the losers. The poor have been forced to rely increasingly on their own resources, making people more dependent on family, friends and neighbours. Thus, paradoxically, the strategy of neoliberalism, which accentuates worldwide economic flows, has resulted in poor people becoming increasingly dependent on the smallest spatial scales of the home and neighbourhood.

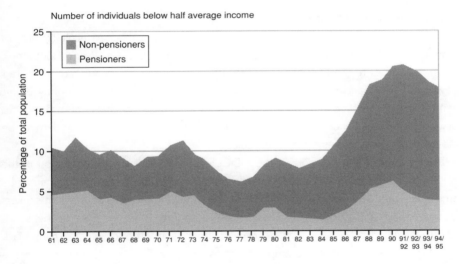

Figure 12.6 *Number of people on low incomes in Britain, 1961–95. Source: adapted from Hills (1998).*

We can see, then, that there is a germ of truth in the culture of poverty theory: the social life of poor residential areas does deepen poverty. But we need to look much more widely to get a full picture of the processes involved. *Actors* other than the poor themselves, and more powerful than them, are deeply involved: employers, better-off residents, national and local governments, and the elites who have pushed forward neoliberal restructuring. And *spatial scales* larger than neighbourhood are central: the organization of housing, services and transport across the locality and region, the decisions of business at all spatial scales, regional and national regulation, and the global strategy of neoliberalism. The implication is that poverty cannot be solved merely by the poor 'pulling themselves up by their own bootstraps', whether individually or in communities. In section 12.7, however, we shall see that the poor can improve their situation through other strategies.

12.6 Poverty and social oppression

In analysing the causes of poverty to this point we have concentrated on class processes. But poverty is constructed also by other forms of social power considered in Part II of the book – gender, racism, age and disability; in this section we consider their role. These forms of social power operate through the structures already considered – employment, the home, neighbourhoods, public services and the state – so that there are strong links with the processes already discussed. But within these fields and spaces, different forms of oppression operate in distinct ways, which we consider in turn.

12.6.1 Poverty and racism

Research on the links between poverty and race is often made difficult by lack of empirical data. In Britain the 1991 census was the first to include a question about ethnic origin, in contrast to the US where both debate and data on poverty and race are better developed. The paucity of official information is partly due to the fear among ethnic minority groups that it could be used to threaten the immigration status of respondents, or used as general 'evidence' for racism (Alcock, 1997:151). Thus the very thing to be researched, racism, makes research difficult.

The poverty of black people in the MDCs is due primarily to their position in the labour market (Jones, 1993). This is constructed partly by direct discrimination by employers, partly by hostility from white workers. Illegal immigrants and asylum-seekers are particularly badly exploited. The residential sphere, however, also deepens this labour market disadvantage. The poverty of the neighbourhoods where many black people live produces barriers to employment, as we saw in the previous section. In some ethnic minority communities, gender relations in the home and community prevent women taking up wage work, or confine them to very low-paid work within the home or community. Poverty in the sense of exclusion from aspects and sites of social life, is enforced on many black people by racism experienced in most public spaces, whether streets, leisure spaces, or private and public services (Amin and Oppenheim, 1992).

12.6.2 Poverty and gender

The conception of poverty adopted by the OECD Development Assistance Committee considered earlier (Fig. 12.1) has gender at its centre. This highlights the fact that, on a global scale, men and women experience poverty differently. Women outnumber men both in terms of being in poverty and the extent of that poverty. Women in poor households receive a lower share of private consumption and public service provision than males, are less likely to have access to security-providing assets than men, and lack time for rest and social interaction. While there are important differences between LDCs and MDCs in gender inequality, the inequalities just mentioned are true of the MDCs. Lewis and Piachaud (1992), for example, have shown that they have been a feature of British society throughout the twentieth century.

This gender difference has, however, been rendered invisible by how poverty has been measured (Millar and Glendinning, 1989; Glendinning and Millar, 1992). Many indicators of poverty have used measures of income for households and assumed that all members are equal recipients of its income, ignoring issues of control over resources within the household. This research 'has ignored, and in practice concealed, the gendered experience of poverty and the different circumstances in which women are poor and deprived' (Alcock, 1997:137). However, recent research has focused on the creation of poverty by gender relations and the 'feminization' of poverty.

Women are far more likely than men to receive low incomes from waged work, due to occupational segregation into low-paid and casualized jobs, and to limitations on hours worked and commuting distances arising from their work within the home (Pillinger, 1992). Women's poverty also directly arises from policies on social security and welfare services (Oppenheim and Harker, 1996). Caring work within the home and neighbourhood, for which women are expected to take the major responsibility, is far more arduous for poor women, due to having less private space and durable appliances, less access to transport, inability to pay for child care, and the use of inferior private and public services. As a result, caring work for poor women takes longer and is more spatially constrained. This then places particularly sharp constraints on poor women's participation in other activities and spaces (Speak, 2000). These forms of female poverty, each involving geographical processes, reinforce each other.

12.6.3 Poverty and age

In contrast to the lack of attention paid to poverty and gender, analysis of poverty and age has a long heritage. Both Booth's and Rowntree's early work highlighted how the experience of poverty varied over the life course. Rowntree identified three main phases of the life-cycle during which the risk of poverty was high, namely childhood, parenthood and old age, the latter also highlighted by Booth. These patterns have been found in more recent studies by Townsend (1979) and Walker (1993). While Chapter 7 notes that older people are often portrayed in terms of the 'huge financial burdens' they impose on the welfare state and wage earners, a burden now often said to constitute a 'crisis', older people themselves have long experienced a crisis of poverty.

Many older people receive their entire income from state pensions and benefits. These are typically set at around official poverty levels; in countries such as Britain their value has been reduced under neoliberal policies (see section 12.4). Private and occupational pensions are very unevenly spread, and savings accumulated over decades can be quickly eroded in times of need or through inflation (Alcock, 1997). Many older people have particular need for high-quality public services; these, too, have been eroded by neoliberal policies, and location in poor neighbourhoods tends to further lower the quality of these services. The daily mobility of some older people is limited by combinations of disability and low income, with consequent impoverishing of their social lives. The house is thus often the dominant space for some groups of older people (see section 7.3.2 of Chapter 7), and this is often made poor by inability to afford adequate space, repairs, heating and home appliances (Wheeler, 1986). Thus for older people too, geographical–social processes are central to creating poverty.

12.6.4 Poverty and disability

'Poverty is disability's close companion' (Groves, 1988:17). In a global context Beresford (1996: 553) notes:

> By all definitions of poverty, disabled people are grossly over-represented among poor people. This is true for all groups who are disabled, including people with physical and sensory impairments, people with learning difficulties and where included, people labelled as mentally ill. They experience levels of economic and social deprivation rarely encountered by other sections of the population.

Over 60 per cent of disabled people in Britain and the US live below the official poverty line (New Internationalist, 1992, cited in Beresford, 1996; see also Martin, Melzer and Elliott, 1988; Berthoud, Lakey and McKay, 1993). These high poverty levels are partly due to discrimination in employment against people with disability, and their consequent high dependence on state benefits. Many disabled people require care by another person, who is often a family member, and many carers are themselves severely restricted in the labour market and consequently have low levels of income (Baldwin and Parker, 1991). Disability also raises the costs of many activities and of transport to them, often due to disabling built environments (see Chapter 8). The specific causes of poverty for people with disabilities, then, like those for the other groups discussed in this section, also involve space.

Three general points on poverty and social oppression can be made in conclusion. Firstly, as with class processes, the scales at which social oppression causes poverty are extremely varied. For example, the global division of labour between North and South has had a major role in the poverty of black people in the MDCs, while, at the other extreme, the poverty of many women and people with disabilities is constructed strongly at the scale of homes, neighbourhoods and localities. Secondly, processes at different spatial scales interact with each other. The role of nursery provision (or lack of it) in creating women's poverty is constructed partly through gender divisions within the home, partly in neighbourhood child care arrangements, partly in patterns of women's commuting, and partly in actions of local and national governments. Thirdly, while these geographical scales are important, they have significance only in relation to social processes, in particular the forms of social oppression. Indeed, we hope that the last

neighbourhoods, especially those located close to central business districts of big cities, have resisted redevelopment of their areas for commercial purposes and the consequent destruction of their communities (Ambrose and Colenutt, 1975). Residents in many poor communities have also organized to combat crime. Neighbourhoods, then, are not only sites where poverty is created and deepened, but also spaces within which people find the solidarity to fight against it. For example, Figure 12.7 shows protest banners in the Scotswood neighbourhood in Newcastle-upon-Tyne, England. In 2000 the city council in Newcastle proposed to demolish 6,000 houses, most of them occupied, in poor neighbourhoods of the city in order to provide green space and, particularly, large sites for higher-income housing development by private developers. The council claimed that the introduction of middle-class residents would be the only way to reverse social decline, but this strategy has been vigorously opposed by residents' organizations. Box 4.2 in Chapter 4 gives more details about this strategy.

Figure 12.7 *Protest in a poor neighbourhood. Credit: D. Fuller.*

The oppressed groups discussed in section 6 have played especially prominent roles in this resistance. Women tend to play the major role in the organization of poor neighbourhoods, since, due to traditional gender roles and men's neglect they take responsibility for the community's living conditions and social life (Campbell, 1993). Black and ethnic minority organizations have also played particularly strong roles, particularly in neighbourhoods where they form a high proportion of residents and hence draw on local networks (see, for example, the Black Environmental Network, 1998).

The geography of this political organization of the poor is complex (Smith, 1993). Poverty itself inhibits organizing at large spatial scales because of lack of money and, specifically, access to transport and means of communication. This is another reason why much organization is at the neighbourhood level. While this takes strength from the immediacy of the issues and from bonds of friendship and trust, it is weakened by its particularity: struggles around a particular issue can be repeated around the country at different times with little or no co-operation or synergy between the campaigns. However, in many fields of anti-poverty campaigning there are networks of local groups. These may start by giving advice to local campaigns, but can develop into nationally co-ordinated campaigns, as with the claimants' organizations in France or the association of outer city estates in Britain. On the other hand, campaigns over issues which are the remit of national government, such as benefits, taxation and employment law, can develop from the first at the national level. Finally, in recent years some transnational campaigns of the poor have emerged, such as the Marches for Jobs in the EU. These are to a large extent a response to the similarities between countries in the worsening of poverty by neoliberalism, as well as the implementation of neoliberal measures by the EU itself. Scales of organization against poverty, then, are as varied and as interlinked as the scales of its creation.

12.8 Conclusion

Human geography and other social sciences have much to contribute to the fight against poverty. Social geography can contribute particularly by showing the complex scales and spaces within which poverty is created, and the way in which policies against poverty may be weakened or strengthened by such geographies. We hope that many readers of this book will use their understanding of geography both to help develop state policies against poverty and to support the organizations and struggles of the poor themselves.

Summary

- Poverty has traditionally been conceived in either absolute or relative terms. Recent approaches often take a hybrid approach, and picture poverty as having many dimensions beyond low monetary income. These definitions of poverty are contentious and are used politically.

- Explanations of poverty are diverse. They differ in the aspects of society and the spatial scale focused on. They include individualist, community and structural explanations. We have argued that the latter is the strongest approach.

- Poor-quality jobs play a central role in creating poverty and its geography. These jobs are generated by fundamental features of capitalist economies and class relations.

- Poverty is spatially concentrated in particular residential areas. Social life and public and private services in these areas deepen poverty, and exacerbate the marginalization of poor people in the labour market.

- In addition to class, other forms of social oppression and their operation in space play central roles in creating poverty, particularly racism, gender, age and disability.

- Economic, social, cultural and political processes at all spatial scales, from the individual and the home to the nation and the world, play roles in creating poverty. Processes within places where poverty is concentrated play a role in deepening it. But poverty is not generated by geography in itself, but by processes which are simultaneously geographical and social.

- Varied groups of the poor organize against diverse aspects of poverty. These organizations use place-specific social networks, but also organize across large scale spaces.

Further reading

The following two publications give overviews of geographies of poverty:

- Leyshon, A. (1995) Missing words: whatever happened to the geography of poverty? *Environment and Planning A* 27, 1021–8.

- Philo, C. (2000) Poverty. In Johnston, R.J. *et al.*, *Dictionary of Human Geography*, 4th edn. Oxford: Blackwell, pp. 627–9.

For examples of different approaches to poverty definition and explanation, and its manifestation in different environments, see:

- Philo, C. (1995) *Off the Map: The Social Geography of Poverty in the UK*. London: Child Poverty Action Group.

- Merrifield, A. and Swyngedouw, E. (1996) (eds) *The Urbanization of Injustice*. London: Lawrence & Wishart.

- Kodras, J. E. (1997) The changing map of American poverty in an era of economic restructuring and political realignment. *Economic Geography* 73, 67–95.

- Pacione, M. (ed.) (1997) *Britain's Cities*. London: Routledge.

References

Abel-Smith, B. and Townsend, P. (1965) *The Poor and the Poorest*. London: Bell.

Abercrombie, N. and Warde, A. (2000) *Contemporary British society*, 3rd edn. Cambridge: Polity Press.

Adams, W. M. (1996) *Future Nature: A Vision for Conservation*. London: Earthscan.

Adler, S. and Brenner, J. (1992) Gender and space: lesbians and gay men in the city. *International Journal of Urban and Regional Research* 16(1), 24–34.

Adorno, T. W. (1991) *The Culture Industry*. London: Routledge.

Agyeman, J. and Spooner, R. (1997) Ethnicity and the rural environment. In Cloke, P. and Little, J. (eds) *Contested Countryside Cultures: Otherness, Marginalisation and Rurality*. London: Routledge.

Aitchison, C. (1999a) New cultural geographies: the spatiality of leisure, gender and sexuality. *Leisure Studies* 18(1), 19–39.

Aitchison, C. (1999b) Heritage and nationalism: gender and the performance of power. In Crouch, D. (ed.) *Leisure/Tourism Geographies*. London: Routledge.

Alcock, P. (1997) *Understanding poverty*. 2nd edn. London: Macmillan.

Allen, J. and Hamnett, C. (eds) (1991) *Housing and Labour Markets*. London: Unwin Hyman.

Allen, J., Massey, D. and Cochrane, A. (1997) *Rethinking the Region: Spaces of Neo-Liberalism*. London: Routledge.

Ambrose, P. and Colenutt, B. (1975) *The Property Machine*. Harmondsworth: Penguin.

Amin, K. and Oppenheim, C. (1992) *Poverty in Black and White: Deprivation and Ethnic Minorities*. London: Child Poverty Action Group.

Anderson, B. (1991) *Imagined Communities: Reflections on the Origins and Spread of Nationalism*. London: Verso.

Anderson, K. (1991) *Vancouver's Chinatown: Racial Discourse in Canada, 1875–1980*. Montreal: McGill-Queens University Press.

Anderson, S. (1998) *Older People, Crime and Crime Prevention*. Edinburgh: Age Concern.

Anderson, S., Kinsey, R., Loader, I. and Smith, C. (1990) *Cautionary Tales: A Study of Young People and Crime in Edinburgh*. Edinburgh: University of Edinburgh.

Andersson, R. (1998) Socio-spatial dynamics: ethnic divisions of mobility and housing in post-Palme Sweden. *Urban Studies* 35, 397–428.

Arber, S. and Ginn, J. (eds) (1995) *Connecting Gender and Ageing: A Sociological Approach*. Buckingham: Open University Press.

Arnup, K., Levesque, A. and Pierson, R. (eds) (1990) *Delivering Motherhood: Maternal Ideologies and Practices in the Nineteenth and Twentieth Centuries*. London: Routledge.

Atkins, P., Simmons, I. and Roberts, B. (1998) *People, Land and Time: An Historical*

Introduction to the Relations between Landscape, Culture and Environment. London: Arnold.

Atkins, S., Husain, S. and Storey, A. (1991) *The Influence of Street Lighting on Crime and the Fear of Crime.* Crime Prevention Unit Paper 29. London: Home Office.

Bailey, R. (1997) DIY for the homeless. In Goodwin, J. and Grant, C. (eds) *Built to Last: Reflections on British Housing Policy.* London: Roof Magazine.

Baker, A. W. and Duncan, S. P. (1985) Child sexual abuse: a study of prevalence in Great Britain. *Child Abuse and Neglect* 9, 453–67.

Balchin, P. (1995) *Housing Policy: An Introduction.* London: Routledge.

Baldwin, J. (1975) Urban criminality and the 'problem' estate. *Local Government Studies* 1, 12–20.

Baldwin, J. and Bottoms, A. E. (1976) *The Urban Criminal.* London: Tavistock.

Baldwin, S. and Parker, G. (1991) Support for informal carers – the role of social security. In Dalley, G. (ed.) *Disability and Social Policy.* London: Policy Studies Institute.

Bank of England (1992) Negative equity in the housing market. *Bank of England Quarterly Bulletin* 32, 266–8.

Barke, M. (1997) The 'right to buy' revisited: an empirical assessment in the Tyne & Wear area. *Northern Economic Review* 26, 63–85.

Barke, M. and Turnbull, G. (1992) *Meadowell: The Biography of an 'Estate with Problems'.* Aldershot: Avebury.

Barker, G. (1996) Alien and native – drawing the line. *ECOS* 17(2), 18–26.

Barnes, C. (1991) *Disabled People in Britain and Discrimination: A Case for Anti-Discrimination.* Hurst & Co. in association with the British Council of Organizations of Disabled People.

Barnes, C. (1996) Theories of disability and the origins of the oppression of disabled people in western society. In Barton, L. (ed.) *Disability and Society: Emerging Issues and Insights.* Harlow: Longman.

Barrett, G. A., Jones, T. P. and McEvoy, D. (1996) Ethnic minority business: theoretical discourse in Britain and North America. *Urban Studies* 33, 783–809.

Barrett, M. (1988) *Women's Oppression Today.* London: Verso.

Barton, L. (ed.) (1996) *Disability and Society: Emerging Issues and Insights.* London: Longman.

Bartram. R. and Shobrook, S. (1998) You have to be twice as good to be equal: 'placing' women in Plymouth's Devonport Dockyard. *Area* 30(1), 59–65.

Beauvoir, S. de (1972) *The Second Sex.* Harmondsworth: Penguin.

Belcove-Shalin, J. (1988) Becoming more of an Eskimo: fieldwork among the Hasidim of New York. In Kugelmass, J. (ed.) *Between Two Worlds: Ethnographic Essays on American Jewry.* Ithaca, New York: Cornell University Press.

Bell, D. (1991) Insignificant others: lesbian and gay geographies. *Area* 23(4), 323–9.

Bell, D. (1994) Bi-sexuality – a place on the margins. In Whittle, S. (ed.) *The Margins of the City.* Aldershot: Ashgate.

Bell, D. and Valentine, G. (1995) Queer country: rural lesbian and gay lives. *Journal of Rural Studies* 11(3), 113–22.

Benson, J. and Roe, M. (eds) (2000) *Urban Lifestyles: Spaces, Places, People, Proceedings of an International Conference.* Rotterdam: Balkema.

Beresford, P. (1996) Poverty and disabled people: challenging dominant debates and policies. *Disability and Society* 11(4), 553–67.

Beresford, P., Green, D., Lister, R., and Woodard, K. (1999) *Poverty Firsthand: Poor People Speak for Themselves*. London: Child Poverty Action Group.

Berry, W. and Jones, H. (1995) Investigating spatial patterns of crime through police statistics, crime surveys and census profiles: findings from Dundee housing estates. *Scottish Geographical Magazine* 111(2), 76–82.

Berthoud, R., Lakey, J. and Mckay, S. (1993) *The Economic Problems of Disabled People*. London: Policy Studies Institute.

Beynon, H., Lewis, J., Sadler, D. and Townsend, A. (1989) 'It's all falling apart here': coming to terms with the future in Teesside. In Cooke, P. (ed.) *Localities*. London: Unwin Hyman, 267–95.

Bines, W. (1994) *The Health of Single Homeless People*. York: Centre for Housing Policy, University of York.

Binnie, J. (1995) Trading places: consumption, sexuality and the production of queer space. In Bell, D. and Valentine, G. (eds) *Mapping Desire*. London: Routledge.

Binnie, J. and Valentine, G. (1999) Geographies of sexuality – a review of progress. *Progress in Human Geography* 23(2), 175–87.

Black Environmental Network (1998) *Ethnic Environmental Participation*, Vol. 1. Llanberis: Black Environment Network.

Blackman, S. J. (1998) Poxy cupid! An ethnographic and feminist account of a resistant female youth culture: the New Wave Girls. In Skelton, T. and Valentine, G. (eds) *Cool Places: Geographies of Youth Cultures*. London: Routledge.

Blasius, M. and Phelan, S. (1997) *We are Everywhere: A Historical Sourcebook of Gay and Lesbian Politics*. London: Routledge.

Blunt, A. and Wills, J. (2000) *Dissident Geographies*. London: Prentice Hall.

Boal, F. W. (1969) Territoriality on the Shankill–Falls divide, Belfast. *Irish Geography* V, 30–50.

Boal, F. W. (1982) Segregating and mixing: space and residence in Belfast. In Boal, F. W. and Douglas, J. N. H. (eds) *Integration and Division: Geographical Perspectives on the Northern Ireland Problem*. London and New York: Academic Press.

Boal, F. W. (1996) Integration and division: sharing and segregating in Belfast. *Planning Practice and Research* 11, 151–58.

Bond, J., Coleman, P. and Peace, S. (eds) (1993) *Ageing in Society: An Introduction to Social Gerontology*, 2nd edn. London: Sage.

Bondi, L. (1991) Gender divisions and gentrification. *Transactions of the Institute of British Geographers; New Series* 16, 190–8.

Bondi, L. (1992) Gender symbols and urban landscapes. *Progress in Human Geography* 16 (2), 157–70.

Bondi, L. (1998) Sexing the city. In Fincher, R. and Jacobs, J. (eds) *Cities of Difference*. New York: Guilford Press.

Bondi, L. (1999) Gender, class and gentrification: enriching the debate. *Environment and Planning D: Society and Space* 17, 261–82.

Bondi, L. and Peake, L. (1988) Gender and the city: urban politics revisited. In Little, J., Peake, L. and Richardson, P. (eds) *Women in Cities: Gender and the Urban Environment*. London: Macmillan.

Bonnett, A. (2000) *White Identities*. Harlow: Prentice Hall.

Booth, C. (1889) *The Life and Labour of the People*. London: Williams & Northgate.

Booth, C. (1892) *Pauperism: A Picture of the Endowment of Old Age: An Argument*. London: Macmillan.

Booth, C. (1894) *The Aged Poor: Condition*. London: Macmillan.

Bottoms, A. E. and Wiles, P. (1997) 'Environmental criminology'. In Maguire, M., Morgan, R. and Reiner, R. (eds) *The Oxford Handbook of Criminology*. Oxford: Clarendon Press.

Bourdieu, P. (1979) *Distinction: A Social Critique of the Judgement of Taste*. London: Routledge & Kegan Paul.

Bowles, S. and Gintis, H. (1976) *Schooling in Capitalist America*. New York: Basic Books.

Brantingham, P. J. and Brantingham, P. L. (1975) Residential burglary and urban form. *Urban Studies* 12, 273–84.

Brown, S. (1995) Crime and safety in whose 'community'? Age, everyday life, and problems for youth policy. *Youth and Policy* 48, 27–48.

Brownill, S. (1994) Selling the inner city: regeneration and place marketing in London's Docklands. In Gold, J. R. and Ward, S. V. (eds) *Place Promotion: The Use of Publicity and Marketing to Sell Towns and Regions*. Chichester: John Wiley.

Brunhes, J. (1920) *Human Geography: An Attempt at a Positive Classification – Principles and Examples*. London: George G. Harrap.

Bryden, J. and Watson, D. (1995) *Community Involvement and Rural Policy*. Edinburgh: Report to the Scottish Office.

Buckser, A. (2000) Jewish identity and the meaning of community in contemporary Denmark. *Ethnic and Racial Studies* 23, 712–34.

Bulmer, M. (1986) *Neighbours: The Work of Philip Abrams*. Cambridge: Cambridge University Press.

Bunce, M. (1994) *The Countryside Ideal: Anglo-American Images of Landscape*. London: Routledge.

Bunge, W. (1973) The point of reproduction: a second front. *Antipode* 9, 60–76.

Burt, M. R. and Estep, R. E. (1981) Apprehension and fear: learning a sense of sexual vulnerability. *Sex Roles* 7(5), 511–22.

Butler, R. (1998) Rehabilitating the images of disabled youths. In Skelton, T. and Valentine, G. (eds) *Cool Places: Geographies of Youth Cultures*. London: Routledge.

Butler, R. and Parr, H. (eds) (1999) *Mind and Body Spaces: Geographies of Disability, Illness and Impairment*. London: Routledge.

Byrne, D. (1998) Class and ethnicity in complex cities – the cases of Leicester and Bradford. *Environment and Planning A* 30, 703–20.

Byrne, D. (1999) *Social Exclusion*. Buckingham: Open University Press.

Bytheway, B. (1995) *Ageism*. Buckingham: Open University Press.

Campbell, B. (1993) *Goliath: Britain's Dangerous Places*. London: Methuen.

Carson, R. (1962) *Silent Spring*. Harmondsworth: Penguin.

Castles, S. and Kosack, G. (1973) *Immigrant Workers and the Class Structure*. London: Oxford University Press.

Chouinard, V. and Grant, A. (1995) On being not anywhere near 'The Project': ways of putting ourselves in the picture. *Antipode* 27(2), 137–66.

Chouinard, V. (1997) Making space for disabling difference: challenging ableist geographies. *Environment and Planning D: Society and Space* 15, 379–87.

Christopherson, S. (1993) Market rules and territorial outcomes: the case of the US. *International Journal of Urban and Regional Research* 17, 272–84.

Christopherson, S. (1994) The fortress city: privatised spaces, consumer citizenship. In Amin, A. (ed.) *Post-Fordism: A Reader*. Oxford: Blackwell.

Clapham, D. (1997) A woman of her time. In Goodwin, J. and Grant, C. (eds) *Built to Last: Reflections on British Housing Policy*. London: Roof Magazine.

Clapham, D. and Smith, S. J. (1990) Housing policy and 'special needs'. *Policy and Politics* 18, 193–205.

Clarke, D. B. and Bradford, M. G. (1998) Public and private consumption and the city. *Urban Studies* 35, 865–88.

Clarke, J. and Critcher, C. (1985) *The Devil Makes Work: Leisure in Capitalist Britain*. London: Macmillan.

Clarke, R. V. (ed.) (1992) *Situational Crime Prevention: Successful Case Studies*. New York: Harrow & Heston.

Cloke, P. (1997) Poor country: marginalization, poverty and rurality. In Cloke, P. and Little, J. (eds) *Contested Countryside Cultures: Otherness, Marginalization and Rurality*. London: Routledge.

Cloke, P., Phillips, M. and Thrift, N. (1995) The new middle classes and the social constructs of rural living. In Butler, T. and Savage, M. (eds) *Social Change and the Middle Classes*. London: UCL Press.

Cloke, P. and Little, J. (eds) (1997) *Contested Countryside Cultures: Otherness, Marginalization and Rurality*. London: Routledge.

Cloonan, M. (1996) *Banned! Censorship of Popular Music in Britain: 1967–92*. Aldershot: Arena.

Cochrane, A. (1993) *Whatever Happened to Local Government?* Buckingham: Open University Press.

Cocks, E. and Cockram, J. (1995) The participatory research paradigm and intellectual disability. *Mental Handicap Research* 8, 25–37.

Cohen, A. (1985) *The Symbolic Construction of Community*. London: Tavistock.

Coleman, A. (1985) *Utopia on Trial*. London: Hilary Shipman.

Cone, J. (1990) *A Black Theology of Liberation*. New York: Orbis.

Connell, R. W. (1995) *Masculinities*. Berkeley: University of California Press.

Cox, G. and Winter, M. (1997) The beleaguered 'other': hunt followers in the countryside. In Milbourne, P. (ed.) *Revealing Rural 'Others': Representation, Power and Identity in the British Countryside*. London: Pinter.

Cox, K. (1993) The local and the global in the new urban politics: a critical view. *Environment and Planning D: Society and Space* 11, 433–48.

Cox, K. (1998) Spaces of dependence, spaces of engagement and the politics of scale; or, looking for local politics. *Political Geography* 17(1), 1–24.

Crouch, D. (ed.) (1999) *Leisure/Tourism Geographies*. London: Routledge.

Cumming, E. and Henry, W. (1961) *Growing Old: The Process of Disengagement*. New York: Basic Books.

Cunningham, H. (1980) *Leisure and the Industrial Revolution*. London: Croom Helm.

Dalley, G. (ed.) (1991) *Disability and Social Policy*. London: Policy Studies.

Daunton, M. J. (1983) House and Home in the Victorian City. London: Edward Arnold.

Davidson, R. N. (1981) *Crime and Environment*. London: Croom Helm.

Davis, M. (1990) *City of Quartz*. London: Verso

Davis, M. (1992) *Beyond Blade Runner Urban Control: The Ecology of Fear*. Westfield, NJ: Open Magazine Pamphlet Series.

Day, G. and Murdoch, J. (1993) Locality and community: coming to terms with place. *Sociological Review* 41, 82–111.

Deakin, N. and Edwards, J. (1993) *The Enterprise Culture and the Inner City*. London: Routledge.

Dear, M. and Scott, A. (eds) (1981) *Urbanization and Urban Planning in Capitalist Society*. London: Methuen.

Dear, M. and Wolch, J. (1987) *Landscapes of Despair: From Deindustrialisation to Homelessness*. Oxford: Polity Press.

Deem, R. (1982) Women, leisure and inequality. *Leisure Studies* 1(1), 29–46.

Department of Social Security (1998) *A New Contract for Welfare: Support for Disabled People*. Consultation paper CM4103, October.

Department of Social Security (2000) *Disability Care and Mobility Benefits – February 2000 Quarterly Statistical Enquiry*. Press Release No. 00/214, 27 July.

Development Assistance Committee (2000) *DAC Guidelines on Poverty Reduction*, Volume 1 (Draft: June 2000). OECD: Development Assistance Committee.

Dicken, P. (1998) *Global Shift*, 3rd edn. London: Paul Chapman.

Dickens, P. (1996) *Reconstructing Nature: Alienation, Emancipation and the Division of Labour*. London: Routledge.

Dickens, P. (1997) Local environments, the division of labour and alienation from nature. *Local Environment* 2(1), 83–7.

Dixey, R. (1988) Eyes Down: a study of Bingo. In Wimbush, E. and Talbot, M. (eds) *Relative Freedoms*. Milton Keynes: Open University Press.

Dorling, D. and Cornford, J. (1995) Who has negative equity? How house price falls in Britain have hit different groups of home buyers. *Housing Studies* 10, 151–78.

Driver, P. (1992) Geography's Empire: histories of geographical empire. *Environment and Planning D: Society and Space* 10, 23–40.

Dumayne-Peaty, L. and Wellens, J. (1998) Gender and physical geography in the United Kingdom. *Area* 30(3), 197–205.

Duncan, C. J. (1997) Victimisation beyond the metropolis: an Australian case study. *Area* 29(2), 119–28.

Duncan, J. S. (1981) *Housing and Identity*. London: Croom Helm.

Duncan, N. (1996) Renegotiating gender and sexuality in public and private spaces. In Duncan, N. (ed.) *Bodyspace: Destabilizing Geographies of Gender and Sexuality*. London: Routledge.

Duncan, O. D. and Duncan, B. (1957) *The Negro Population of Chicago*. Chicago: Chicago University Press.

Duncan, S. (1991) The geography of gender divisions of labour in Britain. *Institute of British Geographers Transactions* 16, 420–39.

Duncan, S. (1994) Theorising differences in patriarchy. *Environment and Planning A*. 26, 1177–95.

Duncan, S. S. and Rowe, A. (1993) Self-provided housing: the First World's hidden housing arm. *Urban Studies* 30, 1331–54.

Dwyer, C. (1998) Contested identities: challenging dominant representations of young British Muslim women. In Skelton, T. and Valentine, G. (eds) *Cool Places: Geographies of Youth Cultures*. London: Routledge, 50–65.

Dyck, I. (1995) Hidden geographies: the changing lifeworlds of women with disabilities. *Social Science and Medicine* 40, 307–20.

Easterbrook, G. (1995) *A Moment on the Earth: The Coming Age of Environmental Optimism*. New York: Penguin.

Eisenschitz, A. and Gough, J. (1993) *The Politics of Local Economic Policy*. Basingstoke: Macmillan.

Esping-Andersen, G. (1990) *Three Worlds of Welfare Capitalism*. Cambridge: Polity Press.

Evans, D. and Oulds, G. (1984) Geographical aspects of the incidence of residential burglary in Newcastle under Lyme, UK. *Tijdschrift voor Economische en Sociale Geografie* 75, 344–55.

Evans, K., Fraser, P. and Walklate, S. (1996) Whom can you trust? The politics of 'grassing' on an inner–city housing estate. *Sociological Review* 44(3), 359–80.

Eyles, J. (1987) Housing advertisements as signs: locality creation and meaning-systems. *Geografiska Annaler* 69B, 93–105.

Eyles, J. (1988) Mental health services, the restructuring of care, and the fiscal crisis of the state: the United Kingdom case study. In Smith, C. J. and Giggs, J. A. (eds) *Location and Stigma: Contemporary Perspectives on Mental Health and Mental Health Care*. Boston: Unwin Hyman.

Fainstein, S., Gordon, I. and Harloe, M. (1992) *Divided Cities: New York and London in the Contemporary World*. Oxford: Blackwell.

Falk, I. and Kilpatrick, S. (2000) What is social capital? A study of interaction in a rural community. *Sociologia Ruralis* 40(1), 87–110.

Family Policy Studies Centre (1992) *Understanding Poverty: A Guide to the Concepts and Measures*. London: Family Policy Studies Centre.

Fasenfest, D. (ed.) (1993) *Community Economic Development: Policy Formation in the US and UK*. Basingstoke: Macmillan.

Featherstone, M. and Hepworth, M. (1989) Ageing and old age: reflections on the postmodern life course. In Bytheway, B., Keil, T., Allatt, P. and Bryman, A. (eds) *Becoming and Being Old: Sociological Approaches to Later Life*. London: Sage.

Finkelstein, V. (1980) *Attitudes and Disabled People: Issues for Discussion*. New York: World Rehabilitation Fund.

Fitzpatrick, S. (1998) Homelessness in the European Union. In Kleinman, M., Matznetter, W. and Stephens, M. (eds) *European Integration and Housing Policy*. London: Routledge.

Fitzpatrick, S. and Stephens, M. (1999) Homelessness, need and desert in the allocation of council housing. *Housing Studies* 14, 413–31.

Ford, J. (1999) Home ownership, mortgage possession and homelessness: public policies and private troubles? In Hutson, S. and Clapham, D. (eds) *Homelessness: Public Policies and Private Troubles*. London and New York: Cassell.

Foord, J. and Gregson, N. (1986) Patriarchy: towards and reconceptinalization. *Antipode* 18, 186–211.

Forrest, B. (1995) West Hollywood as a symbol: the significance of place in the construction of a gay identity. *Environment and Planning D: Society and Space* 13, 133-57.

Forrest, R. and Murie, A. (1991) *Selling the Welfare State: The Privatisation of Public Housing*. London: Routledge.

Foster, H. D. (1988) Reducing the incidence of multiple sclerosis. *Environments* 19, 14–34.

Foucault, M. (1984) *The History of Sexuality*. Harmondsworth: Penguin.

Frazier, E. F. (1967) The Negro family in Chicago. In Burgess, E. W. and Bogue, D. J. (eds) *Urban Sociology*. Chicago: Chicago University Press.

Friedman, A. (1977) *Industry and Labour*. Basingstoke: Macmillan.

Friedrichs, J. and Alpheis, H. (1991) Housing segregation of immigrants in West Germany. In Huttman, E. D. (ed.) *Urban Housing Segregation of Minorities in Western Europe and the United States*. Durham and London: Duke University Press.

Frouws, J. (1998) The contested redefinition of the countryside. An analysis of rural discourses in The Netherlands. *Sociologia Ruralis* 38 (1), 54–68.

Fuller, D. and Jonas, A. E. G. (in press): Institutionalising future geographies of financial inclusion: national legitimacy versus local autonomy in the British Credit Union Movement. *Antipode* 33,5.

Gans, H. J. (1962) *The Urban Villagers*. New York: The Free Press.

Garland, D. (1996) The limits of the sovereign state: strategies of crime control in contemporary society. *British Journal of Criminology* 36(4), 445–71.

Genn, H. (1988) Multiple victimisation. In Maguire, M. and Pointing, J. (eds) *Victims of Crime: A New Deal?* Milton Keynes: Open University Press.

Gertler, M. (1997) The invention of regional culture. In Lee, R. and Wills, J. (eds) *Geographies of Economies*. London: Arnold.

Gibson, K. and Watson, S. (eds) (1994) *Metropolis Now*. Leichhardt: Pluto.

Giddens, A. (1991) *Modernity and Self-Identity: Self and Society in the Late Modern Age*. Cambridge: Polity Press.

Giggs, J. A. (1973) The distribution of schizophrenics in Nottingham. *Transactions of the Institute of British Geographers* 59, 55–76.

Gilchrist, E., Bannister, J., Diton, J. and Farrall, S. (1998) Women and the 'fear of crime': challenging the accepted stereotype. *British Journal of Criminology* 38(2), 283–99.

Gilling, D. (1997) *Crime Prevention*. London, UCL Press.

Gittus, E. (1976) *Flats, Families and the Under-Fives*. London: Routledge & Kegan Paul.

Giulianotti, R. and Williams, J. (eds) (1994) *Game without Frontiers: Football, Identity and Modernity*. Aldershot: Arena.

Gleeson, B. (1996) A geography for disabled people? *Transactions of the Institute of British Geographers* 21(2), 387–96.

Gleeson, B. (1999) *Geographies of Disability*. London: Routledge.

Glendinning, C. and Millar, J. (eds) (1992) *Women and Poverty in Britain: The 1990s*. London: Harvester/Wheatsheaf.

Glyptis, S. A. (1989) *Leisure and Unemployment*. Buckingham: Open University Press.

Gold, J. R. and Gold, M. M. (1994) 'Home at last!': building societies, home ownership and the imagery of English suburban promotion in the interwar years. In Gold, J. R. and Ward, S. V. (eds) *Place Promotion. The Use of Publicity and Marketing to Sell Towns and Regions*. Chichester: John Wiley.

Golledge, R. G. (1993) Geography and the disabled: a survey with special reference to vision-impaired and the blind. *Transactions of the Institute of British Geographers* 18(1), 63–85.

Goodey, J. (1997) Boys don't cry: masculinities, fear of crime and fearlessness. *British Journal of Criminology* 37(3), 401–18.

Gordon, D. (1984) Capitalist development and the history of American cities. In Tabb, W. and Sawers, L. (eds) *Marxism and the Metropolis*, 2nd edn. New York: Oxford University Press.

Gordon, D. *et al.* (2000) *Poverty and Social Exclusion in Britain*. York: Joseph Rowntree Foundation.

Gornostaeva, G. and Campbell, N. (1999) Pubs in Docklands: a new stage of exclusion or the globalisation of public spaces. Paper presented at the conference on 'Leisure and Exclusion', Staffordshire University, September 1999.

Gough, I. (1979) *The Political Economy of the Welfare State*. London: Macmillan.

Gough, J. (1992) Workers' competition, class relations and space, *Environment and Planning D: Society and Space* 10, 265–86.

Granovetter, M. and Swedberg, R. (eds) (1992) *The Sociology of Economic Life*. Boulder: Westview Press.

Green, E., Hebron, S. and Woodward, D. (1990) *Women's Leisure, What Leisure?* London: Macmillan.

Gregson, N. and Lowe, M. (1994) *Servicing the Middle Class: Class, Gender and Waged Domestic Labour in Contemporary Britain*. London: Routledge.

Gregson, N. and Lowe, M. (1995) 'Home'-making: on the spatiality of daily social reproduction in contemporary middle-class Britain. *Transactions of the Institute of British Geographers* 20, 224–35.

Grossin, W. (1986) The relationship between work time and free time and the meaning of retirement. *Leisure Studies* 5, 91–101.

Groves, D. (1988) Poverty, disability and social services. In Becker, S. and MacPherson, S. (eds) *Public Issues and Private Pain: Poverty, Social Work and Social Policy*. London: Insight.

Hahn, H. (1988) Can disability be beautiful? *Social Policy* (Winter), 26-32.

Halfacree, K. (1995) Talking about rurality: social representations of the rural as expressed by residents of six English parishes. *Journal of Rural Studies* 11(1), 1–20.

Halford, S. and Savage, M. (1997) Rethinking restructuring: embodiment, agency and identity in organizational change. In Lee, R. and Wills, J. (eds) *Geographies of Economies*. London: Arnold.

Hall, C. M. and Page, S. J. (1998) *The Geography of Tourism and Recreation: Environment, Place and Space*. London: Routledge.

Hall, R. E. (1985) *Ask Any Woman: A London Enquiry into Rape and Sexual Assault*. Bristol: Falling Wall Press.

Hamnett, C. (1973) Improvement grants as an indicator of gentrification in London. *Area* 5, 252–61.

Hamnett, C. (ed.) (1996) *Social Geography: A Reader*. London, Arnold.

Hamnett, C. and Randolph, B. (1986) Tenurial transformations and the flat break-up market in London: the British condo experience. In Smith, N. and Williams, P. (eds) *Gentrification of the City*. Boston, MA: Allen & Unwin.

Hamnett, C. and Randolph, B. (1988) *Cities, Housing and Profits*. London: Hutchinson.

Hamnett, C., Harmer, M. and Williams, P. (1991) *Safe as Houses*. London: Paul Chapman.

Hanbury-Tenison, R. (1997) Life in the countryside. *Geographical Magazine* (November) 89–95.

Hanmer, J. (1978) Male violence and the social control of women. In Littlejohn, G. (ed.) *Power and the State*. London: Croom Helm.

Hanmer, J. and Saunders, S. (1984) *Well-founded Fear: A Community Study of Violence to Women*. London: Hutchinson.

Haraway, D. (1991) *Simians, Cyborgs and Women: The Reinvention of Nature*. London: Routledge.

Harper, S. (1989) The British rural 'community': an overview of perspectives. *Journal of Rural Studies* 5, 161–84.

Harper, S. (1997) Constructing later life/constructing the body: some thoughts from feminist theory. In Jamieson, A., Harper, S. and Victor, C. (eds) *Critical Approaches to Ageing and Later Life*. Buckingham: Open University Press.

Harper, S. and Laws, G. (1995) Rethinking the geography of ageing. *Progress in Human Geography* 19(2), 199–221.

Harris, A., Cox, E and Smith, R. (1971) *Handicapped and Impaired People in Great Britain*. London: HMSO.

Harrison C. M. and Burgess, J. (1994) Social constructions of nature: a case study of conflicts over the development of the Rainham Marshes. *Transactions of the Institute of British Geographers* 19, 291–310.

Harrison, C. M., Burgess, J. and Clark, J. (1998) Discounted knowledges: farmers' and residents' understandings of nature conservation goals and policies. *Journal of Environmental Management* 54, 305–20.

Hart, R. (1979) *Children's Experience of Place*. New York: Irvington.

Harvey, B. (1999) The problem of homelessness: a European perspective. In Hutson, S. and Clapham, D. (eds) *Homelessness: Public Policies and Private Troubles*. London and New York: Cassell.

Harvey, D. (1982) *The Limits to Capital*. Oxford: Blackwell.

Harvey, D. (1989a) *The Urban Experience*. Oxford: Blackwell.

Harvey, D. (1989b) *The Condition of Postmodernity*. Oxford: Blackwell.

Harvey, D. (1996a) *Justice, Nature and the Geography of Difference*. Oxford: Blackwell.

Harvey, D. (1996b) The geography of capitalist accumulation. In Agnew, J., Livingstone, D. and Rogers, A. (eds) *Human Geography: An Essential Anthology*. Oxford: Blackwell.

Harvey, D. (2000a) Ethnicity. In Johnston, R. J. *et al.* (eds) *Dictionary of Human Geography*. Oxford: Blackwell.

Harvey, D. (2000b) Underclass. In Johnston, R. J. *et al.* (eds) *Dictionary of Human Geography*. Oxford: Blackwell.

Hayden, D. (1981) *The Grand Domestic Revolution: A History of Feminist Designs for American Houses, Neighbourhoods and Cities*. Cambridge, MA: MIT Press.

Haywood, L., Kew, F., Bramham, P., Spink, J., Capenhurst, J. and Henry, I. (1995) *Understanding Leisure*. 2nd edn. Cheltenham: Stanley Thornes.

Henley Centre (1993) *Leisure Futures*, Vol 3. London: Henley Centre.

Henley Centre (1994) *Leisure Tracking Survey*. London: Henley Centre.

Herbert, D. (1982) *The Geography of Urban Crime*. London: Longman.

Herbert, D. and Davidson, N. (1994) Modifying the built environment: the impact of improved street lighting. *Geoforum* 25(3), 339–50.

Herbert, D. T. (1975) Urban neighbourhoods and social geographical research. In Phillips, A. D. M. and Turton, B. J. (eds) *Environment, Man and Economic Change*. London: Longman.

Herbert, D. T. and Raine, J. W. (1976) Defining communities within urban areas. *Town Planning Review* 47, 325–38.

Herbert, D. T. and Hyde, S. W. (1985) Environmental criminology: testing some area hypotheses. *Transactions Institute British Geographers* (NS) 10(13), 259–74.

Herbert, D. T. and Darwood, J. (1992) Crime awareness and urban neighbourhoods. In Evans, D. J., Fyfe, N. and Herbert, D. T. (eds) *Crime, Policing and Place: Essays in Environmental Criminology*. London: Routledge.

Herek, G. M. and Berrill, K. T. (1992) *Hate Crimes: Confronting Violence against Lesbians and Gay men*. London: Sage.

Hewison, R. (1987) *The Heritage Industry: Britain in a Climate of Decline*. London: Methuen.

Hey, V. (1986) *Patriarchy and Pub Culture*. London: Tavistock.

Hillery, G. (1955) Definitions of community: areas of agreement. *Rural Sociology* 20, 111–32.

Hillman, M., Adams, J. and Whitelegg, J. (1990) *One False Move: A Study of Children's Independent Mobility*. London: Policy Studies Institute.

Hills, J. and Walker, R. (1996) *New Inequalities: The Changing Distribution of Income and Wealth in the UK*. Cambridge: Cambridge University Press.

Hills, J. (1998) *Income and Wealth: The Latest Evidence*. York: Joseph Rowntree Foundation.

Hinchcliffe, S. (1996) Helping the earth begins at home: the construction of socio-environmental responsibilities. *Global Environmental Change* 6(1), 53–62.

Hindle, P. (1994) Gay communities and gay space in the city. In Whittle, S. (ed.) *The Margins of the City: Gay Men's Urban Lives*. Arena: Aldershot.

Hirschman, C. (1983) America's melting pot reconsidered. *Annual Review of Sociology* 9, 397–423.

Hobbs, D. (1995) *Bad Business: Professional Crime in Modern Britain*. Oxford: Oxford University Press.

Hoggart, K. (1995) The changing geography of council house sales in England and Wales. *Tijdscrift voor Economische en Sociale Geografie* 86, 137–49.

Hoggart, K. (1997) The middle classes in rural England, 1971–1991. *Journal of Rural Studies* 13(3), 253–273.

Holloway, S. L. (1998) 'She lets me go out once a week': mothers' strategies for obtaining personal time and space. *Area* 30 (4), 321–30.

Holloway, S. L. (1999) Reproducing motherhood. In Laurie, N., Dwyer, C., Holloway, S. L. and Smith, F. *Geographies of New Femininities*. Harlow: Longman.

Hollway, W. and Jefferson, T. (1997) The risk society in an age of anxiety: situating fear of crime. *British Journal of Sociology* 48(2), 255–66.

hooks, b. (1991) *Yearning: Race, Gender and Cultural Politics*. London: Turnaround.

Horna, J. (1994) *The Study of Leisure: An Introduction*. London: Oxford University Press.

Hough, M. and Mayhew, P. (1983) *British Crime Survey: First Report*. London: HMSO.

Hudson, R. and Williams, A. (1995) *Divided Britain*, 2nd edn. Chichester: John Wiley.

Hunt, G. and Satterlee, S. (1987) Darts, drink and the pub: the culture of female drinking. *Sociological Review* (August), 575–601.

Hunter, J. M. (1987) Need and demand for mental health care: Massachusetts 1854. *The Geographical Review* 77, 139–56.

Imrie, R. (1996a) *Disability and the City: International Perspectives*. London: Paul Chapman.

Imrie, R. (1996b) Ableist geographies, disablist spaces: towards a reconstruction of Golledge's 'Geography and the Disabled'. *Transactions of the Institute of British Geographers* 21(2), 397–403.

Imrie, R. (2000a) Geography and disability, In Johnston, R. J. *et al.* (eds) *Dictionary of Human Geography*, 4th edn. Oxford: Blackwall.

Imrie, R. (2000b) Disabling environments and the geography of access policies and practices. *Disability and Society* 15(1), 5-24.

Jackson, P. (1991) The cultural politics of masculinity: towards a social geography. *Transactions of the Institute of British Geographers* 16(2), 199–213.

Jackson, P. (1992) *Maps of Meaning: An Introduction to Cultural Geography*. London : Routledge.

Jackson, P. (2000) Race. In Johnston, R. J., *et al.* (eds) *Dictionary of Human Geography*. Oxford: Blackwell.

Jackson, P. and Smith, S. (1984) *Exploring Social Geography*. London: Edward Arnold.

Jacobs, K., Kemeny, J. and Manzi, T. (1999) The struggle to define homelessness: a constructivist approach. In Hutson, S. and Clapham, D. (eds) *Homelessness: Public Policies and Private Troubles*. London and New York: Cassell.

James, S. (1990) Is there a place for children in geography? *Area* 22(3), 278–83.

Jarvis, H. (1999) The tangled webs we weave: household strategies to co-ordinate home and work. *Work, Employment and Society* 13(2), 225–47.

Jedrej, C. and Nuttall, M. (1996) *White Settlers: The Impact of Rural Repopulation in Scotland*. Luxembourg: Harwood.

Jeffers, S., Hoggett, P. and Harrison, L. (1996) Race, ethnicity and community in three localities. *New Community* 22, 111–26.

Jeffries, M. (2000) Niche broadcasting. *ECOS* 20(3/4), 70–6.

Jenkins, R. (1991) Violence, language and politics: nationalism in Northern Ireland and Wales. *North Atlantic Studies* 3(1), 31–40.

Johnston, L. and Valentine, G. (1995) Wherever I lay my girlfriend, that's my home: the performance and surveillance of lesbian identities in domestic environments. In Bell, D. and Valentine, G. (eds) *Mapping Desire*. London: Routledge.

Johnston, R. J., Gregory, D. and Smith, D. E. (eds) (1994) *The Dictionary of Human Geography*. 3rd edn. Oxford: Blackwell.

Johnston, R. J., Gregory, D., Pratt, G., Watts, M. (eds) (2000) *The Dictionary of Human Geography*. 4th edition. Oxford, Blackwell.

Jones, J. P. and Kodras, J. E. (1990) Restructured regions and families: the feminisation of poverty in the United States. *Annals of the Association of American Geographers* 80, 163–83.

Jones, T. (1993) *Britain's Ethnic Minorities*. London: Policy Studies Institute.

Junger, M. (1987) Women's experiences of sexual harassment: some implications for their fear of crime. *British Journal of Criminology* 22(4), 358–83.

Katz, S. (1992) Alarmist demography: power, knowledge and the elderly population. *Journal of Aging Studies* 6(3), 203–25.

Katz, C. (1993) Growing girls/closing circles: limits on the spaces of knowing in rural Sudan and US cities. In Katz, C. and Monk, J. *Full Circles: Geographies of Women over the Lifecourse*. London: Routledge.

Katz, C. and Monk, J. (1993) *Full Circles: Geographies of Women over the Lifecourse*. London: Routledge.

Kearns, G. and Philo, C. (1993) *Selling Places*. Oxford: Pergamon.

Kearns, R. A. and Smith, C. J. (1993) Housing stressors and mental health among marginalized urban populations. *Area* 25, 267–78.

Keller, S. (1988) The American dream of community: an unfinished agenda. *Sociological Forum* 3, 167–83.

Kelly, J. (1983) *Leisure Identities and Interactions*. London: George. Allen & Unwin.

Kemp, P. (1997) Burying Rachman. In Goodwin, J. and Grant, C. (eds) *Built to Last: Reflections on British Housing Policy*. London: Roof Magazine.

Kemper, F. J. (1998) Restructuring of housing and ethnic segregation: recent developments in Berlin. *Urban Studies* 35, 1765–89.

Kesteloot, C. and Cortie, C. (1998) Housing Turks and Moroccans in Brussels and Amsterdam: the difference between private and public markets. *Urban Studies* 35, 1835–53.

Kitchin, R. (1998) 'Out of Place', 'Knowing One's Place': space, power and the exclusion of disabled people. *Disability and Society* 13(3), 343–56.

Kitchin, R. (1999) Morals and ethics in geographical studies of disability. In Proctor, J. and Smith, D. (eds) *Geography and Ethics: a Journey through Moral Terrain*. London: Routledge.

Knopp, L. (1990) Some theoretical implications of gay involvement in the urban land market. *Political Geography Quarterly* 9, 337–52.

Knopp, L. (1995) Sexuality and urban space: a framework for analysis. In Bell, D. and Valentine, G. (eds) *Mapping Desire*. London: Routledge.

Knox, P. (1995) *Urban Social Geography*. 3rd edn. Harlow: Longman.

Knox, P. and Agnew, P. (1994) *The Geography of the World Economy*. London: Arnold.

Knox, P. L. and Pinch, S. (2000) *Urban Social Geography: An Introduction*. Harlow: Person Education.

Kodras, J. E. (1997) The changing map of American poverty in an era of economic restructuring and political realignment. *Economic Geography* 73, 67–95.

Kong, L., Yuen, B., Sodhi, N. S. and Brieffett C. (1999) The construction and experience of nature: perspectives of urban youths. *Tijdschrift voor Economische en Sociale Geografie* 90(1), 3–16.

Koskela, H. (1997) 'Bold walk and breakings': women's spatial confidence versus fear of violence. *Gender, Place and Culture* 4(3), 301–19.

Koskela, H. (1999) *Fear, Control and Space: Geographies of Gender, Fear of Violence, and Video Surveillance*. PhD thesis, Department of Geography, University of Helsinki.

Koskela, H. (forthcoming) 'The gaze without eyes': video surveillance and the changing nature of urban space. *Progress in Human Geography*.

Koskela, H. and Pain, R. (2000) Revisiting fear and place: women's fear of attack and the built environment. *Geoforum* 31(2), 269–80.

Langan, M. (1996) Hidden and respectable: crime and the market. In Muncie, J. and McLaughlin, E. (eds) *The Problem of Crime*. London: Sage.

Laurie, N., Dwyer, C., Holloway, S. and Smith, F. (1999) *Geographies of New Femininities*. Harlow: Longman.

Lauria, M. and Knopp, L. (1985) Towards an analysis of the role of gay communities in the urban renaissance. *Urban Geography* 6, 152–69.

Laws, G. (1994) Aging, contested meanings, and the built environment. *Environment and Planning A* 26, 1787–802.

Laws, G. (1995) Embodiment and emplacement: identities, representations and landscape in Sun City retirement communities. *International Journal of Aging and Human Development* 40(4), 253–80.

Laws, G. (1997) Spatiality and age relations. In Jamieson, A., Harper, S. and Victor, C. (eds) *Critical Approaches to Ageing and Later Life*. Buckingham: Open University Press.

Lee, R. and Wills, J. (eds) (1997) *Geographies of Economies*. London: Arnold.

Lees, L. (1994) Rethinking gentrification: beyond the positions of economics or culture. *Progress in Human Geography* 18, 137–50.

Levine, M. P. (1979) Gay ghetto. In *Gay Men: The Sociology of Male Homosexuality*. New York: Harper & Row.

Lewis, C. (2000) *A Man's Place in The Home: Fathers and Families in the UK*. Findings No. 440. York: Joseph Rowntree Foundation.

Lewis, J. and Piachaud, D. (1992) Women and poverty in the twentieth century. In Glendinning, C. and Millar, J. (eds) *Women and Poverty in Britain: The 1990s*. London: Harvester/Wheatsheaf.

Lewis, M. (1994) A sociological pub crawl around gay Newcastle. In Whittle, S. *The Margins of the City: Gay Men's Urban Lives*. Aldershot: Arena.

Lewis, O. (1969) The possessions of the poor. *Scientific American* 221, 114–24.

Ley, D. (1986) Alternative explanations for inner-city gentrification: a Canadian assessment. *Annals of the Association of American Geographers* 70, 238–58.

Leyshon, A. (1995) Missing words: whatever happened to the geography of poverty? *Environment and Planning A* 27, 1021–8.

Liepins, R. (2000) New energies for an old idea: reworking approaches to 'community' in contemporary rural studies. *Journal of Rural Studies* 16, 23–35.

Lindén, A. L. and Lindberg, G. (1991) Immigrant housing patterns in Sweden. In Huttman, E. D. (ed.) *Urban Housing Segregation of Minorities in Western Europe and the United States*. Durham NC and London: Duke University Press.

Lipton, M. (1983) *Poverty, Undernutrition and Hunger*. Staff Working Papers No. 597. Washington: World Bank.

Little, J., Peake, L. and Richardson, P. (1988) *Women and Cities*. London: Macmillan.

Loader, I., Girling, E. and Sparks, R. (1998) Narratives of decline: youth, dis/order and community in an English 'Middletown'. *British Journal of Criminology* 38(3), 388–403.

Longhurst, R. (2000) Geography and gender: masculinity, male identity and men. *Progress in Human Geography* 24(3), 439–44.

Lowe, P., Clark, J., Seymour, S. and Ward, N. (1997) *Moralizing the Environment: Countryside Change, Farming and Pollution*. London: UCL Press.

Lowenthal, D. (1991) British national identity and the English landscape. *Rural History* 2(2), 205–30.

Luymes, D. (1997) The fortification of suburbia: investigating the rise of enclave communities. *Landscape and Urban Planning* 39, 187–203.

McArthur, A. (1993) Community business and urban regeneration. *Urban Studies* 30, 849–73.

McCormick, J. (1991) *British Politics and the Environment*. London: Earthscan.

McCreadie, C. (1996) *Elder Abuse: Update on Research*. London: Age Concern Institute of Gerontology, King's College.

McCrone, G. and Stephens, M. (1995) *Housing Policy in Britain and Europe*. London: UCL Press.

McDowell, L. (1983) Towards an understanding of the gender division of urban space. *Environment and Planning D: Society and Space* 1, 59–72.

McDowell, L. (1990) Sex and power in academia. *Area* 22(4), 323–32.

McDowell, L. (1993a) Space, place and gender relations: Part I. Feminist empiricism and the geography of social relations. *Progress in Human Geography* 17(2), 159–79.

McDowell, L. (1993b) Space, place and gender relations: Part II. Identity, difference, feminist geometries and geographies. *Progress in Human Geography* 17(3), 305–18.

McDowell, L. (1995) Body work: heterosexual gender performances in city workplaces. In Bell, D. and Valentine, G. (eds) *Mapping Desire*. London: Routledge, 75-95.

McDowell, L. and Massey, D. (1984) A woman's place. In Massey, D. and Allen, J. (eds) *Geography Matters!* Cambridge: Cambridge University Press.

McDowell, L. and Sharp, J. (1997) *Space, Gender, Knowledge*. London: Arnold.

McDowell, L. and Sharp, J. (1999) *A Feminist Glossary of Human Geography*. London: Arnold.

MacFarlane R. (1998a) One rally and a march, but whose Countryside? *ECOS* 19(1), 87–96.

MacFarlane R. (1998b) What, or who, is rural Britain? *Town and Country Planning* 67(5), 184–8.

McGlone, F. (1992) *Disability and Dependency in Old Age: A Demographic and Social Audit*. London: Family Policy Studies Centre.

McKendrick, J. H. (1997) *Regulating Children's Street Life: A Case Study of Everyday Politics in the Neighbourhood*, SPA Working Paper 39. Manchester: School of Geography, University of Manchester.

MacKenzie, J. M. (1988) *The Empire of Nature: Hunting, Conservation and British Imperialism*. Manchester: Manchester University Press.

Macaghten, P. and Urry, J. (1998) *Contested Natures*. London: Sage.

MacPherson, S. and Silburn, R. (1998) The meaning and measurement of poverty. In Dixon, J. and Macarov, D. (eds) *Poverty: A Persistent Global Reality*. London: Routledge.

Maguire, M. *et al.* (eds) (1994) *Oxford Handbook of Criminology*. Oxford: Clarendon Press.

Malbon, B. (1998) Clubbing: consumption, identity and the spatial practices of everyday life. In Skelton, T. and Valentine, G. (eds) *Cool Places: Geographies of Youth Cultures*. London: Routledge.

Malcolmson, R. W. (1973) *Popular Recreations in English Society, 1700–1850*. Cambridge: Cambridge University Press.

Malik, S. (1992) Colours of the countryside – a whiter shade of pale. *ECOS* 13(4), 33–40.

Marsden, T., Murdoch, J., Lowe P., Munton, R. and Flynn, A. (1993) *Constructing the Countryside*. London: UCL Press.

Martin, J., Melzer, H. and Elliott, D. (1988) *OPCS Report 1: The Prevalence of Disability among Adults*. London: HMSO.

Martin, R., Sunley, P. and Wills, J. (1996) *Union Retreat and the Regions: The Shrinking Landscape of Organised Labour*. London: Jessica Kingsley.

Mason, A. and Palmer, A. (1996) *Queer Bashing: A National Survey of Hate Crimes against Lesbians and Gay Men*. London: Stonewall.

Massey, D. (1984a) *Spatial Divisions of Labour*. London: Macmillan.

Massey, D. (1984b) Geography matters. In Massey, D. and Allen, J. (eds) *Geography Matters!* Cambridge: Cambridge University Press.

Massey, D. (1994) *Space, Place and Gender*. Cambridge: Polity Press.

Massey, D. (1995) The conceptualisation of place. In Massey, D. and Jess, P., *A Place in the World?* Oxford: Oxford University Press.

Massey, D. (1998) Blurring the binaries? High tech in Cambridge. In Ainley, R. (ed.) *New Frontiers of Space, Bodies and Gender*. London: Routledge.

Massey, D. and Denton, N. (1993) *Apartheid American Style*. Cambridge, MA: Harvard University Press.

Matless, D. (1998) *Landscape and Englishness*. London: Reaktion Books.

Matrix Group (1984) *Making Space: Women and the Man-Made Environment*. London: Pluto Press.

Matthews, H. and Vujakovic, P. (1995) Mapping the Environment of Wheelchair Users. *Geography Review* (January), 30–4.

Matthews, H. and Limb, M. (1999) Defining an agenda for the geography of children: review and prospect. *Progress in Human Geography* 13(1), 61–90.

Mawby, R. I. (1977) Defensible space: a theoretical and empirical appraisal. *Urban Studies* 14, 169–79.

Mee, K. (1994) Dressing up the suburbs: representations of western Sydney. In Gibson, K. and Watson, S. (eds) *Metropolis Now*. Leichhardt, NSW: Pluto Press.

Meier, A. and Rudwick, E. M. (1966) *From Plantation to Ghetto: An Interpretive History of American Negroes*. London: Constable.

Meyrowitz, J. (1984) The adult child and the childlike adult. *Daedalus* 113(3), 19–48.

MHLG (Ministry of Housing and Local Government) (1970) *Moving Out of a Slum: A Study of People Moving from Sts Mary's Oldham*. London: HMSO.

Milbourne, P. (ed.) (1997a) *Revealing Rural 'Others': Representation, Power and Identity in the British Countryside*. London: Pinter.

Milbourne, P. (1997b) Challenging the rural: representation, power and identity in the British countryside. In Milbourne, P. (ed.) *Revealing Rural 'Others': Representation, Power and Identity in the British Countryside*. London: Pinter.

Millard-Ball, A. (2000) Moving beyond the gentrification gaps: social change, tenure change and gap theories in Stockholm. *Urban Studies* 37, 1673–93.

Milligan, C. (2000) 'Bearing the burden': towards a restructured geography of caring. *Area* 32(1), 49–58.

Mills, S. (1997) *The American Landscape*. Edinburgh: Keele University Press.

Mirrlees-Black, C., Budd, T., Partridge, S. and Mayhew, P. (1998) *The 1998 British Crime Survey*. Home Office Statistical Bulletin, 21/98. London: Home Office.

Mirrlees-Black, C. and Allen, J. (1998) *Concern about Crime: Findings from the 1998 British Crime Survey*. Research Findings No. 83, Research, Development and Statistics Directorate. London: Home Office.

Mohan, J. (1999) *A United Kingdom? Economic, Social and Political Geographies*. London: Arnold.

Mollenkopf, J. (1981) Community and accumulation. In Dear, M. and Scott, A. (eds) *Urbanization and Urban Planning in Capitalist Society*. London: Methuen.

Moore, R. C. (1986) *Childhood's Domain: Play and Place in Child Development*. London: Croom Helm.

Mordue, T. (1999) Heartbeat Country: conflicting values, coinciding visions. *Environment and Planning* A 31, 629–46.

Mormont, M. (1990) Who is rural? Or, How to be rural: towards a sociology of the rural. In Marsden, T., Lowe, P. and Whatmore, S. (eds) *Rural Restructuring: Global Processes and Their Responses*. London: David Fulton.

Morris, J. (1989) *Able lives – Women's Experience of Paralysis*. London: Women's Press.

Morris, J. (1993) *Independent Lives, Community Care and Disabled People*. Basingstoke: Macmillan.

Mowl, G. and Towner, J. (1995a) Women, gender, leisure and place: towards a more 'humanistic' geography of women's leisure. *Leisure Studies* 14(2), 102–16.

Mowl, G. and Edwards, C. (1995b) *Leisure space and disability: a case study of wheelchair users.* Paper presented at the conference on 'Recreation and the City: Popular values and Policy Directions', Staffordshire University, 8 September 1995.

Mowl, G., Pain, R. and Talbot, C. (2000) The ageing body and the homespace. *Area* 32 (2), 189–98.

Muir, R. (1999) *Approaches to Landscape.* Basingstoke: Macmillan.

Muncie, J. and McLaughlin, E. (eds) (1996) *The Problem of Crime.* London: Sage.

Murdoch, J. and Marsden, T. (1994) *Reconstituting Rurality.* London: UCL Press.

Murray, C. (1990) *The Emerging British Underclass.* London: Institute of Economic Affairs.

Murray, C. (1994) *Underclass: The Crisis Deepens.* London: Institute of Economic Affairs.

Nair, G., Ditton J. and Phillips, S. (1993) Environmental improvements and the fear of crime. *British Journal of Criminology* 33(4), 555–61.

Namaste, K. (1996) Genderbashing: sexuality, gender, and the regulation of public space. *Environment and Planning D* 14, 221–40.

Nassauer, J. (ed.) (1997) *Placing Nature: Culture and Landscape Ecology.* Washington: Island Press.

Nelson, J.G. (1989) Wilderness in Canada: past, present, future. *Natural Resources Journal* 29, 83–102.

Neulinger, J. (1981) *The Psychology of Leisure.* Springfield, IL: Charles C. Thomas.

New Internationalist (1992) *Disabled Lives: Difference and Defiance.* Special Issue, 233 (July).

Newburn, T. and Stanko, E. A. (1994) *Just Boys Doing Business? Men, Masculinities and Crime.* London: Routledge.

Newby, H. (1985) *Green and pleasant land? Social Change in Rural England,* 2nd edn. London: Wildwood.

Newcastle City Council (2000) *Challenging Media Myths about Refugees.* Newcastle upon Tyne: Newcastle City Council.

Newcastle City Council (2000) *Draft Masterplan for the East End and West End of Newcastle.* Newcastle City Council, in association with Richard Rogers Partnership, Andrew Wright Associates and DTZ Pieda Consulting, Newcastle upon Tyne.

Newman, O. (1972) *Defensible Space: Crime Prevention Through Design.* New York: Macmillan.

North, R. D. (1995) *Life on a Modern Planet: A Manifesto for Progress.* Manchester: Manchester University Press.

Office of Population Censuses an Surveys (1987) *The Prevalence of Disability in Great Britian,* Report 1. London, HMSO.

Oliver, M. (1990) *The Politics of Disablement.* Basingstoke: Macmillan.

Oppenheim, C. and Harker, L. (1996) *Poverty: The Facts,* 3rd edn. London: Child Poverty Action Group.

Pacione, M. (ed.) (1997) *Britain's Cities.* London: Routledge.

Pahl, R. (1984) *Divisions of Labour.* Oxford: Blackwell.

Pain, R. (1991) Space, sexual violence and social control: integrating geographical and feminist analyses of women's fear of crime. *Progress in Human Geography* 15(4), 415–31.

Pain, R. H. (1995) Fear of crime and local contexts: elderly people in north east England. *Northern Economic Review* 24, 96–111.

Pain, R. (1997a) 'Old age' and ageism in urban research: the case of fear of crime. *International Journal of Urban and Regional Research* 21(1), 117–28.

Pain, R. (1997b) Social geographies of women's fear of crime. *Transactions of the Institute of British Geographers* 22(2), 231–44.

Pain, R. (2000) Place, social relations and the fear of crime: a review. *Progress in Human Geography* 24(3).

Pain, R., Mowl, G. and Talbot, C. (2000) Difference and the negotiation of 'old age'. *Environment and Planning D: Society and Space* 18, 377–93.

Pain, R. and Williams, S. (2000) Young people and fear of violence in North Tyneside: the exclusionary tensions of 'community safety'. Paper presented to the annual conference of Institute of British Geographers, University of Sussex, Brighton, January 2000.

Pain, R. and Townshend, T. (forthcoming) A safer city centre for all? Meanings of 'community safety' in Newcastle upon Tyne. *Geoforum*.

Painter, K. (1991) Streetlighting and crime: a response to recent Home Office research. *The Lighting Journal* 58(4), 229–31.

Painter, K. (1992) Different worlds: the spatial, temporal and social dimensions of female victimization. In Evans, D. J., Fyfe, N. R. and Herbert, D. T. (eds) *Crime, Policing and Place*. London: Routledge.

Park, D. C., Radford, J. P. and Vickers, M. H. (1998) Disability Studies in Human geography. *Progress in Human Geography* 22(2), 208-33.

Parr, H. (1997) Mental health, public space, and the city: questions of individual and collective access. *Environment and Planning D: Society and Space* 15(4), 435–54.

Patmore, J. A. (1983) *Recreation and Resources*. Oxford: Blackwell.

Pawson, E. and Banks, G. (1993) Rape and fear in a New Zealand city. *Area* 25(1), 55–63.

Paxman, J. (1998) *The English: A Portrait of a People*. London: Michael Joseph.

Peach, C. (1968) *West Indian Migration to Britain: A Social Geography*. London: Oxford University Press.

Peach, C. (1996) Does Britain have ghettos? *Transactions of the Institute of British Geographers* 21, 216–35.

Peach, C. and Rossitter, D. (1997) Level and nature of spatial concentration and segregation of minority ethnic populations in Great Britain, 1991. In Ratcliffe, P. (ed.) *Social Geography and Ethnicity in Britain: Geographical Spread, Spatial Concentration and Internal Migration*, Volume 3 of *Ethnicity in the 1991 Census*. London: HMSO.

Peach, C. (1998) South Asian and Caribbean ethnic minority housing choice in Britain. *Urban Studies* 10, 1657–80.

Pearson, G. (1983) *Hooligan: A History of Respectable Fears*. London: Macmillan.

Peck, J. (1996) *Work-Place: The Social Regulation of Labour Markets*. New York: Guilford Press.

Peck, J. and Tickell, A. (1995) The social regulation of uneven development: 'regulatory deficit', England's South East and the collapse of Thatcherism. *Environment and Planning A* 27(1), 15–40.

Pect, R. (1975) The Geography of crime: a political critique. *Professional Geographer* 27, 277–80.

Peet, R. (1987a) The geography of class struggle and the relocation of US manufacturing industry. In Peet, R. (ed.) *International Capitalism and Industrial Restructuring*. Winchester, MA: Allen & Unwin.

Peet, R. (ed.) (1987b) *International Capitalism and Industrial Restructuring*. Winchester, MA: Allen & Unwin.

Peet, R. and Thrift, N. (eds) (1989) *New Models in Geography*. London: Unwin Hyman.

Penhale, B. (1993) The abuse of elderly people: considerations for practice. *British Journal of Social Work* 23(2), 95–112.

Pepper, D. (1984) *The Roots of Modern Environmentalism*. London: Routledge.

Phillips, D. (1981) The social and spatial segregation of Asians in Leicester. In Jackson, P. and Smith, S. (eds) *Social Interaction and Ethnic Segregation*. London: Academic Press.

Phillips, D. (1998) Black minority ethnic concentration, segregation and dispersal in Britain. *Urban Studies* 35, 1681–702.

Phillipson, C. (1993) The sociology of retirement. In Bond, J., Coleman, P. and Peace, S. (eds) *Ageing in Society: An Introduction to Social Gerontology*. London: Sage.

Philo, C. (1989) Enough to drive one mad: the organisation of space in nineteenth-century lunatic asylums. In Wolch, J. and Dear, M. (eds) *The Power of Geography: How Territory Shapes Social Life*. London: Unwin Hyman.

Philo, C. (ed.) (1995) *Off the Map: The Social Geography of Poverty in the UK*. London: Child Poverty Action Group.

Philo, C. (2000) Poverty. In Johnston, R. J., et al., *Dictionary of Human Geography*, 4th edn. Oxford: Blackwell.

Piachaud, D. (1987) Problems in the definition and measurement of poverty. *Journal of Social Policy* 16(2), 147–64.

Pile, S. and Thrift, N. (1995) *Mapping the Subject, Geographies of Cultural Transformation*. London: Routledge.

Pile, S. (1997) Introduction: opposition, political identities and spaces of resistance. In S. Pile and M. Keith (eds) *Geographies of Resistance*. London Routledge.

Pillinger, J. (1992) *Feminising the Market: Women's Pay and Employment in the EC*. London: Macmillan.

Pinch, S. (1989) Collective consumption. In Wolch, J. and Dear, M. (eds) *The Power of Geography*. Boston: Unwin Hyman.

Pollert, A. (1999) Dismantling flexibility. In Bryson, J., Henry, N., Keeble, D. and Martin, R. (eds) *The Economic Geography Reader: Producing and Consuming Global Capitalism*. Chicester: John Wiley.

Power, A. (1993) *Hovels to High Rise: State Housing in Europe since 1850*. London and New York: Routledge.

Pratt, G. (1989) Reproduction, class, and the spatial structure of the city. In Peet, R. and Thrift, N. (eds) *New Models in Geography*. London: Unwin Hyman, 84–108.

Preece, R. A. (1991) *Designs on the landscape: everyday landscapes, values and practice*. London: Belhaven.

Rao, V. (1982) *Food, nutrition and poverty in India*. Hemel Hempstead: Harvester/Wheatsheaf.

Redfern, P. A. (1997) A new look at gentrification: 1. Gentrification and domestic technologies. *Environment and Planning A* 29, 1275–96.

Rees, P., Phillips, D., and Medway, D. (1995) The socioeconomic geography of ethnic groups in two northern British cities. *Environment and Planning A* 27, 557–91.

Rees, P. and Phillips, D. (1997) Geographical spread: the national picture. In Ratcliffe, P. (ed.) *Social Geography and Ethnicity in Britain: Geographical Spread, Spatial Concentration and Internal Migration,* Volume 3 of *Ethnicity in the 1991 Census.* London: HMSO.

Renzetti, C. M. (1988) Violence in lesbian relationships: a preliminary analysis of causal factors. *Journal of Interpersonal Violence* 3(4), 381–99.

Roberts, K. (1978) *Contemporary Society and the Growth of Leisure.* London: Longman.

Roberts, M. (1991) *Living in a Man-made World: Gender Assumptions in Modern Housing Design.* London: Routledge.

Robinson, V. (1997) Inter-generational differences in ethnic setlement patterns in Britain. In Ratcliffe, P. (ed.) *Social Geography and Ethnicity in Britain: Geographical Spread, Spatial Concentration and Internal Migration,* Volume 3 of *Ethnicity in the 1991 Census.* London: HMSO.

Rodgers, G. and Rodgers, J. (eds) (1989) *Precarious Jobs in Labour Market Regulation: The Growth of Atypical Employment in Western Europe.* Geneva: International Labour Organization.

Rojek, C. (1995) *Decentring Leisure: Rethinking Leisure Theory.* London: Sage.

Rose, G. (1993) *Feminism and Geography: The Limits of Geographical Knowledge.* Cambridge: Polity Press.

Rose, G. (1995) Place and identity: a sense of place. In Massey, D. and Jess, P. (eds) *A Place in the World?* Oxford: Oxford University Press.

Rose, G., Kinnaird, V., Morris, M. and Nash, C. (1997) Feminist geographies of environment, nature and landscape. In Women and Geography Study Group (eds) *Feminist Geographies: Explorations in Diversity and Difference.* Harlow, Essex: Addison Wesley Longman.

Rose, H. M. (1971) *The Black Ghetto: A Spatial Behavioral Perspective.* New York: McGraw-Hill.

Ross, R. (1987) Facing Leviathan: public policy and global capitalism. In Peet, R. (ed.) *International Capitalism and Industrial Restructuring.* Winchester, MA: Allen & Unwin.

Rothenberg, T. (1995) 'And she told two friends': lesbians creating urban social space. In Bell, B. and Valentine, G. (eds) *Mapping Desire.* London: Routledge.

Roulstone, A. (2000) Disability, dependency and the new deal for disabled people. *Disability and Society* 15(3), 427–43.

Rowell, A. (1996) *Green Backlash.* London: Routledge.

Rowles, G. (1983) Place and personal identity in older age. *Journal of Environmental Psychology* 3, 299–313.

Rowntree, S. (1901) *Poverty: A Study of Town Life.* London: Macmillan.

Rowntree, S. (1937) *The Human Needs of Labour.* London: Longman.

Rowntree, S. (1941) *Poverty and progress.* London: Longman.

Rowntree, S. and Laver, G. R. (1951) *Poverty and the Welfare State.* London: Longman.

Rubinstein, R. L. and Parmalee, P. A. (1992) Attachment to place and the representation of the life course by the elderly. In Altman, I. and Low, S. (eds) *Place Attachment.* New York: Plenum Press.

Ryan, J. and Thomas, F. (1980) *The Politics of Mental Handicap.* Harmondsworth: Penguin.

Saegert, S. (1980) Masculine cities and feminine suburbs: polarized ideas and contradictory realities. *Signs* 5(3), 96–111.

Said, E. (1978) *Orientalism*. London: Routledge.

Sande, A. (1997) The family and the social division of labour during industrial restructuring. In Wheelock, J. and Mariussen, A., *Households, Work and Economic Change*. London: Kluwer Academic Publishers.

Sassen, S. (1991) *The Global City*. Princeton, NJ: Princeton University Press.

Savage, M. and Warde, A. (1993) *Urban Sociology, Capitalism and Modernity*. Basingstoke: Macmillan.

Saunders, P. (1989) The meaning of 'home' in contemporary English culture. *Housing Studies* 4, 177–92.

Saunders, P. (1990) *A Nation of Home Owners*. London: Unwin Hyman

Schoenberger, E. (1989) New models of regional development. In Peet, R. and Thrift, N. (eds) *New Models in Geography* Vol. 1. London: Unwin Hyman.

Scope (2000) *Disability Issues: Housing and Support*. Scope Research (www.scope.org.uk)

Scraton, S. and Watson, B. (1998) Gendered cities: women and public leisure space in the 'postmodern city', *Leisure Studies* 17, 123–37.

Scutt, R. and Bonnet, A. (1996) *In Search of England: Popular Representations of Englishness and the English Countryside*. Working Paper 22, Centre for Rural Economy, University of Newcastle upon Tyne.

Seccombe, W. (1993) *Weathering the Storm: Working-class Families from the Industrial Revolution to the Fertility Decline*. London: Verso.

Segal, L. (1990) *Slow Motion: Changing Masculinities, Changing Men*. London: Virago.

Sen, A. (1983) Poor, relatively speaking. *Oxford Economic Papers* 35 (1).

Sennett, R. (1998) *The Corrosion of Character: The Personal Consequences of Work in the New Capitalism*. New York: Norton.

Seymour, S., Lowe, P., Ward, N. and Clark, J. (1997) Environmental 'others' and 'elites': rural pollution and changing power relations in the countryside. In Milbourne, P. (ed.) *Revealing Rural 'Others': Representation, Power and Identity in the British countryside*. London: Pinter.

Shakespeare, T. (1994) Cultural representation of disabled people: dustbins for disavowal. *Disability and Society* 9(3), 283–99.

Shanks, N. and Smith, S. J. (1991) Public policy and the health of homeless people. *Policy and Politics* 20, 35–46.

Shapland, J. and Vagg, J. (1988) *Policing by the Public*. London: Routledge.

Shaw, S. M. (1985) Gender and leisure: inequality in the distribution of leisure time, *Journal of Leisure Research* 17(4), 266–82.

Sheail, J., Treweek, J. R. and Mountford, J. O. (1997) The UK transition from nature preservation to 'creative conservation'. *Environmental Conservation* 24(3), 224–35.

Short J. R. (1991) *Imagined Country: Society, Culture and Environment*. London: Routledge.

Short, J. (1996) *The Urban Order*. Oxford: Blackwell.

Shucksmith, M. (1990) *Housebuilding in Britain's Countryside*. London: Routledge.

Shucksmith, M., Chapman, P. and Clark, G. (1996) *Rural Scotland Today: The Best of Both Worlds?* Aldershot: Avebury.

Sibley, D. (1991) Children's geographies: some problems of representation. *Area* 23(3), 269–70.

Sibley, D. (1995) *Geographies of Exclusion*. London: Routledge.

Sidaway, J. D. (1992) In other worlds: on the politics of research by 'First World' geographers in the 'Third World'. *Area* 24(4), 403.

Silburn, R. (1998) United Kingdom. In Dixon, J. and Macarov, D., *Poverty: A Persistent Global Reality*. London: Routledge.

Simmie, J. (ed.) (1997) *Innovation, Networks and Learning Regions*. London: Jessica Kingsley.

Simmons, M. (1997) *Landscapes – of Poverty: Aspects of Rural England in the Late 1990s*. London: Lemos & Crane.

Sixsmith, A. (1986a) Independence and home in later life. In Phillipson, C., Bernard, M. and Strang, P. (eds) *Dependency and Interdependency in Old Age*. London: Croom Helm.

Sixsmith, J. (1986b) The meaning of home: an exploratory study of environmental experience. *Journal of Environmental Psychology* 6, 281–98.

Skelton, T. and Valentine, G. (1998) *Cool Places: Geographies of Youth Cultures*. London: Routledge.

Skogan, W. G. (1990) *Disorder and Decline: Crime and the Spiral of Decay in American Neighborhoods*. New York: Free Press.

Smith, A. D. (1990) Towards a global culture? In Featherstone, M. (ed.) *Global Culture: Nationalism, Globalization and Modernity*. London: TCS/Sage.

Smith, N. (1979) Towards a theory of gentrification: a back to the city movement by capital, not people. *Journal of the American Planning Association* 45, 538–48.

Smith, N. (1993) Homeless/global: scaling places. In Bird, J., Curtis, B., Putnam, T., Robertson, G. and Tickner, L. (eds) *Mapping the Futures: Local Cultures, Global Change*. London: Routledge.

Smith, N. (1996) *The New Urban Frontier*. London: Routledge.

Smith, S. J. (1989) Social relations, neighbourhood structure, and the fear of crime in Britain. In Evans, D. and Herbert, D. (eds) *The Geography of Crime*. London: Routledge.

Smith, S. J. (1993) Social landscapes: continuity and change. In Johnston, R. J. (ed.) *The Challenge for Geography*. Oxford: Blackwell.

Smith, S. J. (1999) Society–Space. In Cloke, P. Crang, P. and Goodwin, M. (eds) *Introducing Human Geographies*. London: Arnold.

Smith, T. (1994) *Lean Production: A Capitalist Utopia?* Amsterdam: International Institute for Research and Education.

Soja, E. (1996) *Thirdspace: A journey to Los Angeles and Other Real and Imagined Places*. Oxford: Blackwell.

Somerville, P. (1999) The making and unmaking of homelessness legislation. In Hutson, S. and Clapham, D. (eds) *Homelessness: Public Policies and Private Troubles*. London and New York: Cassell.

Sparks, R. (1992) Reason and unreason in 'left realism': some problems in the constitution of the fear of crime. In Matthews, R. and Young, J. (eds) *Issues in Realist Criminology*. London: Sage.

Speak, S. (2000) Barriers to lone parents' employment. *Local Economy* 15(1), 32–44.

Speak, S. and Graham, S. (1999) Service not included: private services restructuring, neighbourhoods, and social marginalisation. *Environment and Planning A* 31, 1985–2001.

Spicker, P. (1999) Definitions of poverty: eleven clusters of meaning. In Gordon, D. and Spicker, P. (eds) *The International Glossary on Poverty*. London: Zed Books.

Stephenson, J. B. (1984) *Ford: A Village in the West Highlands*. Lexington: University of Kentucky Press.

Stacey, M. (1969) The myth of community studies. *British Journal of Sociology* 20, 134–47.

Stanko, E. A. (1987) Typical violence, normal precaution: men, women and interpersonal violence in England, Wales, Scotland and the USA. In Hanmer, J. and Maynard, M. (eds) *Women, Violence and Social Control*. London: Macmillan.

Stanko, E. (1990a) *Everyday Violence: Women's and Men's Experience of Personal Danger*. London: Pandora.

Stanko, E. (1990b) When precaution is normal: a feminist critique of crime prevention. In Gelsthorpe, L. and Morris, A. (eds) *Feminist Perspectives in Criminology*. Milton Keynes: Open University Press.

Stanko, E. A. and Hobdell, K. (1993) Assault on men: masculinity and male victimisation. *British Journal of Criminology* 33(3), 400–15.

Storper, M. (1997) Regional economies as relational assets. In Lee, R. and Wills, J. (eds) *Geographies of Economies*. London: Arnold.

Storper, M. and Walker, R. (1989) *The Capitalist Imperative*. Oxford: Blackwell.

Sullivan, D. (1995) *Virtually Normal: An Argument about Homosexuality*. London: Picador.

Summerfield, C. (1998) *Social Focus on Men and Women*. London: HMSO.

Swenarton, M. (1981) *Homes Fit for Heroes: The Politics and Architecture of Early State Housing*. London: Heinemann.

Taeuber, K.E. and Taeuber, A. (1965) *Negroes in Cities: Residential Segregation and Neighborhood Change*. Chicago: Aldine.

Taylor, G. (ed.) (1951) *Geography in the Twentieth Century: A Study of Growth, Fields, Techniques, Aims and Trends*. London: Methuen.

Taylor, I. (1995) Private homes and public others: an analysis of talk about crime in suburban South Manchester in the mid-1990s. *British Journal of Criminology* 35(2), 263–85.

Therborn, G. (1986) *Why Some Peoples Are More Unemployed Than Others*. London: Verso.

Thompson, P. (1989) *The Nature of Work*, 2nd edn. London: Macmillan.

Thornton, S. (1994) Moral panic, the media and British rave culture. In Ross A. and Rose, T. (eds) *Microphone Fiends: Youth Music and Youth Culture*. London: Routledge, 176–92.

Thrift, N. (1996) Owners' time and own time: the making of a capitalist time-consciousness 1300–1880. In Agnew, J. Livingstone, D. N. and Rogers, A. (eds) *Human Geography: An Essential Anthology*. Oxford: Blackwell.

Thrift, N. and Williams, P. (1987) *Class and Space: The Making of Urban Society*. London: Routledge & Kegan Paul.

Tomlinson, L. (1998) 'This ain't no disco' or is it? Youth culture and the rave phenomenon. In Epstein, J. (ed.) *Youth Culture: Identity in a Postmodern World*. Oxford: Blackwell.

Tonnies, F. (1955) *Community and Association*. London: Routledge & Kegan Paul.

Tonnies, F. (1887) *Community and Society*, new edn 1963, transl. by C.P.Loomis. New York: Harper & Row.

Toogood, M. (1995) Representing ecology and Highland tradition. *Area* 27(2), 102–9.

Topliss, E. (1979) Provision for the Disabled, 2nd edn. Oxford, Blackwell.

Townsend, P. (1979) *Poverty in the United Kingdom: A Survey of Household Resources and Standards of Living*. London: Penguin.

Townsend, P. (1993) *The International Analysis of Poverty*. London: Harvester Wheatsheaf.

Trickett A., Ellingworth, D., Hope, T. and Pease, K. (1995) Crime victimization in the eighties: changes in area and regional inequality. *British Journal of Criminology* 35(3), 343–59.

Tuan, Yi-Fu (1975) Place: an experiential perspective. *The Geographical Review* 56(2), 151–65.

Turner, B. (1996) Sweden. In Balchin, P. (ed.) *Housing Policy in Europe*. London: Routledge.

UPIAS (1976) *Fundamental Principles of Disability*. London: Union of Physically Impaired Against Segregation.

United Nations Development Programme (1995) *Human Development Report*. Oxford: Oxford University Press.

United Nations Development Programme (1997) *Human Development Report*. Oxford: Oxford University Press.

Unwin, T. (1998) *A European Geography*. Harlow: Longman.

Urry, J. (1995) A middle-class countryside? In Butler, T. and Savage, M. (eds) *Social Change and the Middle Classes*. London: UCL Press.

Urry, J. (1999) Sensing leisure spaces. In Crouch, D. (ed.) *Leisure/tourism Geographies*. London: Routledge.

Valentine, G. (1989) The geography of women's fear. *Area* 21(4), 385-90.

Valentine. G. (1992) Images of danger: women's sources of information about the spatial distribution of male violence. *Area* 24(1), 22–9.

Valentine, G. (1993a) Desperately seeking Susan: a geography of lesbian friendships, *Area* 25(2), 109–16.

Valentine G. (1993b) Negotiating and managing multiple sexual identities: lesbian time–space strategies. *Transactions of the Institute of British Geographers* 18(2), 237–481.

Valentine, G. (1996) Children should be seen and not heard: the progression and transgression of adults' public space. *Urban Geography* 17(3), 205–20.

Valentine, G. and McKendrick, J. (1997) Children's outdoor play: exploring parental concerns about children's safety and the changing nature of childhood. *Geoforum* 28(2), 219–35.

Valentine, G. (1998) 'Sticks and stones may break my bones': a personal geography of harassment. *Antipode* 30, 305–32.

Van Kempen, R. and Özüekren, S. (1998) Ethnic segregation in cities: new forms and explanations in a dynamic world. *Urban Studies* 35, 1631–56.

Vrij, A. and Winkel, F. W. (1991) Characteristics of the built environment and fear of crime: a research note on interventions in unsafe locations. *Deviant Behaviour* 12, 203–15.

Wakeford, N. (1998) Urban culture for vitual bodies: comments on lesbian 'identity' and 'community' in San Francisco Bay Area cyberspace. In Ainley, R. (ed.) *New Frontiers of Spaces, Bodies and Gender*. London: Routledge.

Walby, S. (1990) *Theorising Patriarchy*. Oxford: Blackwell.

Walby, S. and Bagguley, P. (1989) Gender restructuring: five labour-markets compared. *Environment and Planning D: Society and Space* 7, 277–92.

Waldinger, R. (1986) *Through the Eye of a Needle: Immigrants and Enterprise in New York's Garment Trades*. New York: New York University Press.

Walker, A. (1987) The social construction of dependency in old age. In Loney, M. (ed.) *The State or the Market*. London: Sage.

Walker, A. (1993) Poverty and inequality in old age. In Bond, J., Coleman, P. and Peace, S. (eds) *Aging in Society: An introduction to Social Gerontology*, 2nd edn. London: Sage.

Walker, A. and Phillipson, C. (eds) (1986) *Ageing and Social Policy: A Critical Assessment*. London: Gower.

Walklate, S. (1995) *Gender and Crime: An Introduction*. London: Prentice Hall.

Ward, R. and Sims, R. (1983) Social status, the market and ethnic segregation. In Peach, C., Robinson,V. and Smith, S. (eds) *Ethnic Segregation in Cities*. London: Croom Helm.

Warde, A. (1988) Industrial restructuring, local politics and the reproduction of labour power. *Environment and Planning D: Society and Space* 6, 75–95.

Warnes, A. M. (ed.) (1982) *Geographical Perspectives on the Elderly*. Chichester: John Wiley.

Warren, R. B. and Warren, D. I. (1977) *The Neighbourhood Organizer's Handbook*. Indiana: University of Notre Dame Press.

Watson, D. R. (1996) Integrating catchment management: the human dimension. In Cresser, M. and Pugh, K. (eds) *Multiple Land Use and Catchment Management*. Proceedings of an International Conference, 11–13 September 1996, Macaulay Land Use Research Institute, Aberdeen.

Watson, J. W. (1951) The sociological aspects of geography. In Taylor, G. (ed.) *Geography in the Twentieth Century: A Study of Growth, Fields, Techniques, Aims and Trends*. London: Methuen.

Watson, S. (1986) Women and housing or feminist housing analysis. *Housing Studies* 1, 1–10.

Wearing, B. and Wearing, S. (1988) 'All in a day's leisure': gender and the concept of leisure. *Leisure Studies* 7, 111–123.

Wellman, B. (1979) The community question. *American Journal of Sociology* 84, 1201–31.

Werbner, P. (1979) Avoiding the ghetto: Pakistani migrants and settlement shifts in Manchester. *New Community* 7, 376–89.

Whatmore, S. (1999) Culture – Nature. In Cloke, P., Crang, P. and Goodwin, M. (eds) *Introducing Human Geographies*. London: Arnold.

Wheeler, R. (1986) Housing policy and elderly people. In Walker, A. and Phillipson, C. (eds) *Ageing and Social Policy: A Critical Assessment*. London: Gower.

Wheelock, J. and Mariussen, A. (1997) *Households, Work and Economic Change*. London: Kluwer Academic Publishers.

White, P. (1999) Ethnicity, racialization and citizenship as divisive elements in Europe. In Hudson, R. and Williams, A. M. (eds) *Divided Europe: Society and Territory*. London: Sage Publications.

Williams, N. J., Sewel, J. B. and Twine, F. E. (1988) Council house sales: an analysis of the factors associated with purchase and implications for the future of public sector housing. *Tijdscrift voor Economische en Sociale Geografie* 79, 39–49.

Williams, P. (1987) Constituting class and gender: a social history of the home, 1700–1901. In Thrift, N. and Williams, P., *Class and Space: The Making of Urban Society*. London: Routledge & Kegan Paul.

Williams, R. (1993) *The Country and the City*. London: Hogarth Press.

Williams, S. (1995) *Outdoor Recreation and the Urban Environment*. London: Routledge.

Williams, S. 1998: *Tourism Geography*. London: Routledge.

Wilson, E. (1991) *The Sphinx in the City: Urban Life, the Control of Disorder, and Women*. London: Virago.

Wilson, G. A. and Bryant, R. L. (1997) *Environmental Management: New Directions for the Twenty-first Century*. London: UCL Press.

Wilson, W. J. (1987) *The Truly Disadvantaged: The Inner City, The Underclass and Public Policy*. Chicago: University of Chicago Press.

Winchester, H. (1991) The geography of children. *Area* 23(4), 357–60.

Wirth, L. (1928) *The Ghetto*. Chicago: University of Chicago Press.

Wirth, L. (1938) Urbanism as a way of life. *American Journal of Sociology* 44, 1–24.

Wolch, J. and Dear, M. (1989a) Introduction, in Wolch, J. and Dear, M. (1989b).

J. Wolch and Dear, M. (eds) (1989b) *The Power of Geography*. Boston: Unwin Hyman.

Wood, E. M. (1995) *Democracy against Capitalism*. Cambridge: Cambridge University Press.

Wright, R. and Decker, S. H. (1994) *Burglars on the Job: Streetlife and Residential Breakins*. Boston: Northeastern University Press.

Wypijewski, J. (1997) *Painting by Numbers: Komar and Melamid's Scientific Guide to Art*. Berkeley: University of California Press.

Yarwood, R. and Gardner, G. (2000): Fear of crime, cultural threat and the countryside. *Area* 32(4), 403–12.

Yeo, E. and Yeo, S. (1981) *Popular Culture and Class Conflict, 1590–1914*. London: Harvester.

Young, I. M. (1981) Beyond the unhappy marriage: a critique of the dual systems theory. In Sargent, L., *Women and Revolution*. Boston: South End Press.

Young, I. M. (1990a) *Justice and the Politics of Difference*. Princeton, NJ: Princeton University Press.

Young, I. M. (1990b) The ideal of community and the politics of difference. In Nicholson, L. (ed.) *Feminism/Postmodernism*. London: Routledge.

Young, M. and Willmott, P. (1957) *Family and Kinship in East London*. London: Routledge & Kegan Paul.

Young, S. C. (1993) *The Politics of the Environment*. Manchester: Baseline Books.

Zangwill, I. (1921) *The Voice of Jerusalem*. New York: Macmillan.

Zukin, S. (1995) *The Cultures of Cities*. London: Blackwell.

Index

three sections have shown that geographical and social patterns of poverty are constructed by processes which are simultaneously social and geographical.

12.7 Political action of the poor and its geography

In the previous three sections we have dwelt on the powerful social-geographical causes of poverty. But these have been contested. We have seen that national and local politics can affect poverty in important ways – through constructing territorial regimes, or through carrying through strategies such as neoliberalism. These politics are created through conflicts and compromises between all social groups (see Chapter 2, sections 2.5 and 2.7). However, the political activity of the poor themselves is also important – the poor are far from being passive victims.

As poverty is multi-faceted, the focuses for campaigns against poverty have been very varied, as have the sections of the poor conducting these struggles. Trade unions, especially those which have most of their members in low-paid jobs, have fought for improvement of poor jobs, or, in recent decades, have attempted to resist their worsening. Sometimes these battles have been conducted by workers in a particular workplace, particularly when faced with deterioration of conditions or redundancy. Particularly exploited groups of workers such as homeworkers have organized at local and national levels to attempt to secure basic employment rights. Organizations of groups strongly dependent on state benefits, particularly pensioners and social security claimants, have campaigned for benefits to be raised above the poverty level. Pensioners in general have had stronger and more stable organizations than claimants. But the latter have conducted some powerful campaigns; in France in 1998–9, for example, occupations of social security offices across the country won concessions from the government. Increases in the tax burden of the poor can elicit militant ad hoc organization. When the British government in 1990–1 introduced a poll tax which shifted local taxation sharply from the rich to the poor, millions of poor people refused to pay it and there were militant demonstrations. This resistance resulted in major reform of the tax (and contributed to the departure of Margaret Thatcher as prime minister). People with disabilities have campaigned against their commonly experienced poverty on many fronts: for better access to paid employment, for better support from public services, and for changes to the built environment.

Much organization against poverty has been concerned with reproduction at the neighbourhood scale (compare with section 12.5). Residents' groups in poor areas have campaigned for improvements in public and private services or against their deterioration (Fasenfest, 1993). Communities have also organized to provide services for themselves: child care clubs, credit unions, and community businesses, such as repair enterprises, are examples. While these start from self-help, they usually also make demands for state financial support, and sometimes, as with credit unions, put political pressure on service providers in the public or private sector (Fuller and Jonas, 2000). Many poor communities have campaigned against pollution of their environments. Poor